Barthes: Selected Writings

Susan Sontag studied philosophy at the University of
Chicago and at Harvard, then taught at Columbia
University before becoming a fulltime writer. Her first
book was a novel, *The Benefactor* (1963). Since then her
publications have included *Death Kit* (1967; a novel), *Trip
to Hanoi* (1968), *Illness as Metaphor* (1978); and *Against
Interpretation* (1966) and *On Photography* (1977), both
books of essays. She has also written and directed three
films – *Duet for Cannibals*, *Brother Carl* and *Promised
Lands* – and has published a selection of the work of
Antonin Artaud.

Barthes: Selected Writings

Barthes: Selected Writings

edited and with an introduction by
Susan Sontag

Fontana/Collins

First published in the USA as *A Barthes Reader* by Hill & Wang Inc. 1982
Published in Great Britain by Jonathan Cape Ltd 1982
First issued as *Barthes: Selected Writings* by Fontana Paperbacks 1983
Selection and introduction copyright © Susan Sontag 1982
Printed and bound in Great Britain at The University Press, Oxford

CONTENTS

Writing Itself: On Roland Barthes

TEACHER, man of letters, moralist, philosopher of culture, connoisseur of strong ideas, protean autobiographer . . . of all the intellectual notables who have emerged since World War II in France, Roland Barthes is the one whose work I am most certain will endure. Barthes was in full flow, incessantly productive as he had been for over three decades, when he was struck by a van as he started across a street in Paris in early 1980—a death felt by friends and admirers to be excruciatingly untimely. But along with the backward look of grief comes the awareness that confers upon his large, chronically mutating body of writing, as on all major work, its retroactive completeness. The development of Barthes's work now seems logical; more than that, exhaustive. It even begins and falls silent on the same subject—that exemplary instrument in the career of consciousness, the writer's journal. As it happens, the first essay Barthes ever published celebrates the model consciousness he found in the *Journal* of André Gide, and what turned out to be the last essay published before he died offers Barthes's musings on his own journal-keeping. The symmetry, however adventitious, is an utterly appropriate one, for Barthes's writing, with its prodigious variety of subjects, has finally one great subject: writing itself.

His early themes were those of the freelance partisan of

letters, on the occasions afforded by cultural journalism, literary debate, theater and book reviews. To these were added topics that originated and were recycled in seminars and from the lecture platform, for Barthes's literary career was run concurrently with a (very successful) academic one, and in part *as* an academic one. But the voice was always singular, and self-referring; the achievement is of another, larger order than can be had even by practicing, with thrilling virtuosity, the most lively and many-tracked of academic disciplines. For all his contributions to the would-be science of signs and structures, Barthes's endeavor was the quintessentially literary one: the writer organizing, under a series of doctrinal auspices, the theory of his own mind. And when the current enclosure of his reputation by the labels of semiology and structuralism crumbles, as it must, Barthes will appear, I think, as a rather traditional *promeneur solitaire*, and a greater writer than even his more fervent admirers now claim.

He always wrote full out, was always concentrated, keen, indefatigable. This dazzling inventiveness seems not just a function of Barthes's extraordinary powers as a mind, as a writer. It seems to have almost the status of a position—as if this is what critical discourse *must* be. "Literature is like phosphorous," he says in his first book, which came out in 1953, *Writing Degree Zero*; "it shines with its maximum brilliance at the moment when it attempts to die." In Barthes's view, literature is already a posthumous affair. His work affirms a standard of vehement brilliance that is indeed one ideal of a cultural moment which believes itself to be having, in several senses, the last word.

Its brilliance aside, Barthes's work has some of the specific traits associated with the style of a late moment in culture—one that presumes an endless discourse anterior to itself, that presumes intellectual sophistication: it is work that, strenuously unwilling to be boring or obvious, favors compact assertion, writing that rapidly covers a great deal of ground. Barthes was an inspired, ingenious practitioner of the essay and the anti-essay—he had a resistance to long forms. Typically, his sentences are complex, comma-ridden and colon-prone, packed with densely worded entailments of ideas deployed as if these were the materials of a supple prose. It is a style of exposition, recognizably French, whose parent tradition is to be found in the tense, idiosyncratic essays published between the two world wars in the *Nouvelle Revue Française*—a perfected version of the *NRF*'s house style which can deliver more ideas per page while retaining the brio of that style, its acuteness of timbre. His vocabulary is large, fastidious, fearlessly mandarin. Even Barthes's less fleet, more jargon-haunted writings—most of them from the 1960s—are full of flavor; he manages to make an exuberant use of neologisms. While exuding straight-ahead energy, his prose constantly reaches for the summative formulation; it is irrepressibly aphoristic. (Indeed, one could go through Barthes's work extracting superb bits—epigrams, maxims—to make a small book, as has been done with Wilde and Proust.) Barthes's strengths as an aphorist suggest a sensibility gifted, before any intervention of theory, for the perception of structure. Being a method of condensed assertion by means of symmetrically counterposed terms, the maxim or aphorism inevitably displays the symmetries and complementarities of situations or ideas—that design, their shape. Like a markedly greater feeling for drawings than for paintings, a talent for aphorism is one of the signs of what could be called the formalist temperament.

The formalist temperament is just one variant of a sensibility shared by many who speculate in an era of hypersaturated awareness. What characterizes such a sensibility more generally is its reliance on the criterion of taste, and its proud refusal to propose anything that does not bear the stamp of subjectivity.

Confidently assertive, it nevertheless insists that its assertions are no more than provisional. (To do otherwise would be . . . bad taste.) Indeed, adepts of this sensibility usually make a point of claiming and reclaiming amateur status. "In linguistics I have never been anything but an amateur," Barthes told an interviewer in 1975. Throughout his late writings Barthes repeatedly disavows the, as it were, vulgar roles of system-builder, authority, mentor, expert, in order to reserve for himself the privileges and freedoms of delectation: the exercise of taste for Barthes means, usually, to praise. What makes the role a choice one is his unstated commitment to finding something new and unfamiliar to praise (which requires having the right dissonance with established taste); or to praising a familiar work differently.

An early example is his second book—it appeared in 1954—which is on Michelet. Through an inventory of the recurrent metaphors and themes in the great nineteenth-century historian's epic narratives, Barthes discloses a more intimate narration: Michelet's history of his own body and the "lyric resurrection of past bodies." Barthes is always after another meaning, a more eccentric—often utopian—discourse. What pleased him was to show insipid and reactionary works to be quirky and implicitly subversive; to display in the most extravagant projects of the imagination an opposite extreme—in his essay on Sade, a sexual ideal that was really an exercise in delirious rationality; in his essay on Fourier, a rationalist ideal that was really an exercise in sensual delirium. Barthes did take on central figures of the literary canon when he had something polemical to offer: in 1960 he wrote a short book on Racine, which scandalized academic critics (the ensuing controversy ended with Barthes's complete triumph over his detractors); he also wrote on Proust and Flaubert. But more often, armed with his essentially adversary notion of the "text," he applied his ingenuity to the marginal literary subject: an unimportant "work"—say, Balzac's *Sarrasine*, Chateaubriand's *Life of Rancé*—could be a marvelous "text." Considering something as a "text" means for Barthes precisely to suspend conventional evaluations (the difference between major and minor literature), to subvert established classifications (the separation of genres, the distinctions among the arts).

Though work of every form and worth qualifies for citizenship in the great democracy of "texts," the critic will tend to avoid the texts that everyone has handled, the meaning that everyone knows. The formalist turn in modern criticism—from its pristine phase, as in Shklovsky's idea of defamiliarizing, onward—dictates just this. It charges the critic with the task of discarding worn-out meanings for fresh ones. It is a mandate to scout for new meanings. *Etonne-moi.*

The same mandate is supplied by Barthes's notions of "text" and "textuality." These translate into criticism the modernist ideal of an open-ended, polysemous literature; and thereby make the critic, just like the creators of that literature, the inventor of meaning. (The aim of literature, Barthes asserts, is to put "meaning" into the world but not "a meaning.") To decide that the point of criticism is to alter and to relocate meaning—adding, subtracting, multiplying it—is in effect to base the critic's exertions on an enterprise of avoidance, and thereby to recommit criticism (if it had ever left) to the dominion of taste. For it is, finally, the exercise of taste which identifies meanings that are familiar; a judgment of taste which discriminates against such meanings as too familiar; an ideology of taste which makes of the familiar something vulgar and facile. Barthes's formalism at its most decisive, his ruling that the critic is called on to reconstitute not the "message" of a work but only its "system"—its form, its structure—is perhaps best understood thus, as the liberating avoidance of the obvious, as an immense gesture of good taste.

For the modernist—that is, formalist—critic, the work with

its received valuations already exists. Now, what *else* can be said? The canon of great books has been fixed. What can we add or restore to it? The "message" is already understood, or is obsolete. Let's ignore it.

Of a variety of means Barthes possessed for giving himself something to say—he had an exceptionally fluent, ingenious generalizing power—the most elementary was his aphorist's ability to conjure up a vivacious duality: anything could be split either into itself and its opposite, or into two versions of itself; and one term then fielded against the other to yield an unexpected relation. The point of Voltairean travel, he remarks, is "to manifest an immobility"; Baudelaire "had to protect theatricality from the theater"; the Eiffel Tower "makes the city into a kind of Nature"—Barthes's writing is seeded with such ostensibly paradoxical, epigrammatic formulas as these, whose point is to sum something up. It is the nature of aphoristic thinking to be always in a state of concluding; a bid to have the final word is inherent in all powerful phrase-making.

Less elegant, indeed making a point of dogged explicitness, and far more powerful as an instrument for giving himself something to say, are the classifications that Barthes lays out in order to topple himself into a piece of argument—dividing into two, three, even four parts the matter to be considered. Arguments are launched by announcing that there are two main classes and two subclasses of narrative units, two ways in which myth lends itself to history, two facets of Racinean eros, two musics, two ways to read La Rochefoucauld, two kinds of writers, two forms of his own interest in photographs. That there are three types of corrections a writer makes, three Mediterraneans and three tragic sites in Racine, three levels on which to read the plates of the *Encyclopedia*, three areas of spectacle and three types of gesture in Japanese puppet theater, three attitudes toward speech and writing, equivalent to three vocations: writer, intellectual, and teacher. That there are four kinds of readers, four reasons for keeping a journal . . .

And so on. This is the codifying, frontal style of French intellectual discourse, a branch of the rhetorical tactics that the French call, not quite accurately, Cartesian. Although a few of the classifications Barthes employs are standard, such as semiology's canonical triad of signified, signifier, and sign, many are inventions devised by Barthes in order to *make* an argument, such as his assertion in a late book, *The Pleasure of the Text*, that the modern artist seeks to destroy art, "this effort taking three forms." The aim of this implacable categorizing is not just to map the intellectual territory: Barthes's taxonomies are never static. Often the point is precisely for one category to subvert the other, as do the two forms, which he calls *punctum* and *studium*, of his interest in photographs. Barthes offers classifications to keep matters open—to reserve a place for the uncodified, the enchanted, the intractable, the histrionic. He was fond of bizarre classifications, of classificatory excess (Fourier's, for example), and his boldly physical metaphors for mental life stress not topography but transformation. Drawn to hyperbole, as all aphorists are, Barthes enlists ideas in a drama, often a sensual melodrama or a faintly Gothic one. He speaks of the quiver, thrill, or shudder of meaning, of meanings that themselves vibrate, gather, loosen, disperse, quicken, shine, fold, mutate, delay, slide, separate, that exert pressure, crack, rupture, fissure, are pulverized. Barthes offers something like a poetics of thinking, which identifies the meaning of subjects with the very mobility of meaning, with the kinetics of consciousness itself; and liberates the critic as artist. The uses that binary and triadic thinking had for Barthes's imagination were always provisional, available to correction, destabilization, condensation.

As a writer he preferred short forms, and had been planning

to give a seminar on them; he was particularly drawn to miniature ones, like the haiku and the quotation; and, like all true writers, what enthralled him was "the detail" (his word) —experience's model short form. Even as an essayist, Barthes mostly wrote short, and the books he did write tend to be multiples of short forms rather than "real" books, itineraries of topics rather than unified arguments. His *Michelet*, for example, keys its inventory of the historian's themes to a large number of brief excerpts from Michelet's prolific writings. The most rigorous example of the argument as an itinerary by means of quotation is *S/Z*, published in 1970, his model exegesis of Balzac's *Sarrasine*. From staging the texts of others, he passed inevitably to the staging of his own ideas. And, in the same series on great writers (*"Ecrivains de toujours"*) to which he contributed the Michelet volume, he eventually did one on himself in 1975: that dazzling oddity in the series, *Roland Barthes* by Roland Barthes. The high-velocity arrangements of Barthes's late books dramatize both his fecundity (insatiability *and* lightness) and his desire to subvert all tendencies to system-making.

An animus against the systematizers has been a recurrent feature of intellectual good taste for more than a century; Kierkegaard, Nietzsche, Wittgenstein are among the many voices that proclaim, from a superior if virtually unbearable burden of singularity, the absurdity of systems. In its strong modern form, scorn for systems is one aspect of the protest against Law, against Power itself. An older, milder refusal is lodged in the French sceptic tradition, from Montaigne to Gide: writers who are epicures of their own consciousness are likely to decry "the sclerosis of systems," a phrase Barthes used in his first essay, on Gide. And along with these refusals a distinctive modern stylistics has evolved, the prototypes of which go back at least to Sterne and the German Romantics— the invention of anti-linear forms of narration: in fiction, the destruction of the "story"; in nonfiction, the abandonment of linear argument. The presumed impossibility (or irrelevance) of producing a continuous systematic argument has led to a remodeling of the standard long forms—the treatise, the long book—and a recasting of the genres of fiction, autobiography, and essay. Of this stylistics, Barthes is a particularly inventive practitioner.

The Romantic and post-Romantic sensibility discerns in every book a first-person performance: to write is a dramatic act, subject to dramatic elaboration. One strategy is to use multiple pseudonyms, as Kierkegaard did, concealing and multiplying the figure of the author. When autobiographical, the work invariably includes avowals of reluctance to speak in the first person. One of the conventions of *Roland Barthes* is for the autobiographer to refer to himself sometimes as "I," sometimes as "he." All this, Barthes announces on the first page of this book about himself, "must be considered as if spoken by a character in a novel." Under the meta-category of performance, not only the line between autobiography and fiction is muted, but that between essay and fiction as well. "Let the essay avow itself almost a novel," he says in *Roland Barthes*. Writing registers new forms of dramatic stress, of a self-referring kind: writing becomes the record of compulsions and of resistances to write. (In the further extension of this view, writing itself becomes the writer's subject.)

For the purpose of achieving an ideal digressiveness and an ideal intensity, two strategies have been widely adopted. One is to abolish some or all of the conventional demarcations or separations of discourse, such as chapters, paragraphing, even punctuation, whatever is regarded as impeding formally the continuous production of (the writer's) voice—the run-on method favored by writers of philosophical fictions such as Hermann Broch, Joyce, Stein, Beckett. The other strategy is the opposite one: to multiply the ways in which discourse is segmented, to invent further ways of breaking it up. Joyce and Stein used this method, too; Shklovsky in his best books, from the 1920s, writes in one-sentence paragraphs. The multiple openings and closures produced by the start-and-stop method permit discourse to become as differentiated, as polyphonous, as possible. Its most common shape in expository discourse is that of short, one- or two-paragraph units separated by spaces. "Notes on . . ." is the usual literary title—a form Barthes uses in the essay on Gide, and returns to often in his later work. Much of his writing proceeds by techniques of interruption, sometimes in the form of an excerpt alternating with a disjunctive commentary, as in *Michelet* and *S/Z*. To write in fragments or sequences or "notes" entails new, serial (rather than linear) forms of arrangements. These sequences may be staged in some arbitrary way. For example, they may be numbered— a method practiced with great refinement by Wittgenstein. Or they may be given headings, sometimes ironic or overemphatic —Barthes's strategy in *Roland Barthes*. Headings allow an additional possibility: for the elements to be arranged alphabetically, to emphasize further the arbitrary character of their sequence—the method of *A Lover's Discourse* (1977), whose real title evokes the notion of the fragment; it is *Fragments d'un discours amoureux*.

Barthes's late writing is his boldest formally: all major work was organized in a serial rather than linear form. Straight essay writing was reserved for the literary good deed (prefaces, for example, of which Barthes wrote many) or journalistic whim. However, these strong forms of the late writing only bring forward a desire implicit in all of his work— Barthes's wish to have a superior relation to assertion: the relation that art has, of pleasure. Such a conception of writing excludes the fear of contradiction. (In Wilde's phrase: "A truth in art is that whose contradiction is also true.") Barthes repeatedly compared teaching to play, reading to eros, writing to seduction. His voice became more and more personal, more full of grain, as he called it; his intellectual art more openly a performance, like that of the other great anti-systematizers. But whereas Nietzsche addresses the reader in many tones, mostly aggressive—exulting, berating, coaxing, prodding, taunting, inviting complicity—Barthes invariably performs in an affable register. There are no rude or prophetic claims, no pleadings with the reader, and no efforts *not* to be understood. This is seduction as play, never violation. All of Barthes's work is an exploration of the histrionic or ludic; in many ingenious modes, a plea for savor, for a festive (rather than dogmatic or credulous) relation to ideas. For Barthes, as for Nietzsche, the point is not to teach us something in particular. The point is to make us bold, agile, subtle, intelligent, detached. And to give pleasure.

Writing is Barthes's perennial subject—indeed, perhaps no one since Flaubert (in his letters) has thought as brilliantly, as passionately as Barthes has about what writing is. Much of his work is devoted to portraits of the vocation of the writer: from the early debunking studies included in *Mythologies* (1957) of the writer as seen by others, that is, the writer as fraud, such as "The Writer on Holiday," to more ambitious essays on writers writing, that is, the writer as hero and martyr, such as "Flaubert and the Sentence," about the writer's "agony of style." Barthes's wonderful essays on writers must be considered as different versions of his great apologia for the vocation of the writer. For all his admiration for the self-punishing standards of integrity set by Flaubert, he dares to conceive of writing as a kind of happiness: the point of his essay on Voltaire ("The Last Happy Writer"), and of his portrait of Fourier, unvexed by the sense of evil. In his late work he speaks directly of his own practice, scruples, bliss.

Barthes construes writing as an ideally complex form of

consciousness: a way of being both passive and active, social
and asocial, present and absent in one's own life. His idea of
the writer's vocation excludes the sequestration that Flaubert
thought inevitable, would appear to deny any conflict between
the writer's necessary inwardness and the pleasures of world-
liness. It is, so to speak, Flaubert strongly amended by Gide:
a more well-bred, casual rigor, an avid, guileful relation to
ideas that excludes fanaticism. Indeed, the ideal self-portrait—
the portrait of the self as writer—that Barthes sketched
throughout his work is virtually complete in the first essay, on
Gide's "work of egoism," his *Journal*. Gide supplied Barthes
with the patrician model for the writer who is supple, multiple;
never strident or vulgarly indignant; generous . . . but also
properly egotistical; incapable of being deeply influenced. He
notes how little Gide was altered by his vast reading ("so
many self-recognitions"), how his "discoveries" were never
"denials." And he praises the profusion of Gide's scruples,
observing that Gide's "situation at the intersection of great
contradictory currents has nothing facile about it . . ." Barthes
subscribes as well to Gide's idea of writing that is elusive,
willing to be minor. His relation to politics also recalls Gide's:
a willingness in times of ideological mobilization to take the
right stands, to be political—but, finally, not: and thereby,
perhaps, to tell the truth that hardly anybody else is telling.
(See the short essay Barthes wrote after a trip to China in
1974.) Barthes had many affinities with Gide, and much of
what he says of Gide applies unaltered to himself. How remarkable to find it all laid out—including the program of
"perpetual self-correction"—well before he embarked on his
career. (Barthes was twenty-seven, a patient in a sanatorium
for tubercular students, when he wrote this essay in 1942 for
the sanatorium's magazine; he did not enter the Paris literary
arena for another five years.)

    When Barthes, who began under the aegis of Gide's doctrine

of psychic and moral availability, started writing regularly, Gide's important work was long over, his influence already negligible (he died in 1951); and Barthes put on the armor of postwar debate about the responsibility of literature, the terms of which were set up by Sartre—the demand that the writer be in a militant relation to virtue, which Sartre described by the tautological notion of "commitment." Gide and Sartre were, of course, the two most influential writer-moralists of this century in France, and the work of these two sons of French Protestant culture suggests quite opposed moral and aesthetic choices. But it is just this kind of polarization that Barthes, another Protestant in revolt against Protestant moralism, seeks to avoid. Supple Gidean that he is, Barthes is eager to acknowledge the model of Sartre as well. While a quarrel with Sartre's view of literature lies at the heart of his first book, *Writing Degree Zero* (Sartre is never mentioned by name), an agreement with Sartre's view of the imagination, and its obsessional energies, surfaces in Barthes's last book, *Camera Lucida* (written "in homage" to the early Sartre, the author of *L'Imaginaire*). Even in the first book, Barthes concedes a good deal to Sartre's view of literature and language—for example, putting poetry with the other "arts" and identifying literature with prose, with argument. Barthes's view of literature in his subsequent writing was more complex. Though he never wrote on poetry, his standards for literature approached those of the poet: language that has undergone an upheaval, has been displaced, liberated from ungrateful contexts; that, so to speak, lives on its own. Although Barthes agrees with Sartre that the writer's vocation has an ethical imperative, he insists on its complexity and ambiguity. Sartre appeals to the morality of ends. Barthes invokes "the morality of form"— what makes literature a problem rather than a solution; what makes literature.

To conceive of literature as successful "communication"

and position-taking, however, is a sentiment that must inevitably become conformist. The instrumental view expounded in Sartre's *What Is Literature?* (1948) makes of literature something perpetually obsolete, a vain—and misplaced—struggle between ethical good soldiers and literary purists, that is, modernists. (Contrast the latent philistinism of this view of literature with the subtlety and acuity of what Sartre had to say about visual images.) Riven by his love of literature (the love recounted in his own perfect book, *The Words*) and an evangelical contempt for literature, one of the century's great *littérateurs* spent the last years of his life insulting literature and himself with that indigent idea, "the neurosis of literature." His defense of the writer's project of commitment is no more convincing. Accused of thereby reducing literature (to politics), Sartre protested that it would be more correct to accuse him of overestimating it. "If literature isn't *everything*, it's not worth a single hour of someone's trouble," he declared in an interview in 1960. "That's what I mean by 'commitment.' " But Sartre's inflation of literature to "everything" is another brand of depreciation.

Barthes, too, might be charged with overestimating literature—with treating literature as "everything"—but at least he made a good case for doing so. For Barthes understood (as Sartre did not) that literature is first of all, last of all, language. It is language that is everything. Which is to say that all of reality is presented in the form of language—the poet's wisdom, and also the structuralist's. And Barthes takes for granted (as Sartre, with his notion of writing as communication, did not) what he calls the "radical exploration of writing" undertaken by Mallarmé, Joyce, Proust, and their successors. That no venture is valuable unless it can be conceived as a species of radicalism, radicalism thereby unhinged from any distinctive content, is perhaps the essence of what we call modernism.

Barthes's work belongs to the sensibility of modernism in the extent to which it assumes the necessity of the adversary stance: literature conceived by modernist standards but not necessarily a modernist literature. Rather, all varieties of counterposition are available to it.

Perhaps the most striking difference between Sartre and Barthes is the deep one, of temperament. Sartre has an intellectually brutal, *bon enfant* view of the world, a view that wills simplicity, resolution, transparence; Barthes's view is irrevocably complex, self-conscious, refined, irresolute. Sartre was eager, too eager, to seek confrontation, and the tragedy of this great career, of the use he made of his stupendous intellect, was just his willingness to simplify himself. Barthes preferred to avoid confrontation, to evade polarization. He defines the writer as "the watcher who stands at the crossroads of all other discourses"—the opposite of an activist or a purveyor of doctrine.

Barthes's utopia of literature has an ethical character almost the opposite of Sartre's. It emerges in the connections he makes between desire and reading, desire and writing—his insistence that his own writing is, more than anything, the product of appetite. The words "pleasure," "bliss," "happiness" recur in his work with a weight, reminiscent of Gide, that is both voluptuous and subversive. As a moralist—Puritan or anti-Puritan—might solemnly distinguish sex for procreation from sex for pleasure, Barthes divides writers into those who write *something* (what Sartre meant by a writer) and the real writers, who do not write something but, rather, *write*. This intransitive sense of the verb "to write" Barthes endorses as not only the source of the writer's felicity but the model of freedom. For Barthes, it is not the commitment that writing makes to something outside of itself (to a social or moral goal) that makes literature an instrument of opposition and subversion but a certain practice of writing itself: excessive, playful, intricate, subtle, sensuous—language which can never be that of power.

Barthes's praise of writing as a gratuitous, free activity is, in one sense, a political view. He conceives of literature as a perpetual renewal of the right of individual assertion; and all rights are, finally, political ones. Still, Barthes is in an evasive relation to politics, and he is one of the great modern refusers of history. Barthes started publishing and mattering in the aftermath of World War II, which, astonishingly, he never mentions; indeed, in all his writings he never, as far as I recall, mentions the word "war." Barthes's friendly way of understanding subjects domesticates them, in the best sense. He lacks anything like Walter Benjamin's tragic awareness that every work of civilization is also a work of barbarism. The ethical burden for Benjamin was a kind of martyrdom; he could not help connecting it with politics. Barthes regards politics as a kind of constriction of the human (and intellectual) subject which has to be outwitted; in *Roland Barthes* he declares that he likes political positions "lightly held." Hence, perhaps, he was never gripped by the project that is central for Benjamin, as for all true modernists: to try to fathom the nature of "the modern." Barthes, who was not tormented by the catastrophes of modernity or tempted by its revolutionary illusions, had a post-tragic sensibility. He refers to the present literary era as "a moment of gentle apocalypse." Happy indeed the writer who can pronounce such a phrase.

Much of Barthes's work is devoted to the repertoire of pleasure—"the great adventure of desire," as he calls it in the essay on Brillat-Savarin's *Physiology of Taste*. Collecting a model of felicity from each thing he examines, he assimilates intellectual practice itself to the erotic. Barthes called the life of the mind desire, and was concerned to defend "the plurality of desire." Meaning is never monogamous. His joyful wisdom or gay science offers the ideal of a free yet capacious, satisfied consciousness; of a condition in which one does not have to choose between good and bad, true and false, in which it is not necessary to justify. The texts and enterprises that engaged Barthes tend to be those in which he could read a defiance of these antitheses. For example, this is how Barthes construes fashion: as a domain, like eros, where contraries do not exist ("Fashion seeks equivalences, validities—not verities"); where one can allow oneself to be gratified; where meaning—and pleasure—is profuse.

To construe in this way, Barthes requires a master category through which everything can be refracted, which makes possible the maximum number of intellectual moves. That most inclusive category is language, the widest sense of language— meaning form itself. Thus, the subject of *Système de la mode* (1967) is not fashion but the language of fashion. Barthes assumes, of course, that the language of fashion *is* fashion; that, as he said in an interview, "fashion exists only through the discourse on it." Assumptions of this sort (myth is a language, fashion is a language) have become a leading, often reductive convention of contemporary intellectual endeavor. In Barthes's work the assumption is less a reductive one than it is proliferative—embarrassment of riches for the critic as artist. To stipulate that there is no understanding outside of language is to assert that there is meaning *everywhere.*

By so extending the reach of meaning, Barthes takes the notion over the top, to arrive at such triumphant paradoxes as the empty subject that contains everything, the empty sign to which all meaning can be attributed. With this euphoric sense of how meaning proliferates, Barthes reads that "zero degree of the monument," the Eiffel Tower, as "this pure— virtually empty—sign" that (his italics) *"means everything."* (The characteristic point of Barthes's arguments-by-paradox is to vindicate subjects untrammeled by utility: it is the use-lessness of the Eiffel Tower that makes it infinitely useful as a sign, just as the uselessness of genuine literature is what makes it morally useful.) Barthes found a world of such liberating absences of meaning, both modernist and simply non-Western, in Japan; Japan, he noted, was full of empty signs. In place of moralistic antitheses—true versus false, good versus bad— Barthes offers complementary extremes. "Its form is empty but present, its meaning absent but full," he writes about myth in an essay in the 1950s. Arguments about many sub-jects have this identical climax: that absence is really presence, emptiness repletion, impersonality the highest achievement of the personal.

Like that euphoric register of religious understanding which discerns treasures of meaning in the most banal and meaning-less, which designates as the richest carrier of meaning one vacant of meaning, the brilliant descriptions in Barthes's work bespeak an ecstatic experience of understanding; and ecstasy— whether religious, aesthetic, or sexual—has perennially been described by the metaphors of being empty and being full, the zero state and the state of maximal plentitude: their alterna-tion, their equivalence. The very transposing of subjects into the discourse about them is the same kind of move: emptying subjects out to fill them up again. It is a method of under-standing that, presuming ecstasy, fosters detachment. And his very idea of language also supports both aspects of Barthes's sensibility: while endorsing a profusion of meaning, the Saus-surean theory—that language *is* form (rather than substance) —is wonderfully congruent with a taste for elegant, that is, reticent, discourse. Creating meaning through the intellectual equivalent of negative space, Barthes's method has one never talking about subjects in themselves: fashion is the language of fashion, a country (Japan) is "the empire of signs"—the ultimate accolade. For reality to exist *as* signs conforms to a maximum idea of decorum: all meaning is deferred, indirect, elegant.

Barthes's ideals of impersonality, of reticence, of elegance, are set forth most beautifully in his appreciation of Japanese culture: in the book called *Empire of Signs* (1970) and in his essay on the Bunraku puppets. This essay, "Lesson in Writing," recalls Kleist's "On the Puppet Theater," which similarly celebrates the tranquillity, lightness, and grace of beings free of thinking, of meaning—free of "the disorders of consciousness." Like the puppets in Kleist's essay, the Bunraku puppets are seen as incarnating an ideal "impassivity, clarity, agility, subtlety." To be both impassive and fantastic, inane and profound, unselfconscious and supremely sensuous —these qualities that Barthes discerned in various facets of Japanese civilization project an ideal of taste and deportment, the ideal of the aesthete in its larger meaning that has been in general circulation since the dandies of the late eighteenth century. Barthes was hardly the first Western observer for whom Japan has meant an aesthete's utopia, the place where one finds aesthete views everywhere and exercises one's own at liberty. The culture where aesthete goals are central—not, as in the West, eccentric—was bound to elicit a strong response. (Japan is mentioned in the Gide essay written in 1942.)

Of the available models of the aesthetic way of looking at the world, perhaps the most eloquent are French and Japanese. In France it has largely been a literary tradition, though with annexes in two popular arts, gastronomy and fashion. Barthes did take up the subject of food as ideology, as classification, as taste—he talks often of savoring; and it seems inevitable that he found the subject of fashion congenial. Writers from Baudelaire to Cocteau have taken fashion seriously, and one of the founding figures of literary modernism, Mallarmé, edited a fashion magazine. French culture, where aesthete ideals have been more explicit and influential than in any other European culture, allows a link between ideas of vanguard art and of fashion. (The French have never shared the Anglo-American conviction that makes the fashionable the opposite of the serious.) In Japan, aesthete standards appear to imbue the whole culture, and long predate the modern ironies; they were formulated as early as the late tenth century, in Sei Shōnagon's *Pillow Book*, that breviary of consummate dandy attitudes, written in what is for us an astonishingly modern, disjunctive form—notes, anecdotes, and lists. Barthes's interest in Japan expresses the attraction to a less defensive, more innocent, and far more elaborated version of the aesthete sensibility: emptier and prettier than the French, more straightforward (no beauty in ugliness, as in Baudelaire); pre-apocalyptic, refined, serene.

In Western culture, where it remains marginal, the dandy attitude has the character of an exaggeration. In one form, the older one, the aesthete is a willful exclusionist of taste, holding attitudes that make it possible to like, to be comfortable with, to give one's assent to the smallest number of things; reducing things to the smallest expression of them. (When taste distributes its plusses and minuses, it favors diminutive adjectives, such as—for praise—happy, amusing, charming, agreeable, suitable.) Elegance equals the largest amount of refusal. As language, this attitude finds its consummate expression in the rueful quip, the disdainful one-liner. In the other form, the aesthete sustains standards that make it possible to be pleased with the largest number of things; annexing new, unconventional, even illicit sources of pleasure. The literary device that best projects this attitude is the list (*Roland Barthes* has many)—the whimsical aesthete polyphony that juxtaposes things and experiences of a starkly different, often incongruous nature, turning them all, by this technique, into artifacts, aesthetic objects. Here elegance equals the wittiest acceptances. The aesthete's posture alternates between *never* being satisfied and *always* finding a way of being satisfied, being pleased with virtually everything.[1]

Although both directions of dandy taste presuppose detachment, the exclusivist version is cooler. The inclusivist version can be enthusiastic, even effusive; the adjectives used for praise tend to be over- rather than understatements. Barthes, who had much of the high exclusivist taste of the dandy, was more inclined to its modern, democratizing form: aesthete leveling —hence his willingness to find charm, amusement, happiness, pleasure in so many things. His account of Fourier, for example, is finally an aesthete's appraisal. Of the "little details" that, he says, make up the "whole of Fourier," Barthes writes: "I am carried away, dazzled, convinced by a sort of charm of expressions . . . Fourier is swarming with these felicities . . . I cannot resist these pleasures; they seem 'true' to me." Similarly: what another *flâneur*, less committed to finding pleasure everywhere, might experience as the oppressive overcrowdedness of streets in Tokyo signifies for Barthes "the transformation of quality by quantity," a new relation that is "a source of endless jubilation."

Many of Barthes's judgments and interests are implicitly affirmations of the aesthete's standards. His early essays championing the fiction of Robbe-Grillet, which gave Barthes the misleading reputation as an advocate of literary modernism, were in effect aesthete polemics. The "objective," the "literal"—these austere, minimalist ideas of literature are in fact Barthes's ingenious recycling of one of the aesthete's principal theses: that surface is as telling as depth. What Barthes discerned in Robbe-Grillet in the 1950s was a new,

[1] The version of the aesthete sensibility I once tried to include under the name "camp" can be regarded as a technique of taste for making the aesthete taste less exclusionary (a way of liking more than one really wants to like) and as part of the democratizing of dandy attitudes. Camp taste, however, still presupposes the older, high standards of discrimination—in contrast to the taste incarnated by, say, Andy Warhol, the franchiser and mass marketer of the dandyism of leveling.

high-tech version of the dandy writer; what he hailed in Robbe-Grillet was the desire "to establish the novel on the surface," thereby frustrating our desire to "fall back on a psychology." The idea that depths are obfuscating, demagogic, that no human essence stirs at the bottom of things, and that freedom lies in staying on the surface, the large glass on which desire circulates—this is the central argument of the modern aesthete position, in the various exemplary forms it has taken over the last hundred years. (Baudelaire. Wilde. Duchamp. Cage.)

Barthes is constantly making an argument against depth, against the idea that the most real is latent, submerged. Bunraku is seen as refusing the antinomy of matter and soul, inner and outer. "*Myth hides nothing*," he declares in "Myth Today" (1956). The aesthete position not only regards the notion of depths, of hiddenness, as a mystification, a lie, but opposes the very idea of antitheses. Of course, to speak of depths and surfaces is already to misrepresent the aesthetic view of the world—to reiterate a duality, like that of form and content, it precisely denies. The largest statement of this position was made by Nietzsche, whose work constitutes a criticism of fixed antitheses (good versus evil, right versus wrong, true versus false).

But while Nietzsche scorned "depths," he exalted "heights." In the post-Nietzschean tradition, there are neither depths nor heights; there are only various kinds of surface, of spectacle. Nietzsche said that every profound nature needs a mask, and spoke—profoundly—in praise of intellectual ruse; but he was making the gloomiest prediction when he said that the coming century, ours, would be the age of the actor. An ideal of seriousness, of sincerity, underlies all of Nietzsche's work, which makes the overlap of his ideas and those of a true aesthete (like Wilde, like Barthes) so problematic. Nietzsche was a histrionic thinker but not a lover of the histrionic.

His ambivalence toward spectacle (after all, his criticism of Wagner's music was finally that it was a seduction), his insistence on the authenticity of spectacle, means that criteria other than the histrionic are in effect. In the aesthete's position, the notions of reality and spectacle precisely reinforce and infuse each other, and seduction is always something positive. In this respect, Barthes's ideas have an exemplary coherence. Notions of the theater inform, directly or indirectly, all his work. (Divulging the secret, late, he declares in *Roland Barthes* that there was no single text of his "which did not treat of a certain theater, and the spectacle is the universal category through whose forms the world is seen.") Barthes explains Robbe-Grillet's empty, "anthological" description as a technique of theatrical distancing (presenting an object "as if it were in itself a spectacle"). Fashion is, of course, another casebook of the theatrical. So is Barthes's interest in photography, which he treats as a realm of pure haunted spectatorship. In the account of photography given in *Camera Lucida* there are hardly any photographers—the subject is photographs (treated virtually as found objects) and those who are fascinated by them: as objects of erotic reverie, as *memento mori*.

What he wrote about Brecht, whom he discovered in 1954 (when the Berliner Ensemble visited Paris with their production of *Mother Courage*) and helped make known in France, has less to do with the theatrical than does his treatment of some subjects as *forms* of the theatrical. In his frequent use of Brecht in seminars of the 1970s, he cited the prose writings, which he took as a model of critical acuity; it was not Brecht the maker of didactic spectacles but Brecht the didactic intellectual who finally mattered to Barthes. In contrast, with Bunraku what Barthes valued was the element of theatricality as such. In Barthes's early work, the theatrical is the domain of liberty, the place where identities are only roles and one can *change* roles, a zone where meaning itself may be refused.

(Barthes speaks of Bunraku's privileged "exemption from meaning.") Barthes's talk about the theatrical, like his evangelism of pleasure, is a way of proselytizing for the attenuating, lightening, baffling of the Logos, of meaning itself.

To affirm the notion of the spectacle is the triumph of the aesthete's position: the promulgation of the ludic, the refusal of the tragic. All of Barthes's intellectual moves have the effect of voiding work of its "content," the tragic of its finality. That is the sense in which his work is genuinely subversive, liberating—playful. It is outlaw discourse, in the great aesthete tradition, which often assumes the liberty of rejecting the "substance" of discourse in order better to appreciate its "form": outlaw discourse turned respectable, as it were, with the help of various theories known as varieties of formalism. In numerous accounts of his intellectual evolution, Barthes describes himself as the perpetual disciple—but the point that he really wants to make is that he remains, finally, untouched. He spoke of his having worked under the aegis of a succession of theories and masters. In fact, Barthes's work has altogether more coherence, and ambivalence. For all his connection with tutelary doctrines, Barthes's submission to doctrine was superficial. In the end, it was necessary that all intellectual gadgetry be discarded. His last books are a kind of unraveling of his ideas. *Roland Barthes*, he says, is the book of his resistance to his ideas, the dismantling of his own authority. And in the inaugural lecture that marked his acceding to a position of the highest authority—the Chair of Literary Semiology at the Collège de France in 1977—Barthes chooses, characteristically enough, to argue for a soft intellectual authority. He praises teaching as a permissive, not a coercive, space where one can be relaxed, disarmed, floating.

Language itself, which Barthes called a "utopia" in the euphoric formulation that ends *Writing Degree Zero*, now comes under attack, as another form of "power," and his very effort to convey his sensitivity to the ways in which language is "power" gives rise to that instantly notorious hyperbole in his Collège de France lecture: the power of language is "quite simply fascist." To assume that society is ruled by monolithic ideologies and repressive mystifications is necessary to Barthes's advocacy of egoism, post-revolutionary but nevertheless antinomian: his notion that the affirmation of the unremittingly personal is a subversive act. This is a classic extension of the aesthete attitude, in which it becomes a politics: a politics of radical individuality. Pleasure is largely identified with unauthorized pleasure, and the right of individual assertion with the sanctity of the asocial self. In the late writings, the theme of protest against power takes the form of an increasingly private definition of experience (as fetishized involvement) and a ludic definition of thought. "The great problem," Barthes says in a late interview, "is to outplay the signified, to outplay law, to outplay the father, to outplay the repressed—I do not say to explode it, but to outplay it." The aesthete's ideal of detachment, of the selfishness of detachment, allows for avowals of passionate, obsessed involvement: the selfishness of ardor, of fascination. (Wilde speaks of his "curious mixture of ardour and of indifference . . . I would go to the stake for a sensation and be a sceptic to the last.") Barthes has to keep affirming the aesthete's detachment, and undermining it—with passions.

Like all great aesthetes, Barthes was an expert at having it both ways. Thus he identifies writing both with a generous relation to the world (writing as "perpetual production") and with a defiant relation (writing as "a perpetual revolution of language," outside the bounds of power). He wants a politics and an anti-politics, a critical relation to the world and one beyond moral considerations. The aesthete's radicalism is the radicalism of a privileged, even a replete, consciousness —but a genuine radicalism nonetheless. All genuine moral views are founded on a notion of refusal, and the aesthete's view, which can be conformist, does provide certain potentially powerful, not just elegant, grounds for a great refusal.

The aesthete's radicalism: to be multiple, to make multiple identifications; to assume fully the privilege of the personal. Barthes's work—he avows that he writes by obsessions—consists of continuities and detours; the accumulation of points of view; finally, their disburdenment: a mixture of progress and caprice. For Barthes, liberty is a state that consists in remaining plural, fluid, vibrating with doctrine; whose price is being indecisive, apprehensive, fearful of being taken for an impostor. The writer's freedom that Barthes describes is, in part, flight. The writer is the deputy of his own ego—of that self in perpetual flight before what is fixed by writing, as the mind is in perpetual flight from doctrine. "Who *speaks* is not who *writes*, and who *writes* is not who *is*." Barthes wants to move on—that is one of the imperatives of the aesthete's sensibility.

Throughout his work Barthes projects himself into his subject. He is Fourier: unvexed by the sense of evil, aloof from politics, "that necessary purge"; he "vomits it up." He is the Bunraku puppet: impersonal, subtle. He is Gide: the writer who is ageless (always young, always mature); the writer as egoist—a triumphant species of "simultaneous being" or plural desire. He is the subject of all the subjects that he praises. (That he must, characteristically, praise may be connected with his project of defining, creating standards for himself.) In this sense, much of what Barthes wrote now appears autobiographical.

Eventually, it became autobiographical in the literal sense. A brave meditation on the personal, on the self, is at the center of his late writings and seminars. Much of Barthes's work, especially the last three books with their poignant themes of loss, constitutes a candid defense of his sensuality (as well as his sexuality)—his flavor, his way of tasting the world. The books are also artfully anti-confessional. *Camera Lucida* is a meta-book: a meditation on the even more personal auto-biographical book that he planned to write about photographs of his mother, who died in 1978, and then put aside. Barthes starts from the modernist model of writing that is superior to any idea of intention or mere expressiveness; a mask. "The work," Valéry insists, "should not give the person it affects anything that can be reduced to an idea of the author's person and thinking."[2] But this commitment to impersonality does not preclude the avowal of the self; it is only another variation on the project of self-examination: the noblest project of French literature. Valéry offers one ideal of self-absorption—impersonal, disinterested. Rousseau offers another ideal—passionate, avowing vulnerability. Many themes of Barthes's work lie in the classic discourse of French literary culture: its taste for elegant abstraction, in particular for the formal analysis of the sentiments; its disdain for mere psychology; and its coquetry about the impersonal (Flaubert declaring *"Madame Bovary, c'est moi"* but also insisting in letters on his novel's "impersonality," its lack of connection with himself).

Barthes is the latest major participant in the great national literary project, inaugurated by Montaigne: the self as vocation, life as a reading of the self. The enterprise construes the self as the locus of all possibilities, avid, unafraid of contradiction (nothing need be lost, everything may be gained), and the exercise of consciousness as a life's highest aim, be-

---

[2] This modernist dictum that writing is, ideally, a form of impersonality or absence underlies Barthes's move to eliminate the "author" when considering a book. (The method of his *S/Z*: an exemplary reading of a Balzac novella as virtually an authorless text.) One of the things Barthes does as a critic is to formulate the mandate for one kind of modernism (Flaubert, Valéry, Eliot) for the writer as a general program for *readers*. Another is to contravene that mandate in practice—for most of Barthes's writing is precisely devoted to personal singularity.

cause only through becoming fully conscious may one be free. The distinctive French utopian tradition is this vision of reality redeemed, recovered, transcended by consciousness; a vision of the life of the mind as a life of desire, of full intelligence and pleasure—so different from, say, the traditions of high moral seriousness of German and of Russian literature.

Inevitably, Barthes's work had to end in autobiography. "One must choose between being a terrorist and being an egoist," he once observed in a seminar. The options seem very French. Intellectual terrorism is a central, respectable form of intellectual practice in France—tolerated, humored, rewarded: the "Jacobin" tradition of ruthless assertion and shameless ideological about-faces; the mandate of incessant judgment, opinion, anathematizing, overpraising; the taste for extreme positions, then casually reversed, and for deliberate provocation. Alongside this, how modest egoism is!

Barthes's voice became steadily more intimate, his subjects more inward. An affirmation of his own idiosyncrasy (which he does not "decipher") is the main theme of *Roland Barthes*. He writes about the body, taste, love; solitude; erotic desolation; finally, death, or rather desire and death: the twin subjects of the book on photography. As in the Platonic dialogues, the thinker (writer, reader, teacher) and the lover—the two main figures of the Barthesian self—are joined. Barthes, of course, means his erotics of literature more literally, as literally as he can. (The text *enters*, *fills*, it *grants* euphoria.) But finally he seems fairly Platonic after all. The monologue of *A Lover's Discourse*, which obviously draws on a story of disappointment in love, ends in a spiritual vision in the classic Platonic way, in which lower loves are transmuted into higher, more inclusive ones. Barthes avows that he "wants to unmask, no longer to interpret, but to make of consciousness itself a drug, and thus accede to a vision of irreducible reality, to the great drama of clarity, to prophetic love."

As he divested himself of theories, he gave less weight to the modernist standard of the intricate. He does not want, he says, to place any obstacles between himself and the reader. The last book is part memoir (of his mother), part meditation on eros, part treatise on the photographic image, part invocation of death—a book of piety, resignation, desire; a certain brilliance is being renounced, and the view itself is of the simplest. The subject of photography provided the great exemption, perhaps release, from the exactions of formalist taste. In choosing to write about photography, Barthes takes the occasion to adopt the warmest kind of realism: photographs fascinate because of what they are about. And they may awaken a desire for a further divestment of the self. ("Looking at certain photographs," he writes in *Camera Lucida*, "I wanted to be a primitive, without culture.") The Socratic sweetness and charm become more plaintive, more desperate: writing is an embrace, a being embraced; every idea is an idea reaching out. There is a sense of disaggregation of his ideas, and of himself—represented by his increasing fascination with what he calls "the detail." In the preface to *Sade/Fourier/Loyola,* Barthes writes: "Were I a writer, and dead, how pleased I would be if my life, through the efforts of some friendly and detached biographer, were to reduce itself to a few details, a few preferences, a few inflections, let us say: to 'biographemes' whose distinction and mobility might travel beyond the limits of any fate, and come to touch, like Epicurean atoms, some future body, destined to the same dispersion." The need to touch, even in the perspective of his own mortality.

Barthes's late work is filled with signals that he has come to the end of something—the enterprise of the critic as artist—and was seeking to become another kind of writer. (He announced his intention to write a novel.) There were exalted avowals of vulnerability, of being forlorn. Barthes more and more entertained an idea of writing which resembles the mystical idea of *kenosis*, emptying out. He acknowledged that not only systems—his ideas were in a state of melt—but the "I" as well has to be dismantled. (True knowledge, says Barthes, depends on the "unmasking of the 'I.'") The aesthetics of absence—the empty sign, the empty subject, the exemption from meaning—were all intimations of the great project of depersonalization which is the aesthete's highest gesture of good taste. Toward the close of Barthes's work, this ideal took on another inflection. A spiritual ideal of depersonalization—that is perhaps the characteristic terminus of every serious aesthete's position. (Think of Wilde, of Valéry.) It is the point at which the aesthete's view self-destructs: what follows is either silence —or becoming something else.

Barthes harbored spiritual strivings that could not be supported by his aesthete's position. It was inevitable that he pass beyond it, as he did in his very last work and teaching. At the end, he had done with the aesthetics of absence, and now spoke of literature as the embrace of subject and object. There was an emergence of a vision of "wisdom" of the Platonic sort—tempered, to be sure, by wisdom of a worldly kind: skeptical of dogmatisms, conscientious about gratification, wistfully attached to utopian ideals. Barthes's temperament, style, sensibility, had run its course. And from this vantage point his work now appears to unfold, with more grace and poignancy and with far greater intellectual power than that of any other contemporary, the considerable truths vouchsafed to the aesthete's sensibility, to a commitment to intellectual adventure, to the talent for contradiction and inversion— those "late" ways of experiencing, evaluating, reading the world; and surviving in it, drawing energy, finding consolation (but finally not), taking pleasure, expressing love.

Susan Sontag

Note

This selection of Barthes's work was devised over a year before death closed the canon, and without consulting the author.

The ordering is chronological, and has three parts, corresponding to the three decades in which Barthes did the bulk of his work. Part One, which starts with the first text Barthes published, in 1942, includes work that appeared in the 1950s. Part Two includes work from the 1960s. Part Three, the work from the 1970s, ends with the last essay published before he died. So conventional a grouping is not meant to suggest a notion about how, if at all, Barthes's work falls into periods; it is just a formal way of taking a breath.

These are the first English translations of the opening and closing essays in the Reader. The Inaugural Lecture, which Barthes gave when he was elected to a chair at the Collège de France in 1977, appears here in English for the first time in book form.

Most selections, being essays, are of course complete. Whole sections from several larger works, such as *Writing Degree Zero*, are given uncut. In the case of the short sections drawn from different parts of *The Pleasure of the Text* and *Roland Barthes*, the jumps in the text are indicated by three dots.

Some writings were chosen because they seemed so representative of Barthes's work, or have been so influential. Mostly I chose writings that I find particularly fortifying; or, in a few cases, that seem to me irresistibly odd.

Barthes is such a glorious writer that there has to be a problem about what to exclude. It seemed unwise to try to make a larger, more compendious volume than this. But, inevitably, I have had some afterthoughts. How I wish now that I had included Barthes's essay on La Rochefoucauld, his "From Work to Text," and "The Death of the Author," his preface to Brillat-Savarin's *The Physiology of Taste*, and "Change the Object Itself," his second thoughts on mythology (from 1971). As my admiration for and pleasure in Barthes's work is unending, the list is actually longer, but I cannot resist these few rueful commendations. And, obviously, no excerpts can do justice to Barthes's last and deepest books, the three installments of one of the most intelligent, subtle, and gallant of autobiographical projects: *Roland Barthes*, *A Lover's Discourse*, and *Camera Lucida*. I implore readers of this Reader to go on, or back, to them.

S.S.
December 1981

PART ONE

On Gide and His Journal

Reluctant to enclose Gide in a system I knew would never content me, I was vainly trying to find some connection among these notes. Finally I decided it would be better to offer them as such—notes—and not try to disguise their lack of continuity. Incoherence seems to me preferable to a distorting order.

I. *THE JOURNAL*

I doubt that the *Journal* has much interest, if reading the work has not awakened some initial curiosity as to the man.

In Gide's *Journal* the reader will find his ethic—the genesis and the life of his books—his readings—the basis for a critique of his work—silences—exquisite instances of wit—trivial avowals which make him man par excellence, another Montaigne.

"Notes sur André Gide et son Journal" was published in July 1942 in *Existences*, the magazine of the Sanatorium des Etudiants de France at Saint-Hilaire-du-Touvet (Isère). Barthes, who had tuberculosis, was a patient there in 1942 and 1943–5.
Translated by Richard Howard.

Many entries in the *Journal* will doubtless irritate those who have some prejudice, secret or otherwise, against Gide. These same entries will delight those who have some reason, secret or otherwise, to believe themselves like Gide. This is true of any personality which *compromises itself*.

The *Journal* is not an explanatory, an external work; it is not a chronicle (though actuality is often caught in its web). It is not like Jules Renard's journals, or like Saint-Simon, and those who scan it for important judgments on the work of some contemporary (Valéry or Claudel, of whom Gide often speaks) will certainly be disappointed. It is a work of *egoism*, in fact, and especially when it speaks of others. Though Gide's aim is always good, it is valid only because of its reflexive force, turning back on Gide himself.

"What must appear here is precisely what is too insignificant to have been retained by the sieve of any *work*. Here I must write, and without prearrangement, *details* (1929)." Hence we must not suppose that the *Journal* is in opposition to the work and not itself a work of art. There are sentences which are halfway between confession and creation; they require only to be inserted into a novel and are already less sincere (or rather: their sincerity counts less than something else, which is the pleasure we take in reading them). I should prefer to say this: it is not "Edouard's Journal" which resembles Gide's; on the contrary, many entries in Gide's *Journal* have the autonomy of "Edouard's Journal." They are no longer completely Gide; they begin to be outside him, en route for some unspecified work in which they want to appear, which they summon into being.

Nietzsche writes: "Far from being superficial, a great Frenchman has his superficies to the extreme degree, a natural envelope which surrounds his depths" (*Dawn,* aphorism 192).

Gide's work constitutes his depths; let us say that his *Journal* is his superficies; he draws his contours and juxtaposes his extremes; readings, reflections, narratives show how distant these extremes are, how enormous is Gide's superficies.

II. *DAS SCHAUDERN*

Goethe, quoted by Gide: "Fear and trembling (*das Schaudern*) is the best of man."

Goethe's *Schaudern* is very much like Montaigne's "marvelously supple man." I don't know if we have accorded enough importance to Gide's Goethean aspect; the same is also true of his affinities with Montaigne (Gide's predilections indicate not an influence but an identity); it is never without a reason that Gide writes a critical work. His preface to selections from Montaigne, indeed his very choice of texts, tells us as much about Gide as about Montaigne.

The Dialogues. Nothing more characteristic of French literature, nothing more precious than these duets which occur, from century to century, between writers of the same class: Pascal and Montaigne, Rousseau and Molière, Hugo and Voltaire, Valéry and Descartes, Montaigne and Gide. Nothing offers better proof of the perenniality of this literature, and also, precisely, of its *Schaudern*, its suppleness, by which it manages to escape the sclerosis of systems, by which its remotest past is renewed upon contact with a present intelligence. If the great classics of French literature are eternal, it is because they can still be modified. The stream is more durable than marble . . .

A critic of Gide must not attempt to produce a portrait of him in terms of good and evil, as biographers are in the habit of doing; his role should be to keep us from misjudging—out of ignorance, or even worse, out of preterition, deliberate or otherwise—certain of his works, or of his expressions. It is a matter of being "infinitely respectful of personality," as Gide himself was of others'. Indeed, the *Journal* is often written to correct some notion of Gide we might have arrived at because of quotations out of context, false reports, inexact words. It is a perpetual self-correction; like a scrupulous *projector*, Gide constantly adjusts his image to counteract the public's lazy or spiteful vision. "They want to make me into a dreadfully anxious being. My only anxiety is to find my thoughts misinterpreted" (*Journal*, 1927).

Let those who blame Gide for his contradictions (his refusal to choose among them) remember this page of Hegel: "For common sense, an opposition between true and false is something fixed; common sense expects us to approve or to reject an existing system *en bloc*. It does not conceive the difference among philosophical systems as the gradual development of truth; for common sense diversity means only contradiction . . . The mind which grasps contradiction cannot release it and keep it in its unilateralness and recognize (in the form of what seems to oppose and contradict itself) mutually necessary moments."

Gide is a simultaneous being. To a greater or lesser degree, Nature has posited him as complete, from the very first. He has merely taken the time to reveal the various aspects of himself in succession, but we must always remember that these aspects are in fact contemporaries of each other, as are his works: "It is still hard for them to admit that these books have cohabited, and cohabit even now in my mind. They succeed each other only on paper and because it was impossible to write them simultaneously. Whatever book I am writing, I never give myself up to it altogether, and the subject which next demands me most insistently is even now developing at the other end of myself" (*Journal*, 1909). Whence: fidelity and contradictions. *Fidelity*: All of Gide is in André Walter, and André Walter is still in Gide's 1939 *Journal*. It follows that Gide is ageless; he is always young, always mature; he is always sage, always fervent. Perhaps the latter half of his life, because of his great age, has assumed a darker tonality, in the manner of the Greek tragic poets. But he has been able to incarnate certain of his tendencies—or certain aspects—in young men quite as well as in old (Gide's characters are never objective without being purely himself), in Lafcadio as well as in La Pérouse. Gide has a loyal heart, a loyal soul. Indeed, it is odd how little his vast reading has altered his physiognomy. His discoveries have never been denials. When he read Nietzsche, Dostoevsky, Whitman, Blake, or Browning (except for Goethe, whose influence he admits), these encounters were so many self-recognitions, hence so many reasons for continuity. Gide's situation at the intersection of great contradictory currents has nothing facile about it. Which makes his perseverance admirable: indeed, it is his very *raison d'être*, the thing that makes him great. How many would have made a conversion into an ending? This fidelity to the truth of his life is heroic. "How much easier to proceed according to a given aesthetic and a given ethic! Writers who subscribe to a recognized religion advance confidently enough. I must invent everything. Sometimes this results in endless groping toward an almost imperceptible light. And sometimes I whisper to myself: What's the use?" (*Journal*, 1930).

Contradictions. In what direction, then, could this loyal nature move, though each of his works leaves an impression of iridescence and transformation—so that he has often been accused of inconsistency and evasion? Here we must dissipate the prejudice of rigidity: certain minds seem consistent because they are forever harping on one and the same quality;

they spirit away their hesitations and present only the hardened surface of their new opinion, which they solidify by doing
violence to a great many others. Gide's attitude, confronted
with such minds, is humbler and more measured. Possessing a
conscience which ordinary morality has the odd habit of calling
sickly, Gide explains himself, surrenders himself, delicately
retracts or asserts himself bravely enough, but never abuses
the reader as to his mutations; Gide puts everything in the
movement of his thought and not in its brutal profession. I
see several reasons for this attitude: (1) the impulses of a
soul are the mark of its authenticity (Gide's entire effort is to
render himself and others "authentic"); (2) the aesthetic
pleasure he takes in slowly revealing the infinitesimal changes
of his nature (*movement* remaining for Gide the best of man);
(3) the profusion of his scruples in the search for truth,
pursued through the finest nuances (truth is never brutal);
(4) lastly, the moral importance accorded to states of conflict, perhaps because they are warrants of humility.

In Japan, where the conflict between Catholicism and Prot-
estantism, between Hellenism and Christianity, may not have
much meaning, Gide is nonetheless widely read. What is it that
is admired in this writer? The image of a conscience which
honestly pursues its truth.

The only point where we can speak of Gide's *development*
is this: at a certain moment the social question assumed a
larger importance for him than the ethical one. In 1901, he
wrote: "Social questions? Of course. But the ethical ones
come first. Man is more interesting than men: it is *he* and not
them whom God created in His image. Each is more precious
than all" (*Journal*). Then, in 1934, when world revolutions
take him from the world of art: ". . . I feel almost nothing but

sympathy. Wherever I look, I see nothing but distress. To remain contemplative today, a spectator, is to give evidence of an inhuman philosophy or a monstrous blindness" (*Journal*). But does this represent a true development? At most, in Gide, a recrudescence of the evangelical ferment to which he surrenders all the more freely, no longer bearing the shackles of his youth; and also the weight of actuality which he has always felt in human terms.

Some choose a path and keep to it; others change paths, each time with the same conviction. Gide has remained at an intersection, constantly, loyally, at the most important, the most populous one, where the two greatest roads of the West cross—the Greek and the Christian; he has preferred this *total* situation, where he could receive both lights, both energies. In this heroic situation, protected by nothing but also enclosed by nothing, he has subjected himself to every attack, offered himself to every affection. For him to endure in so perilous a situation, this man required a certain hardness, out of which masterpieces are made . . .

Yet this cannot be denied: "He who loveth his life shall lose it." This saying of Christ's is the basis of every one of Gide's works. His entire output can be considered as a certain mythology of pride. Pride, for him, is the capital moral phenomenon. Every critic must insist on this and show the place this subject occupies, from *Dostoevsky* to *Numquid et tu?* and the diptych of *The Immoralist* and *Strait Is the Gate*. It is no use claiming to know Gide to any degree if we do not have a clear conception of the importance of this evangelical saying.

In the last hundred years, there have been three men who have had the most intense, the most intimate, and even what I

might call the most fraternal attraction to Christ's person—
outside of a dogmatic or mystical knowledge: Nietzsche (as a
frère ennemi), Rozanov, and Gide.

"Confronting this Asiaticism," Gide writes (he is talking
about Renan, Barrès, Loti, Lemaître), "how Dorian I feel!"
(*Journal*, 1932). Gide's Hellenism is fulfilled during his old
age. From the time of *Fruits of the Earth* there was always
something Hellenistic about him: Pierre Louÿs was not far
away. But of late he has become truly Greek, i.e., tragic. In
the last years of the *Journal*, there are admirable pages to
which wisdom and suffering give an extraordinary resonance
of purity and proximity. Now the difficult thing, so successfully achieved by the fifth-century Greeks, is to be wise without necessarily being reasonable, to be happy without necessarily renouncing suffering. In Gide's ultimate wisdom, there is
no assurance, but always that trembling (*das Schaudern*); the
demons are not frozen out, and his eyelid, drooping with age,
does not stare at God with an insulting serenity. In the last
Journal pages I seem to be seeing Oedipus, but Oedipus at
Colonus, and no longer Oedipus the King.

III. THE WORK OF ART

"It is from the point of view of art that what I write should
be judged, a point of view never taken, or almost never taken
by the critics . . . Moreover, it is the only point of view which
is not exclusive of any other" (*Journal*, 1918).

"I first regarded myself as a mere artist, and concerned
myself, à la Flaubert, with nothing but the good quality of my
work. Its profound meaning, strictly speaking, escaped me altogether" (*Journal*, 1931). Gide became aware of this profound meaning of his work only when confronted with others'
reactions; and he systematized it in his critical works. Books

like *Fruits of the Earth* would not be so fine, so lasting, if he had consciously assigned them an intention antecedent to the work, of which the work would be no more than a convenient scaffolding. These are specifically poetic books, in which the author is, like the Latin *vates*, no more than an interpreter; his message transcends him and indeed he may not understand it very well himself; it proceeds from something stronger than himself, from something or someone that inhabits him, from a god. Once created, his work almost surprises him; it is already to such a degree not himself that he can fall in love with it, as Pygmalion with the statue.

The Legitimate Excuse. Let us make no mistake about Gide's critical labors; it is here that he preserves the deepest part of himself. These are his systematic books—admitting that Gide has a system; the others are too much works of art, too gratuitous. It is only at second hand, illuminated by these critical works, but so to speak in spite of himself, that *Fruits of the Earth* or *Oedipus* can assume the contour of gospels and their message be discerned as that of a new ethic. Gide's work is a net of which no mesh can be dropped. I believe it is quite futile to divide it up by chronological or methodical slices. It almost requires to be read in the fashion of certain Bibles, with a synoptic table of references, or even like those pages of the *Encyclopedia* where marginal notes gave the text its explosive value. Gide is often his own scholiast. This was necessary in order to permit the work to retain its gratuitousness, its freedom. Gide's version of the work of art is deliberately evasive; it escapes—God be thanked—any annexation of parties or dogmas, even if they were revolutionary. If anything else were the case, it would not be a work of art. But from this to infer that Gide's *thought* is evasive is a mistake. Gide permits us to grasp and define him very clearly in his critical works, in his *Journal*. When we know this latter Gide, there emanates from his poetic work certain new resonances, a courageously systematic view of man.

"I wanted to indicate in this *'tentative amoureuse'* the book's influence on the person who is writing it, and during the writing itself. For as it leaves us, it changes us, it modifies the movement of our life . . . Our actions have a retroaction upon us" (*Journal*, 1893). Compare these words with Michelet's: "History, in the march of time, makes the historian much more than it is made by him. My book has created me. I am its work" (Preface of 1869). If we admit that the work is an expression of Gide's will (Lafcadio's life, Michel's, Edouard's), the *Journal* is actually the converse of the work, its contrary complement. The work: Gide as he should (would) be. The *Journal*: Gide as he is, or more exactly: as Edouard, Michel, and Lafcadio have made him (any number of fine passages from the *Journal* on this subject) . . .

It is because at a certain moment he wanted to be someone that he summoned up Ménalque, Lafcadio, Michel, or Edouard, that Gide wrote *Fruits of the Earth*, *The Immoralist*, and *The Counterfeiters*. "The desire to portray characters one has encountered is, I believe, quite common. But the creation of new characters becomes a natural need only in those tormented by an imperious complexity and whom their own gesture does not exhaust" (*Journal*, 1924).

Novels and Récits. Gide's aesthetic includes two currents which exhaust, on the one hand, the importance he assigns to man's moral nature, and on the other the organic pleasure he takes in imagining himself in someone else's skin.

Récits (*André Walter*, *The Pastoral Symphony*, *The Immoralist*, *Strait Is the Gate*). Fictionalization—if that—of a case, of a theme, of a pathology. Were it not for Gide's extraordinary art, this would be virtually an apology, but an apology attached to no particular theory. In short, these narratives are almost so many myths. There is a Gidean mythology (a Promethean and not an Olympian mythology), each of whose characters does not fear to reproduce the others somewhat, and which, like any mythology, tends toward allegory, toward the symbol, or at least which can be so interpreted. Each hero engages the reader, promulgates example or iconoclasm. Mythology, as in these récits of Gide's, proves nothing: it is a work of art in which a great deal of faith circulates; a fine fiction in which one agrees to believe because it explains life and at the same time is a little stronger, a little larger than life (it affords the image of an ideal; every mythology is a dream). And these récits of Gide's, like every myth, are an equivalence between an abstract reality and a concrete fiction. All these books are Christian works.

Novels (*Lafcadio's Adventures, The Counterfeiters*). Characteristic of these novels is their utter gratuitousness; they are games. (The game in relation to the obligation is what is done "for nothing.") They prove nothing and are not even psychological except insofar as they present an imbroglio and an incoherence quite proper to life itself. They are born of the superior pleasure of imagining stories into which one introduces oneself under the most numerous and piquant aspects possible (everything which one cannot be). It is the same instinct of fabulation as is found among children which imparts so much lightness, so much sparkling irreverence to *Lafcadio's Adventures*, and to *The Counterfeiters* so much unlikely complexity. That Gide conceived his characters with a deep pleasure and that it was his desire to *be* them, that in them he is incarnated, I see proved in any number of humble details which cannot deceive us: Lafcadio's pleasure in wearing new clothes, scrupulously described (as a child details a toy he wants, especially when it is imaginary); Edouard's attitude to Olivier. As in children's games, reality suddenly spills over into the fantastic: real episodes are inserted into the novel, without Gide's bothering to change the names: the episode of the old La Pérouse, Georges's theft, etc.

The Counterfeiters. "What do I want this novel to be? A crossroads—a rendez-vous of problems" (*Journal*, 1923). It would be of a certain interest to criticism, no doubt, to consider this book as a great Russian novel conceived and executed by a great French writer. The tone, the spirit of the episode of the boys in *The Brothers Karamazov* recurs almost entirely in the first scene of *The Counterfeiters*. Like all of Dostoevsky's novels (except perhaps *The Eternal Husband*), *The Counterfeiters* is a knot of discrepant stories, whose connections are not immediately apparent. (It was on Martin du Gard's advice that Gide gathered these independent plots into a single sheaf.) Like *Lafcadio's Adventures*, *The Counterfeiters* is a diabolic novel; I mean that unity of action is dissolved for the sake of unpredictable and frequently unexploited perspectives, so that we rediscover here an infernal fantasy. A proof *a contrario*: Gide's récits are evangelical works; their tone and plot have the simplicity of angels.

Onomastics of Gide's characters: We can distinguish the heroes with a first name from the characters with a family name. The patronyms are most often characteristic or ironic (though chosen with such finesse!): Baraglioul, Profitendieu, Fleurissoire. By their family names, Gide mocks what most people are proudest of but what in his eyes keeps them from being authentic. The first names, on the contrary, are always vague, impersonal: Edouard, Michel, Bernard, Robert. They are loose garments which betray nothing; the personality of these heroes is in something else than their name (i.e.: their family, their society), for which they are not responsible. There are also the mythological or exotic first names (also chosen quite simply because they are splendid): Ménalque, Lafcadio, whose historical or geographic eccentricity declasses or dislocates the hero, warns us that we will not encounter him in our time or our place, and—perhaps ironically—justifies the strangeness of his ethic or his actions. They seem to say: "Rest easy, you will find no Ménalque, no Lafcadio among us; but that may be too bad."

Gide's novels. Note that the habitual aspect of novels (observations, atmosphere, psychology) is passed over in silence. All this is regarded as *given*. The novel has been written *beyond*, starting from the ordinary warp and woof; it relies on the reader's quality.

Our period, in several of its greatest writers (as a matter of fact, since Poe), might well be defined by this, that the artist himself dismantles the procedures of creation and is interested in them almost as much as in his work itself. This is because we have realized that art is a game, a technique (this dates from the French invention of the formula *l'Art pour l'Art.* See Nietzsche's *Beyond Good and Evil*, aphorism 254). I do not think I misinterpret Valéry when I say he made himself a poet to be able to afford an exact account of the procedures of poetics. Whence Edouard's astonishing Journal, and also many passages of Gide's own *Journal*.

Natural Sciences. The *Journal* will lead the future critic to consider Gide's affection for the Natural Sciences. ". . . I missed my vocation; I wanted to be a naturalist, and should have been one" (*Journal*, 1938). This affection has permitted him to regard the formal world most attentively. Scratch a poet and you will always find a naturalist. The Natural Sciences afforded Gide many comparisons, even whole sectors of demonstration (in *Corydon*, in his attacks on Maeterlinck's scientific books). This is because nothing raises the ontological problem better than such analogies. Many great minds make use of Science to render this problem explicit, at first to themselves, then to their readers. The attention that Valéry gives to epistemology, that Gide gives to the Natural Sciences, should make us reflect . . .

Commonplaces. Sometimes, in Gide, we meet the shadow of a commonplace, but clothed in that always admirable style, which perhaps at this moment has somewhat led him on, deceived him. But I am not at all sure that this "neutral" thought was not deliberate, in order to contrast all the more vividly with the grace of his expression or even out of humility; i.e., out of that conscience which makes him explain at such length (in the *Journal*) the minor problems of translation. With this man, you never know; he has put himself in a position to forestall you in the estimation of his weaknesses, so that you are hard put to impute them to him. You cannot be certain he does not yield them up deliberately, but without warning, without informing us whether or not he is conscious of them.

Coquetry of the uniform. This consists in the fact that it is harder to shine where everyone possesses equal and ordinary weapons; the victory is only the more valuable. For Gide, too, there is a certain coquetry of the commonplace, of the uniform. With the same ideas and the same words as everyone else, he manages to say something valid. This is the classical rule: to have the courage of saying splendidly what is obvious, so that it is never on a first reading that a classical author delights us; he actually seduces us by what he has not said, but which we will be quite naturally led to discover, so clearly drawn are the essential lines. But furthermore the accessory lines are suppressed. This is characteristic of all art (see in this regard certain significant drawings by Picasso). As Montesquieu said: "We do not describe without omitting the intermediate notions." And Gide adds: "There is no work of art without foreshortenings." This does not occur without an initial obscurity, or an extreme simplicity, which makes a mediocre mind say that it does not "understand." In this sense, the Classics are the great masters of the obscure, even of the equivocal; i.e., of the preterition of the superfluous (that superfluous of which the vulgar mind is so fond), or if you prefer, masters of the shadow propitious to meditation and to individual discovery. To oblige us to think for ourselves, that is a possible definition of classical culture; whereby it is no longer the monopoly of a century, but of all rigorous minds, whether they are called Racine, Stendhal, Baudelaire, or Gide.

1942

The World of Wrestling

"The grandiloquent truth of gestures on life's great occasions."
—BAUDELAIRE

THE virtue of all-in wrestling is that it is the spectacle of excess. Here we find a grandiloquence which must have been that of ancient theaters. And in fact wrestling is an open-air spectacle, for what makes the circus or the arena what they are is not the sky (a romantic value suited rather to fashionable occasions), it is the drenching and vertical quality of the flood of light. Even hidden in the most squalid Parisian halls, wrestling partakes of the nature of the great solar spectacles, Greek drama and bullfights: in both, a light without shadow generates an emotion without reserve.

There are people who think that wrestling is an ignoble sport. Wrestling is not a sport, it is a spectacle, and it is no more ignoble to attend a wrestled performance of Suffering than a performance of the sorrows of Arnolphe or Andromaque.[1] Of course, there exists a false wrestling, in which the participants unnecessarily go to great lengths to make a show of a fair fight; this is of no interest. True wrestling, wrongly called amateur wrestling, is performed in second-rate

From *Mythologies*, translated by Annette Lavers (New York: Hill and Wang, 1972).

[1] In Molière's *L'École des Femmes* and Racine's *Andromaque*.

halls, where the public spontaneously attunes itself to the spectacular nature of the contest, like the audience at a suburban
cinema. Then these same people wax indignant because wrestling is a stage-managed sport (which ought, by the way, to
mitigate its ignominy). The public is completely uninterested
in knowing whether the contest is rigged or not, and rightly so;
it abandons itself to the primary virtue of the spectacle, which
is to abolish all motives and all consequences: what matters is
not what it thinks but what it sees.

This public knows very well the distinction between wrestling and boxing; it knows that boxing is a Jansenist sport,
based on a demonstration of excellence. One can bet on the
outcome of a boxing match: with wrestling, it would make no
sense. A boxing match is a story which is constructed before
the eyes of the spectator; in wrestling, on the contrary, it is
each moment which is intelligible, not the passage of time. The
spectator is not interested in the rise and fall of fortunes; he
expects the transient image of certain passions. Wrestling
therefore demands an immediate reading of the juxtaposed
meanings, so that there is no need to connect them. The logical conclusion of the contest does not interest the wrestling
fan, while on the contrary a boxing match always implies a
science of the future. In other words, wrestling is a sum of
spectacles, of which no single one is a function: each moment
imposes the total knowledge of a passion which rises erect and
alone, without ever extending to the crowning moment of a
result.

Thus the function of the wrestler is not to win; it is to go
exactly through the motions which are expected of him. It is
said that judo contains a hidden symbolic aspect; even in the
midst of efficiency, its gestures are measured, precise but restricted, drawn accurately but by a stroke without volume.
Wrestling, on the contrary, offers excessive gestures, exploited
to the limit of their meaning. In judo, a man who is down is

hardly down at all, he rolls over, he draws back, he eludes defeat, or, if the latter is obvious, he immediately disappears; in wrestling, a man who is down is exaggeratedly so, and completely fills the eyes of the spectators with the intolerable spectacle of his powerlessness.

This function of grandiloquence is indeed the same as that of ancient theater, whose principle, language and props (masks and buskins) concurred in the exaggeratedly visible explanation of a Necessity. The gesture of the vanquished wrestler signifying to the world a defeat which, far from disguising, he emphasizes and holds like a pause in music, corresponds to the mask of antiquity meant to signify the tragic mode of the spectacle. In wrestling, as on the stage in antiquity, one is not ashamed of one's suffering, one knows how to cry, one has a liking for tears.

Each sign in wrestling is therefore endowed with an absolute clarity, since one must always understand everything on the spot. As soon as the adversaries are in the ring, the public is overwhelmed with the obviousness of the roles. As in the theater, each physical type expresses to excess the part which has been assigned to the contestant. Thauvin, a fifty-year-old with an obese and sagging body, whose type of asexual hideousness always inspires feminine nicknames, displays in his flesh the characters of baseness, for his part is to represent what, in the classical concept of the *salaud*, the "bastard" (the key concept of any wrestling match), appears as organically repugnant. The nausea voluntarily provoked by Thauvin shows therefore a very extended use of signs: not only is ugliness used here in order to signify baseness, but in addition ugliness is wholly gathered into a particularly repulsive quality of matter: the pallid collapse of dead flesh (the public calls Thauvin *la barbaque*, "stinking meat"), so that the passionate condemnation of the crowd no longer stems from its judgment, but instead from the very depth of its humors. It will thereafter

let itself be frenetically embroiled in an idea of Thauvin which
will conform entirely with this physical origin: his actions will
perfectly correspond to the essential viscosity of his personage.

It is therefore in the body of the wrestler that we find the
first key to the contest. I know from the start that all of
Thauvin's actions, his treacheries, cruelties, and acts of cowardice, will not fail to measure up to the first image of ignobil-
ity he gave me; I can trust him to carry out intelligently and
to the last detail all the gestures of a kind of amorphous baseness, and thus fill to the brim the image of the most repugnant
bastard there is: the bastard octopus. Wrestlers therefore have
a physique as peremptory as those of the characters of the
Commedia dell'Arte, who display in advance, in their costumes and attitudes, the future contents of their parts: just as
Pantaloon can never be anything but a ridiculous cuckold,
Harlequin an astute servant, and the Doctor a stupid pedant,
in the same way Thauvin will never be anything but an ignoble
traitor, Reinières (a tall blond fellow with a limp body and
unkempt hair) the moving image of passivity, Mazaud (short
and arrogant like a cock) that of grotesque conceit, and Or-
sano (an effeminate teddy boy first seen in a blue-and-pink
dressing gown) that, doubly humorous, of a vindictive *salope*,
or bitch (for I do not think that the public of the Elysée-
Montmartre, like Littré, believes the word *salope* to be a masculine).

The physique of the wrestlers therefore constitutes a basic
sign, which like a seed contains the whole fight. But this seed
proliferates, for it is at every turn during the fight, in each new
situation, that the body of the wrestler casts to the public the
magical entertainment of a temperament which finds its natural expression in a gesture. The different strata of meaning
throw light on each other, and form the most intelligible of
spectacles. Wrestling is like a diacritic writing: above the fundamental meaning of his body, the wrestler arranges com-

ments which are episodic but always opportune, and constantly help the reading of the fight by means of gestures, attitudes, and mimicry which make the intention utterly obvious. Sometimes the wrestler triumphs with a repulsive sneer while kneeling on the good sportsman; sometimes he gives the crowd a conceited smile which forebodes an early revenge; sometimes, pinned to the ground, he hits the floor ostentatiously to make evident to all the intolerable nature of his situation; and sometimes he erects a complicated set of signs meant to make the public understand that he legitimately personifies the ever-entertaining image of the grumbler, endlessly confabulating about his displeasure.

We are therefore dealing with a real Human Comedy, where the most socially inspired nuances of passion (conceit, rightfulness, refined cruelty, a sense of "paying one's debts") always felicitously find the clearest sign which can receive them, express them, and triumphantly carry them to the confines of the hall. It is obvious that at such a pitch, it no longer matters whether the passion is genuine or not. What the public wants is the image of passion, not passion itself. There is no more a problem of truth in wrestling than in the theater. In both, what is expected is the intelligible representation of moral situations which are usually private. This emptying out of interiority to the benefit of its exterior signs, this exhaustion of the content by the form, is the very principle of triumphant classical art. Wrestling is an immediate pantomime, infinitely more efficient than the dramatic pantomime, for the wrestler's gesture needs no anecdote, no decor, in short no transference in order to appear true.

Each moment in wrestling is therefore like an algebra which instantaneously unveils the relationship between a cause and its represented effect. Wrestling fans certainly experience a kind of intellectual pleasure in *seeing* the moral mechanism function so perfectly. Some wrestlers, who are great comedians, entertain as much as a Molière character, because they succeed in imposing an immediate reading of the inner nature: Armand Mazaud, a wrestler of an arrogant and ridiculous character (as one says that Harpagon[2] is a character), always delights the audience by the mathematical rigor of his transcriptions, carrying the form of his gestures to the furthest reaches of their meaning, and giving to his manner of fighting the kind of vehemence and precision found in a great scholastic disputation, in which what is at stake is at once the triumph of pride and the formal concern with truth.

What is thus displayed for the public is the great spectacle of Suffering, Defeat, and Justice. Wrestling presents man's suffering with all the amplification of tragic masks. The wrestler who suffers in a hold which is reputedly cruel (an arm lock, a twisted leg) offers an excessive portrayal of Suffering; like a primitive Pietà, he exhibits for all to see his face, exaggeratedly contorted by an intolerable affliction. It is obvious, of course, that in wrestling reserve would be out of place, since it is opposed to the voluntary ostentation of the spectacle, to this Exhibition of Suffering which is the very aim of the fight. This is why all the actions which produce suffering are particularly spectacular, like the gesture of a conjurer who holds out his cards clearly to the public. Suffering which appeared without intelligible cause would not be understood; a concealed action that was actually cruel would transgress the unwritten rules of wrestling and would have no more sociological efficacy than a mad or parasitic gesture. On the contrary, suffering appears as inflicted with emphasis and conviction, for everyone must not only see that the man suffers but also and above all understand why he suffers. What wrestlers call a hold, that is, any figure which allows one to immobilize the adversary indefinitely and to have him at one's mercy, has precisely the function of pre-

[2] In Molière's *L'Avare*.

paring in conventional, therefore intelligible, fashion the spectacle of suffering, of methodically establishing the conditions of suffering. The inertia of the vanquished allows the (temporary) victor to settle in his cruelty and to convey to the public this terrifying slowness of the torturer who is certain about the outcome of his actions; to grind the face of one's powerless adversary or to scrape his spine with one's fist with a deep and regular movement, or at least to produce the superficial appearance of such gestures: wrestling is the only sport which gives such an externalized image of torture. But here again, only the image is involved in the game, and the spectator does not wish for the actual suffering of the contestant; he only enjoys the perfection of an iconography. It is not true that wrestling is a sadistic spectacle: it is only an intelligible spectacle.

There is another figure, more spectacular still than a hold; it is the forearm smash, this loud slap of the forearm, this embryonic punch with which one clouts the chest of one's adversary, and which is accompanied by a dull noise and the exaggerated sagging of a vanquished body. In the forearm smash, catastrophe is brought to the point of maximum obviousness, so much so that ultimately the gesture appears as no more than a symbol; this is going too far, this is transgressing the moral rules of wrestling, where all signs must be excessively clear, but must not let the intention of clarity be seen. The public then shouts, "He's laying it on!", not because it regrets the absence of real suffering, but because it condemns artifice: as in the theater, one fails to put the part across as much by an excess of sincerity as by an excess of formalism.

We have already seen to what extent wrestlers exploit the resources of a given physical style, developed and put to use in order to unfold before the eyes of the public a total image of Defeat. The flaccidity of tall white bodies which collapse with one blow or crash into the ropes with arms flailing, the inertia

of massive wrestlers rebounding pitiably off all the elastic surfaces of the ring, nothing can signify more clearly and more
passionately the exemplary abasement of the vanquished. Deprived of all resilience, the wrestler's flesh is no longer anything but an unspeakable heap spread out on the floor, where
it solicits relentless reviling and jubilation. There is here a
paroxysm of meaning in the style of antiquity, which can only
recall the heavily underlined intentions in Roman triumphs. At
other times, there is another ancient posture which appears in
the coupling of the wrestlers, that of the suppliant who, at the
mercy of his opponent, on bended knees, his arms raised
above his head, is slowly brought down by the vertical pressure of the victor. In wrestling, unlike judo, Defeat is not a
conventional sign, abandoned as soon as it is understood; it is
not an outcome, but quite the contrary, it is a duration, a
display, it takes up the ancient myths of public Suffering and
Humiliation: the cross and the pillory. It is as if the wrestler is
crucified in broad daylight and in the sight of all. I have heard
it said of a wrestler stretched on the ground: "He is dead, little
Jesus, there, on the cross," and these ironic words revealed the
hidden roots of a spectacle which enacts the exact gestures of
the most ancient purifications.

But what wrestling is above all meant to portray is a purely
moral concept: that of justice. The idea of "paying" is essential to wrestling, and the crowd's "Give it to him" means
above all else "Make him pay." This is therefore, needless to
say, an immanent justice. The baser the action of the "bastard,"
the more delighted the public is by the blow which he justly
receives in return. If the villain—who is of course a coward—
takes refuge behind the ropes, claiming unfairly to have a right
to do so by a brazen mimicry, he is inexorably pursued there
and caught, and the crowd is jubilant at seeing the rules broken
for the sake of a deserved punishment. Wrestlers know very
well how to play up to the capacity for indignation of the

public by presenting the very limit of the concept of Justice, this outermost zone of confrontation where it is enough to infringe the rules a little more to open the gates of a world without restraints. For a wrestling fan, nothing is finer than the revengeful fury of a betrayed fighter who throws himself vehemently not on a successful opponent but on the smarting image of foul play. Naturally, it is the pattern of Justice which matters here, much more than its content: wrestling is above all a quantitative sequence of compensations (an eye for an eye, a tooth for a tooth). This explains why sudden changes of circumstances have in the eyes of wrestling habitués a sort of moral beauty: they enjoy them as they would enjoy an inspired episode in a novel, and the greater the contrast between the success of a move and the reversal of fortune, the nearer the good luck of a contestant to his downfall, the more satisfying the dramatic mime is felt to be. Justice is therefore the embodiment of a possible transgression; it is from the fact that there is a Law that the spectacle of the passions which infringe it derives its value.

It is therefore easy to understand why out of five wrestling matches, only about one is fair. One must realize, let it be repeated, that "fairness" here is a role or a genre, as in the theater: the rules do not at all constitute a real constraint; they are the conventional appearance of fairness. So that in actual fact a fair fight is nothing but an exaggeratedly polite one: the contestants confront each other with zeal, not rage; they can remain in control of their passions, they do not punish their beaten opponent relentlessly, they stop fighting as soon as they are ordered to do so, and congratulate each other at the end of a particularly arduous episode, during which, however, they have not ceased to be fair. One must of course understand here that all these polite actions are brought to the notice of the public by the most conventional gestures of fairness: shaking hands, raising the arms, ostensibly avoiding a fruitless hold which would detract from the perfection of the contest.

Conversely, foul play exists only in its excessive signs: administering a big kick to one's beaten opponent, taking refuge behind the ropes while ostensibly invoking a purely formal right, refusing to shake hands with one's opponent before or after the fight, taking advantage of the end of the round to rush treacherously at the adversary from behind, fouling him while the referee is not looking (a move which obviously only has any value or function because in fact half the audience can see it and get indignant about it). Since Evil is the natural climate of wrestling, a fair fight has chiefly the value of being an exception. It surprises the aficionado, who greets it when he sees it as an anachronism and a rather sentimental throwback to the sporting tradition ("Aren't they playing fair, those two"); he feels suddenly moved at the sight of the general kindness of the world, but would probably die of boredom and indifference if wrestlers did not quickly return to the orgy of evil which alone makes good wrestling.

Extrapolated, fair wrestling could lead only to boxing or judo, whereas true wrestling derives its originality from all the excesses which make it a spectacle and not a sport. The ending of a boxing match or a judo contest is abrupt, like the full stop which closes a demonstration. The rhythm of wrestling is quite different, for its natural meaning is that of rhetorical amplification: the emotional magniloquence, the repeated paroxysms, the exasperation of the retorts can only find their natural outcome in the most baroque confusion. Some fights, among the most successful kind, are crowned by a final charivari, a sort of unrestrained fantasia where the rules, the laws of the genre, the referee's censuring and the limits of the ring are abolished, swept away by a triumphant disorder which overflows into the hall and carries off pell-mell wrestlers, seconds, referee, and spectators.

It has already been noted that in America wrestling represents a sort of mythological fight between Good and Evil (of a quasi-political nature, the "bad" wrestler always being supposed to be a Red). The process of creating heroes in French wrestling is very different, being based on ethics and not on politics. What the public is looking for here is the gradual construction of a highly moral image: that of the perfect "bastard." One comes to wrestling in order to attend the continuing adventures of a single major leading character, permanent and multiform like Punch or Scapino, inventive in unexpected figures and yet always faithful to his role. The "bastard" is here revealed as a Molière character or a "portrait" by La Bruyère, that is to say, as a classical entity, an essence, whose acts are only significant epiphenomena arranged in time. This stylized character does not belong to any particular nation or party, and whether the wrestler is called Kuzchenko (nicknamed Mustache after Stalin), Yerpazian, Gaspardi, Jo Vignola or Nollières, the aficionado does not attribute to him any country except "fairness"—observing the rules.

What then is a "bastard" for this audience composed in part, we are told, of people who are themselves outside the rules of society? Essentially someone unstable, who accepts the rules only when they are useful to him and transgresses the formal continuity of attitudes. He is unpredictable, therefore asocial. He takes refuge behind the law when he considers that it is in his favor, and breaks it when he finds it useful to do so. Sometimes he rejects the formal boundaries of the ring and goes on hitting an adversary legally protected by the ropes, sometimes he re-establishes these boundaries and claims the protection of what he did not respect a few minutes earlier. This inconsistency, far more than treachery or cruelty, sends the audience beside itself with rage: offended not in its morality but in its logic, it considers the contradiction of arguments as the basest of crimes. The forbidden move becomes dirty only when it destroys a quantitative equilibrium and disturbs the rigorous reckoning of compensations; what is condemned by the audience is not at all the transgression of insipid official rules, it is the lack of revenge, the absence of a punishment. So that there is nothing more exciting for a crowd than the grandiloquent kick given to a vanquished "bastard"; the joy of punishing is at its climax when it is supported by a mathematical justification; contempt is then unrestrained. One is no longer dealing with a *salaud* but with a *salope*—the verbal gesture of the ultimate degradation.

Such a precise finality demands that wrestling should be exactly what the public expects of it. Wrestlers, who are very experienced, know perfectly how to direct the spontaneous episodes of the fight so as to make them conform to the image which the public has of the great legendary themes of its mythology. A wrestler can irritate or disgust, he never disappoints, for he always accomplishes completely, by a progressive solidification of signs, what the public expects of him. In wrestling, nothing exists except in the absolute, there is no symbol, no allusion, everything is presented exhaustively. Leaving nothing in the shade, each action discards all parasitic meanings and ceremonially offers to the public a pure and full signification, rounded like Nature. This grandiloquence is nothing but the popular and age-old image of the perfect intelligibility of reality. What is portrayed by wrestling is therefore an ideal understanding of things; it is the euphoria of men raised for a while above the constitutive ambiguity of everyday situations and placed before the panoramic view of a univocal Nature, in which signs at last correspond to causes, without obstacle, without evasion, without contradiction.

When the hero or the villain of the drama, the man who was seen a few minutes earlier possessed by moral rage, magnified into a sort of metaphysical sign, leaves the wrestling hall, impassive, anonymous, carrying a small suitcase and arm-in-arm with his wife, no one can doubt that wrestling holds that power of transmutation which is common to the Spectacle and to Religious Worship. In the ring, and even in the depths of their voluntary ignominy, wrestlers remain gods because they are, for a few moments, the key which opens Nature, the pure gesture which separates Good from Evil, and unveils the form of a Justice which is at last intelligible.

1952

from *Writing Degree Zero*

PART ONE

WHAT IS WRITING?

W<small>E</small> know that a language is a corpus of prescriptions and habits common to all the writers of a period. Which means that a language is a kind of natural ambience wholly pervading the writer's expression, yet without endowing it with form or content: it is, as it were, an abstract circle of truths, outside of which alone the solid residue of an individual *logos* begins to settle. It enfolds the whole of literary creation much as the earth, the sky, and the line where they meet outline a familiar habitat for mankind. It is not so much a stock of materials as a horizon, which implies both a boundary and a perspective; in short, it is the comforting area of an ordered space. The writer literally takes nothing from it; a language is for him rather a frontier, to overstep which alone might lead to the linguistically supernatural; it is a field of action, the definition of, and hope for, a possibility. It is not the locus of a social commitment, but merely a reflex response involving no choice, the undivided property of men, not of writers; it remains outside

Writing Degree Zero, translated by Annette Lavers and Colin Smith (New York: Hill and Wang, 1977).

the ritual of Letters; it is a social object by definition, not by option. No one can without formalities pretend to insert his freedom as a writer into the resistant medium of language because, behind the latter, the whole of History stands unified and complete in the manner of a Natural Order. Hence, for the writer, a language is nothing but a human horizon which provides a distant setting of *familiarity*, the value of which, incidentally, is entirely negative: to say that Camus and Queneau speak the same language is merely to presume, by a differential operation, all languages, archaic and futuristic, that they do not use. Suspended between forms either disused or as yet unknown, the writer's language is not so much a fund to be drawn on as an extreme limit; it is the geometrical *locus* of all that he could not say without, like Orpheus looking back, losing the stable meaning of his enterprise and his essential gesture as a social being.

A language is therefore on the hither side of Literature. Style is almost beyond it: imagery, delivery, vocabulary spring from the body and the past of the writer and gradually become the very reflexes of his art. Thus under the name of style a self-sufficient language is evolved which has its roots only in the depths of the author's personal and secret mythology, that subnature of expression where the first coition of words and things takes place, where once and for all the great verbal themes of his existence come to be installed. Whatever its sophistication, style has always something crude about it: it is a form with no clear destination, the product of a thrust, not an intention, and, as it were, a vertical and lonely dimension of thought. Its frame of reference is biological or biographical, not historical: it is the writer's "thing," his glory and his prison, it is his solitude. Indifferent to society and transparent to it, a closed personal process, it is in no way the product of a choice or of a reflection on Literature. It is the private portion of the ritual, it rises up from the writer's myth-laden depths and unfolds beyond his area of control. It is the decorative voice of hidden, secret flesh; it works as does Necessity, as if, in this kind of floral growth, style were no more than the outcome of a blind and stubborn metamorphosis starting from a sub-language elaborated where flesh and external reality come together. Style is properly speaking a germinative phenomenon, the transmutation of a Humor. Hence stylistic overtones are distributed in depth; whereas speech has a horizontal structure, its secrets are on a level with the words in which they are couched, and what it conceals is revealed by the very duration of its flow. In speech, everything is held forth, meant for immediate consumption, and words, silences, and their common mobility are launched toward a meaning superseded: it is a transfer leaving no trace and brooking no delay. Style, on the other hand, has only a vertical dimension, it plunges into the closed recollection of the person and achieves its opacity from a certain experience of matter; style is never anything but metaphor, that is, equivalence of the author's literary intention and carnal structure (it must be remembered that structure is the residual deposit of duration). So that style is always a secret; but the occult aspect of its implications does not arise from the mobile and ever-provisional nature of language; its secret is recollection locked within the body of the writer. The allusive virtue of style is not a matter of speed, as in speech, where what is unsaid nevertheless remains as an interim of language, but a matter of density, for what stands firmly and deeply beneath style, brought together harshly or tenderly in its figures of speech, are fragments of a reality entirely alien to language. The miracle of this transmutation makes style a kind of supra-literary operation which carries man to the threshold of power and magic. By reason of its biological origin, style resides outside art, that is, outside the pact which binds the writer to society. Authors may therefore be imagined who prefer the security of art to the loneliness of style. The very type of an author without a style is Gide, whose craftsmanlike approach exploits the pleasure the moderns derive from a certain classical ethos, just as Saint-Saëns has composed in Bach's idiom, or Poulenc in Schubert's. In contrast, modern poetry—such as Hugo's, Rimbaud's or Char's—is saturated with style and is *art* only by virtue of an intention to be Poetry. It is the Authority of style, that is, the entirely free relationship between language and its fleshly double, which places the writer above History as the freshness of Innocence.

A language is therefore a horizon, and style a vertical dimension, which together map out for the writer a Nature, since he does not choose either. The language functions negatively, as the initial limit of the possible, style is a Necessity which binds the writer's humor to his form of expression. In the former, he finds a familiar History, in the latter, a familiar personal past. In both cases he deals with a Nature, that is, a familiar repertory of gestures, a gestuary, as it were, in which the energy expended is purely operative, serving here to enumerate, there to transform, but never to appraise or signify a choice.

Now every Form is also a Value, which is why there is room, between a language and a style, for another formal reality: writing. Within any literary form, there is a general choice of tone, of ethos, if you like, and this is precisely where the writer shows himself clearly as an individual because this is where he commits himself. A language and a style are data prior to all problematics of language, they are the natural product of Time and of the person as a biological entity; but the formal identity of the writer is truly established only outside the permanence of grammatical norms and stylistic constants, where the written continuum, first collected and enclosed within a perfectly innocent linguistic nature, at last becomes a total sign, the choice of a human attitude, the affirmation of a certain Good. It thus commits the writer to manifest and communicate a state of happiness or malaise, and links the form of his utterance, which is at once normal and singular, to the vast History of the Others. A language and a style are blind forces; a mode of writing is an act of historical solidarity. A language and a style are objects; a mode of writing is a function: it is the relationship between creation and society, the literary language transformed by its social finality, form considered as a human intention and thus linked to the great crises of History. Mérimée and Fénelon, for instance, are separated by linguistic phenomena and contingent features of style; yet they make use of a language charged with the same intentionality, their ideas of form and content share a common framework, they accept the same type of conventions, the same technical reflexes work through both of them. Although separated by a century and a half, they use exactly the same instrument in the same way: an instrument perhaps a little changed in outward appearance, but not at all in the place and manner of its employment. In short, they have the same mode of writing. In contrast, writers who are almost contemporaries, Mérimée and Lautréamont, Mallarmé and Céline, Gide and Queneau, Claudel and Camus, who have shared or who share our language at the same stage of its historical development use utterly different modes of writing. Everything separates them: tone, delivery, purpose, ethos, and naturalness of expression: the conclusion is that to live at the same time and share the same language is a small matter compared with modes of writing so dissimilar and so sharply defined by their very dissimilarity.

These modes of writing, though different, are comparable, because they owe their existence to one identical process, namely the writer's consideration of the social use which he has chosen for his form, and his commitment to this choice. Placed at the center of the problematics of literature, which cannot exist prior to it, writing is thus essentially the morality of form, the choice of that social area within which the writer elects to situate the nature of his language. But this social area is by no means that of an actual consumption. It is not a question for the writer of choosing the social group for which he is to write: well he knows that, save for the possibility of a Revolution, it can only be for the self-same society. His choice is a matter of conscience, not of efficacy. His writing is a way of conceiving Literature, not of extending its limits. Or better still: it is because the writer cannot modify in any way the objective data which govern the consumption of Literature (these purely historical data are beyond his control even if he is aware of them) that he voluntarily places the need for a free language at the sources of this language and not in its eventual consumption. So that writing is an ambiguous reality: on the one hand, it unquestionably arises from a confrontation of the writer with the society of his time; on the other hand, from this social finality, it refers the writer back, by a sort of tragic reversal, to the sources, that is to say, the instruments of creation. Failing the power to supply him with a freely consumed language, History suggests to him the demand for one freely produced.

Thus the choice of, and afterward the responsibility for, a mode of writing point to the presence of Freedom, but this Freedom has not the same limits at different moments of History. It is not granted to the writer to choose his mode of writing from a kind of non-temporal store of literary forms. It is under the pressure of History and Tradition that the possible modes of writing for a given writer are established; there is a History of Writing. But this History is dual: at the very moment when general History proposes—or imposes—new problematics of the literary language, writing still remains full of the recollection of previous usage, for language is never innocent: words have a second-order memory which mysteriously persists in the midst of new meanings. Writing is precisely this compromise between freedom and remembrance, it is this freedom which remembers and is free only in the gesture of choice, but is no longer so within duration. True, I can today select such and such mode of writing, and in so doing assert my freedom, aspire to the freshness of novelty or to a tradition; but it is impossible to develop it within duration without gradually becoming a prisoner of someone else's words and even of my own. A stubborn after-image, which comes from all the previous modes of writing and even from the past of my own, drowns the sound of my present words. Any written trace precipitates, as inside a chemical at first transparent, innocent and neutral, mere duration gradually reveals in suspension a whole past of increasing density, like a cryptogram.

Writing as Freedom is therefore a mere moment. But this moment is one of the most explicit in History, since History is always and above all a choice and the limits of this choice. It is because writing derives from a meaningful gesture of the writer that it reaches the deeper layers of History, much more palpably than does any other cross-section of literature. The unity of classical writing, which remained uniform for centuries, the plurality of its modes in modern times, increased in the last hundred years until it came near to questioning the very fact of literature, this kind of disintegration of French writing does indeed correspond to a great crisis in general History, which is noticeable in literary History proper, only much more confusedly. What separates the "thought" of a Balzac from that of a Flaubert is a variation within the same school; what contrasts their modes of writing is an essential break, at the precise moment when a new economic structure is joined on to an older one, thereby bringing about decisive changes in mentality and consciousness.

POLITICAL MODES OF WRITING

All modes of writing have in common the fact of being "closed" and thus different from spoken language. Writing is in no way an instrument for communication, it is not an open route through which there passes only the intention to speak. A whole disorder flows through speech and gives it this self-devouring momentum which keeps it in a perpetually suspended state. Conversely, writing is a hardened language which is self-contained and is in no way meant to deliver to its own duration a mobile series of approximations. It is on the contrary meant to impose, thanks to the shadow cast by its system of signs, the image of a speech which had a structure even before it came into existence. What makes writing the opposite of speech is that the former always *appears* symbolical, introverted, ostensibly turned toward an occult side of language, whereas the second is nothing but a flow of empty signs, the movement of which alone is significant. The whole of speech is epitomized in this expendability of words, in this froth ceaselessly swept onward, and speech is found only where language self-evidently functions like a devouring process which swallows only the moving crest of the words. Writing, on the contrary, is always rooted in something beyond language, it develops like a seed, not like a line, it manifests an essence and holds the threat of a secret, it is an anti-communication, it is intimidating. All writing will therefore contain the ambiguity of an object which is both language and coercion: there exists fundamentally in writing a "circumstance" foreign to language, there is, as it were, the weight of a gaze conveying an intention which is no longer linguistic. This gaze may well express a passion of language, as in literary modes of writing;

it may also express the threat of retribution, as in political ones: writing is then meant to unite at a single stroke the reality of the acts and the ideality of the ends. This is why power, or the shadow cast by power, always ends in creating an axiological writing, in which the distance which usually separates fact from value disappears within the very space of the word, which is given at once as description and as judgment. The word becomes an alibi, that is, an elsewhere and a justification. This, which is true of the literary modes of writing, in which the unity of the signs is ceaselessly fascinated by zones of infra- or ultra-language, is even truer of the political ones, in which the alibi stemming from language is at the same time intimidation and glorification: for it is power or conflict which produces the purest types of writing.

We shall see later that classical writing was a ceremonial which manifested the implantation of the writer into a particular political society, and that to speak like Vaugelas meant in the first place to be connected with the exercise of power. The Revolution did not modify the norms of this writing, since its force of thinkers remained, all things considered, the same, having merely passed from intellectual to political power; but the exceptional conditions of the struggle nevertheless brought about, within the great Form of classicism, a revolutionary mode of writing proper, defined not by its structure (which was more conventional than ever) but by its closed character and by its counterpart, since the use of language was then linked, as never before in history, to the Blood which had been shed. The Revolutionaries had no reason to wish to alter classical writing; they were in no way aware of questioning the nature of man, still less his language, and an "instrument" they had inherited from Voltaire, Rousseau, or Vauvenargues could not appear to them as compromised. It was the singularity of the historical circumstances which produced the identity of the revolutionary mode of writing. Baudelaire spoke somewhere of the "grandiloquent truth of gestures on life's great occasions." The Revolution was in the highest degree one of those great occasions when truth, through the bloodshed that it costs, becomes so weighty that its expression demands the very forms of theatrical amplification. Revolutionary writing was the one and only grand gesture commensurate with the daily presence of the guillotine. What today appears turgid was then no more than life-size. This writing, which bears all the signs of inflation, was an exact writing: never was language more incredible, yet never was it less spurious. This grandiloquence was not only form modeled on drama; it was also the awareness of it. Without this extravagant pose, typical of all the great revolutionaries, which enabled Guadet, the Girondin, when arrested at Saint-Emilion, to declare without looking ridiculous, since he was about to die: "Yes, I am Guadet. Executioner, do your duty. Go take my head to the tyrants of my country. It has always turned them pale; once severed, it will turn them paler still," the Revolution could not have been this mythical event which made History fruitful, along with all future ideas on revolution. Revolutionary writing was so to speak the entelechy of the revolutionary legend: it struck fear into men's hearts and imposed upon them a citizen's sacrament of Bloodshed.

Marxist writing is of a different order. Here the closed character of the form does not derive from rhetorical amplification or from grandiloquence in delivery, but from a lexicon as specialized and as functional as a technical vocabulary; even metaphors are here severely codified. French revolutionary writing always proclaimed a right founded on bloodshed or moral justification, whereas from the very start Marxist writing is presented as the language of knowledge. Here, writing is univocal, because it is meant to maintain the cohesion of a Nature; it is the lexical identity of this writing which allows it to impose a stability in its explanations and a permanence in its method; it is only in the light of its whole linguistic system that Marxism is perceived in all its political implications. Marxist writing is as much given to understatement as revolutionary writing is to grandiloquence, since each word is no longer anything but a narrow reference to the set of principles which tacitly underlie it. For instance, the word "imply," frequently encountered in Marxist writing, does not there have its neutral dictionary meaning; it always refers to a precise historical process, and is like an algebraical sign representing a whole bracketed set of previous postulates.

Being linked to action, Marxist writing has rapidly become, in fact, a language expressing value judgments. This character, already visible in Marx, whose writing however remains in general explanatory, has come to pervade writing completely in the era of triumphant Stalinism. Certain outwardly similar notions, for which a neutral vocabulary would not seek a dual designation, are evaluatively parted from each other, so that each element gravitates toward a different noun: for instance, "cosmopolitanism" is the negative of "internationalism" (already in Marx). In the Stalinist world, in which *definition*, that is to say, the separation between Good and Evil, becomes the sole content of all language, there are no more words without values attached to them, so that finally the function of writing is to cut out one stage of a process: there is no more lapse of time between naming and judging, and the closed character of language is perfected, since in the last analysis it is a value which is given as explanation of another value. For instance, it may be alleged that such and such a criminal has engaged in activities harmful to the interests of the state; which boils down to saying that a criminal is someone who commits a crime. We see that this is in fact a tautology, a device constantly used in Stalinist writing. For the latter no longer aims at founding a Marxist version of the facts, or a revolutionary rationale of actions, but at presenting reality in a prejudged form, thus imposing a reading which involves immediate condemnation: the objective content of the word "deviationist" puts it into a penological category. If two deviationists band together, they become "fractionists," which does not involve an objectively different crime but an increase in the sentence imposed. One can enumerate a properly Marxist writing (that of Marx and Lenin) and a writing of triumphant Stalinism; there certainly is as well a Trotskyist writing and a tactical writing, for instance that of the French Communist Party with its substitution of "people," then of "plain folk," for "working class," and the willful ambiguity of terms like "democracy," "freedom," "peace," etc.

There is no doubt at all that each regime has its own writing, no history of which has yet been written. Since writing is the spectacular commitment of language, it contains at one and the same time, thanks to a valuable ambiguity, the reality and the appearance of power, what it is, and what it would like to be thought to be: a history of political modes of writing would therefore be the best of social phenomenologies. For instance, the French Restoration evolved a class writing by means of which repression was immediately given as a condemnation spontaneously arising from classical "Nature": workers claiming rights were always "troublemakers," strikebreakers were "good workmen," and the subservience of judges became, in this language, the "paternal vigilance of magistrates" (it is thanks to a similar procedure that Gaullism today calls Communists "separatists"). We see that here the function of writing is to maintain a clear conscience and that its mission is fraudulently to identify the original fact with its remotest subsequent transformation by bolstering up the justification of actions with the additional guarantee of its own reality. This fact about writing is, by the way, typical of all authoritarian regimes; it is what might be called police-state writing: we know, for example, that the content of the word "Order" always indicates repression.

The spreading influence of political and social facts into the literary field of consciousness has produced a new type of scriptor, halfway between the party member and the writer, deriving from the former an ideal image of committed man, and from the latter the notion that a written work is an act. Thus while the intellectual supersedes the writer, there appears in periodicals and in essays a militant mode of writing entirely freed from stylistic considerations, and which is, so to speak, a professional language signifying "presence." In this mode of writing, nuances abound. Nobody will deny that there is such a thing, for instance, as a writing typical of *Esprit* or of *Les Temps Modernes*.[1] What these intellectual modes of writing have in common is that in them language, instead of being a privileged area, tends to become the sufficient sign of commitment. To come to adopt a closed sphere of language under the pressure of all those who do not speak it, is to proclaim one's act of choosing, if not necessarily one's agreement with that choice. Writing here resembles the signature one affixes at the foot of a collective proclamation one has not written oneself. So that to adopt a mode of writing—or, even better, to make it one's own—means to save oneself all the preliminaries of a choice, and to make it quite clear that one takes for granted the reasons for such a choice. Any intellectual writing is therefore the first of the "leaps of the intellect." Whereas an ideally free language never could function as a sign of my own person and would give no information whatsoever about my history and my freedom, the writing to which I entrust myself already exists entirely as an institution; it reveals my past and my choice, it gives me a history, it blazons forth my situation,

[1] *Esprit* and *Les Temps Modernes* are two prominent monthlies, the first left-wing Catholic and the second directed by J.-P. Sartre.

it commits me without my having to declare the fact. Form thus becomes more than ever an autonomous object, meant to signify a property which is collective and protected, and this object is a trouble-saving device: it functions as an economy signal whereby the scriptor constantly imposes his conversion without ever revealing how it came about.

This duplicity of today's intellectual modes of writing is emphasized by the fact that in spite of the efforts made in our time, it has proved impossible successfully to liquidate Literature entirely: it still constitutes a verbal horizon commanding respect. The intellectual is still only an incompletely transformed writer, and unless he scuttles himself and becomes forever a militant who no longer writes (some have done so, and are therefore forgotten), he cannot but come back to the fascination of former modes of writing, transmitted through Literature as an instrument intact but obsolete. These intellectual modes of writing are therefore unstable, they remain literary to the extent that they are powerless, and are political only through their obsession with commitment. In short, we are still dealing with ethical modes of writing, in which the conscience of the scriptor (one no longer ventures to call him a writer) finds the comforting image of collective salvation.

But just as, in the present state of History, any political mode of writing can only uphold a police world, so any intellectual mode of writing can only give rise to a para-literature, which no longer dares to speak its name. Both are therefore in a complete blind alley, they can lead only to complicity or impotence, which means, in either case, to alienation.

WRITING AND THE NOVEL

The Novel and History have been closely related in the very century which witnessed their greatest development. Their link in depth, that which should allow us to understand at once Balzac and Michelet, is that in both we find the construction of an autarkic world which elaborates its own dimensions and limits, and organizes within these its own Time, its own Space, its population, its own set of objects and its myths.

This sphericity of the great works of the nineteenth century found its expression in those long recitatives, the Novel and History, which are, as it were, plane projections of a curved and organic world of which the serial story which came into being at that precise moment, presents, through its involved complications, a degraded image. And yet narration is not necessarily a law of the form. A whole period could conceive novels in letters, for instance; and another can evolve a practice of History by means of analyses. Therefore Narration, as a form common to both the Novel and to History, does remain, in general, the choice or the expression of a historical moment.

Obsolete in spoken French, the preterite, which is the cornerstone of Narration, always signifies the presence of Art; it is a part of a ritual of Letters. Its function is no longer that of a tense. The part it plays is to reduce reality to a point of time, and to abstract, from the depth of a multiplicity of experiences, a pure verbal act, freed from the existential roots of knowledge, and directed toward a logical link with other acts, other processes, a general movement of the world: it aims at maintaining a hierarchy in the realm of facts. Through the preterite, the verb implicitly belongs with a causal chain, it partakes of a set of related and orientated actions, it functions as the algebraic sign of an intention. Allowing as it does an ambiguity between temporality and causality, it calls for a sequence of events, that is, for an intelligible Narrative. This is why it is the ideal instrument for every construction of a world; it is the unreal time of cosmogonies, myths, History, and Novels. It presupposes a world which is constructed, elaborated, self-sufficient, reduced to significant lines, and not one which has been sent sprawling before us, for us to take or leave. Behind the preterite there always lurks a demiurge, a God, or a reciter. The world is not unexplained since it is told like a story; each one of its accidents is but a circumstance, and the preterite is precisely this operative sign whereby the narrator reduces the exploded reality to a slim and pure logos, without density, without volume, without spread, and whose sole function is to unite as rapidly as possible a cause and an end. When the historian states that the duc de Guise died on December 23, 1588, or when the novelist relates that the Marchioness went out at five o'clock,[2] such actions emerge from a past without substance; purged of the uncertainty of existence, they have the stability and outline of an algebra, they are a recollection, but a useful recollection, the interest of which far surpasses its duration.

So that finally the preterite is the expression of an order, and consequently of a euphoria. Thanks to it, reality is neither mysterious nor absurd; it is clear, almost familiar, repeatedly gathered up and contained in the hand of a creator; it is subjected to the ingenious pressure of his freedom. For all the great storytellers of the nineteenth century, the world may be full of pathos but it is not derelict, since it is a grouping of coherent relations, since there is no overlapping between the written facts, since he who tells the story has the power to do away with the opacity and the solitude of the existences which made it up, since he can in all sentences bear witness to a communication and a hierarchy of actions and since, to tell the truth, these very actions can be reduced to mere signs.

The narrative past is therefore a part of a security system for Belles-Lettres. Being the image of an order, it is one of those numerous formal pacts made between the writer and society for the justification of the former and the serenity of the latter. The preterite *signifies* a creation: that is, it pro-

---

[2] The sentence which for Valéry epitomized the conventions of the novel.

claims and imposes it. Even from the depth of the most somber realism, it has a reassuring effect because, thanks to it, the verb expresses a closed, well-defined, substantival act, the Novel has a name, it escapes the terror of an expression without laws: reality becomes slighter and more familiar, it fits within a style, it does not outrun language. Literature remains the currency in use in a society apprised, by the very form of words, of the meaning of what it consumes. On the contrary, when the Narrative is rejected in favor of other literary genres, or when, within the narration, the preterite is replaced by less ornamental forms, fresher, more full-blooded and nearer to speech (the present tense or the present perfect), Literature becomes the receptacle of existence in all its density and no longer of its meaning alone. The acts it recounts are still separated from History, but no longer from people.

We now understand what is profitable and what is intolerable in the preterite as used in the Novel: it is a lie made manifest, it delineates an area of plausibility which reveals the possible in the very act of unmasking it as false. The teleology common to the Novel and to narrated History is the alienation of the facts: the preterite is the very act by which society affirms its possession of its past and its possibility. It creates a content credible, yet flaunted as an illusion; it is the ultimate term of a formal dialectics which clothes an unreal fact in the garb first of truth then of a lie denounced as such. This has to be related to a certain mythology of the universal typifying the bourgeois society of which the Novel is a characteristic product; it involves giving to the imaginary the formal guarantee of the real, but while preserving in the sign the ambiguity of a double object, at once believable and false. This operation occurs constantly in the whole of Western art, in which the false is equal to the true, not through any agnosticism or poetic duplicity, but because the true is supposed to contain a germ of the universal, or to put it differently, an essence capable of fecundating by mere reproduction, several orders of things among which some differ by their remoteness and some by their fictitious character.

It is thanks to an expedient of the same kind that the triumphant bourgeoisie of the last century was able to look upon its values as universal and to carry over to sections of society which were absolutely heterogeneous to it all the Names which were parts of its ethos. This is strictly how myths function, and the Novel—and within the Novel, the preterite—are mythological objects in which there is, superimposed upon an immediate intention, a second-order appeal to a corpus of dogmas, or better, to a pedagogy, since what is sought is to impart an essence in the guise of an artifact. In order to grasp the significance of the preterite, we have but to compare the Western art of the novel with a certain Chinese tradition, for instance, in which art lies solely in the perfection with which reality is imitated. But in this tradition no sign, absolutely nothing, must allow any distinction to be drawn between the natural and the artificial objects: this wooden walnut must not impart to me, along with the image of a walnut, the intention of conveying to me the art which gave birth to it. Whereas, on the contrary, this is what writing does in the novel. Its task is to put the mask in place and at the same time to point it out.

This ambiguous function disclosed in the preterite is found in another fact relating to this type of writing: the third person in the Novel. The reader will perhaps recall a novel by Agatha Christie in which all the invention consisted in concealing the murderer beneath the use of the first person of the narrative. The reader looked for him behind every "he" in the plot: he was all the time hidden under the "I." Agatha Christie knew perfectly well that, in the novel, the "I" is usually a spectator, and that it is the "he" who is the actor. Why? The "he" is a typical novelistic convention; like the narrative tense, it signifies and carries through the action of the novel; if the third person is absent, the novel is powerless to come into being, and even wills its own destruction. The "he" is a formal manifestation of the myth, and we have just seen that, in the West at least, there is no art which does not point to its own mask. The third person, like the preterite, therefore performs this service for the art of the novel, and supplies its consumers with the security born of a credible fabrication which is yet constantly held up as false.

Less ambiguous, the "I" is thereby less typical of the novel: it is therefore at the same time the most obvious solution, when the narration remains on this side of convention (Proust's work, for instance, purports to be a mere introduction to Literature), and the most sophisticated, when the "I" takes its place beyond convention and attempts to destroy it, by conferring on the narrative the spurious naturalness of taking the reader into its confidence (such is the guileful air of some stories by Gide). In the same way the use of the "he" in a novel involves two opposed systems of ethics: since it represents an unquestioned convention, it attracts the most conformist and the least dissatisfied, as well as those others who have decided that, finally, this convention is necessary to the novelty of their work. In any case, it is the sign of an intelligible pact between society and the author; but it is also, for the latter, the most important means he has of building the world in the way that he chooses. It is therefore more than a literary experiment: it is a human act which connects creation to History or to existence.

In Balzac, for instance, the multiplicity of "he's," this vast network of characters, slight in terms of solid flesh, but consistent by the duration of their acts, reveals the existence of a world of which History is the first datum. The Balzacian "he" is not the end product of a development starting from some transformed and generalized "I"; it is the original and crude

element of the novel, the material, not the outcome, the creative activity: there is no Balzacian history prior to the history
of each third person in the novels of Balzac. His "he" is
analogous to Caesar's "he": the third person here brings about
a kind of algebraic state of the action, in which existence plays
the smallest possible part, in favor of elements which connect,
clarify, or show the tragedy inherent in human relationships.
Conversely—or at any rate previously—the function of "he"
in the novel can be that of expressing an existential experience. In many modern novelists the history of the man is
identified with the course of the conjugation: starting from an
"I" which is still the form which expresses anonymity most
faithfully, man and author little by little win the right to the
third person, in proportion as existence becomes fate, and
soliloquy becomes a Novel. Here the appearance of the "he"
is not the starting point of History, it is the end of an effort
which has been successful in extracting from a personal world
made up of humors and tendencies, a form which is pure,
significant, and which therefore vanishes as soon as it is born,
thanks to the totally conventional and ethereal decor of the
third person. This certainly was the course displayed in the
first novels of Jean Cayrol, whose case can be taken as an
exemplar. But whereas in the classics—and we know that
where writing is concerned classicism lasts until Flaubert—the
withdrawal of the biological person testifies to the establishment of essential man, in novelists such as Cayrol, the inva-
sion of the "he" is a progressive conquest over the profound
darkness of the existential "I": so true it is that the Novel,
identified as it is by its most formal signs, is a gesture of
sociability; it establishes Literature as an institution.

Maurice Blanchot has shown, in the case of Kafka, that the
elaboration of the impersonal narrative (let us notice, apropos
of this term, that the "third person" is always presented as a
negative degree of the person) was an act of fidelity to the

essence of language, since the latter naturally tends toward its own destruction. We therefore understand how "he" is a victory over "I," inasmuch as it conjures up a state at once more literary and more absent. Nonetheless this victory is ceaselessly threatened: the literary convention of the "he" is necessary to the belittling of the person, but runs at every moment the risk of encumbering it with an unexpected density. For Literature is like phosphorus: it shines with its maximum brilliance at the moment when it attempts to die. But as, on the other hand, it is an act which necessarily implies a duration—especially in the Novel—there can never be any Novel independently of Belles-Lettres. So that the third person in the Novel is one of the most obsessive signs of this tragic aspect of writing which was born in the last century, when under the weight of History, Literature became dissociated from the society which consumes it. Between the third person as used by Balzac and that used by Flaubert, there is a world of difference (that of 1848): in the former we have a view of History which is harsh but coherent and certain of its principles, the triumph of an order; in the latter, an art which in order to escape its pangs of conscience either exaggerates conventions or frantically attempts to destroy them. Modernism begins with the search for a Literature which is no longer possible.

Thus we find, in the Novel too, this machinery directed toward both destruction and resurrection, and typical of the whole of modern art. What must be destroyed is duration, that is, the ineffable binding force running through existence: for order, whether it be that of poetic flow or of narrative signs, that of Terror or plausibility, is always a murder in intention. But what reconquers the writer is again duration, for it is impossible to develop a negative within time, without elaborating a positive art, an order which must be destroyed anew. So that the greater modern works linger as long as possible, in a sort of miraculous stasis, on the threshold of Literature, in this anticipatory state in which the breadth of life is given, stretched but not yet destroyed by this crowning phase, an order of signs. For instance, we have the first person in Proust, whose whole work rests on a slow and protracted effort toward Literature. We have Jean Cayrol, whose acquiescence to the Novel comes only as the very last stage of soliloquy, as if the literary act, being supremely ambiguous, could be delivered of a creation consecrated by society, only at the moment when it has at last succeeded in destroying the existential density of a hitherto meaningless duration.

The Novel is a Death; it transforms life into destiny, a memory into a useful act, duration into an orientated and meaningful time. But this transformation can be accomplished only in full view of society. It is society which imposes the Novel, that is, a complex of signs, as a transcendence and as the History of a duration. It is therefore by the obviousness of its intention, grasped in that of the narrative signs, that one can recognize the path which, through all the solemnity of art, binds the writer to society. The preterite and the third person in the Novel are nothing but the fateful gesture with which the writer draws attention to the mask which he is wearing. The whole of Literature can declare *Larvatus prodeo*,[3] As I walk forward, I point out my mask. Whether we deal with the inhuman experience of the poet, who accepts the most momentous of all breaks, that from the language of society, or with the plausible untruth of the novelist, sincerity here feels a need of the signs of falsehood, and of conspicuous falsehood in order to last and to be consumed. Writing is the product, and ultimately the source, of this ambiguity. This specialized language, the use of which gives the writer a glorious but none the less superintended function, evinces a kind of servitude, invis-

---

[3] *Larvatus prodeo* was the motto of Descartes.

ible at first, which characterizes any responsibility. Writing, free in its beginnings, is finally the bond which links the writer to a History which is itself in chains: society stamps upon him the unmistakable signs of art so as to draw him along the more inescapably in its own process of alienation.

IS THERE ANY POETIC WRITING?

In the classical period, prose and poetry are quantities, their difference can be measured; they are neither more nor less separated than two different numbers, contiguous like them, but dissimilar because of the very difference in their magnitudes. If I use the word prose for a minimal form of speech, the most economical vehicle for thought, and if I use the letters a, b, c for certain attributes of language, which are useless but decorative, such as meter, rhyme or the ritual of images, all the linguistic surface will be accounted for in M. Jourdain's[4] double equation:

$$\text{Poetry} = \text{Prose} + a + b + c$$
$$\text{Prose} = \text{Poetry} - a - b - c$$

whence it clearly follows that Poetry is always different from Prose. But this difference is not one of essence, it is one of quantity. It does not, therefore, jeopardize the unity of language, which is an article of classical dogma. One may effect a different dosage in manner of speech, according to the social occasion: here, prose or rhetoric, there, poetry or precosity, in accordance with a whole ritual of expression laid down by good society, but there remains everywhere a single language, which reflects the eternal categories of the mind. Classical poetry is felt to be merely an ornamental variation of prose, the fruit of an *art* (that is, a technique), never a different language, or the product of a particular sensibility. Any poetry

[4] Molière's *Bourgeois Gentilhomme*.

is then only the decorative equation, whether allusive or forced, of a possible prose which is latent, virtually and potentially, in any conceivable manner of expression. "Poetic," in the days of classicism, never evokes any particular domain, any particular depth of feeling, any special coherence, or separate universe, but only an individual handling of a verbal technique, that of "expressing oneself" according to rules more artistic, therefore more sociable, than those of conversation, in other terms, the technique of projecting out an inner thought, springing fully armed from the Mind, a speech which is made more socially acceptable by virtue of the very conspicuousness of its conventions.

We l ₀w that nothing of this structure remains in modern poetry, which springs not from Baudelaire but from Rimbaud, unless it is in cases where one takes up again, in a revised traditional mode, the formal imperatives of classical poetry: henceforth, poets give to their speech the status of a closed Nature, which covers both the function and the structure of language. Poetry is then no longer a Prose either ornamental or shorn of liberties. It is a quality *sui generis* and without antecedents. It is no longer an attribute but a substance, and therefore it can very well renounce signs, since it carries its own nature within itself, and does not need to signal its identity outwardly: poetic language and prosaic language are sufficiently separate to be able to dispense with the very signs of their difference.

Furthermore, the alleged relations between thought and language are reversed; in classical art, a ready-made thought generates an utterance which "expresses" or "translates" it. Classical thought is devoid of duration, classical poetry has it only in such degree as is necessary to its technical arrangement. In modern poetics, on the contrary, words produce a kind of formal continuum from which there gradually emanates an intellectual or emotional density which would have been impossible without them; speech is then the solidified time of a more spiritual gestation, during which the "thought" is prepared, installed little by little by the contingency of words. This verbal luck, which will bring down the ripe fruit of a meaning, presupposes therefore a poetic time which is no longer that of a "fabrication" but that of a possible adventure, the meeting point of a sign and intention. Modern poetry is opposed to classical art by a difference which involves the whole structure of language, without leaving between those two types of poetry anything in common except the same sociological intention.

The economy of classical language (Prose and Poetry) is relational, which means that in it words are abstracted as much as possible in the interest of relationships. In it, no word has a density by itself, it is hardly the sign of a thing, but rather the means of conveying a connection. Far from plunging into an inner reality consubstantial to its outer configuration, it extends, as soon as it is uttered, toward other words, so as to form a superficial chain of intentions. A glance at the language of mathematics will perhaps enable us to grasp the relational nature of classical prose and poetry: we know that in mathematical language, not only is each quantity provided with a sign, but also that the relations between these quantities are themselves transcribed, by means of a sign expressing operative equality or difference. It may be said that the whole movement of mathematical flow derives from an explicit reading of its relations. The language of classicism is animated by an analogous, although of course less rigid, movement: its "words," neutralized, made absent by rigorous recourse to a tradition which desiccates their freshness, avoid the phonetic or semantic accident which would concentrate the flavor of language at one point and halt its intellectual momentum in the interest of an unequally distributed enjoyment. The classical flow is a succession of elements whose density is even; it is exposed to the same emotional pressure, and relieves those elements of any tendency toward an individual meaning appearing at all invented. The poetic vocabulary itself is one of usage, not of invention: images in it are recognizable in a body; they do not exist in isolation; they are due to long custom, not to individual creation. The function of the classical poet is not therefore to find new words, with more body or more brilliance, but to follow the order of an ancient ritual, to perfect the symmetry or the conciseness of a relation, to bring a thought exactly within the compass of a meter. Classical conceits involve relations, not words: they belong to an art of expression, not of invention. The words, here, do not, as they later do, thanks to a kind of violent and unexpected abruptness, reproduce the depth and singularity of an individual experience; they are spread out to form a surface, according to the exigencies of an elegant or decorative purpose. They delight us because of the formulation which brings them together, not because of their own power or beauty.

True, classical language does not reach the functional perfection of the relational network of mathematics: relations are not signified, in it, by any special signs, but only by accidents of form and disposition. It is the restraint of the words in itself, their alignment, which achieves the relational nature of classical discourse. Overworked in a restricted number of ever-similar relations, classical words are on the way to becoming an algebra where rhetorical figures of speech, clichés, function as virtual linking devices; they have lost their density and gained a more interrelated state of speech; they operate in the manner of chemical valences, outlining a verbal area full of symmetrical connections, junctions and networks from which arise, without the respite afforded by wonder, fresh intentions towards signification. Hardly have the fragments of classical discourse yielded their meaning than they become messengers or harbingers, carrying ever further a meaning which refuses to settle within the depths of a word, but tries instead to spread widely enough to become a total gesture of intellection, that is, of communication.

Now the distortion to which Hugo tried to subject the alexandrine, which is of all meters the most interrelational, already contains the whole future of modern poetry, since what is attempted is to eliminate the intention to establish relationships and to produce instead an explosion of words. For modern poetry, since it must be distinguished from classical poetry and from any type of prose, destroys the spontaneously functional nature of language, and leaves standing only its lexical basis. It retains only the outward shape of relationships, their music, but not their reality. The Word shines forth above a line of relationships emptied of their content, grammar is bereft of its purpose, it becomes prosody and is no longer anything but an inflection which lasts only to present the Word. Connections are not properly speaking abolished, they are merely reserved areas, a parody of themselves, and this void is necessary for the density of the Word to rise out of a magic vacuum, like a sound and a sign devoid of background, like "fury and mystery."

In classical speech, connections lead the word on, and at once carry it toward a meaning which is an ever-deferred project; in modern poetry, connections are only an extension of the word, it is the Word which is "the dwelling place," it is rooted like a *fons et origo* in the prosody of functions, which are perceived but unreal. Here, connections only fascinate, and it is the Word which gratifies and fulfills like the sudden revelation of a truth. To say that this truth is of a poetic order is merely to say that the Word in poetry can never be untrue, because it is a whole; it shines with an infinite freedom and prepares to radiate toward innumerable uncertain and possible connections. Fixed connections being abolished, the word is left only with a vertical project, it is like a monolith, or a pillar which plunges into a totality of meanings, reflexes, and recollections: it is a sign which stands. The poetic word is here an act without immediate past, without environment, and which holds forth only the dense shadow of reflexes from all sources which are associated with it. Thus under each Word in modern poetry there lies a sort of existential geology, in which is gathered the total content of the Name, instead of a chosen content as in classical prose and poetry. The Word is no longer guided *in advance* by the general intention of a socialized discourse; the consumer of poetry, deprived of the guide of selective connections, encounters the Word frontally, and receives it as an absolute quantity, accompanied by all its possible associations. The Word, here, is encyclopedic, it contains simultaneously all the acceptations from which a relational discourse might have required it to choose. It therefore achieves a state which is possible only in the dictionary or in poetry—places where the noun can live without its article—and is reduced to a sort of zero degree, pregnant with all past and future specifications. The word here has a generic form; it is a category. Each poetic word is thus an unexpected object, a Pandora's box from which fly out all the potentialities of language; it is therefore produced and consumed with a peculiar curiosity, a kind of sacred relish. This Hunger of the Word, common to the whole of modern poetry, makes poetic speech terrible and inhuman. It initiates a discourse full of gaps and full of lights, filled with absences and overnourishing signs, without foresight or stability of intention, and thereby so opposed to the social function of language that merely to have recourse to a discontinuous speech is to open the door to all that stands above Nature.

For what does the rational economy of classical language mean, if not that Nature is a plenum, that it can be possessed, that it does not shy away or cover itself in shadows, but is in its entirety subjected to the toils of language? Classical language is always reducible to a persuasive continuum, it postulates the possibility of dialogue, it establishes a universe in which men are not alone, where words never have the terrible weight of things, where speech is always a meeting with the others. Classical language is a bringer of euphoria because it is immediately social. There is no genre, no written work of classicism which does not suppose a collective consumption, akin to speech; classical literary art is an object which circulates among several persons brought together on a class basis; it is a product conceived for oral transmission, for a consumption regulated by the contingencies of society: it is essentially a spoken language, in spite of its strict codification.

We have seen that on the contrary modern poetry destroyed relationships in language and reduced discourse to words as static things. This implies a reversal in our knowledge of Nature. The interrupted flow of the new poetic language initiates a discontinuous Nature, which is revealed only piecemeal. At the very moment when the withdrawal of functions obscures the relations existing in the world, the object in discourse assumes an exalted place: modern poetry is a poetry of the object. In it, Nature becomes a fragmented space, made of objects solitary and terrible, because the links between them are only potential. Nobody chooses for them a privileged meaning, or a particular use, or some service; nobody imposes a hierarchy on them, nobody reduces them to the manifestation of a mental behavior, or of an intention, of some evidence of tenderness, in short. The bursting upon us of the poetic word then institutes an absolute object; Nature becomes a succession of verticalities, of objects, suddenly standing erect, and filled with all their possibilities: one of these can be only a landmark in an unfulfilled, and thereby terrible, world. These unrelated objects—words adorned with all the violence of their irruption, the vibration of which, though wholly mechanical, strangely affects the next word, only to die out immediately—these poetic words exclude men: there is no humanism of modern poetry. This erect discourse is full of terror, that is to say, it relates man not to other men but to the most inhuman images in Nature: heaven, hell, holiness, childhood, madness, pure matter, etc.

At such a point, it is hardly possible to speak of a poetic mode of writing, for this is a language in which a violent drive toward autonomy destroys any ethical scope. The verbal gesture here aims at modifying Nature, it is the approach of a demiurge; it is not an attitude of the conscience but an act of coercion. Such, at least, is the language of those modern poets who carry their intention to the limit, and assume Poetry not as a spiritual exercise, a state of the soul or a placing of oneself in a situation, but as the splendor and freshness of a dream language. For such poets, it is as vain to speak about a mode of writing as of poetic feeling. Modern Poetry, in Char, for instance, is beyond this diffuse tone, this precious *aura*, which *are*, indeed, a mode of writing, usually termed poetic feeling. There is no objection to speaking of a poetic mode of writing concerning the classical writers and their epigones, or even concerning poetic prose in the manner of Gide's *Fruits of the Earth*, in which Poetry is in fact a certain linguistic ethos. In both cases, the mode of writing soaks up the style, and we can imagine that for people living in the seventeenth century, it was not easy to perceive an *immediate* difference between Racine and Pradon (and even less a difference of a poetic kind), just as it is not easy for a modern reader to pass judgment on those contemporary poets who use the same uniform and indecisive poetic mode of writing, because for them Poetry is a *climate* which means, essentially, a linguistic convention. But when the poetic language radically questions Nature by virtue of its very structure, without any resort to the content of the discourse and without falling back on some ideology, there is no mode of writing left, there are only styles, thanks to which man turns his back on society and confronts the world of objects without going through any of the forms of History or of social life.

1953

The World as Object

Hᴀɴɢɪɴɢ in the Dutch museums are works by a minor master who may be as deserving of literary renown as Vermeer. Saenredam painted neither faces nor objects, but chiefly vacant church interiors, reduced to the beige and innocuous unction of butterscotch ice cream. These churches, where there is nothing to be seen but expanses of wood and white-washed plaster, are irremediably unpeopled, and this negation goes much further than the destruction of idols. Never has nothingness been so confident. Saenredam's sugary, stubborn surfaces calmly reject the Italian overpopulation of statues, as well as the horror vacui professed by other Dutch painters. Saenredam is in effect a painter of the absurd; he has achieved a privative state of the subject, more insidious than the dislocations of our contemporaries. To paint so lovingly these meaningless surfaces, and to paint nothing else—that is already a "modern" aesthetic of silence.

Saenredam is a paradox: he articulates by antithesis the nature of classical Dutch painting, which has washed away religion only to replace it with man and his empire of things.

From *Critical Essays*, translated by Richard Howard (Evanston: Northwestern University Press, 1972).

Where once the Virgin presided over ranks of angels, man
stands now, his feet upon the thousand objects of everyday
life, triumphantly surrounded by his functions. Behold him,
then, at the pinnacle of history, knowing no other fate than a
gradual appropriation of matter. No limits to this humanization, and above all, no horizon: in the great Dutch seascapes
(Cappelle's or Van de Venne's), the ships are crammed with
people or cargo, the water is a ground you could walk on, the
sea completely urbanized. A foundering vessel is always close
to a shore covered with men and help; the human, here, is a
virtue of numbers. As if the destiny of the Dutch landscape is
to swarm with men, to be transformed from an elemental infinity to the plenitude of the registry office. This canal, this mill,
these trees, these birds (Essaias van de Velde's) are linked by
a crowded ferry; the overloaded boat connects the two shores
and thus closes the movement of trees and water by the intention of a human movement, reducing these forces of Nature to
the rank of objects and transforming the Creation into a facility. In the season most contrary to mankind, during one of
those savage winters only history describes, Ruysdael still
manages to put in a bridge, a house, a man walking down the
road; the first warm spring shower is still a long way off, yet
this man walking is actually the seed in the earth, for man
himself is the seed, stubbornly pushing through this huge ocher
sheet.

Here, then, men inscribe themselves upon space, immediately covering it with familiar gestures, memories, customs,
and intentions. They establish themselves by means of a path,
a mill, a frozen canal, and as soon as they can they arrange
their objects in space as in a room; everything in them tends
toward the *habitat* pure and simple: it is their heaven. There
has been (eloquent) testimony to the domiciliary power of the
Dutch canal boat; sturdy, securely decked, concave, it is as full
as an egg and produces the egg's felicity: an absence of the

void. Consider the Dutch still life: the object is never alone, and never privileged; it is merely there, among many others, painted between one function and another, participating in the disorder of the movements which have picked it up, put it down—in a word, *utilized*. There are objects wherever you look, on the tables, the walls, the floor: pots, pitchers overturned, a clutter of baskets, a bunch of vegetables, a brace of game, milk pans, oyster shells, glasses, cradles. All this is man's space; in it he measures himself and determines his humanity, starting from the memory of his gestures: his *chronos* is covered by functions, there is no other authority in his life but the one he imprints upon the inert by shaping and manipulating it.

This universe of fabrication obviously excludes terror, as it excludes style. The concern of the Dutch painters is not to rid the object of its qualities in order to liberate its essence but, quite the contrary, to accumulate the secondary vibrations of appearance, for what must be incorporated into human space are layers of air, surfaces, and not forms or ideas. The only logical issue of such painting is to coat substance with a kind of glaze against which man may move without impairing the object's usefulness. Still-life painters like Van de Velde or Heda always render matter's most superficial quality: *sheen*. Oysters, lemon pulp, heavy goblets full of dark wine, long clay pipes, gleaming chestnuts, pottery, tarnished metal cups, three grape seeds—what can be the justification of such an assemblage if not to lubricate man's gaze amid his domain, to facilitate his daily business among objects whose riddle is dissolved and which are no longer anything but easy surfaces?

An object's *use* can only help dissipate its essential form and emphasize instead its attributes. Other arts, other ages may have pursued, under the name of style, the essential core of things; here, nothing of the kind: each object is accompanied by its adjectives, substance is buried under its myriad qualities, man never confronts the object, which remains dutifully subjugated to him by precisely what it is assigned to provide. What need have I of the lemon's principal form? What my quite empirical humanity needs is a lemon ready for use, half-peeled, half-sliced, half-lemon, half-juice, caught at the precious moment it exchanges the scandal of its perfect and useless ellipse for the first of its economic qualities, astringency. The object is always open, exposed, accompanied, until it has destroyed itself as closed substance, until it has cashed in all the functional virtues man can derive from stubborn matter. I regard the Dutch "kitchen scenes" (Buelkelaer's, for instance) less as a nation's indulgence of its own appetites (which would be more Belgian than Dutch; patricians like Ruyter and Tromp ate meat only once a week) than as a series of explanations concerning the *instrumentality* of foodstuffs: the units of nourishment are always destroyed as still lifes and restored as moments of a domestic *chronos*; whether it is the crisp greenness of cucumbers or the pallor of plucked fowls, everywhere the object offers man its *utilized* aspect, not its principal form. Here, in other words, is never a generic state of the object, but only circumstantial states.

Behold then a real transformation of the object, which no longer has an essence but takes refuge entirely within its attributes. A more complete subservience of things is unimaginable. The entire city of Amsterdam, indeed, seems to have been built with a view to this domestication: few substances here are not annexed to the empire of merchandise. Take the rubble in the corner of a vacant lot or near a railroad siding— what seems more indescribable: not an object, but an element! Yet in Amsterdam, consider this same rubble sifted and loaded onto a barge, led through the canals—you will see objects as clearly defined as cheeses, crates, vats, logs. Add to the vehicular movement of the water the vertical plane of the houses which retain, absorb, interpose, or restore the merchandise: that whole concert of pulleys, chutes, and docks effects a permanent mobilization of the most shapeless substances. Each house—narrow, flat, tilting forward as though to meet the merchandise halfway—suddenly opens at the top: here, pushing up into the sky, is nothing more than a kind of mystical mouth, the attic, as if each human habitat were merely the rising path of storage, hoarding, that great ancestral gesture of animals and children. As the city is built on water, there are no cellars, everything is taken up to the attic, raised there from outside. Thus objects interrupt every horizon, glide along the water and along the walls. It is objects which articulate space.

The object is by and large constituted by this mobility. Hence the defining power of all these Dutch canals. What we have, clearly, is a water-merchandise complex; it is water which makes the object, giving it all the nuances of a calm, planar mobility, collecting supplies, shifting them without perceptible transition from one exchange to another, making the entire city into a census of agile goods. Take a look at the canals of another minor master, Berckheyde, who has painted virtually nothing but this mild traffic of ownership: everything is, for the object, a means of procession; this bit of wharf is a cynosure of kegs, logs, tarpaulins; man has only to overturn or to hoist; space, obedient creature, does the rest—carries back and forth, selects, distributes, recovers, seems to have no other goal than to complete the projected movement of all these things, separated from matter by the sleek, firm film of *use*; here all objects are prepared for manipulation, all have the detachment and the density of Dutch cheeses: round, waxed, prehensible.

This separation is the extreme limit of the concrete, and I know only one French work which can claim to equal in its itemizing power that of the Dutch canals—our Civil Code. Consider the list of real estate and chattels: "domestic pigeons, wild rabbits, beehives, pond fish, wine presses, stills, ovens, manure and stable litter, wall hangings, mirrors, books and medals, linens, weapons, seeds, wines, hay," etc. Is this not exactly the universe of Dutch painting? Each represents the triumph of an entirely self-sufficient nominalism. Every definition and every manipulation of property produce an art of the catalogue, in other words, of the concrete itself, divided, countable, mobile. The Dutch scenes require a gradual and complete reading; we must begin at one edge and finish at the other, audit the painting like an accountant, not forgetting this corner, that margin, that background, in which is inscribed yet another perfectly rendered object adding its unit to this patient weighing of property or of merchandise.

When applied to social groups regarded by the period as inferior, this enumerative power constitutes certain men as objects. Van Ostade's peasants or Averkamp's skaters are entitled only to the existence of number, and the scenes grouping them must be read not as a repertory of fully human gestures, but rather as an anecdotic catalogue dividing and combining the various elements of a prehumanity; we must decipher the scene the way we read a puzzle. This is because Dutch painting obviously deals with two anthropologies, as distinctly separated as Linnaeus' zoological classes. It is no accident that the word "class" applies to both notions: there is the patrician class (*homo patricius*) and the peasant class (*homo paganicus*), and each encompasses human beings not only of the same social condition but also of the same morphology.

Van Ostade's peasants have abortive, shapeless faces; as if they were unfinished creatures, rough drafts of men, arrested at an earlier stage of human development. Even the children have neither age nor sex; they are identified only by their size. As the ape is separated from man, here the peasant is separated from the burgher precisely insofar as he is deprived of the ultimate characteristics of humanity, those of the *person*.

This subclass of men is never represented frontally, an attitude which presupposes at least a gaze: this privilege is reserved for the patrician or the cow, the Dutch totem animal and national provider. From the neck up, these peasants have only a blob which has not yet become a face, its lower part invariably slashed or blurred or somehow twisted askew; it is a shifting prehumanity which reels across space like so many objects endowed with an additional power of drunkenness or hilarity.

Turn now to the young patrician (Verspronck's, for example) frozen into the proposition of an idle god. He is an ultra-person, endowed with the extreme signs of humanity. Just as the peasant face falls short of creation, the patrician face achieves the ultimate degree of identity. This zoological class of rich Dutch burghers possesses, further, its characteristic features: chestnut hair, brown or plum-colored eyes, pinkish skin, prominent nose, soft red lips, and a play of fragile shadows round the salient points of the face. Virtually no portraits of women, except as regents of hospitals, dispensers of public funds, not private fun. Woman is assigned only an instrumental role, as an administrator of charity or a guardian of domestic economy. Man, and man alone, is human. Hence all Dutch painting—still lifes, seascapes, peasant scenes, regents—culminate in a purely masculine iconography whose obsessive expression is the guild portrait.

The guilds or *Doelen* are the subject of so many paintings that we cannot help suspecting the presence of a myth. The *Doelen* are rather like Italian Madonnas, Greek ephebes, Egyptian pharaohs, or German fugues—a classical theme which indicates to the artist the limits of nature. And just as all Madonnas, all ephebes, all pharaohs, and all fugues are somewhat alike, all guild faces are isomorphic. Here, once again, is proof that the face is a social sign, that there is a possible history of faces, and that the most direct product of nature is as subject to process and to signification as the most socialized institutions.

In the guild portraits, one thing is striking: the great size of the heads, the lighting, the excessive truth of the face. The face becomes a kind of hothouse flower, brought to perfection by careful forcing. All these faces are treated as units of one and the same horticultural species, combining generic resemblance and individual identity. There are huge fleshy blooms (Hals) or tawny nebulae (Rembrandt), but this universality has nothing to do with the glabrous neutrality of medieval portraits, which are entirely accessible, ready to receive the signs of the soul, and not those of the person: pain, joy, piety, and pity, a whole fleshless iconography of the passions. The similarity of faces in medieval art is of an ontological order, that of the *Doelen* portraits of a genetic one. A social class unequivocally defined by its economy (identity of commercial function, after all, justifies these guild paintings) is here presented in its anthropological aspect, and this aspect has nothing to do with the secondary characteristics of the physiognomy: it is not because of their seriousness or their confidence that these heads look alike, contrary to socialist-realist portraits, for example, which unify a representation of the workers, say, under a single sign of virility and tension (this is the method of a primitive art). Here the matrix of the human face is not of an ethical order, it is of a carnal order; it consists not of a community of intentions, but of an identity of blood and food; it is formed after a long sedimentation which has accumulated all the characteristics of a social particularity within a class: age, size, morphology, wrinkles, veins, the very order of biology separates the patrician caste from the functional substance (objects, peasants, landscapes) and imprisons it within its own authority.

Entirely identified by their social heredity, these Dutch faces

are engaged in none of those visceral adventures which ravage
the countenance and expose the body in its momentary destitution. What have they to do with the *chronos* of passion?
Theirs is the *chronos* of biology; their flesh has no need, in
order to exist, to anticipate or to endure events; it is blood
which causes it to be and to command recognition; passion
would be pointless, it would add nothing to existence. Consider the exception: Rembrandt's David does not weep, but
half veils his head in a curtain; to close the eyes is to close the
world, and in all Dutch painting no scene is more aberrant.
This is because for once man is endowed with an adjectival
quality; he slips from being to having, rejoins a humanity at
grips with something else. If we could consider a painting out
of the context of its technical or aesthetic rules, there would be
no difference between a tearful fifteenth-century *Pietà* and
some combative Lenin of contemporary Soviet imagery; for in
either case, an attribute is provided, not an identity. This is
precisely the converse of the little cosmos of Dutch art, where
objects exist only by their qualities, whereas man, and man
alone, possesses existence-in-itself. A substantive world of
man, an adjectival world of things: such is the order of a
creation dedicated to contentment.

What is it then which distinguishes these men at the pinnacle of their empire? It is the *numen*. The ancient *numen* was
that simple gesture by which divinity signified its decisions,
disposing of human destiny by a sort of infra-language consisting of pure demonstration. Omnipotence does not speak (perhaps because it does not think), it is content with gesture,
even with a half gesture, a hint of a gesture, swiftly absorbed
into the slothful serenity of the Divine. The modern prototype
of the *numen* might be that circumspect tension, mixed with
lassitude and confidence, by which Michelangelo's God draws
away from Adam after having created him, and with a sus-

pended gesture assigns him his imminent humanity. Each time the ruling class is represented, it must expose its *numen* or else the painting would be unintelligible. Consider the hagiography of the First Empire: Napoleon is a purely numinous figure, unreal by the very convention of his gesture. At first, this gesture still exists: the emperor is never represented idle; he points or signifies or acts. But there is nothing human about his gesture; it is not the gesture of the workman, *homo faber*, whose functional movement encompasses him in search of its own effect; it is a gesture immobilized in the least stable moment of its course; it is the idea of power, not its density, which is thus eternalized. The hand which rises slightly or gently comes to rest—the very suspension of movement— produces the phantasmagoria of a power alien to man. The gesture creates, it does not complete, and consequently its indication matters more than its course. Consider *The Battle of Eylau* (a painting to remove from its context, if ever there was one): what a difference in density between the excessive gestures of the ordinary mortals—shouting, supporting a wounded man, caracoling rhetorically—and the waxy impasto of the emperor-God, surrounded by motionless air, raising a hand huge with every signification at once, designating everything and nothing, creating with a terrible languor a future of unknown acts. This exemplary painting shows us just how the *numen* is constituted: it *signifies* infinite movement yet does not accomplish it, merely eternalizing the notion of power and not its substance in an embalmed gesture, a gesture arrested at the most fragile point of its fatigue, imposing on the man who contemplates and endures it the plenitude of an intelligible power.

Naturally, there is nothing warlike about the *numen* of these merchants, these Dutch burghers at banquets or grouped around a table to draw up their accounts, this class at once social and zoological. How, then, does it impose its unreality? By looking. It is the gaze which is the *numen* here, the gaze which disturbs, intimidates, and makes man the ultimate term of a problem. To be stared at by a portrait is always disconcerting. Nor is this a Dutch specialty. But here the gaze is collective; these men, even these lady regents virilized by age and function, all these patricians rest upon you the full weight of their smooth, bare faces. They are gathered together not to count their money—which they never bother with, despite the table, the ledger, the pile of gold—not to eat the food—despite its abundance—but to look at you, thereby signifying an existence and an authority beyond which you cannot go. Their gaze is their proof and it is yours. Consider Rembrandt's cloth merchants—one of them even stands up to get a better look at you. You become a matter of capital, you are an element of humanity doomed to participate in a *numen* issuing finally from man and not from God. There is no sadness and no cruelty in that gaze; it is a gaze without adjectives, it is only, completely, a gaze which neither judges you nor appeals to you; it posits you, implicates you; makes you exist. But this creative gesture is endless; you keep on being born, you are sustained, carried to the end of a movement which is one of infinite origin, source, and which appears in an eternal state of suspension. God and the emperor had the power of the hand, man has the gaze. All history reaches the grandeur of its own mystery in an endless look.

It is because the gaze of the *Doelen* institutes a final suspension of history, at the pinnacle of social happiness, that Dutch painting is not satiated, and that its class orientation culminates after all in something which also belongs to other men. What happens when men are, by their own means, content? What is left of man? The *Doelen* answer: a look is left. In this perfectly content patrician world, absolute master of matter and evidently rid of God, the gaze produces a strictly human interrogation and proposes an infinite postponement of history. There is, in these Dutch *Doelen*, the very contrary of a realistic art.

Consider Courbet's *Atelier*: it is a complete allegory. Shut up in a room, the artist is painting a landscape he does not see, turning his back to his (naked) model, who is watching him paint. In other words, the painter establishes himself in a space carefully emptied of any gaze but his own. Now, all art which has only two dimensions, that of the work and that of the spectator, can create only a platitude, since it is no more than the capture of a shopwindow spectacle by a painter-voyeur. Depth is born only at the moment the spectacle itself slowly turns its shadow toward man and begins to look at him.

1953

Baudelaire's Theater

WHAT is interesting about Baudelaire's plays[1] is not their dramatic content but their embryonic state: the critic's role is therefore not to dissect these sketches for the image of an achieved theater but, on the contrary, to determine in them the vocation of their failure. It would be futile—and probably cruel to Baudelaire's memory—to imagine the plays these germs might have produced; it is not so to seek out the reasons which kept Baudelaire in this state of imperfect creation, so far from the aesthetic of *Les Fleurs du mal.* How well Sartre has shown us that nonfulfillment itself is a choice, and that to have projected a dramatic *oeuvre* without writing it was for Baudelaire a significant form of his fate.

One notion is essential to the understanding of Baudelairean

From *Critical Essays.*

[1] We know of four projects: the first, *Ideolus* (or *Manoel*), is an unfinished drama in alexandrines written about 1843 (Baudelaire was twenty-two), in collaboration with Ernest Praron. The other three are scenarios: *La Fin de Don Juan* is little more than a plot outline; *Le Marquis du Iᵉʳ Houzards* is a kind of historical drama in which Baudelaire planned to study the case of an *émigré's* son, Wolfgang de Cadolles, torn between the ideas of his parents and his enthusiasm for the emperor. *L'Ivrogne,* the most Baudelairean of these scenarios, is the story of a crime: a drunk and lazy workman pushes his wife down a well he then fills with cobblestones; the play was to develop the situation indicated in a poem from *Les Fleurs du mal, Le Vin de l'assassin.*

theater: theatricality. What is theatricality? It is theater-minus-text, it is a density of signs and sensations built up on stage starting from the written argument; it is that ecumenical perception of sensuous artifice—gesture, tone, distance, substance, light—which submerges the text beneath the profusion of its external language. Of course theatricality must be present in the first written germ of a work, it is a datum of creation not of production. There is no great theater without a devouring theatricality—in Aeschylus, in Shakespeare, in Brecht, the written text is from the first carried along by the externality of bodies, of objects, of situations; the utterance immediately explodes into substances. One thing strikes us on the contrary in the three scenarios by Baudelaire (I set no store by *Ideolus*): these are purely narrative scenarios whose theatricality, even potentially, is very weak.

We must not let Baudelaire deceive us by such naïve indications as "very active, bustling production, great military pomp, settings of a poetic effect, fantastic statue, costumes of various nations," etc. This concern for externals, manifested intermittently, like a sudden remorse, affords no profound theatricality. Quite the contrary, it is the very generality of the Baudelairean impression which is alien to the theater: here, as elsewhere, Baudelaire is too intelligent; he substitutes concept for object, replaces the tavern of *L'Ivrogne* by the idea, the "atmosphere" of the tavern, offers the pure concept of military pomp instead of the materiality of flags or uniforms. Paradoxically, nothing attests better to impotence in the theater than this *total* character, somehow romantic, at least exotic, of vision. Each time Baudelaire refers to "production values," he sees them, naïvely, with a spectator's eye—in other words, fulfilled, static, ready-made, precooked and offering a seamless deception which has had time to do away with all traces of its own artifice. The "color of crime" necessary, for example, in the last act of *L'Ivrogne* is a critic's truth, not a dramatist's. In its initial movement, the production can be based only on the plurality and the literalness of objects. Baudelaire, on the other hand, conceives things in the theater only as accompanied by their dreamed-of doubles, endowed with a spirituality vaporous enough to unify them, to alienate them all the more. Now, nothing is more contrary to dramaturgy than the dream. The germs of true theater are always elementary movements of prehension or distancing: the sur-reality of theater objects is of a sensorial, not an oneiric order.

It is therefore not when Baudelaire speaks of production, of staging, that he is closest to a concrete theater. His authentic theatricality is the sentiment, indeed one might say the torment, of the actor's disturbing corporeality. In one scenario he proposes that Don Juan's son be played by a girl, in another that the hero be surrounded by lovely women each assigned a domestic function, and in a third that the drunkard's wife offer in her very body that appearance of modesty and fragility which call down rape and murder upon her. This is because for Baudelaire the actor's condition is a prostitution ("In a spectacle, in a dance, each takes his pleasure from all the participants"); his charm is therefore not experienced as an episodic and decorative character (contrary to the "bustling" staging, the movements of gypsies or the atmosphere of taverns), it is necessary to the theater as the manifestation of a primary category of the Baudelairean universe: artificiality.

The actor's body is artificial, but its duplicity is much more profound than that of the painted sets or the fake furniture of the stage; the grease paint, the imitation of gestures or intonation, the accessibility of an exposed body—all this is artificial but not factitious, and thereby a part of that delicate transcendence, of an exquisite, essential savor, by which Baudelaire has defined the power of the artificial paradise: the actor bears in himself the very overprecision of an excessive world, like that of hashish, where nothing is invented, but where everything exists in a multiplied intensity. This suggests that Baudelaire had an acute sense of the most secret and also the most disturbing theatricality, the kind which puts the actor at the center of the theatrical prodigy and constitutes the theater as the site of an ultra-incarnation, in which the body is double, at once a living body deriving from a trivial nature, and an emphatic, formal body, frozen by its function as an artificial object.

However, this powerful theatricality is merely vestigial in Baudelaire's projects for plays, whereas it flows powerfully through the rest of his work. It would seem that Baudelaire put his theater everywhere except, precisely, in his projects for plays. It is, moreover, a general fact of creation, this kind of marginal development of the elements of a genre—drama, novel, or poetry—within works which nominally are not made to receive them. For instance, France has put her historical drama everywhere in her literature except on stage. Baudelaire's theatricality is animated by the same power of evasion: wherever we do not expect it, it explodes; first and foremost in *Les Paradis artificiels*: here Baudelaire describes a sensory transmutation which is of the same nature as theatrical perception, since in both cases reality is assigned an emphatic accent, which is the stress of an ideality of things. Then in his poetry, at least wherever objects are united by the poet in a kind of radiant perception of matter, amassed, condensed as though on a stage, glowing with colors, lights, and cosmetics, touched here and there by the grace of the artificial; in every description of scenes, finally, for here the preference for a space deeper and stabilized by the painter's theocratic gesture is satisfied in the same manner as in the theater (conversely, "scenes" abound in the scenario of *Le Marquis du Ier Houzards*, which seems to come all of a piece out of Gros or Delacroix, just as *La Fin de Don Juan* or *L'Ivrogne* seem to come from a poetic rather than a strictly theatrical intention).

Thus Baudelaire's theatricality evades his theater in order to spread through the rest of his work. By a converse process, though one just as revealing, elements deriving from extra-dramatic orders abound in these scenarios, as if this theater were striving to destroy itself by a double movement of evasion and intoxication. As soon as it is conceived, the Baudelairean scenario is immediately steeped in novelistic categories: *La Fin de Don Juan*, at least the opening fragment we have of it, ends curiously with a pastiche of Stendhal; Don Juan speaks almost like Mosca: the few words he exchanges with his servant suggest the dialogue of the novel, in which the language of the characters, direct as it may be, retains that precious glaze, that chastened transparency we know Baudelaire applied to all the objects of his creation. Of course the text is no more than a sketch, and Baudelaire might have given his dialogue that absolute literality which is the fundamental status of language in the theater. But we are analyzing here the vocation of a failure and not the potentiality of a project: it is significant that in its nascent state, this ghost of a scenario should have the very tonality of a written literature, frozen by the page, without voice, without viscera.

Time and place, each time they are indicated, testify to the same horror of the theater, at least of the theater as we can imagine it in Baudelaire's day: act and scene are units which immediately hamper Baudelaire, which he repeatedly overflows and whose regulation he always postpones: sometimes he feels that the act is too short, sometimes too long: in Act III of *Le Marquis du Ier Houzards* he inserts a flashback which even today only the cinema could manage; in *La Fin de Don Juan*, the scene gradually shifts from city to country, as in some abstract theater (*Faust*): in a general manner, even in its germ, this theater explodes, turns like an unstable chemical mixture, divides into "scenes" (in the pictorial sense of the term) or narratives. This is because, contrary to any true man of the theater, Baudelaire imagines a story entirely narrated, instead of starting from the stage; genetically, the theater is the subsequent creation of a fiction around an initial datum, which is always of a gestural order (liturgy in Aeschylus, actors' intrigues in Molière); Baudelaire evidently conceives the theater as a purely formal avatar, imposed after the fact upon a creative principle of a symbolic order (*Le Marquis du Ier Houzards*) or an existential one (*L'Ivrogne*). "I confess I have not given a thought to the staging," Baudelaire says at one point; impossible naïveté in any playwright, however minor.

Not that Baudelaire's scenarios are absolutely alien to an aesthetic of performance; but precisely insofar as they belong to a generally novelistic order, it is not theater but cinema which might best articulate them, for it is from the novel that cinema derives and not from the theater. The shifting locales, the flashbacks, the exoticism of the scenes, the temporal disproportion of the episodes, in short that torment of laying out the narration, to which Baudelaire's pre-theater testifies, might nourish a pure cinema. From this point of view, *Le Marquis du Ier Houzards* is a complete scenario: even the actors in this drama suggest the classical typology of cinema roles. This is because the actor, deriving from a novelistic character and not from a corporeal dream (as is still the case for Don Juan's son, played by a woman, or the drunkard's wife, object of sadism), has no need of the stage's dimension in order to exist: he belongs to a sentimental or social typology, not a morphological one: he is a pure narrative sign, as in the novel and as in the cinema.

What remains, then, which is strictly theatrical in Baudelaire's projects? Nothing, except precisely a pure recourse to the theater. It is as if the mere intention of someday writing plays had sufficed for Baudelaire and had exempted him from sustaining these projects with a strictly theatrical substance, suggested throughout his work but rejected in just those places where it might have been fulfilled. For to this theater which Baudelaire momentarily sought out, he eagerly lent the features most likely to eliminate it at once: a certain triviality, a certain puerility (surprising in relation to Baudelairean dandyism), deriving visibly from the supposed pleasures of the crowd, the "Odeonic" imagination of spectacular scenes (a battle, the emperor reviewing troops, a country dance hall, a gypsy camp, a complicated murder), a whole aesthetic of crude impressiveness, cut off from its dramatic motives or, one might say, a formalism of the theatrical act conceived in its effects most flattering to *petit bourgeois* sensibility.

With such a conception of theater, Baudelaire had to protect theatricality from the theater; fearing the sovereign artifice would be threatened by the collective character of the occasion, he hid it far from the stage, gave it refuge in his solitary literature, in his poems, his essays, his *Salons*; so that there is nothing left in this imaginary theater but the prostitution of the actor, the supposed pleasure of the public in the lies (and not in the artifice) of a grandiloquent production. This theater is trivial, but it is a triviality painful precisely insofar as it is pure conduct, mutilated as though deliberately of any poetic or dramatic depth, cut off from any development which might have justified it, crudely indicating that zone in which Baudelaire created himself from project to project, from failure to failure, until he built up that pure murder of literature, which we know since Mallarmé to be the torment and the justification of the modern writer.

It is therefore because the theater, abandoned by a theatricality which seeks refuge everywhere else, then fulfills to perfection a vulgar social nature, that Baudelaire chooses it briefly as the nominal site of an impulse and as the sign of what we would today call a commitment. By this pure gesture (pure because it transmits only his intention, and because this theater exists only as a project), Baudelaire rejoins, but this time on the level of creation, that sociability he pretended to postulate and to flee, according to the dialectic of a choice Sartre has so decisively analyzed. To bring a play to Holstein, the director of the Gaîté, was an action as reassuring as to flatter Sainte-Beuve, to canvas votes for the Academy, or to want the Legion of Honor.

And that is why these theatrical projects touch us so deeply: they belong in Baudelaire to that vast background of negativity against which rises finally the success of *Les Fleurs du mal* like an act which no longer owes anything to talent, that is, to literature. It took General Aupik, Ancelle, Théophile Gautier, Sainte-Beuve, the Academy, the ribbon of the Legion, and this pseudo-Odeonic theater, all these complacencies, accursed or abandoned moreover as soon as they were consented to, for Baudelaire's fulfilled work to be that responsible choice which made, in the end, his life into a great destiny. We would be ungrateful for *Les Fleurs du mal* if we failed to incorporate into its creator's history this agonizing Passion of vulgarity.

1954

The Face of Garbo

GARBO still belongs to that moment in cinema when capturing the human face still plunged audiences into the deepest ecstasy, when one literally lost oneself in a human image as one would in a philter, when the face represented a kind of absolute state of the flesh, which could be neither reached nor renounced. A few years earlier the face of Valentino was causing suicides; that of Garbo still partakes of the same rule of Courtly Love, where the flesh gives rise to mystical feelings of perdition.

It is indeed an admirable face-object. In *Queen Christina*, a film which has again been shown in Paris in the last few years, the makeup has the snowy thickness of a mask: it is not a painted face, but one set in plaster, protected by the surface of the color, not by its lineaments. Amid all this snow at once fragile and compact, the eyes alone, black like strange soft flesh, but not in the least expressive, are two faintly tremulous wounds. In spite of its extreme beauty, this face, not drawn but sculpted in something smooth and friable, that is, at once perfect and ephemeral, comes to resemble the flour-white

From *Mythologies*.

complexion of Charlie Chaplin, the dark vegetation of his eyes, his totem-like countenance.

Now the temptation of the absolute mask (the mask of antiquity, for instance) perhaps implies less the theme of the secret (as is the case with Italian half mask) than that of an archetype of the human face. Garbo offered to one's gaze a sort of Platonic Idea of the human creature, which explains why her face is almost sexually undefined, without however leaving one in doubt. It is true that this film (in which Queen Christina is by turns a woman and a young cavalier) lends itself to this lack of differentiation; but Garbo does not perform in it any feat of transvestism; she is always herself, and carries without pretense, under her crown or her wide-brimmed hats, the same snowy solitary face. The name given to her, *the Divine*, probably aimed to convey less a superlative state of beauty than the essence of her corporeal person, descended from a heaven where all things are formed and perfected in the clearest light. She herself knew this: how many actresses have consented to let the crowd see the ominous maturing of their beauty. Not she, however; the essence was not to be degraded, her face was not to have any reality except that of its perfection, which was intellectual even more than formal. The Essence became gradually obscured, progressively veiled with dark glasses, broad hats and exiles: but it never deteriorated.

And yet, in this deified face, something sharper than a mask is looming: a kind of voluntary and therefore human relation between the curve of the nostrils and the arch of the eyebrows; a rare, individual function relating two regions of the face. A mask is but a sum of lines; a face, on the contrary, is above all their thematic harmony. Garbo's face represents this fragile moment when the cinema is about to draw an existential from an essential beauty, when the archetype leans toward the fascination of mortal faces, when the clarity of the flesh as essence yields its place to a lyricism of Woman.

Viewed as a transition the face of Garbo reconciles two iconographic ages, it assures the passage from awe to charm. As is well known, we are today at the other pole of this evolution: the face of Audrey Hepburn, for instance, is individualized, not only because of its peculiar thematics (woman as child, woman as kitten), but also because of her person, of an almost unique specification of the face, which has nothing of the essence left in it, but is constituted by an infinite complexity of morphological functions. As a language, Garbo's singularity was of the order of the concept, that of Audrey Hepburn is of the order of the substance. The face of Garbo is an Idea, that of Hepburn, an Event.

1955

Striptease

STRIPTEASE—at least Parisian striptease—is based on a contradiction: Woman is desexualized at the very moment when she is stripped naked. We may therefore say that we are dealing in a sense with a spectacle based on fear, or rather on the pretense of fear, as if eroticism here went no further than a sort of delicious terror, whose ritual signs have only to be announced to evoke at once the idea of sex and its conjuration.

It is only the time taken in shedding clothes which makes voyeurs of the public; but here, as in any mystifying spectacle, the decor, the props, and the stereotypes intervene to contradict the initially provocative intention and eventually bury it in insignificance: evil is *advertised* the better to impede and exorcise it. French striptease seems to stem from what I have earlier called "Operation Margarine," a mystifying device which consists in inoculating the public with a touch of evil, the better to plunge it afterward into a permanently immune Moral Good: a few particles of eroticism, highlighted by the very situation on which the show is based, are in fact absorbed in a reassuring ritual which negates the flesh as surely as the

From *Mythologies*.

vaccine or the taboo circumscribe and control the illness or the crime.

There will therefore be in striptease a whole series of coverings placed upon the body of the woman in proportion as she pretends to strip it bare. Exoticism is the first of these barriers, for it is always of a petrified kind which transports the body into the world of legend or romance: a Chinese woman equipped with an opium pipe (the indispensable symbol of "Sininess"), an undulating vamp with a gigantic cigarette holder, a Venetian decor complete with gondola, a dress with panniers and a singer of serenades: all aim at establishing the woman *right from the start* as an object in disguise. The end of the striptease is then no longer to drag into the light a hidden depth, but to signify, through the shedding of an incongruous and artificial clothing, nakedness as a *natural* vesture of woman, which amounts in the end to regaining a perfectly chaste state of the flesh.

The classic props of the music hall, which are invariably rounded up here, constantly make the unveiled body more remote, and force it back into the all-pervading ease of a well-known rite: the furs, the fans, the gloves, the feathers, the fish-net stockings, in short, the whole spectrum of adornment, constantly makes the living body return to the category of luxurious objects which surround man with a magical decor. Covered with feathers or gloved, the woman identifies herself here as a stereotyped element of music hall, and to shed objects as ritualistic as these is no longer a part of a further, genuine undressing. Feathers, furs, and gloves go on pervading the woman with their magical virtue even once removed, and give her something like the enveloping memory of a luxurious shell, for it is a self-evident law that the whole of striptease is given in the very nature of the initial garment: if the latter is improbable, as in the case of the Chinese woman or the woman in furs, the nakedness which follows remains itself unreal, smooth, and enclosed like a beautiful slippery object, with-drawn by its very extravagance from human use: this is the underlying significance of the G-string covered with diamonds or sequins which is the very end of striptease. This ultimate triangle, by its pure and geometrical shape, by its hard and shiny material, bars the way to the sexual parts like a sword of purity, and definitively drives the woman back into a mineral world, the (precious) stone being here the irrefutable symbol of the absolute object, that which serves no purpose.

Contrary to the common prejudice, the dance which accom-panies the striptease from beginning to end is in no way an erotic element. It is probably quite the reverse: the faintly rhythmical undulation in this case exorcises the fear of immo-bility. Not only does it give to the show the alibi of Art (the dances in strip shows are always "artistic"), but above all it constitutes the last barrier, and the most efficient of all: the dance, consisting of ritual gestures which have been seen a thousand times, acts on movements as a cosmetic, it hides nudity, and smothers the spectacle under a glaze of superflu-ous yet essential gestures, for the act of becoming bare is here relegated to the rank of parasitical operations carried out in an improbable background. Thus we see the professionals of striptease wrap themselves in the miraculous ease which con-stantly clothes them, makes them remote, gives them the icy indifference of skillful practitioners, haughtily taking refuge in the sureness of their technique: their science clothes them like a garment.

All this, this meticulous exorcism of sex, can be verified *a contrario* in the "popular contests" (*sic*) of amateur strip-tease: there, "beginners" undress in front of a few hundred spectators without resorting or resorting very clumsily to magic, which unquestionably restores to the spectacle its erotic power. Here we find at the beginning far fewer Chinese or Spanish women, no feathers or furs (sensible suits, ordinary coats), few disguises as a starting point—gauche steps, unsatisfactory dancing, girls constantly threatened by immobility, and above all by a "technical" awkwardness (the resistance of briefs, dress or bra) which gives to the gestures of unveiling an unexpected importance, denying the woman the alibi of art and the refuge of being an object, imprisoning her in a condition of weakness and timorousness.

And yet, at the Moulin Rouge, we see hints of another kind of exorcism, probably typically French, and one which in actual fact tends less to nullify eroticism than to tame it: the compère tries to give striptease a reassuring petit-bourgeois status. To start with, striptease is a *sport*: there is a Striptease Club, which organizes healthy contests whose winners come out crowned and rewarded with edifying prizes (a subscription to physical training lessons), a novel (which can only be Robbe-Grillet's *Voyeur*), or useful prizes (a pair of nylons, five thousand francs). Then, striptease is identified with a *career* (beginners, semi-professionals, professionals), that is, to the honorable practice of a specialization (strippers are skilled workers). One can even give them the magical alibi of work: *vocation*; one girl is, say, "*doing well*" or "*well on the way to fulfilling her promise,*" or on the contrary "*taking her first steps*" on the arduous path of striptease. Finally and above all, the competitors are socially situated: one is a salesgirl, another a secretary (there are many secretaries in the Striptease Club). Striptease here is made to rejoin the world of the public, is made familiar and bourgeois, as if the French, unlike the American public (at least according to what one hears), following an irresistible tendency of their social status, could not conceive eroticism except as a household property, sanctioned by the alibi of weekly sport much more than by that of a magical spectacle: and this is how, in France, striptease is nationalized.

1955

The Lady of the Camellias

THEY still perform, in some part of the world or other, *The Lady of the Camellias* (it had in fact another run in Paris some time ago). This success must alert us to a mythology of Love which probably still exists, for the alienation of Marguerite Gautier in relation to the class of her masters is not fundamentally different from that of today's petit-bourgeois women in a world which is just as stratified.

Yet in fact, the central myth in *The Lady of the Camellias* is not Love, it is Recognition. Marguerite loves in order to achieve recognition, and this is why her passion (in the etymological, not the libidinal sense) has its source entirely in other people. Armand, on the other hand (who is the son of a District Collector of Taxes), gives an example of classical love: bourgeois, descended from essentialist culture, and one which will live on in Proust's analyses. This is a segregative love, that of the owner who carries off his prey; an internalized love, which acknowledges the existence of the world only intermittently and always with a feeling of frustration, as if the world were never anything but the threat of some theft (jealousy, quarrels, misunderstandings, worry, coolness, irritation,

From *Mythologies*.

etc.). Marguerite's Love is the perfect opposite of this. She was first touched to feel herself *recognized* by Armand, and passion, to her, was thereafter nothing but the permanent demand for this recognition; this is why the sacrifice which she grants M. Duval in renouncing Armand is by no means moral (in spite of the phraseology used), it is existential; it is only the logical consequence of the postulate of recognition, a superlative means (much better than love) of winning recognition from the world of the masters. And if Marguerite hides her sacrifice and gives it the mask of cynicism, this can only be at the moment when the argument really becomes Literature: the grateful and recognizing gaze of the bourgeois class is here delegated to the reader who in his turn *recognizes* Marguerite through the very mistake of her lover.

All this is to say that the misunderstandings which make the plot progress are not here of a psychological nature (even if the language in which they are expressed is abusively so): Armand and Marguerite do not belong socially to the same world and there can be no question between them of tragedy in the manner of Racine or subtle flirting in the manner of Marivaux. The conflict is exterior to them: we do not deal here with one passion divided against itself but with two passions of different natures, because they come from different situations in society. Armand's passion, which is bourgeois in type, and appropriative, is by definition a murder of the other; and that of Marguerite can only crown her effort to achieve recognition by a sacrifice which will in its turn constitute an indirect murder of Armand's passion. A simple social disparity, taken up and amplified by the opposition of two ideologies of love, cannot but produce here a hopeless entanglement, a hopelessness of which Marguerite's death (however cloying it is on the stage) is, so to speak, the algebraic symbol.

The difference between the two types of love stems of course from the difference of awareness in the two partners:

Armand lives in the essence of eternal love, Marguerite lives in the awareness of her alienation, she lives only through it: she knows herself to be, and in a sense *wills* herself to be a courtesan. And the behavior she adopts in order to adjust consists entirely in behavior meant to secure recognition: now she endorses her own legend exaggeratedly, and plunges into the whirlwind of the typical courtesan's life (like those homosexuals whose way of accepting their condition is to make it obvious), sometimes she makes one guess at a power to transcend her rank which aims to achieve recognition less for a "natural" virtue than for a devotion suited to her station, as if her sacrifice had the function, not of making manifest the murder of the courtesan she is, but on the contrary of flaunting a superlative courtesan, enhanced, without losing anything of her nature, with a bourgeois feeling of a high order.

Thus we begin to see better the mythological content of this love, which is the archetype of petit-bourgeois sentimentality. It is a very particular state of myth, defined by a semi-awareness, or to be more precise, a parasitic awareness. Marguerite *is aware* of her alienation, that is to say, she sees reality as an alienation. But she follows up this awareness by a purely servile behavior: either she plays the part which the masters expect from her, or she tries to reach a *value* which is in fact a part of this same world of the masters. In either case, Marguerite is never anything more than an alienated awareness: she sees that she suffers, but imagines no remedy which is not parasitic to her own suffering; she knows herself to be an object but cannot think of any destination for herself other than that of ornament in the museum of the masters. In spite of the grotesqueness of the plot, such a character does not lack a certain dramatic richness: true, it is neither tragic (the fate which weighs on Marguerite is social, not metaphysical), nor comic (Marguerite's behavior stems from her condition, not from her essence), nor as yet, of course, revolutionary (Marguerite brings no criticism to bear on her alienation). But at bottom she would need very little to achieve the status of the Brechtian character, which is an alienated object but a source of criticism. What puts this out of her reach—irremediably— is her positive side: Marguerite Gautier, "touching" because of her tuberculosis and her lofty speech, spreads to the whole of her public the contagion of her blindness: patently stupid, she would have opened their petit-bourgeois eyes. Magniloquent and noble, in one word, "serious," she only sends them to sleep.

1956

Myth Today

WHAT is a myth, today? I shall give at the outset a first, very simple answer, which is perfectly consistent with etymology: *myth is a type of speech*.[1]

MYTH IS A TYPE OF SPEECH

Of course, it is not *any* type: language needs special conditions in order to become myth: we shall see them in a minute. But what must be firmly established at the start is that myth is a system of communication, that it is a message. This allows one to perceive that myth cannot possibly be an object, a concept, or an idea; it is a mode of signification, a form. Later, we shall have to assign to this form historical limits, conditions of use, and reintroduce society into it: we must nevertheless first describe it as a form.

It can be seen that to purport to discriminate among mythical objects according to their substance would be entirely illusory: since myth is a type of speech, everything can be a myth provided it is conveyed by a discourse. Myth is not

From *Mythologies*.

[1] Innumerable other meanings of the word "myth" can be cited against this. But I have tried to define things, not words.

defined by the object of its message, but by the way in which it utters this message: there are formal limits to myth, there are no "substantial" ones. Everything, then, can be a myth? Yes, I believe this, for the universe is infinitely fertile in suggestions. Every object in the world can pass from a closed, silent existence to an oral state, open to appropriation by society, for there is no law, whether natural or not, which forbids talking about things. A tree is a tree. Yes, of course. But a tree as expressed by Minou Drouet is no longer quite a tree, it is a tree which is decorated, adapted to a certain type of consumption, laden with literary self-indulgence, revolt, images, in short with a type of social *usage* which is added to pure matter.

Naturally, everything is not expressed at the same time: some objects become the prey of mythical speech for a while, then they disappear, others take their place and attain the status of myth. Are there objects which are *inevitably* a source of suggestiveness, as Baudelaire suggested about Woman? Certainly not: one can conceive of very ancient myths, but there are no eternal ones; for it is human history which converts reality into speech, and it alone rules the life and the death of mythical language. Ancient or not, mythology can only have a historical foundation, for myth is a type of speech chosen by history: it cannot possibly evolve from the "nature" of things.

Speech of this kind is a message. It is therefore by no means confined to oral speech. It can consist of modes of writing or of representations; not only written discourse, but also photography, cinema, reporting, sport, shows, publicity, all these can serve as a support to mythical speech. Myth can be defined neither by its object nor by its material, for any material can arbitrarily be endowed with meaning: the arrow which is brought in order to signify a challenge is also a kind of speech. True, as far as perception is concerned, writing and pictures, for instance, do not call upon the same type of consciousness;

and even with pictures, one can use many kinds of reading: a
diagram lends itself to signification more than a drawing, a
copy more than an original, and a caricature more than a
portrait. But this is the point: we are no longer dealing here
with a theoretical mode of representation: we are dealing with
this particular image, which is given for *this* particular signification. Mythical speech is made of a material which has
already been worked on so as to make it suitable for communication: it is because all the materials of myth (whether pictorial or written) presuppose a signifying consciousness, that
one can reason about them while discounting their substance.
This substance is not unimportant: pictures, to be sure, are
more imperative than writing, they impose meaning at one
stroke, without analyzing or diluting it. But this is no longer
a constitutive difference. Pictures become a kind of writing as
soon as they are meaningful: like writing, they call for a *lexis*.

We shall therefore take *language, discourse, speech*, etc., to
mean any significant unit or synthesis, whether verbal or visual: a photograph will be a kind of speech for us in the same
way as a newspaper article; even objects will become speech, if
they mean something. This generic way of conceiving language
is in fact justified by the very history of writing: long before
the invention of our alphabet, objects like the Inca *quipu*, or
drawings, as in pictographs, have been accepted as speech.
This does not mean that one must treat mythical speech like
language; myth in fact belongs to the province of a general
science, coextensive with linguistics, which is *semiology*.

MYTH AS A SEMIOLOGICAL SYSTEM

For mythology, since it is the study of a type of speech, is
but one fragment of this vast science of signs which Saussure
postulated some forty years ago under the name of *semiology*.
Semiology has not yet come into being. But since Saussure
himself, and sometimes independently of him, a whole section

of contemporary research has constantly been referred to the problem of meaning: psychoanalysis, structuralism, eidetic psychology, some new types of literary criticism of which Bachelard has given the first examples, are no longer concerned with facts except inasmuch as they are endowed with significance. Now to postulate a signification is to have recourse to semiology. I do not mean that semiology could account for all these aspects of research equally well: they have different contents. But they have a common status: they are all sciences dealing with values. They are not content with meeting the facts: they define and explore them as tokens for something else.

Semiology is a science of forms, since it studies significations apart from their content. I should like to say one word about the necessity and the limits of such a formal science. The necessity is that which applies in the case of any exact language. Zhdanov made fun of Alexandrov the philosopher, who spoke of *"The spherical structure of our planet." "It was thought until now,"* Zhdanov said, *"that form alone could be spherical."* Zhdanov was right: one cannot speak about structures in terms of forms, and vice versa. It may well be that on the plane of "life," there is but a totality where structures and forms cannot be separated. But science has no use for the ineffable: it must speak about "life" if it wants to transform it. Against a certain quixotism of synthesis, quite platonic incidentally, all criticism must consent to the *ascesis*, to the artifice of analysis; and in analysis, it must match method and language. Less terrorized by the specter of "formalism," historical criticism might have been less sterile; it would have understood that the specific study of forms does not in any way contradict the necessary principles of totality and History. On the contrary: the more a system is specifically defined in its forms, the more amenable it is to historical criticism. To parody a well-known saying, I shall say that a little formalism turns one away from History, but that a lot brings one back to it. Is there a better example of total criticism than the description of saintliness, at once formal and historical, semiological and ideological, in Sartre's *Saint-Genet*? The danger, on the contrary, is to consider forms as ambiguous objects, half form and half substance, to endow form with a substance of form, as was done, for instance, by Zhdanovian realism. Semiology, once its limits are settled, is not a metaphysical trap: it is a science among others, necessary but not sufficient. The important thing is to see that the unity of an explanation cannot be based on the amputation of one or other of its approaches, but, as Engels said, on the dialectical coordination of the particular sciences it makes use of. This is the case with mythology: it is a part both of semiology inasmuch as it is a formal science, and of ideology inasmuch as it is a historical science: it studies ideas-in-form.[2]

Let me therefore restate that any semiology postulates a relation between two terms, a signifier and a signified. This relation concerns objects which belong to different categories, and this is why it is not one of equality but one of equivalence. We must here be on our guard, for despite common parlance which simply says that the signifier *expresses* the signified, we are dealing, in any semiological system, not with two, but with three different terms. For what we grasp is not at all one term after the other but the correlation which unites them: there are, therefore, the signifier, the signified, and the sign, which is the associative total of the first two terms. Take a bunch of roses: I use it to signify my passion. Do we have here, then,

---

[2] The development of publicity, of a national press, of radio, of illustrated news, not to speak of the survival of a myriad rites of communication which rule social appearances makes the development of a semiological science more urgent than ever. In a single day, how many really non-signifying fields do we cross? Very few, sometimes none. Here I am, before the sea; it is true that it bears no message. But on the beach, what material for semiology! Flags, slogans, signals, signboards, clothes, suntan even, which are so many messages to me.

only a signifier and a signified, the roses and my passion? Not even that: to put it accurately, there are here only "passioni-fied" roses. But on the plane of analysis, we do have three terms; for these roses weighted with passion perfectly and cor-rectly allow themselves to be decomposed into roses and pas-sion: the former and the latter existed before uniting and forming this third object, which is the sign. It is as true to say that on the plane of experience I cannot dissociate the roses from the message they carry, as to say that on the plane of analysis I cannot confuse the roses as signifier and the roses as sign: the signifier is empty, the sign is full, it is a meaning. Or take a black pebble: I can make it signify in several ways, it is a mere signifier; but if I weigh it with a definite signified (a death sentence, for instance, in an anonymous vote), it will become a sign. Naturally, there are between the signifier, the signified, and the sign, functional implications (such as that of the part to the whole) which are so close that to analyze them may seem futile; but we shall see in a moment that this distinc-tion has a capital importance for the study of myth as semio-logical schema.

Naturally these three terms are purely formal, and different contents can be given to them. Here are a few examples: for Saussure, who worked on a particular but methodologically exemplary semiological system—the language or *langue*—the signified is the concept, the signifier is the acoustic image (which is mental), and the relation between concept and image is the sign (the word, for instance), which is a concrete entity.[3] For Freud, as is well known, the human psyche is a stratification of tokens or representatives. One term (I refrain from giving it any precedence) is constituted by the manifest meaning of behavior, another, by its latent or real meaning (it is, for instance, the substratum of the dream); as for the third

---

[3] The notion of *word* is one of the most controversial in linguistics. I keep it here for the sake of simplicity.

term, it is here also a correlation of the first two: it is the dream itself in its totality, the parapraxis (a mistake in speech or behavior) or the neurosis, conceived as compromises, as economies effected thanks to the joining of a form (the first term) and an intentional function (the second term). We can see here how necessary it is to distinguish the sign from the signifier: a dream, to Freud, is no more its manifest datum than its latent content: it is the functional union of these two terms. In Sartrean criticism, finally (I shall keep to these three well-known examples), the signified is constituted by the original crisis in the subject (the separation from his mother for Baudelaire, the naming of the theft for Genet); Literature as discourse forms the signifier; and the relation between crisis and discourse defines the work, which is a signification. Of course, this tri-dimensional pattern, however constant in its form, is actualized in different ways: one cannot therefore say too often that semiology can have its unity only at the level of forms, not contents; its field is limited, it knows only one operation: reading, or deciphering.

In myth, we find again the tri-dimensional pattern which I have just described: the signifier, the signified, and the sign. But myth is a peculiar system, in that it is constructed from a semiological chain which existed before it: it *is a second-order semiological system*. That which is a sign (namely the associative total of a concept and an image) in the first system, becomes a mere signifier in the second. We must here recall that the materials of mythical speech (the language itself, photography, painting, posters, rituals, objects, etc.), however different at the start, are reduced to a pure signifying function as soon as they are caught by myth. Myth sees in them only the same raw material; their unity is that they all come down to the status of a mere language. Whether it deals with alphabetical or pictorial writing, myth wants to see in them only a sum of signs, a global sign, the final term of a first semiological chain. And it is precisely this final term which will become the first term of the greater system which it builds and of which it is only a part. Everything happens as if myth shifted the formal system of the first significations sideways. As this lateral shift is essential for the analysis of myth, I shall represent it in the following way, it being understood, of course, that the spatialization of the pattern is here only a metaphor:

	1. Signifier	2. Signified	
Language	3. Sign I SIGNIFIER		II SIGNIFIED
MYTH	III SIGN		

It can be seen that in myth there are two semiological systems, one of which is staggered in relation to the other: a linguistic system, the language (or the modes of representation which are assimilated to it), which I shall call the *language-object*, because it is the language which myth gets hold of in order to build its own system; and myth itself, which I shall call *metalanguage*, because it is a second language, *in which* one speaks about the first. When he reflects on a metalanguage, the semiologist no longer needs to ask himself questions about the composition of the language-object, he no longer has to take into account the details of the linguistic schema; he will only need to know its total term, or global sign, and only inasmuch as this term lends itself to myth. This is why the semiologist is entitled to treat in the same way writing and pictures: what he retains from them is the fact that they are both *signs*, that they both reach the threshold of myth endowed with the same signifying function, that they constitute, one just as much as the other, a language-object.

It is now time to give one or two examples of mythical speech. I shall borrow the first from an observation by

Valéry.[4] I am a pupil in the second form in a French *lycée*. I open my Latin grammar, and I read a sentence, borrowed from Aesop or Phaedrus: *quia ego nominor leo*. I stop and think. There is something ambiguous about this statement: on the one hand, the words in it do have a simple meaning: *because my name is lion*. And on the other hand, the sentence is evidently there in order to signify something else to me. Inasmuch as it is addressed to me, a pupil in the second form, it tells me clearly: I am a grammatical example meant to illustrate the rule about the agreement of the predicate. I am even forced to realize that the sentence in no way *signifies* its meaning to me, that it tries very little to tell me something about the lion and what sort of name he has; its true and fundamental signification is to impose itself on me as the presence of a certain agreement of the predicate. I conclude that I am faced with a particular, greater, semiological system, since it is co-extensive with the language: there is, indeed, a signifier, but this signifier is itself formed by a sum of signs, it is in itself a first semiological system (*my name is lion*). Thereafter, the formal pattern is correctly unfolded: there is a signified (*I am a grammatical example*) and there is a global signification, which is none other than the correlation of the signifier and the signified; for neither the naming of the lion nor the grammatical example is given separately.

And here is now another example: I am at the barber's, and a copy of *Paris-Match* is offered to me. On the cover, a young Negro in a French uniform is saluting, with his eyes uplifted, probably fixed on a fold of the tricolor. All this is the *meaning* of the picture. But, whether naïvely or not, I see very well what it signifies to me: that France is a great Empire, that all her sons, without any color discrimination, faithfully serve under her flag, and that there is no better answer to the de-

---

[4] *Tel Quel*, II.

tractors of an alleged colonialism than the zeal shown by this Negro in serving his so-called oppressors. I am therefore again faced with a greater semiological system: there is a signifier, itself already formed with a previous system (*a black soldier is giving the French salute*); there is a signified (it is here a purposeful mixture of Frenchness and militariness); finally, there is a presence of the signified through the signifier.

Before tackling the analysis of each term of the mythical system, one must agree on terminology. We now know that the signifier can be looked at, in myth, from two points of view: as the final term of the linguistic system, or as the first term of the mythical system. We therefore need two names. On the plane of language, that is, as the final term of the first system, I shall call the signifier: *meaning* (*my name is lion, a Negro is giving the French salute*); on the plane of myth, I shall call it: *form*. In the case of the signified, no ambiguity is possible: we shall retain the name *concept*. The third term is the correlation of the first two: in the linguistic system, it is the *sign*; but it is not possible to use this word again without ambiguity, since in myth (and this is the chief peculiarity of the latter), the signifier is already formed by the *signs* of the language. I shall call the third term of myth the *signification*. This word is here all the better justified since myth has in fact a double function: it points out and it notifies, it makes us understand something and it imposes it on us.

THE FORM AND THE CONCEPT

The signifier of myth presents itself in an ambiguous way: it is at the same time meaning and form, full on one side and empty on the other. As meaning, the signifier already postulates a reading, I grasp it through my eyes, it has a sensory reality (unlike the linguistic signifier, which is purely mental), there is a richness in it: the naming of the lion, the Negro's salute are credible wholes, they have at their disposal a sufficient rationality. As a total of linguistic signs, the meaning of the myth has its own value, it belongs to a history, that of the lion or that of the Negro: in the meaning, a signification is already built, and could very well be self-sufficient if myth did not take hold of it and did not turn it suddenly into an empty, parasitical form. The meaning is *already* complete, it postulates a kind of knowledge, a past, a memory, a comparative order of facts, ideas, decisions.

When it becomes form, the meaning leaves its contingency behind; it empties itself, it becomes impoverished, history evaporates, only the letter remains. There is here a paradoxical permutation in the reading operations, an abnormal regression from meaning to form, from the linguistic sign to the mythical signifier. If one encloses *quia ego nominor leo* in a purely linguistic system, the clause finds again there a fullness, a richness, a history: I am an animal, a lion, I live in a certain country, I have just been hunting, they would have me share my prey with a heifer, a cow and a goat; but being the stronger, I award myself all the shares for various reasons, the last of which is quite simply that *my name is lion*. But as the form of the myth, the clause hardly retains anything of this long story. The meaning contained a whole system of values: a history, a geography, a morality, a zoology, a Literature. The form has put all this richness at a distance: its newly acquired penury calls for a signification to fill it. The story of the lion must recede a great deal in order to make room for the grammatical example, one must put the biography of the Negro in parentheses if one wants to free the picture, and prepare it to receive its signified.

But the essential point in all this is that the form does not suppress the meaning, it only impoverishes it, it puts it at a distance, it holds it at one's disposal. One believes that the meaning is going to die, but it is a death with reprieve; the meaning loses its value, but keeps its life, from which the form of the myth will draw its nourishment. The meaning will be for the form like an instantaneous reserve of history, a tamed richness, which it is possible to call and dismiss in a sort of rapid alternation: the form must constantly be able to be rooted again in the meaning and to get there what nature it needs for its nutriment; above all, it must be able to hide there. It is this constant game of hide-and-seek between the meaning and the form which defines myth. The form of myth is not a symbol: the Negro who salutes is not the symbol of the French Empire; he has too much presence, he appears as a rich, fully experienced, spontaneous, innocent, *indisputable* image. But at the same time this presence is tamed, put at a distance, made almost transparent; it recedes a little, it becomes the accomplice of a concept which comes to it fully armed, French imperiality: once made use of, it becomes artificial.

Let us now look at the signified: this history which drains out of the form will be wholly absorbed by the concept. As for the latter, it is determined, it is at once historical and intentional; it is the motivation which causes the myth to be uttered. Grammatical exemplarity, French imperiality, are the very drives behind the myth. The concept reconstitutes a chain of causes and effects, motives and intentions. Unlike the form, the concept is in no way abstract: it is filled with a situation. Through the concept, it is a whole new history which is implanted in the myth. Into the naming of the lion, first drained of its contingency, the grammatical example will attract my whole existence: Time, which caused me to be born at a certain period when Latin grammar is taught; History, which sets me apart, through a whole mechanism of social segregation, from the children who do not learn Latin; pedagogic tradition, which caused this example to be chosen from Aesop or Phaedrus; my own linguistic habits, which see the agreement of the predicate as a fact worthy of notice and illustration. The same goes for the Negro-giving-the-salute: as form, its meaning is shallow, isolated, impoverished; as the concept of French imperiality, here it is again tied to the totality of the world: to the general History of France, to its colonial adventures, to its present difficulties. Truth to tell, what is invested in the concept is less reality than a certain knowledge of reality; in passing from the meaning to the form, the image loses some knowledge: the better to receive the knowledge in the concept. In actual fact, the knowledge contained in a mythical concept is confused, made of yielding, shapeless associations. One must firmly stress this open character of the concept; it is not at all an abstract, purified essence; it is a formless, unstable, nebulous condensation, whose unity and coherence are above all due to its function.

In this sense, we can say that the fundamental character of the mythical concept is to be *appropriated*: grammatical exemplarity very precisely concerns a given form of pupils, French imperiality must appeal to such and such group of readers and not another. The concept closely corresponds to a function, it is defined as a tendency. This cannot fail to recall the signified in another semiological system, Freudianism. In Freud, the second term of the system is the latent meaning (the content) of the dream, of the parapraxis, of the neurosis. Now Freud does remark that the second-order meaning of behavior is its real meaning, that which is appropriate to a complete situation, including its deeper level; it is, just like the mythical concept, the very intention of behavior.

A signified can have several signifiers: this is indeed the case in linguistics and psychoanalysis. It is also the case in the mythical concept: it has at its disposal an unlimited mass of signifiers: I can find a thousand Latin sentences to actualize for me the agreement of the predicate, I can find a thousand images which signify to me French imperiality. This means that *quantitively*, the concept is much poorer than the signifier, it often does nothing but re-present itself. Poverty and richness are in reverse proportion in the form and the concept: to the qualitative poverty of the form, which is the repository of a rarefied meaning, there corresponds the richness of the concept which is open to the whole of History; and to the quantitative abundance of the forms there corresponds a small number of concepts. This repetition of the concept through different forms is precious to the mythologist, it allows him to decipher the myth: it is the insistence of a kind of behavior which reveals its intention. This confirms that there is no regular ratio between the volume of the signified and that of the signifier. In language, this ratio is proportionate, it hardly exceeds the word, or at least the concrete unit. In myth, on the contrary, the concept can spread over a very large expanse of signifier. For instance, a whole book may be the signifier of a single concept; and conversely, a minute form (a word, a gesture, even incidental, so long as it is noticed) can serve as signifier to a concept filled with a very rich history. Although unusual in language, this disproportion between signifier and signified is not specific to myth: in Freud, for instance, the parapraxis is a signifier whose thinness is out of proportion to the real meaning which it betrays.

As I said, there is no fixity in mythical concepts: they can come into being, alter, disintegrate, disappear completely. And it is precisely because they are historical that history can very easily suppress them. This instability forces the mythologist to use a terminology adapted to it, and about which I should now like to say a word, because it often is a cause for irony: I mean neologism. The concept is a constituting element of myth: if I want to decipher myths, I must somehow be able to name concepts. The dictionary supplies me with a few: Goodness, Kindness, Wholeness, Humaneness, etc. But by definition, since it is the dictionary which gives them to me, these particular concepts are not historical. Now what I need most often is ephemeral concepts, in connection with limited contingencies:

neologism is then inevitable. China is one thing, the idea which a French petit-bourgeois could have of it not so long ago is another: for this peculiar mixture of bells, rickshaws and opium dens, no other word possible but *Sininess*.[5] Unlovely? One should at least get some consolation from the fact that conceptual neologisms are never arbitrary: they are built according to a highly sensible proportional rule.

THE SIGNIFICATION

In semiology, the third term is nothing but the association of the first two, as we saw. It is the only one which is allowed to be seen in a full and satisfactory way, the only one which is consumed in actual fact. I have called it: the signification. We can see that the signification is the myth itself, just as the Saussurean sign is the word (or more accurately the concrete unit). But before listing the characters of the signification, one must reflect a little on the way in which it is prepared, that is, on the modes of correlation of the mythical concept and the mythical form.

First we must note that in myth, the first two terms are perfectly manifest (unlike what happens in other semiological systems): one of them is not "hidden" behind the other, they are both given *here* (and not one here and the other there). However paradoxical it may seem, *myth hides nothing*: its function is to distort, not to make disappear. There is no latency of the concept in relation to the form: there is no need of an unconscious in order to explain myth. Of course, one is dealing with two different types of manifestation: form has a literal, immediate presence; moreover, it is extended. This stems—this cannot be repeated too often—from the nature of the mythical signifier, which is already linguistic: since it is constituted by a meaning which is already outlined, it can

[5] Or perhaps *Sinity*? Just as if Latin/latinity = Basque/x, x = Basquity.

appear only through a given substance (whereas in language, the signifier remains mental). In the case of oral myth, this extension is linear (*for my name is lion*); in that of visual myth, it is multidimensional (in the center, the Negro's uniform, at the top, the blackness of his face, on the left, the military salute, etc.). The elements of the form therefore are related as to place and proximity: the mode of presence of the form is spatial. The concept, on the contrary, appears in global fashion, it is a kind of nebula, the condensation, more or less hazy, of a certain knowledge. Its elements are linked by associative relations: it is supported not by an extension but by a depth (although this metaphor is perhaps still too spatial): its mode of presence is memorial.

The relation which unites the concept of the myth to its meaning is essentially a relation of *deformation*. We find here again a certain formal analogy with a complex semiological system such as that of the various types of psychoanalysis. Just as for Freud the manifest meaning of behavior is distorted by its latent meaning, in myth the meaning is distorted by the concept. Of course, this distortion is possible only because the form of the myth is already constituted by a linguistic meaning. In a simple system like the language, the signified cannot distort anything at all because the signifier, being empty, arbitrary, offers no resistance to it. But here, everything is different: the signifier has, so to speak, two aspects: one full, which is the meaning (the history of the lion, of the Negro soldier), one empty, which is the form (*for my name is lion; Negro-French-soldier-saluting-the-tricolor*). What the concept distorts is of course what is full, the meaning: the lion and the Negro are deprived of their history, changed into gestures. What Latin exemplarity distorts is the naming of the lion, in all its contingency; and what French imperiality obscures is also a primary language, a factual discourse which was telling me about the salute of a Negro in uniform. But this distortion is not an obliteration: the lion and the Negro remain here, the concept needs them; they are half-amputated, they are deprived of memory, not of existence: they are at once stubborn, silently rooted there, and garrulous, a speech wholly at the service of the concept. The concept, literally, deforms, but does not abolish the meaning; a word can perfectly render this contradiction: it alienates it.

What must always be remembered is that myth is a double system; there occurs in it a sort of ubiquity: its point of departure is constituted by the arrival of a meaning. To keep a spatial metaphor, the approximative character of which I have already stressed, I shall say that the signification of the myth is constituted by a sort of constantly moving turnstile which presents alternately the meaning of the signifier and its form, a language-object and a metalanguage, a purely signifying and a purely imagining consciousness. This alternation is, so to speak, gathered up in the concept, which uses it like an ambiguous signifier, at once intellective and imaginary, arbitrary and natural.

I do not wish to prejudge the moral implications of such a mechanism, but I shall not exceed the limits of an objective analysis if I point out that the ubiquity of the signifier in myth exactly reproduces the physique of the *alibi* (which is, as one realizes, a spatial term): in the alibi too, there is a place which is full and one which is empty, linked by a relation of negative identity ("I am not where you think I am; I am where you think I am not"). But the ordinary alibi (for the police, for instance) has an end; reality stops the turnstile revolving at a certain point. Myth is a *value*, truth is no guarantee for it; nothing prevents it from being a perpetual alibi: it is enough that its signifier has two sides for it always to have an "elsewhere" at its disposal. The meaning is always there to *present* the form; the form is always there to *outdistance* the meaning. And there never is any contradiction, conflict, or split between the meaning and the form: they are never at the same place. In the same way, if I am in a car and I look at the scenery through the window, I can at will focus on the scenery or on the windowpane. At one moment I grasp the presence of the glass and the distance of the landscape; at another, on the contrary, the transparence of the glass and the depth of the landscape; but the result of this alternation is constant: the glass is at once present and empty to me, and the landscape unreal and full. The same thing occurs in the mythical signifier: its form is empty but present, its meaning absent but full. To wonder at this contradiction I must voluntarily interrupt this turnstile of form and meaning, I must focus on each separately, and apply to myth a static method of deciphering, in short, I must go against its own dynamics: to sum up, I must pass from the state of reader to that of mythologist.

And it is again this duplicity of the signifier which determines the characters of the signification. We now know that myth is a type of speech defined by its intention (*I am a grammatical example*) much more than by its literal sense (*my name is lion*); and that in spite of this, its intention is somehow frozen, purified, eternalized, *made absent* by this literal sense (*The French Empire? It's just a fact: look at this good Negro who salutes like one of our own boys*). This constituent ambiguity of mythical speech has two consequences for the signification, which henceforth appears both like a notification and like a statement of fact.

Myth has an imperative, buttonholing character: stemming from a historical concept, directly springing from contingency (a Latin class, a threatened Empire), it is *I* whom it has come to seek. It is turned toward me, I am subjected to its intentional force, it summons me to receive its expansive ambiguity. If, for instance, I take a walk in Spain, in the Basque country,[6] I may well notice in the houses an architectural unity, a common style, which leads me to acknowledge the Basque house as a definite ethnic product. However, I do not feel personally concerned, nor, so to speak, attacked by this unitary style: I see only too well that it was here before me, without me. It is a complex product which has its determinations at the level of a very wide history: it does not call out to me, it does not provoke me into naming it, except if I think of inserting it into a vast picture of rural habitat. But if I am in the Paris region and I catch a glimpse, at the end of the rue Gambetta or the rue Jean Jaurès, of a natty white chalet with red tiles, dark brown half timbering, an asymmetrical roof and a wattle-and-daub front, I feel as if I were personally receiving an imperious injunction to name this object a Basque chalet: or even better, to see it as the very essence of *basquity*. This is because the concept appears to me in all its appropriative nature: it comes and seeks me out in order to oblige me to acknowledge the body of intentions which have motivated it and arranged it there as the signal of an individual history, as a confidence and a complicity: it is a real call, which the owners of the chalet send out to me. And this call, in order to be more imperious, has agreed to all manner of impoverishments: all that justified the Basque house on the plane of technology—the barn, the outside stairs, the dovecote, etc.—has been dropped; there remains only a brief order, not to be disputed. And the adhomination is so frank that I feel this chalet has just been created on the spot, *for me*, like a magical object springing up in my present life without any trace of the history which has caused it.

For this interpellant speech is at the same time a frozen speech: at the moment of reaching me, it suspends itself, turns away and assumes the look of a generality: it stiffens, it makes

[6] I say "in Spain" because, in France, petit-bourgeois advancement has caused a whole "mythical" architecture of the Basque chalet to flourish.

itself look neutral and innocent. The appropriation of the concept is suddenly driven away once more by the literalness of
the meaning. This is a kind of *arrest*, in both the physical and
the legal sense of the term: French imperiality condemns the
saluting Negro to be nothing more than an instrumental signifier, the Negro suddenly hails me in the name of French imperiality; but at the same moment the Negro's salute thickens,
becomes vitrified, freezes into an eternal reference meant to
establish French imperiality. On the surface of language something has stopped moving: the use of the signification is here,
hiding behind the fact, and conferring on it a notifying look;
but at the same time, the fact paralyzes the intention, gives it
something like a malaise producing immobility: in order to
make it innocent, it freezes it. This is because myth is speech
stolen and restored. Only, speech which is restored is no
longer quite that which was stolen: when it was brought back,
it was not put exactly in its place. It is this brief act of larceny,
this moment taken for a surreptitious faking, which gives
mythical speech its benumbed look.

One last element of the signification remains to be exam-
ined: its motivation. We know that in a language, the sign is
arbitrary: nothing compels the acoustic image *tree* "naturally"
to mean the concept *tree*: the sign, here, is unmotivated. Yet
this arbitrariness has limits, which come from the associative
relations of the word: the language can produce a whole fragment of the sign by analogy with other signs (for instance one
says *aimable* in French, and not *amable*, by analogy with
aime). The mythical signification, on the other hand, is never
arbitrary; it is always in part motivated, and unavoidably contains some analogy. For Latin exemplarity to meet the naming
of the lion, there must be an analogy, which is the agreement
of the predicate; for French imperiality to get hold of the
saluting Negro, there must be identity between the Negro's
salute and that of the French soldier. Motivation is necessary

to the very duplicity of myth: myth plays on the analogy between meaning and form, there is no myth without motivated form.[7] In order to grasp the power of motivation in myth, it is enough to reflect for a moment on an extreme case. I have here before me a collection of objects so lacking in order that I can find no *meaning* in it; it would seem that here, deprived of any previous meaning, the form could not root its analogy in anything, and that myth is impossible. But what the form can always give one to read is disorder itself: it can give a signification to the absurd, make the absurd itself a myth. This is what happens when common sense mythifies surrealism, for instance. Even the absence of motivation does not embarrass myth; for this absence will itself be sufficiently objectified to become legible: and finally, the absence of motivation will become a second-order motivation, and myth will be re-established.

Motivation is unavoidable. It is nonetheless very fragmentary. To start with, it is not "natural": it is history which supplies its analogies to the form. Then, the analogy between the meaning and the concept is never anything but partial: the form drops many analogous features and keeps only a few: it keeps the sloping roof, the visible beams in the Basque chalet, it abandons the stairs, the barn, the weathered look, etc. One must even go further: a *complete* image would exclude myth, or at least would compel it to seize only its very completeness. This is just what happens in the case of bad painting, which is wholly based on the myth of what is "filled

---

[7] From the point of view of ethics, what is disturbing in myth is precisely that its form is motivated. For if there is a "health" of language, it is the arbitrariness of the sign which is its grounding. What is sickening in myth is its resort to a false nature, its superabundance of significant forms, as in these objects which decorate their usefulness with a natural appearance. The will to weigh the signification with the full guarantee of nature causes a kind of nausea: myth is too rich, and what is in excess is precisely its motivation. This nausea is like the one I feel before the arts which refuse to choose between *physis* and *anti-physis*, using the first as an ideal and the second as an economy. Ethically, there is a kind of baseness in hedging one's bets.

out" and "finished" (it is the opposite and symmetrical case of the myth of the absurd: here, the form mythifies an "absence," there, a surplus). But in general myth prefers to work with poor, incomplete images, where the meaning is already relieved of its fat, and ready for a signification, such as caricatures, pastiches, symbols, etc. Finally, the motivation is chosen among other possible ones: I can very well give to French imperiality many other signifiers beside a Negro's salute: a French general pins a decoration on a one-armed Senegalese, a nun hands a cup of tea to a bedridden Arab, a white schoolmaster teaches attentive pickaninnies: the press undertakes every day to demonstrate that the store of mythical signifiers is inexhaustible.

The nature of the mythical signification can in fact be well conveyed by one particular simile: it is neither more nor less arbitrary than an ideograph. Myth is a pure ideographic system, where the forms are still motivated by the concept which they represent while not yet, by a long way, covering the sum of its possibilities for representation. And just as, historically, ideographs have gradually left the concept and have become associated with the sound, thus growing less and less motivated, the worn-out state of a myth can be recognized by the arbitrariness of its signification: the whole of Molière is seen in a doctor's ruff.

READING AND DECIPHERING MYTH

How is a myth received? We must here once more come back to the duplicity of its signifier, which is at once meaning and form. It can produce three different types of reading by focusing on the one, or the other, or both at the same time.[8]

1. If I focus on an empty signifier, I let the concept fill the

---

[8] The freedom in choosing what one focuses on is a problem which does not belong to the province of semiology: it depends on the concrete situation of the subject.

form of the myth without ambiguity, and I find myself before a simple system, where the signification becomes literal again: the Negro who salutes is an *example* of French imperiality, he is a *symbol* for it. This type of focusing is, for instance, that of the producer of myths, of the journalist who starts with a concept and seeks a form for it.[9]

2. If I focus on a full signifier, in which I clearly distinguish the meaning and the form, and consequently the distortion which the one imposes on the other, I undo the signification of the myth, and I receive the latter as an imposture: the saluting Negro becomes the *alibi* of French imperiality. This type of focusing is that of the mythologist: he deciphers the myth, he understands a distortion.

3. Finally, if I focus on the mythical signifier as on an inextricable whole made of meaning and form, I receive an ambiguous signification: I respond to the constituting mechanism of myth, to its own dynamics, I become a reader of myths. The saluting Negro is no longer an example or a symbol, still less an alibi: he is the very *presence* of French imperiality.

The first two types of focusing are static, analytical; they destroy the myth, either by making its intention obvious, or by unmasking it: the former is cynical, the latter demystifying. The third type of focusing is dynamic, it consumes the myth according to the very ends built into its structure: the reader lives the myth as a story at once true and unreal.

If one wishes to connect a mythical schema to a general history, to explain how it corresponds to the interests of a definite society, in short, to pass from semiology to ideology, it is obviously at the level of the third type of focusing that one must place oneself: it is the reader of myths himself who must reveal their essential function. How does he receive this par-

---

[9] We receive the naming of the lion as a pure *example* of Latin grammar because we are, *as grownups*, in a creative position in relation to it. I shall come back later to the value of the context in this mythical schema.

ticular myth *today*? If he receives it in an innocent fashion, what is the point of proposing it to him? And if he reads it using his powers of reflection, like the mythologist, does it matter which alibi is presented? If the reader does not see French imperiality in the saluting Negro, it was not worth weighing the latter with it; and if he sees it, the myth is nothing more than a political proposition, honestly expressed. In one word, either the intention of the myth is too obscure to be efficacious, or it is too clear to be believed. In either case, where is the ambiguity?

This is but a false dilemma. Myth hides nothing and flaunts nothing: it distorts; myth is neither a lie nor a confession: it is an inflection. Placed before the dilemma which I mentioned a moment ago, myth finds a third way out. Threatened with disappearance if it yields to either of the first two types of focusing, it gets out of this tight spot thanks to a compromise —it *is* this compromise. Entrusted with "glossing over" an intentional concept, myth encounters nothing but betrayal in language, for language can only obliterate the concept if it hides it, or unmask it if it formulates it. The elaboration of a second-order semiological system will enable myth to escape this dilemma: driven to having either to unveil or to liquidate the concept, it will *naturalize* it.

We reach here the very principle of myth: it transforms history into Nature. We now understand why, *in the eyes of the myth consumer*, the intention, the adhomination of the concept can remain manifest without however appearing to have an interest in the matter: what causes mythical speech to be uttered is perfectly explicit, but it is immediately frozen into something natural; it is not read as a motive, but as a reason. If I read the Negro-saluting as symbol pure and simple of imperiality, I must renounce the reality of the picture, it discredits itself in my eyes when it becomes an instrument. Conversely, if I decipher the Negro's salute as an alibi of coloniality, I shatter the myth even more surely by the obviousness of its motivation. But for the myth reader, the outcome is quite different: everything happens as if the picture *naturally* conjured up the concept, as if the signifier *gave a foundation* to the signified: the myth exists from the precise moment when French imperiality achieves the natural state: myth is speech justified *in excess*.

Here is a new example which will help understand clearly how the myth reader is led to rationalize the signified by means of the signifier. We are in the month of July, I read a big headline in *France-Soir*: THE FALL IN PRICES: FIRST INDICATIONS. VEGETABLES: PRICE DROP BEGINS. Let us quickly sketch the semiological schema: the example being a sentence, the first system is purely linguistic. The signifier of the second system is composed here of a certain number of accidents, some lexical (the words: *first, begins, the* [fall]), some typographical (enormous headlines where the reader usually sees news of world importance). The signified or concept is what must be called by a barbarous but unavoidable neologism: *governmentality*, the Government presented by the national press as the Essence of efficacy. The signification of the myth follows clearly from this: fruit and vegetable prices are falling *because* the government has so decided. Now it so happens in this case (and this is on the whole fairly rare) that the newspaper itself has, two lines below, allowed one to see through the myth which it had just elaborated—whether this is due to self-assurance or honesty. It adds (in small type, it is true): "The fall in prices is helped by the return of seasonal abundance." This example is instructive for two reasons. Firstly it conspicuously shows that myth essentially aims at causing an immediate impression—it does not matter if one is later allowed to see through the myth, its action is assumed to be stronger than the rational explanations which may later belie it. This means that the reading of a myth is exhausted at one stroke. I cast a quick glance at my neighbor's *France-Soir*: I cull only a *meaning* there, but I read a true signification; I *receive* the presence of governmental action in the fall in fruit and vegetable prices. That is all, and that is enough. A more attentive reading of the myth will in no way increase its power or its ineffectiveness: a myth is at the same time imperfectible and unquestionable; time or knowledge will not make it better or worse.

Secondly, the naturalization of the concept, which I have just identified as the essential function of myth, is here exemplary. In a first (exclusively linguistic) system, causality would be, literally, natural: fruit and vegetable prices fall because they are in season. In the second (mythical) system, causality is artificial, false; but it creeps, so to speak, through the back door of Nature. This is why myth is experienced as innocent speech: not because its intentions are hidden—if they were hidden, they could not be efficacious—but because they are naturalized.

In fact, what allows the reader to consume myth innocently is that he does not see it as a semiological system but as an inductive one. Where there is only an equivalence, he sees a kind of causal process: the signifier and the signified have, in his eyes, a natural relationship. This confusion can be expressed otherwise: any semiological system is a system of values; now the myth consumer takes the signification for a system of facts: myth is read as a factual system, whereas it is but a semiological system.

MYTH AS STOLEN LANGUAGE

What is characteristic of myth? To transform a meaning into form. In other words, myth is always a language robbery. I rob the Negro who is saluting, the white and brown chalet, the seasonal fall in fruit prices, not to make them into examples or symbols, but to naturalize through them the Empire, my taste for Basque things, the Government. Are all primary languages a prey for myth? Is there no meaning which can resist this capture with which form threatens it? In fact, nothing can be safe from myth, myth can develop its second-order schema from any meaning and, as we saw, start from the very lack of meaning. But all languages do not resist equally well.

Articulated language, which is most often robbed by myth, offers little resistance. It contains in itself some mythical dispositions, the outline of a sign structure meant to manifest the intention which led to its being used: it is what could be called the *expressiveness* of language. The imperative or the subjunctive mode, for instance, are the form of a particular signified, different from the meaning: the signified is here my will or my request. This is why some linguists have defined the indicative, for instance, as a zero state or degree, compared to the subjunctive or the imperative. Now in a fully constituted myth, the meaning is never at zero degree, and this is why the concept can distort it, naturalize it. We must remember once again that the privation of meaning is in no way a zero degree: this is why myth can perfectly well get hold of it, give it for instance the signification of the absurd, of surrealism, etc. At bottom, it would only be the zero degree which could resist myth.

Language lends itself to myth in another way: it is very rare that it imposes at the outset a full meaning which it is impossible to distort. This comes from the abstractness of its concept: the concept of *tree* is vague, it lends itself to multiple contingencies. True, a language always has at its disposal a whole appropriating organization (*this* tree, *the* tree *which*, etc.). But there always remains, around the final meaning, a halo of virtualities where other possible meanings are floating: the meaning can almost always be *interpreted*. One could say that a language offers to myth an open-work meaning. Myth can easily insinuate itself into it, and swell there: it is a robbery by colonization (for instance: *the* fall in prices has started. But what fall? That due to the season or that due to the government? the signification becomes here a parasite of the article, in spite of the latter being definite).

When the meaning is too full for myth to be able to invade it, myth goes around it, and carries it away bodily. This is what happens to mathematical language. In itself, it cannot be distorted, it has taken all possible precautions against *interpretation*: no parasitical signification can worm itself into it. And this is why, precisely, myth takes it away en bloc; it takes a certain mathematical formula ($E = mc^2$), and makes of this unalterable meaning the pure signifier of mathematicity. We can see that what is here robbed by myth is something which resists, something pure. Myth can reach everything, corrupt everything, and even the very act of refusing oneself to it. So that the more the language-object resists at first, the greater its final prostitution; whoever here resists completely yields completely: Einstein on one side, *Paris-Match* on the other. One can give a temporal image of this conflict: mathematical language is a *finished* language, which derives its very perfection from this acceptance of death. Myth, on the contrary, is a language which does not want to die: it wrests from the meanings which give it its sustenance an insidious, degraded survival, it provokes in them an artificial reprieve in which it settles comfortably, it turns them into speaking corpses.

Here is another language which resists myth as much as it can: our poetic language. Contemporary poetry[10] is *a regressive semiological system*. Whereas myth aims at an ultra-signification, at the amplification of a first system, poetry, on the

---

[10] Classical poetry, on the contrary, would be, according to such norms, a strongly mythical system, since it imposes on the meaning one extra signified, which is *regularity*. The alexandrine, for instance, has value both as meaning of a discourse and as signifier of a new whole, which is its poetic signification. Success, when it occurs, comes from the degree of apparent fusion of the two systems. It can be seen that we deal in no way with a harmony between content and form, but with an *elegant* absorption of one form into another.

contrary, attempts to regain an infra-signification, a pre-semio-logical state of language; in short, it tries to transform the sign back into meaning: its ideal, ultimately, would be to reach not the meaning of words, but the meaning of things them-selves.[11] This is why it clouds the language, increases as much as it can the abstractness of the concept and the arbitrariness of the sign and stretches to the limit the link between signifier and signified. The open-work structure of the concept is here maximally exploited: unlike what happens in prose, it is all the potential of the signified that the poetic sign tries to actualize, in the hope of at last reaching something like the transcendent quality of the thing, its natural (not human) meaning. Hence the essentialist ambitions of poetry, the conviction that it alone catches *the thing in itself*, inasmuch, precisely, as it wants to be an anti-language. All told, of all those who use speech, poets are the least formalist, for they are the only ones who believe that the meaning of the words is only a form, with which they, being realists, cannot be content. This is why our modern poetry always asserts itself as a murder of language, a kind of spatial, tangible analogue of silence. Poetry occupies a position which is the reverse of that of myth: myth is a semio-logical system which has the pretension of transcending itself into a factual system; poetry is a semiological system which has the pretension of contracting into an essential system.

But here again, as in the case of mathematical language, the very resistance offered by poetry makes it an ideal prey for myth: the apparent lack of order of signs, which is the poetic facet of an essential order, is captured by myth, and trans-formed into an empty signifier, which will serve to *signify*

By *elegance* I mean the most economical use of the means employed. It is because of an age-old abuse that critics confuse *meaning* and *content*. The language is never anything but a system of forms, and the meaning is a form.

[11] We are again dealing here with the *meaning*, in Sartre's use of the term, as a natural quality of things, situated outside a semiological system (*Saint-Genet*).

poetry. This explains the *improbable* character of modern poetry: by fiercely refusing myth, poetry surrenders to it bound hand and foot. Conversely, the *rules* in classical poetry constituted an accepted myth, the conspicuous arbitrariness of which amounted to perfection of a kind, since the equilibrium of a semiological system comes from the arbitrariness of its signs.

A voluntary acceptance of myth can in fact define the whole of our traditional Literature. According to our norms, this Literature is an undoubted mythical system: there is a meaning, that of the discourse; there is a signifier, which is this same discourse as form or writing; there is a signified, which is the concept of literature; there is a signification, which is the literary discourse. I began to discuss this problem in *Writing Degree Zero*, which was, all told, nothing but a mythology of literary language. There I defined writing as the signifier of the literary myth, that is, as a form which is already filled with meaning and which receives from the concept of Literature a new signification.[12] I suggested that history, in modifying the writer's consciousness, had provoked, a hundred years or so ago, a moral crisis of literary language: writing was revealed as signifier, Literature as signification; rejecting the false nature of traditional literary language, the writer violently shifted his position in the direction of an anti-nature of language. The subversion of writing was the radical act by which a number of writers have attempted to reject Literature as a mythical system. Every revolt of this kind has been a murder of Literature as signification: all have postulated the reduction of literary

[12] *Style*, at least as I defined it then, is not a form, it does not belong to the province of a semiological analysis of Literature. In fact, style is a substance constantly threatened with formalization. To start with, it can perfectly well become degraded into a mode of writing: there is a "Malraux-type" writing, and even in Malraux himself. Then, style can also become a particular language, that used by the writer *for himself and for himself alone*. Style then becomes a sort of solipsistic myth, the language which the writer speaks *to himself*. It is easy to understand that at such a degree of solidification, style calls for a deciphering. The works of J. P. Richard are an example of this necessary critique of styles.

discourse to a simple semiological system, or even, in the case of poetry, to a pre-semiological system. This is an immense task, which required radical types of behavior: it is well known that some went as far as the pure and simple scuttling of the discourse, silence—whether real or transposed—appearing as the only possible weapon against the major power of myth: its recurrence.

It thus appears that it is extremely difficult to vanquish myth from the inside: for the very effort one makes in order to escape its stranglehold becomes in its turn the prey of myth: myth can always, as a last resort, signify the resistance which is brought to bear against it. Truth to tell, the best weapon against myth is perhaps to mythify it in its turn, and to produce an *artificial myth*: and this reconstituted myth will in fact be a mythology. Since myth robs language of something, why not rob myth? All that is needed is to use it as the departure point for a third semiological chain, to take its signification as the first term of a second myth. Literature offers some great examples of such artificial mythologies. I shall only evoke here Flaubert's *Bouvard and Pécuchet*. It is what could be called an experimental myth, a second-order myth. Bouvard and his friend Pécuchet represent a certain kind of bourgeoisie (which is incidentally in conflict with other bourgeois strata): their discourse *already* constitutes a mythical type of speech; its language does have a meaning, but this meaning is the empty form of a conceptual signified, which here is a kind of technological unsatedness. The meeting of meaning and concept forms, in this first mythical system, a signification which is the rhetoric of Bouvard and Pécuchet. It is at this point (I am breaking the process into its components for the sake of analysis) that Flaubert intervenes: to this first mythical system, which already is a second semiological system, he superimposes a third chain, in which the first link is the signification, or final term, of the first myth. The rhetoric of Bouvard and Pécuchet becomes the form of the new system; the concept here is due to Flaubert himself, to Flaubert's gaze on the myth which Bouvard and Pécuchet had built for themselves: it consists of their natively ineffectual inclinations, their inability to feel satisfied, the panic succession of their apprenticeships, in short what I would very much like to call (but I see storm clouds on the horizon): bouvard-and-pécuchet-ity. As for the final signification, it is the book, it is *Bouvard and Pécuchet* for us. The power of the second myth is that it gives the first its basis as a naïveté which is looked at. Flaubert has undertaken a real archaeological restoration of a given mythical speech: he is the Viollet-le-Duc of a certain bourgeois ideology. But less naïve than Viollet-le-Duc, he has strewn his reconstitution with supplementary ornaments which demystify it. These ornaments (which are the form of the second myth) are subjunctive in kind: there is a semiological equivalence between the subjunctive restitution of the discourse of Bouvard and Pécuchet and their ineffectualness.[13]

Flaubert's great merit (and that of all artificial mythologies: there are remarkable ones in Sartre's work) is that he gave to the problem of realism a frankly semiological solution. True, it is a somewhat incomplete merit, for Flaubert's ideology, since the bourgeois was for him only an aesthetic eyesore, was not at all realistic. But at least he avoided the major sin in literary matters, which is to confuse ideological with semiological reality. As ideology, literary realism does not depend at all on the language spoken by the writer. Language is a form, it cannot possibly be either realistic or unrealistic. All it can do is either to be mythical or not, or perhaps, as in *Bouvard and Pécuchet*, countermythical. Now, unfortunately, there is no antipathy between realism and myth. It is well known how often our

---

[13] A subjunctive form because it is in the subjunctive mode that Latin expressed "indirect style or discourse," which is an admirable instrument for demystification.

"realistic" literature is mythical (if only as a crude myth of realism) and how our "literature of the unreal" has at least the merit of being only slightly so. The wise thing would of course be to define the writer's realism as an essentially ideological problem. This certainly does not mean that there is no responsibility of form toward reality. But this responsibility can be measured only in semiological terms. A form can be judged (since forms are on trial) only as signification, not as expression. The writer's language is not expected to *represent* reality, but to signify it. This should impose on critics the duty of using two rigorously distinct methods: one must deal with the writer's realism either as an ideological substance (Marxist themes in Brecht's work, for instance) or as a semiological value (the props, the actors, the music, the colors in Brechtian dramaturgy). The ideal of course would be to combine these two types of criticism; the mistake which is constantly made is to confuse them: ideology has its methods, and so has semiology.

THE BOURGEOISIE AS A JOINT-STOCK COMPANY

Myth lends itself to history in two ways: by its form, which is only relatively motivated; by its concept, the nature of which is historical. One can therefore imagine a diachronic study of myths, whether one submits them to a retrospection (which means founding an historical mythology) or whether one follows some of yesterday's myths down to their present forms (which means founding prospective history). If I keep here to a synchronic sketch of contemporary myths, it is for an objective reason: our society is the privileged field of mythical significations. We must now say why.

Whatever the accidents, the compromises, the concessions and the political adventures, whatever the technical, economic, or even social changes which history brings us, our society is still a bourgeois society. I am not forgetting that since 1789, in

France, several types of bourgeoisie have succeeded one another in power; but the same status—a certain regime of ownership, a certain order, a certain ideology—remains at a
deeper level. Now a remarkable phenomenon occurs in the
matter of naming this regime: as an economic fact, the bourgeoisie is *named* without any difficulty: capitalism is openly
professed.[14] As a political fact, the bourgeoisie has some difficulty in acknowledging itself: there are no "bourgeois" parties
in the Chamber. As an ideological fact, it completely disappears: the bourgeoisie has obliterated its name in passing from
reality to representation, from economic man to mental man.
It comes to an agreement with the facts, but does not compromise about values, it makes its status undergo a real *ex-
nominating* operation: the bourgeoisie is defined as *the social
class which does not want to be named*. "Bourgeois," "petit-
bourgeois," "capitalism,"[15] "proletariat"[16] are the locus of an
unceasing hemorrhage: meaning flows out of them until their
very name becomes unnecessary.

This ex-nominating phenomenon is important; let us examine it a little more closely. Politically, the hemorrhage of the
name "bourgeois" is effected through the idea of *nation*. This
was once a progressive idea, which has served to get rid of the
aristocracy; today, the bourgeoisie merges into the nation,
even if it has, in order to do so, to exclude from it the elements
which it decides are allogenous (the Communists). This
planned syncretism allows the bourgeoisie to attract the nu-
merical support of its temporary allies, all the intermediate,
therefore "shapeless" classes. A long-continued use of the

[14] "The fate of capitalism is to make the worker wealthy," *Paris-Match* tells us.
[15] The word "capitalism" is taboo, not economically, but ideologically; it cannot possibly enter the vocabulary of bourgeois representations. Only in
Farouk's Egypt could a prisoner be condemned by a tribunal for "anti-
capitalist plotting" in so many words.
[16] The bourgeoisie never uses the word "Proletariat," which is supposed to be
a left-wing myth, except when it is in its interest to imagine the Proletariat
being led astray by the Communist Party.

word *nation* has failed to depoliticize it in depth; the political substratum is there, very near the surface, and some circumstances make it suddenly manifest. There are in the Chamber some "national" parties, and nominal syncretism here makes conspicuous what it had the ambition of hiding: an essential disparity. Thus the political vocabulary of the bourgeoisie already postulates that the universal exists: for it, politics is already a representation, a fragment of ideology.

Politically, in spite of the universalistic effort of its vocabulary, the bourgeoisie eventually strikes against a resisting core which is, by definition, the revolutionary party. But this party can constitute only a political richness: in a bourgeois culture, there is neither proletarian culture nor proletarian morality, there is no proletarian art; ideologically, all that is not bourgeois is obliged to *borrow* from the bourgeoisie. Bourgeois ideology can therefore spread over everything and in so doing lose its name without risk: no one here will throw this name of bourgeois back at it. It can without resistance subsume bourgeois theater, art, and humanity under their eternal analogues; in a word, it can ex-nominate itself without restraint when there is only one single human nature left: the defection from the name "bourgeois" is here complete.

True, there are revolts against bourgeois ideology. This is what one generally calls the avant-garde. But these revolts are socially limited, they remain open to salvage. First, because they come from a small section of the bourgeoisie itself, from a minority group of artists and intellectuals, without public other than the class which they contest, and who remain dependent on its money in order to express themselves. Then, these revolts always get their inspiration from a very strongly made distinction between the ethically and the politically bourgeois: what the avant-garde contests is the bourgeois in art or morals—the shopkeeper, the Philistine, as in the heyday of Romanticism; but as for political contestation, there is none.[17] What the avant-garde does not tolerate about the bourgeoisie is its language, not its status. This does not necessarily mean that it approves of this status; simply, it leaves it aside. Whatever the violence of the provocation, the nature it finally endorses is that of "derelict" man, not alienated man; and derelict man is still Eternal Man.[18]

This anonymity of the bourgeoisie becomes even more marked when one passes from bourgeois culture proper to its derived, vulgarized, and applied forms, to what one could call public philosophy, that which sustains everyday life, civil ceremonials, secular rites, in short, the unwritten norms of interrelationships in a bourgeois society. It is an illusion to reduce the dominant culture to its inventive core: there also is a bourgeois culture which consists of consumption alone. The whole of France is steeped in this anonymous ideology: our press, our films, our theater, our pulp literature, our rituals, our Justice, our diplomacy, our conversations, our remarks about the weather, a murder trial, a touching wedding, the cooking we dream of, the garments we wear, everything, in everyday life, is dependent on the representation which the bourgeoisie *has and makes us have* of the relations between man and the world. These "normalized" forms attract little attention, by the very fact of their extension, in which their origin is easily lost. They enjoy an intermediate position: being neither directly political nor directly ideological, they live peacefully between the action of the militants and the quarrels of the intellectuals; more or less abandoned by the former and the latter, they gravitate toward the enormous

[17] It is remarkable that the adversaries of the bourgeoisie on matters of ethics or aesthetics remain for the most part indifferent, or even attached, to its political determinations. Conversely, its political adversaries neglect to issue a basic condemnation of its representations: they often go so far as to share them. This diversity of attacks benefits the bourgeoisie, it allows it to camouflage its name. For the bourgeoisie should be understood only as synthesis of its determinations and its representations.
[18] There can be figures of derelict man which lack all order (Ionesco, for example). This does not affect in any way the security of the Essences.

mass of the undifferentiated, of the insignificant, in short, of Nature. Yet it is through its ethic that the bourgeoisie pervades France: practiced on a national scale, bourgeois norms are experienced as the evident laws of a natural order—the further the bourgeois class propagates its representations, the more naturalized they become. The fact of the bourgeoisie becomes absorbed into an amorphous universe, whose sole inhabitant is Eternal Man, who is neither proletarian nor bourgeois.

It is therefore by penetrating the intermediate classes that the bourgeois ideology can most surely lose its name. Petit-bourgeois norms are the residue of bourgeois culture, they are bourgeois truths which have become degraded, impoverished, commercialized, slightly archaic, or shall we say, out of date? The political alliance of the bourgeoisie and the petite bourgeoisie has for more than a century determined the history of France; it has rarely been broken, and each time only temporarily (1848, 1871, 1936). This alliance got closer as time passed, it gradually became a symbiosis; transient awakenings might happen, but the common ideology was never questioned again. The same "natural" varnish covers up all "national" representations: the big wedding of the bourgeoisie, which originates in a class ritual (the display and consumption of wealth), can bear no relation to the economic status of the lower middle class: but through the press, the news, and literature, it slowly becomes the very norm as dreamed, though not actually lived, of the petit-bourgeois couple. The bourgeoisie is constantly absorbing into its ideology a whole section of humanity which does not have its basic status and cannot live up to it except in imagination, that is, at the cost of an immobilization and an impoverishment of consciousness.[19] By spreading its representations over a whole catalogue of collective

---

[19] To induce a collective content for the imagination is always an inhuman undertaking, not only because dreaming essentializes life into destiny, but also because dreams are impoverished, and the alibi of an absence.

images for petit-bourgeois use, the bourgeoisie countenances the illusory lack of differentiation of the social classes: it is as from the moment when a typist earning twenty pounds a month *recognizes herself* in the big wedding of the bourgeoisie that bourgeois ex-nomination achieves its full effect.

The flight from the name "bourgeois" is not therefore an illusory, accidental, secondary, natural, or insignificant phenomenon: it is the bourgeois ideology itself, the process through which the bourgeoisie transforms the reality of the world into an image of the world, History into Nature. And this image has a remarkable feature: it is upside down.[20] The status of the bourgeoisie is particular, historical: man as represented by it is universal, eternal. The bourgeois class has precisely built its power on technical, scientific progress, on an unlimited transformation of nature: bourgeois ideology yields in return an unchangeable nature. The first bourgeois philosophers pervaded the world with significations, subjected all things to an idea of the rational, and decreed that they were meant for man: bourgeois ideology is of the scientistic or the intuitive kind, it records facts or perceives values, but refuses explanations; the order of the world can be seen as sufficient or ineffable, it is never seen as significant. Finally, the basic idea of a perfectible mobile world produces the inverted image of an unchanging humanity, characterized by an indefinite repetition of its identity. In a word, in the contemporary bourgeois society, the passage from the real to the ideological is defined as that from an *anti-physis* to a *pseudo-physis*.

MYTH IS DEPOLITICIZED SPEECH

And this is where we come back to myth. Semiology has taught us that myth has the task of giving a historical intention

---

[20] "If men and their conditions appear throughout ideology inverted as in a camera obscura, this phenomenon follows from their historical vital process . . ." (Marx, *The German Ideology*).

a natural justification, and making contingency appear eternal. Now this process is exactly that of bourgeois ideology. If our society is objectively the privileged field of mythical significations, it is because formally myth is the most appropriate instrument for the ideological inversion which defines this society: at all the levels of human communication, myth operates the inversion of *anti-physis* into *pseudo-physis*.

What the world supplies to myth is a historical reality, defined, even if this goes back quite a while, by the way in which men have produced or used it; and what myth gives in return is a *natural* image of this reality. And just as bourgeois ideology is defined by the abandonment of the name "bourgeois," myth is constituted by the loss of the historical quality of things: in it, things lose the memory that they once were made. The world enters language as a dialectical relation between activities, between human actions; it comes out of myth as a harmonious display of essences. A conjuring trick has taken place; it has turned reality inside out, it has emptied it of history and has filled it with Nature, it has removed from things their human meaning so as to make them signify a human insignificance. The function of myth is to empty reality: it is, literally, a ceaseless flowing out, a hemorrhage, or perhaps an evaporation, in short, a perceptible absence.

It is now possible to complete the semiological definition of myth in a bourgeois society: *myth is depoliticized speech*. One must naturally understand *political* in its deeper meaning, as describing the whole of human relations in their real, social structure, in their power of making the world; one must above all give an active value to the prefix *de-*: here it represents an operational movement, it permanently embodies a defaulting. In the case of the soldier Negro, for instance, what is got rid of is certainly not French imperiality (on the contrary, since what must be actualized is its presence); it is the contingent, historical, in one word: *fabricated*, quality of colonialism.

Myth does not deny things, on the contrary, its function is to talk about them; simply, it purifies them, it makes them innocent, it gives them a natural and eternal justification, it gives them a clarity which is not that of an explanation but that of a statement of fact. If I *state the fact* of French imperiality without explaining it, I am very near to finding that it is natural and *goes without saying:* I am reassured. In passing from history to Nature, myth acts economically: it abolishes the complexity of human acts, it gives them the simplicity of essences, it does away with all dialectics, with any going back beyond what is immediately visible, it organizes a world which is without contradictions because it is without depth, a world wide open and wallowing in the evident, it establishes a blissful clarity: things appear to mean something by themselves.[21]

However, is myth always depoliticized speech? In other words, is reality always political? Is it enough to speak about a thing naturally for it to become mythical? One could answer with Marx that the most natural object contains a political trace, however faint and diluted, the more or less memorable presence of the human act which has produced, fitted up, used, subjected, or rejected it.[22] The language-object, which *"speaks things,"* can easily exhibit this trace; the metalanguage, which *speaks of things*, much less easily. Now myth always comes under the heading of metalanguage: the depoliticization which it carries out often supervenes against a background which is already naturalized, depoliticized by a general metalanguage which is trained to *celebrate* things, and no longer to *"act them."* It goes without saying that the force needed by myth to distort its object is much less in the case of a tree than in the case of a Sudanese: in the latter case, the political load is very near the surface, a large quantity of

---

[21] To the pleasure principle of Freudian man could be added the clarity principle of mythological humanity. All the ambiguity of myth is there: its clarity is euphoric.

[22] Cf. Marx and the example of the cherry tree (*The German Ideology*).

artificial nature is needed in order to disperse it; in the former case, it is remote, purified by a whole century-old layer of metalanguage. There are, therefore, strong myths and weak myths; in the former, the political quantum is immediate, the depoliticization is abrupt; in the latter, the political quality of the object has *faded* like a color, but the slightest thing can bring back its strength brutally: what is more *natural* than the sea? And what more "political" than the sea celebrated by the makers of the film *The Lost Continent*?

In fact, metalanguage constitutes a kind of preserve for myth. Men do not have with myth a relationship based on truth but on use: they depoliticize according to their needs. Some mythical objects are left dormant for a time; they are then no more than vague mythical schemata whose political load seems almost neutral. But this indicates only that their situation has brought this about, not that their structure is different. This is the case with our Latin-grammar example. We must note that here mythical speech works on a material which has long been transformed: the sentence by Aesop belongs to literature, it is at the very start mythified (therefore made innocent) by its being fiction. But it is enough to replace the initial term of the chain for an instant into its nature as language-object, to gauge the emptying of reality operated by myth: can one imagine the feelings of a *real* society of animals on finding itself transformed into a grammar example, into a predicative nature! In order to gauge the political load of an object and the mythical hollow which espouses it, one must never look at things from the point of view of the signification, but from that of the signifier, of the thing which has been robbed; and within the signifier, from the point of view of the language-object, that is, of the meaning. There is no doubt that if we consulted a *real* lion, he would maintain that the grammar example is a *strongly* depoliticized state, he would qualify as fully *political* the jurisprudence which leads him to claim a

prey because he is the strongest, unless we deal with a bourgeois lion who would not fail to mythify his strength by giving
it the form of a duty.

One can clearly see that in this case the political insignificance of the myth comes from its situation. Myth, as we know,
is a value: it is enough to modify its circumstances, the general
(and precarious) system in which it occurs, in order to regu-
late its scope with great accuracy. The field of the myth is in
this case reduced to the second form of a French *lycée*. But I
suppose that a child *enthralled* by the story of the lion, the
heifer, and the cow, and recovering through the life of the
imagination the actual reality of these animals, would appreciate with much less unconcern than we do the disappearance of
this lion changed into a predicate. In fact, we hold this myth to
be politically insignificant only because it is not meant for
us.

MYTH ON THE LEFT

If myth is depoliticized speech, there is at least one type of
speech which is the opposite of myth: that which *remains*
political. Here we must go back to the distinction between
language-object and metalanguage. If I am a woodcutter and I
am led to name the tree which I am felling, whatever the form
of my sentence, I "speak the tree," I do not speak about it.
This means that my language is operational, transitively linked
to its object; between the tree and myself, there is nothing but
my labor, that is to say, an action. This is a political language:
it represents Nature for me only inasmuch as I am going to
transform it, it is a language thanks to which I *"act the object"*; the tree is not an image for me, it is simply the meaning
of my action. But if I am not a woodcutter, I can no longer
"speak the tree," I can only speak *about* it, *on* it. My language
is no longer the instrument of an "acted-upon tree," it is the
"tree celebrated" which becomes the instrument of my lan-

guage. I no longer have anything more than an intransitive relationship with the tree; this tree is no longer the meaning of reality as a human action, it is an *image-at-one's-disposal*. Compared to the real language of the woodcutter, the language I create is a second-order language, a metalanguage in which I shall henceforth not "act the things" but "act their names," and which is to the primary language what the gesture is to the act. This second-order language is not entirely mythical, but it is the very locus where myth settles; for myth can work only on objects which have already received the mediation of a first language.

There is therefore one language which is not mythical, it is the language of man as a producer: wherever man speaks in order to transform reality and no longer to preserve it as an image, wherever he links his language to the making of things, metalanguage is referred to a language-object, and myth is impossible. This is why revolutionary language proper cannot be mythical. Revolution is defined as a cathartic act meant to reveal the political load of the world: it *makes* the world; and its language, all of it, is functionally absorbed in this making. It is because it generates speech which is *fully*, that is to say initially and finally, political, and not, like myth, speech which is initially political and finally natural, that Revolution excludes myth. Just as bourgeois ex-nomination characterizes at once bourgeois ideology and myth itself, revolutionary denomination identifies revolution and the absence of myth. The bourgeoisie hides the fact that it is the bourgeoisie and thereby produces myth; revolution announces itself openly as revolution and thereby abolishes myth.

I have been asked whether there are myths "on the left." Of course, inasmuch, precisely, as the left is not revolution. Left-wing myth supervenes precisely at the moment when revolution changes itself into "the left," that is, when it accepts to wear a mask, to hide its name, to generate an innocent metalanguage and to distort itself into "Nature." This revolutionary ex-nomination may or may not be tactical, this is no place to discuss it. At any rate, it is sooner or later experienced as a process contrary to revolution, and it is always more or less in relation to myth that revolutionary history defines its "deviations." There came a day, for instance, when it was socialism itself which defined the Stalin myth. Stalin, as a spoken object, has exhibited for years, in their pure state, the constituent characters of mythical speech: a meaning, which was the real Stalin, that of history; a signifier, which was the ritual invocation to Stalin, and the *inevitable* character of the "natural" epithets with which his name was surrounded; a signified, which was the intention to respect orthodoxy, discipline, and unity, *appropriated* by the Communist Parties to a definite situation; and a signification, which was a sanctified Stalin, whose historical determinants found themselves grounded in Nature, sublimated under the name of Genius, that is, something irrational and inexpressible: here, depoliticization is evident, it fully reveals the presence of a myth.[23]

Yes, myth exists on the left, but it does not at all have there the same qualities as bourgeois myth. *Left-wing myth is inessential.* To start with, the objects which it takes hold of are rare—only a few political notions—unless it has itself recourse to the whole repertoire of the bourgeois myths. Left-wing myth never reaches the immense field of human relationships, the very vast surface of "insignificant" ideology. Everyday life is inaccessible to it: in a bourgeois society, there are no "left-wing" myths concerning marriage, cooking, the home, the theater, the law, morality, etc. Then, it is an incidental myth, its use is not part of a strategy, as is the case with

[23] It is remarkable that Khrushchevism presented itself not as a political change, but essentially and only as a *linguistic conversion*. An incomplete conversion, incidentally, for Khrushchev devalued Stalin, but did not explain him —did not repoliticize him.

bourgeois myth, but only of a tactics, or, at the worst, of a deviation; if it occurs, it is as a myth suited to a convenience, not to a necessity.

Finally, and above all, this myth is, in essence, poverty-stricken. It does not know how to proliferate; being produced on order and for a temporally limited prospect, it is invented with difficulty. It lacks a major faculty, that of fabulizing. Whatever it does, there remains about it something stiff and literal, a suggestion of something done to order. As it is expressively put, it remains barren. In fact, what can be more meager than the Stalin myth? No inventiveness here, and only a clumsy appropriation: the signifier of the myth (this form whose infinite wealth in bourgeois myth we have just seen) is not varied in the least: it is reduced to a litany.

This imperfection, if that is the word for it, comes from the nature of the "left": whatever the imprecision of the term, the left always defines itself in relation to the oppressed, whether proletarian or colonized.[24] Now the speech of the oppressed can only be poor, monotonous, immediate: his destitution is the very yardstick of his language: he has only one, always the same, that of his actions; metalanguage is a luxury, he cannot yet have access to it. The speech of the oppressed is real, like that of the woodcutter; it is a transitive type of speech: it is quasi-unable to lie; lying is a richness, a lie presupposes property, truths, and forms to spare. This essential barrenness produces rare, threadbare myths: either transient, or clumsily indiscreet; by their very being, they label themselves as myths, and point to their masks. And this mask is hardly that of a pseudo-physis: for that type of physis is also a richness of a sort, the oppressed can only borrow it: he is unable to throw out the real meaning of things, to give them the luxury of an

---

[24] Today it is the colonized peoples who assume to the full the ethical and political condition described by Marx as being that of the proletariat.

empty form, open to the innocence of a false Nature. One can say that in a sense, left-wing myth is always an artificial myth, a reconstituted myth: hence its clumsiness.

MYTH ON THE RIGHT

Statistically, myth is on the right. There, it is essential; well-fed, sleek, expansive, garrulous, it invents itself ceaselessly. It takes hold of everything, all aspects of the law, of morality, of aesthetics, of diplomacy, of household equipment, of Literature, of entertainment. Its expansion has the very dimensions of bourgeois ex-nomination. The bourgeoisie wants to keep reality without keeping the appearances: it is therefore the very negativity of bourgeois appearance, infinite like every negativity, which solicits myth infinitely. The oppressed is nothing, he has only one language, that of his emancipation; the oppressor is everything, his language is rich, multiform, supple, with all the possible degrees of dignity at its disposal: he has an exclusive right to metalanguage. The oppressed *makes* the world, he has only an active, transitive (political) language; the oppressor conserves it, his language is plenary, intransitive, gestural, theatrical: it is Myth. The language of the former aims at transforming, of the latter at eternalizing.

Does this completeness of the myths of Order (this is the name the bourgeoisie gives to itself) include inner differences? Are there, for instance, bourgeois myths and petit-bourgeois myths? There cannot be any fundamental differences, for whatever the public which consumes it, myth always postulated the immobility of Nature. But there can be degrees of fulfillment or expansion: some myths ripen better in some social strata: for myth also, there are micro-climates.

The myth of Childhood-as-Poet, for instance, is an *advanced* bourgeois myth: it has hardly come out of inventive culture (Cocteau, for example) and is just reaching consumer culture (*L'Express*). Part of the bourgeoisie can still find it too obviously invented, not mythical enough to feel entitled to countenance it (a whole part of bourgeois criticism works only with duly mythical materials). It is a myth which is not yet well run in, it does not yet contain enough *Nature*: in order to make the Child-Poet part of a cosmogony, one must renounce the prodigy (Mozart, Rimbaud, etc.), and accept new norms, those of psychopedagogy, Freudianism, etc.: as a myth, it is still unripe.

Thus every myth can have its history and its geography; each is in fact the sign of the other: a myth ripens because it spreads. I have not been able to carry out any real study of the social geography of myths. But it is perfectly possible to draw what linguists would call the isoglosses of a myth, the lines which limit the social region where it is spoken. As this region is shifting, it would be better to speak of the waves of implantation of the myth. The Minou Drouet myth has thus had at least three waves of amplification: (1) *L'Express;* (2) *Paris-Match, Elle*; (3) *France-Soir*. Some myths hesitate: will they pass into tabloids, the home of the suburbanite of private means, the hairdresser's salon, the Métro? The social geography of myths will remain difficult to trace as long as we lack an analytical sociology of the press.[25] But we can say that its place already exists.

Since we cannot yet draw up the list of the dialectal forms of bourgeois myth, we can always sketch its rhetorical forms. One must understand here by *rhetoric* a set of fixed, regulated, insistent figures, according to which the varied forms of the mythical signifier arrange themselves. These figures are trans-

---

[25] The circulation of newspapers is an insufficient datum. Other information comes only by accident. *Paris-Match* has given—significantly, as publicity— the composition of its public in terms of standard of living (*Le Figaro*, July 12, 1955): out of each 100 readers living in town, 53 have a car, 49 a bathroom, etc., whereas the average standard of living in France is reckoned as follows: car, 22 percent; bathroom, 13 percent. That the purchasing power of the *Paris-Match* reader is high could have been predicted from the mythology of this publication.

parent inasmuch as they do not affect the plasticity of the signifier; but they are already sufficiently conceptualized to adapt to a historical representation of the world (just as classical rhetoric can account for a representation of the Aristotelian type). It is through their rhetoric that bourgeois myths outline the general prospect of this *pseudo-physis* which defines the dream of the contemporary bourgeois world. Here are its principal figures:

1. *The inoculation.* I have already given examples of this very general figure, which consists in admitting the accidental evil of a class-bound institution the better to conceal its principial evil. One immunizes the contents of the collective imagination by means of a small inoculation of acknowledged evil; one thus protects it against the risk of a generalized subversion. This *liberal* treatment would not have been possible only a hundred years ago. Then, the bourgeois Good did not compromise with anything, it was quite stiff. It has become much more supple since: the bourgeoisie no longer hesitates to acknowledge some localized subversions: the avant-garde, the irrational in childhood, etc. It now lives in a balanced economy: as in any sound joint-stock company, the smaller shares —in law but not in fact—compensate the big ones.

2. *The privation of History.* Myth deprives the object of which it speaks of all History.[27] In it, history evaporates. It is a kind of ideal servant: it prepares all things, brings them, lays them out, the master arrives, it silently disappears: all that is left for one to do is to enjoy this beautiful object without wondering where it comes from. Or even better: it can only come from eternity: since the beginning of time, it has been made for bourgeois man, the Spain of the *Blue Guide* has been made for the tourist, and "primitives" have prepared their

---

[26] Marx: ". . . we must pay attention to this history, since ideology boils down to either an erroneous conception of this history, *or to a complete abstraction from it*" (*The German Ideology*).

dances with a view to an exotic festivity. We can see all the disturbing things which this felicitous figure removes from sight: both determinism and freedom. Nothing is produced, nothing is chosen: all one has to do is to possess these new objects from which all soiling trace of origin or choice has been removed. This miraculous evaporation of history is another form of a concept common to most bourgeois myths: the irresponsibility of man.

3. *Identification.* The petit bourgeois is a man unable to imagine the Other.[27] If he comes face to face with him, he blinds himself, ignores and denies him, or else transforms him into himself. In the petit-bourgeois universe, all the experiences of confrontation are reverberating, any otherness is reduced to sameness. The spectacle and the tribunal, which are both places where the Other threatens to appear in full view, become mirrors. This is because the Other is a scandal which threatens his essence. Dominici cannot have access to social existence unless he is previously reduced to the state of a small simulacrum of the president of the Assizes or the Public Prosecutor: this is the price one must pay in order to condemn him justly, since Justice is a weighing operation and since scales can only weigh like against like. There are, in any petit-bourgeois consciousness, small simulacra of the hooligan, the parricide, the homosexual, etc., which periodically the judiciary extracts from its brain, puts in the dock, admonishes and condemns: one never tries anybody but analogues *who have gone astray*: it is a question of direction, not of Nature, for *that's how men are.* Sometimes—rarely—the Other is revealed as irreducible: not because of a sudden scruple, but because *common sense* rebels: a man does not have a white skin, but a black one, another drinks pear juice, not Pernod. How can one assimilate

[27] Marx: ". . . what makes them representative of the petit-bourgeois class, is that their minds, their consciousnesses do not extend beyond the limits which this class has set to its activities" (*The Eighteenth Brumaire*). And Gorky: "the petit bourgeois is the man who has preferred himself to all else."

the Negro, the Russian? There is here a figure for emergencies: exoticism. The Other becomes a pure object, a spectacle, a clown. Relegated to the confines of humanity, he no longer threatens the security of the home. This figure is chiefly petit-bourgeois. For, even if he is unable to experience the Other in himself, the bourgeois can at least imagine the place where he fits in: this is what is known as liberalism, which is a sort of intellectual equilibrium based on recognized places. The petit-bourgeois class is not liberal (it produces Fascism, whereas the bourgeoisie uses it): it follows the same route as the bourgeoisie, but lags behind.

4. *Tautology*. Yes, I know, it's an ugly word. But so is the thing. Tautology is this verbal device which consists in defining like by like (*"Drama is drama"*). We can view it as one of those types of magical behavior dealt with by Sartre in his *Outline of a Theory of the Emotions*: one takes refuge in tautology as one does in fear, or anger, or sadness, when one is at a loss for an explanation: the accidental failure of language is magically identified with what one decides is a natural resistance of the object. In tautology, there is a double murder: one kills rationality because it resists one; one kills language because it betrays one. Tautology is a faint at the right moment, a saving aphasia, it is a death, or perhaps a comedy, the indignant "representation" of the *rights* of reality over and above language. Since it is magical, it can of course only take refuge behind the argument of authority: thus do parents at the end of their tether reply to the child who keeps on asking for explanations: *"because that's how it is,"* or even better: *"just because, that's all"*—a magical act ashamed of itself, which verbally makes the gesture of rationality, but immediately abandons the latter, and believes itself to be even with causality because it has uttered the word which introduces it. Tautology testifies to a profound distrust of language, which is

rejected because it has failed. Now any refusal of language is a death. Tautology creates a dead, a motionless world.

5. *Neither-Norism*. By this I mean this mythological figure which consists in stating two opposites and balancing the one by the other so as to reject them both. (I want *neither* this *nor* that.) It is on the whole a bourgeois figure, for it relates to a modern form of liberalism. We find again here the figure of the scales: reality is first reduced to analogues; then it is weighed; finally, equality having been ascertained, it is got rid of. Here also there is magical behavior: both parties are dismissed because it is embarrassing to choose between them; one flees from an intolerable reality, reducing it to two opposites which balance each other only inasmuch as they are purely formal, relieved of all their specific weight. Neither-Norism can have degraded forms: in astrology, for example, ill luck is always followed by equal good luck; they are always predicted in a prudently compensatory perspective: a final equilibrium immobilizes values, life, destiny, etc.: one no longer needs to choose, but only to endorse.

6. *The quantification of quality*. This is a figure which is latent in all the preceding ones. By reducing any quality to quantity, myth economizes intelligence: it understands reality more cheaply. I have given several examples of this mechanism which bourgeois—and especially petit-bourgeois—mythology does not hesitate to apply to aesthetic realities which it deems on the other hand to partake of an immaterial essence. Bourgeois theater is a good example of this contradiction: on the one hand, theater is presented as an essence which cannot be reduced to any language and reveals itself only to the heart, to intuition. From this quality, it receives an irritable dignity (it is forbidden as a crime of "lese-essence" to speak about the theater *scientifically*: or rather, any intellectual way of viewing the theater is discredited as scientism or pedantic

language). On the other hand, bourgeois dramatic art rests on a pure quantification of effects: a whole circuit of computable appearances establishes a quantitative equality between the cost of a ticket and the tears of an actor or the luxuriousness of a set: what is currently meant by the "naturalness" of an actor, for instance, is above all a conspicuous quantity of effects.

7. *The statement of fact.* Myths tend toward proverbs. Bourgeois ideology invests in this figure interests which are bound to its very essence: universalism, the refusal of any explanation, an unalterable hierarchy of the world. But we must again distinguish the language-object from the metalanguage. Popular, ancestral proverbs still partake of an instrumental grasp of the world as object. A rural statement of fact, such as *"the weather is fine,"* keeps a real link with the usefulness of fine weather. It is an implicitly technological statement; the word, here, in spite of its general, abstract form, paves the way for actions, it inserts itself into a fabricating order: the farmer does not speak *about* the weather, he "acts it," he draws it into his labor. All our popular proverbs thus represent active speech which has gradually solidified into reflexive speech, but where reflection is curtailed, reduced to a statement of fact, and so to speak timid, prudent, and closely hugging experience. Popular proverbs foresee more than they assert, they remain the speech of a humanity which is making itself, not one which is. Bourgeois aphorisms, on the other hand, belong to metalanguage; they are a second-order language which bears on objects already prepared. Their classical form is the maxim. Here the statement is no longer directed toward a world to be made; it must overlay one which is already made, bury the traces of this production under a self-evident appearance of eternity: it is a counter-explanation, the decorous equivalent of a tautology, of this peremptory *because* which

parents in need of knowledge hang above the heads of their children. The foundation of the bourgeois statement of fact is *common sense*, that is, truth when it stops on the arbitrary order of him who speaks it.

I have listed these rhetorical figures without any special order, and there may well be many others: some can become worn out, others can come into being. But it is obvious that those given here, such as they are, fall into two great categories, which are like the Zodiacal Signs of the bourgeois universe: the Essences and the Scales. Bourgeois ideology continuously transforms the products of history into essential types. Just as the cuttlefish squirts its ink in order to protect itself, it cannot rest until it has obscured the ceaseless making of the world, fixated this world into an object which can be forever possessed, catalogued its riches, embalmed it, and injected into reality some purifying essence which will stop its transformation, its flight toward other forms of existence. And these riches, thus fixated and frozen, will at last become computable: bourgeois morality will essentially be a weighing operation, the essences will be placed in scales of which bourgeois man will remain the motionless beam. For the very end of myths is to immobilize the world: they must suggest and mimic a universal order which has fixated once and for all the hierarchy of possessions. Thus, every day and everywhere, man is stopped by myths, referred by them to this motionless prototype which lives in his place, stifles him in the manner of a huge internal parasite and assigns to his activity the narrow limits within which he is allowed to suffer without upsetting the world: bourgeois pseudo-physis is in the fullest sense a prohibition for man against inventing himself. Myths are nothing but this ceaseless, untiring solicitation, this insidious and inflexible demand that all men recognize themselves in this image, eternal yet bearing a date, which was built of them one day as if for all time. For the Nature, in which they are locked up under the pretext of being eternalized, is nothing but a Usage. And it is this Usage, however lofty, that they must take in hand and transform.

NECESSITY AND LIMITS OF MYTHOLOGY

I must, as a conclusion, say a few words about the mythologist himself. This term is rather grand and self-assured. Yet one can predict for the mythologist, if there ever is one, a few difficulties, in feeling if not in method. True, he will have no trouble in feeling justified: whatever its mistakes, mythology is certain to participate in the making of the world. Holding as a principle that man in a bourgeois society is at every turn plunged into a false Nature, it attempts to find again under the assumed innocence of the most unsophisticated relationships, the profound alienation which this innocence is meant to make one accept. The unveiling which it carries out is therefore a political act: founded on a responsible idea of language, mythology thereby postulates the freedom of the latter. It is certain that in this sense mythology *harmonizes* with the world, not as it is, but as it wants to create itself (Brecht had for this an efficiently ambiguous word: *Einverstandnis*, at once an understanding of reality and a complicity with it).

This harmony justifies the mythologist but does not fulfill him: his status still remains basically one of being excluded. Justified by the political dimension, the mythologist is still at a distance from it. His speech is a metalanguage, it "acts" nothing; at the most, it unveils—or does it? To whom? His task always remains ambiguous, hampered by its ethical origin. He can live revolutionary action only vicariously: hence the self-conscious character of his function, this something a little stiff and painstaking, muddled and excessively simplified which brands any intellectual behavior with an openly political foundation ("uncommitted" types of literature are infinitely more "elegant"; they are in their place in metalanguage).

Also, the mythologist cuts himself off from all the myth consumers, and this is no small matter. If this applied to a particular section of the collectivity, well and good.[28] But when a myth reaches the entire community, it is from the latter that the mythologist must become estranged if he wants to liberate the myth. Any myth with some degree of generality is in fact ambiguous, because it represents the very humanity of those who, having nothing, have borrowed it. To decipher the Tour de France or the "good French wine" is to cut oneself off from those who are entertained or warmed up by them. The mythologist is condemned to live in a theoretical sociality; for him, to be in society is, at best, to be truthful: his utmost sociality dwells in his utmost morality. His connection with the world is of the order of sarcasm.

One must even go further: in a sense, the mythologist is excluded from this history in the name of which he professes to act. The havoc which he wreaks in the language of the community is absolute for him, it fills his assignment to the brim: he must live this assignment without any hope of going back or any assumption of payment. It is forbidden for him to imagine what the world will concretely be like, when the immediate object of his criticism has disappeared. Utopia is an impossible luxury for him: he greatly doubts that tomorrow's truths will be the exact reverse of today's lies. History never ensures the triumph pure and simple of something over its opposite: it unveils, while making itself, unimaginable solutions, unforeseeable syntheses. The mythologist is not even in

[28] It is not only from the public that one becomes estranged; it is sometimes also from the very object of the myth. In order to demystify Poetic Childhood, for instance, I have had, so to speak, *to lack confidence* in Minou Drouet, the child. I have had to ignore, in her, under the enormous myth with which she is cumbered, something like a tender, open, possibility. It is never a good thing to speak *against* a little girl.

a Moses-like situation: he cannot see the Promised Land. For him, tomorrow's positivity is entirely hidden by today's negativity. All the values of his undertaking appear to him as acts of destruction: the latter accurately cover the former, nothing protrudes. This subjective grasp of history in which the potent seed of the future *is nothing but* the most profound apocalypse of the present has been expressed by Saint-Just in a strange saying: *"What constitutes the Republic is the total destruction of what is opposed to it."* This must not, I think, be understood in the trivial sense of: "One has to clear the way before reconstructing." The copula has an exhaustive meaning: there is for some men a subjective dark night of history where the future becomes an essence, the essential destruction of the past.

One last exclusion threatens the mythologist: he constantly runs the risk of causing the reality which he purports to protect, to disappear. Quite apart from all speech, the *D.S. 19* is a technologically defined object: it is capable of a certain speed, it meets the wind in a certain way, etc. And this type of reality cannot be spoken of by the mythologist. The mechanic, the engineer, even the user, *"speak* the object"; but the mythologist is condemned to metalanguage. This exclusion already has a name: it is what is called ideologism. Zhdanovism has roundly condemned it (without proving, incidentally, that it was, *for the time being*, avoidable) in the early Lukács, in Marr's linguistics, in works like those of Bénichou or Goldmann, opposing to it the reticence of a reality inaccessible to ideology, such as that of language according to Stalin. It is true that ideologism resolves the contradiction of alienated reality by an amputation, not a synthesis (but as for Zhdanovism, it does not even resolve it): wine is objectively good, and *at the same time*, the goodness of wine is a myth: here is the aporia. The mythologist gets out of this as best he can: he deals with the goodness of wine, not with the wine itself, just as the historian deals with Pascal's ideology, not with the *Pensées* in themselves.[29]

It seems that this is a difficulty pertaining to our times: there is as yet only one possible choice, and this choice can bear only on two equally extreme methods: either to posit a reality which is entirely permeable to history, and ideologize; or, conversely, to posit a reality which is *ultimately* impenetrable, irreducible, and, in this case, poetize. In a word, I do not yet see a synthesis between ideology and poetry (by poetry I understand, in a very general way, the search for the inalienable meaning of things).

The fact that we cannot manage to achieve more than an unstable grasp of reality doubtless gives the measure of our present alienation: we constantly drift between the object and its demystification, powerless to render its wholeness. For if we penetrate the object, we liberate it but we destroy it; and if we acknowledge its full weight, we respect it, but we restore it to a state which is still mystified. It would seem that we are condemned for some time yet always to speak *excessively* about reality. This is probably because ideologism and its opposite are types of behavior which are still magical, terrorized, blinded, and fascinated by the split in the social world. And yet, this is what we must seek: a reconciliation between reality and men, between description and explanation, between object and knowledge.

1956

---

[29] Even here, in these mythologies, I have used trickery: finding it painful constantly to work on the evaporation of reality, I have started to make it excessively dense, and to discover in it a surprising compactness which I savored with delight, and I have given a few examples of "substantial psychoanalysis" about some mythical objects.

The Last Happy Writer

WHAT have we in common, today, with Voltaire? From a modern point of view, his philosophy is outmoded. It is possible to believe in the fixity of essences and in the chaos of history, but no longer in the same way as Voltaire. In any case, atheists no longer throw themselves at the feet of deists, who moreover no longer exist. Dialectics has killed off Manicheanism, and we rarely discuss the ways of Providence. As for Voltaire's enemies, they have disappeared, or been transformed: there are no more Jansenists, no Socinians, no Leibnizians; the Jesuits are no longer named Nonotte or Patouillet.

I was about to say: there is no longer an Inquisition. This is wrong, of course. What has disappeared is the theater of persecution, not persecution itself: the *auto-da-fé* has been subtilized into a police operation, the stake has become the concentration camp, discreetly ignored by its neighbors. In return for which, the figures have changed: in 1721 nine men and eleven women were burned at Grenada in the four ovens of the scaffold, and in 1723 nine men were burned at Madrid to celebrate the arrival of the French princess: they had doubt-

From *Critical Essays*.

less married their cousins or eaten meat on Friday. A horrible repression, whose absurdity sustains Voltaire's entire *oeuvre*. But between 1939 and 1945, six million human beings were killed, among others, because they were Jews—they, or their parents, or their grandparents.

We have not had a single pamphlet against that. But perhaps it is precisely because the figures have changed. Simplistic as it may appear, there is a proportion between the lightness of the Voltairean artillery and the sporadic artillery of religious crime in the eighteenth century: quantitatively limited, the stake became a principle, i.e., a target: a tremendous advantage for its opponent: such is the stuff of which triumphant writers are made. For the very enormity of racist crimes, their organization by the State, the ideological justifications with which they are masked—all this involves today's writer in much more than a pamphlet, demands a philosophy rather than an irony, an explanation rather than an astonishment. Since Voltaire, history has been imprisoned in a difficulty which lacerates any committed literature and which Voltaire never knew: *no freedom for the enemies of freedom*: no one can any longer give lessons in tolerance to anyone.

In short, what separates us from Voltaire is that he was a happy writer. Better than anyone else, he gave reason's combat a festive style. Everything is spectacle in his battles: the adversary's name—always ridiculous; the disputed doctrine—reduced to a proposition (Voltairean irony is invariably the exposure of a disproportion); the points scored, exploding in every direction until they seem to be a game, dispensing the onlooker from all respect and all pity; the very mobility of the combatant, here disguised under a thousand transparent pseudonyms, there making his European journeys a kind of feinting farce, a perpetual Scapinade. For the skirmishes between Voltaire and the world are not only a spectacle but a superlative spectacle, proclaiming themselves such in the fashion of those Punchinello shows Voltaire loved so much—he had a puppet theater of his own at Cirey.

Voltaire's first happiness was doubtless that of his times. Let there be no mistake: the times were very harsh, and Voltaire has everywhere described their horrors. Yet no period has helped a writer more, given him more assurance that he was fighting for a just and natural cause. The bourgeoisie, the class from which Voltaire came, already held most of its economic positions; a power in commerce and industry, in the ministries, in culture and the sciences, it knew that its triumph coincided with the nation's prosperity and the happiness of each citizen. On its side, potential power, certainty of method, and the still-pure heritage of taste; against it, all a dying world could display of corruption, stupidity, and ferocity. It was indeed a great happiness, a great peace to combat an enemy so uniformly condemnable. The tragic spirit is severe because it acknowledges, by obligation of Nature, its adversary's greatness: Voltaire had no tragic spirit: he had to measure himself against no living force, against no idea or individual that could induce him to reflect (except the past: Pascal, and the future: Rousseau; but he conjured them both away): Jesuits, Jansenists, or parliaments, these were great frozen bodies, drained of all intelligence and filled with no more than a ferocity intolerable to the heart and the mind. Authority, even in its bloodiest manifestations, was no more than a decor; merely subject such machinery to human eyes, and it would collapse. Voltaire had that sly and tender gaze (*Zaïre's very heart*, Mme de Genlis tells us, *was in his eyes*), whose destructive power lay in simply bearing life among those great blind masks which still ruled society.

It was, then, a singular happiness to have to do battle in a world where force and stupidity were continually on the same tack: a privileged situation for the mind. The writer was on history's side, all the happier in that he perceived history as a consummation, not as a transcendence which risked sweeping him along with it.

Voltaire's second happiness was precisely to forget history, at the very moment it was supporting him. In order to be happy, Voltaire suspended time; if he has a philosophy, it is that of immobility. We know what he thought: God created the world as a geometer, not as a father. Which means that He does not bother to accompany His creation and that, once regulated, the world no longer sustains relations with God. An original intelligence established a certain type of causality once and for all: there are no objects without ends, no effects without causes, and the relation between one and the other is immutable. Voltairean metaphysics is therefore never anything but an introduction to physics, and Providence a mechanics. For once God has left the world He created (like the clockmaker his clock), neither God nor man ever moves again. Of course good and evil exist; but we are to translate them as happiness and misery, not sin or innocence; for they are merely the elements of a universal causality; they have a necessity, but this necessity is mechanical, not moral: evil does not punish, good does not reward: they do not signify that God is, that He surveys all, but that He has been, that He has created.

If man should take it upon himself to turn from evil to good by a moral impulse, it is the universal order of causes and effects which he injures; he can produce, by this movement, only a farcical chaos (as Memnon does, the day he decides to be wise). Then what can man do with regard to good and evil? Not much: in this machinery which is the Creation, there is room only for a *game*, that is, the very slight amplitude the constructor allows his pieces in which to move. This game is reason. It is capricious—i.e., it attests to no direction of history: reason appears, disappears, with no other law than the very personal effort of certain minds: among the benefits of history (useful inventions, great works) there is a relation of contiguity, never of function. Voltaire's opposition to any intelligence of time is very intense. For Voltaire, there is no history in the modern sense of the word, nothing but chronologies. Voltaire wrote historical works expressly to say that he did not believe in history: the age of Louis XIV is not an organism, it is a cluster of chance meetings, here the dragonnades, there Racine. Nature itself, of course, is never historical: being essentially art, i.e., God's artifice, it cannot move or have moved: the mountains were not wrought by the earth and the waters, God created them once and for all for the use of His creatures, and the fossil fishes—whose discovery so excited the age—are only the prosaic leavings of picnicking pilgrims: there is no evolution.

The philosophy of time will be the contribution of the nineteenth century (and singularly of Germany). We might assume that the relativist lesson of the past is at least replaced in Voltaire, as in his entire age, by that of space. At first glance, this is what occurs: the eighteenth century is not only a great age of travel, the age in which modern capitalism, then preponderantly British, definitively organizes its world market from China to South America; it is above all the age when travel accedes to literature and engages a philosophy. We know the role of the Jesuits, by their *Edifying and Curious Letters*, in the birth of exoticism. From early in the century, these materials were transformed and soon produced a veritable typology of exotic man: we have the Egyptian Sage, the Mohammedan Arab, the Turk, the Chinese, the Siamese, and, most prestigious of all, the Persian. All these Orientals are philosophy teachers; but before saying which philosophy, we must note that just when Voltaire begins writing his Tales, which owe a great deal to Oriental folklore, the century has already elaborated a veritable rhetoric of exoticism, a kind of digest whose figures are so well formed and so well known that they can henceforth be utilized without troubling further over descriptions and astonishments; Voltaire will not fail to utilize them in this fashion, for he never troubled to be "original" (an entirely modern notion, moreover); for him, as indeed for any of his contemporaries, the Oriental is not the object, the term of a genuine consideration, but simply a cipher, a convenient sign of communication.

The result of this conceptualization is that the Voltairean journey has no density; the space Voltaire covers so obsessively (we do nothing but travel in his Tales) is not an explorer's space, it is a surveyor's space, and what Voltaire borrows from the allogeneous humanity of the Chinese and the Persian is a new limit, not a new substance; new habitations are attributed to the human essence, it flourishes from the Seine to the Ganges, and Voltaire's novels are less investigations than inspections of an owner whom we "orient" in no particular order because his estate never varies, and whom we interrupt by incessant stops during which we discuss not what we have seen but what we are. This explains why the Voltairean journey is neither realistic nor baroque (the picaresque vein of the century's first narratives has completely dried up); it is not even an operation of knowledge, but merely of affirmation; it is the element of a logic, the figure of an equation; these Oriental countries, which today have so heavy a weight, so pronounced an individuation in world politics, are for Voltaire so many forms, mobile signs without actual content, humanity at zero degrees (Centigrade), which one nimbly grasps in order to signify . . . oneself.

For such is the paradox of Voltairean travel: to manifest an immobility. There are of course other manners, other laws, other moralities than ours, and this is what the journey teaches; but this diversity belongs to the human essence and consequently finds its point of equilibrium very rapidly; it is enough to acknowledge it in order to be done with it: let man (that is, Occidental man) multiply himself a little, let the European philosopher be doubled by the Chinese Sage, the ingenious Huron, and universal man will be created. To aggrandize oneself in order to confirm, not in order to transform oneself—such is the meaning of the Voltairean voyage.

It was doubtless Voltaire's second happiness to be able to depend upon the world's immobility. The bourgeoisie was so close to power that it could already begin not to believe in history. It could also begin to reject any system, to suspect any organized philosophy, that is, to posit its own thinking, its own good sense as a Nature which any doctrine, any intellectual system would offend. This is what Voltaire did so brilliantly, and it was his third happiness: he ceaselessly dissociated intelligence and intellectuality, asserting that the world is an order if we do not try too much to order it, that it is a system if only we renounce systematizing it: this conduct of mind has had a great career subsequently: today we call it anti-intellectualism.

Notable is the fact that all of Voltaire's enemies could be named, that is, their being derived from their certainty: Jesuits, Jansenists, Socinians, Protestants, atheists, all enemies among themselves, but united under Voltaire's attack by their capacity to be defined by a word. Conversely, on the level of denominative systems, Voltaire escapes. Doctrinally, was he a deist? a Leibnizian? a rationalist? Each time, yes and no. He has no system except the hatred of system (and we know that there is nothing grimmer than this very system); today his enemies would be the doctrinaires of history, of science (*vide* his mockery of pure science in *The Man with Forty Ecus*), or of existence; Marxists, existentialists, leftist intellectuals— Voltaire would have hated them, covered them with incessant *lazzi*, as he did the Jesuits in his own day. By continuously setting intelligence against intellectuality, by using one to undermine the other, by reducing the conflicts of ideas to a kind of Manichean struggle between stupidity and intelligence, by identifying all system with stupidity and all freedom of mind with intelligence, Voltaire grounded liberalism on a contradiction. As system of the nonsystem, anti-intellectualism eludes and gains on both counts, perpetually ricocheting between bad faith and good conscience, between a pessimism of substance and a jig of form, between a proclaimed skepticism and a terrorist doubt.

The Voltairean festivity is constituted by this incessant alibi. Voltaire cudgels and dodges at the same time. The world is simple for a man who ends all his letters with the cordial salutation *Ecrasons l'infâme* (i.e., dogmatism). We know that this simplicity and this happiness were bought at the price of an ablation of history and of an immobilization of the world. Further, it is a happiness which excluded many, despite its dazzling victory over obscurantism. Thus, in accord with the legend, the anti-Voltaire is indeed Rousseau. By forcefully positing the idea of man's corruption by society, Rousseau set history moving again, established the principle of a permanent transcendence of history. But by doing so he bequeathed to literature a poisoned legacy. Henceforth, ceaselessly athirst and wounded by a responsibility he can never again completely honor or completely elude, the intellectual will be defined by his bad conscience: Voltaire was a happy writer, but doubtless the last.

1958

Buffet Finishes Off New York

Bᴇʀɴᴀʀᴅ ʙᴜꜰꜰᴇᴛ's New York will not unsettle many preju-
dices: it is a city of geometric heights, a petrified desert of
grids and lattices, an inferno of greenish abstraction under a
flat sky, a real Metropolis from which man is absent by his
very accumulation; the implicit morality of our new Greuze is
that we are distinctly happier in Belleville than in Manhattan.
This is a folklore New York rather like Bizet's Spain or the
Italy of the Théâtre Mogador: an exoticism which confirms the
Frenchman in the excellence of his habitat.

According to Buffet, the architecture of this city is uniformly
longiform and quadrangular. Here the grid reigns under its
most ill-favored aspect: the contour, this black line which encloses everything, obviously intends to expel man from the
city. By obsessively multiplying the window, by inlaying it
with black, Buffet empties it, destroys it, makes the living
edifice into a dead surface, as if number, unless it is swarming,
must fatally establish an abstract order; Buffet geometrizes
New York the better to depopulate it: everyone knows that
abstraction is "sterile." Now, to my sense of it, one of the

From *The Eiffel Tower and Other Mythologies*, translated by Richard
Howard (New York: Hill and Wang, 1979).

lessons of this marvelous city is that abstraction is alive, and it must paradoxically be a painter who denies us this truth. But no doubt only an "abstract" painter could do justice to New York, could understand that planes and lines, form and meaning are as intensely alive here as in one of Mondrian's compositions: here figuration cunningly serves to destroy: to paint is to deceive. Buffet has "figured" New York in order to get rid of it.

The same aggression is to be noted with regard to the city's great commonplace, the skyscraper. What is astonishing about the skyscraper is that it does not astonish. When we actually see one (but do we ever see one, actually?), the feeling it inspires is: *why not?* For Buffet, on the contrary, the skyscraper always seems to remain in an anthological state, and this is always what he presents, refining on the needle, that obsessive shape of his thin and angular style. As if his very canvas, in its material proportions, *makes* the skyscraper; for him the skyscraper is a Being, and a prejudged one. Of course Buffet is sometimes sensitive to the city's magnificent *breadth*, to the scope of its *base* (for New York is a splendidly *set* city, like all fabulous metropolises); hence he paints a veritable façade of structures, he sees New York full-face, which is a good way of freeing himself from it, or he suspends the great scroll of a bridge in his foreground; but even in these efforts at enlargement, height surreptitiously reappears: the panorama spreads out the skyscrapers only to profile them in a jerky succession, the bridge dominates them only to manifest their aggressive vigor in the distance. There is a mythic combat here between *the Base and the Summit*, as Char says; but instead of altitude being absorbed in the foreground mass (for New York is in fact a deep city, not a high one), Buffet bequeaths it his absurd solitude; he paints the skyscrapers as if they were empty cathedrals: he flattens the "landscape."

Buffet finishes off New York by depopulating the streets. I

am not saying that the truth of New York is a *swarm*, which is a Neapolitan, a European notion. Urbanism itself, this checkerboard of nameless streets, is the price that has to be paid in order that the streets be useful and no longer picturesque, in order that men and objects circulate, adapt themselves to the distances, rule effectively over this enormous urban nature: the biggest city in the world (with Tokyo) is also the one we possess in an afternoon, by the most exciting of operations, since here *to possess* is *to understand*: New York exposes itself to intellection, and our familiarity with it comes very quickly. This is the purpose of these numbered streets, inflexibly distributed according to regular distances: not to make the city into a huge machine and man into an automaton, as we are repeatedly and stupidly told by those for whom tortuosity and dirt are the gauges of spirituality, but on the contrary to master the distances and orientations by the mind, to put at one man's disposal the space of these twelve million, this fabulous reservoir, this world emporium in which *all* goods exist except the metaphysical variety. This is the purpose of New York's geometry: that each individual should be *poetically* the owner of the capital of the world. It is not up, toward the sky, that you must look in New York; it is down, toward men and merchandise: by an admirable static paradox, the skyscraper establishes the block, the block creates the street, the street offers itself to man. Buffet of course proceeds in the opposite direction: he empties the street, climbs up the façades, grazes the surfaces, he rarefies: his New York is an anti-city.

To paint New York from above, at the top, is to rely once again on the first spiritualist myth, i.e., that geometry kills man. In his way, Buffet follows in the wake of our venerable moralists, for whom the refrigerator is antipathetic to the soul. The intentional desolation of his New York—what can it mean except that it is bad for man to live in groups, that number kills the spirit, that too many bathrooms are harmful to the spiritual health of a nation, that a world that is too "modern" is a sinister world, that we are bored when we are comfortable, in short, according to the most reactionary remark of human history, the alibi of all exploitations, that "money doesn't make happiness"? Myself, I can readily imagine that working in New York is a terrible thing, but it is not New York which is terrible, it is work. By making this city into a petrified, infantile necropolis looming up out of an "abstract" age (but not, alas! out of an abstract art), Buffet once again diverts history into metaphysics. Black looks at America always begin with the skyscrapers, and stick there. Yet what the Pilgrims unloaded from the *Mayflower* was not only empiricism, the spirit of enterprise, in short the seed which has doubtless produced the most stupendous city in the world, but also Puritanism and profit, money and metaphysics. What is good, Buffet discredits. And what is bad, he passes over in silence.

1959

Tacitus and
the Funerary Baroque

COUNTED, the murders in the *Annals* are few enough (some fifty for three principates); but read, their effect is apocalyptic: from element to mass, a new quality appears, the world is transformed.[1] Perhaps that is what the baroque is: a growing contradiction between unit and totality, an art in which extent is not additive but multiplicative, in short, the density of an acceleration: In Tacitus, from year to year, death *gels*, and the more divided the moments of this solidification become, the more inseparable their sum: generic Death is massive, not conceptual; the idea, here, is not the product of a reduction, but of a repetition. We know of course that terrorism is not a quantitative phenomenon; we know that during our Revolution the number of tortures was laughable; but we also know that for the next century, from Büchner to Jouve (I am thinking of his preface to selections from Danton), we have seen terrorism as a being, not a volume. A stoic during an enlightened despotism, a creature of the Flavians writing under Trajan the history of the Julio-Claudian tyranny,

From *Critical Essays*.

[1] "In the ninth year of the emperor's reign, Fortune suddenly deranged everything: Tiberius became a cruel tyrant, as well as an abettor of cruelty in others" (IV.1).

Tacitus is in the situation of a liberal living the atrocities of sans-culottism: for him the past is an hallucination, an obsessional theater, a scene even more than a lesson: death is a protocol.

And first of all, in order to destroy number starting from number, what must be paradoxically established is the unit. In Tacitus the great anonymous slaughters scarcely rank as facts, they are not values: such things are always slave massacres: collective death is not human, death begins only with the individual, in other words, with the patrician. Tacitean death always discloses a civil status; the victim holds office, he is a unit, *one*, enclosing his history, his character, his function, his name. Death itself is not algebraic: death is always a dying; it is almost never an effect; however rapidly evoked, death appears as a duration, a process to be relished; we can tell from certain vibrations of the sentence that each victim knew he was dying; Tacitus always gives this ultimate consciousness to the victims of torture, which is probably how he establishes these deaths in terrorism: because he cites man at the purest moment of his end; it is the contradiction between object and subject, between thing and consciousness, it is this final stoic suspense which makes dying a strictly human act: we kill like animals, we die like men: all the deaths in Tacitus are instants, both immobility and catastrophe, both silence and vision.

The act outshines its cause: there is no distinction between murder and suicide, it is the same dying, sometimes administered, sometimes prescribed: the presentation of death establishes death; whether the centurion delivers a blow or an order, it suffices that he appear, like an angel, for the irreversible to occur: the instant is there, the outcome accedes to the present. All these murders have scarcely any causes: delation is enough—a kind of death ray which works by remote control: crime is immediately absorbed into its magical denomination: once you are called guilty, by anyone, you are already doomed; innocence raises no problem, once you are branded. Moreover, it is because death is a raw fact, and not the element of a reason, that it is contagious: the wife follows her husband into suicide without being obliged to do so, relatives die in clusters as soon as one of them is condemned.[2] For those who fling themselves into it—like Gribouille, who leaps into the river to avoid the rain—death is life because it puts an end to the ambiguity of signs, it shifts us from the unnamed to the named. The act yields to its name: if the law forbids killing a virgin, then it suffices to rape her before strangling her: it is the name which is rigid, it is the name which is the order of the world. To accede to the security of the fatal name, the reprieved or pardoned person commits suicide. Not to die is not only an accident but a negative, almost a ridiculous state: it occurs only by inadvertence. Supreme reason of this absurd structure, Cocceius Nerva enumerates all his reasons for living (he is neither poor, nor ill, nor under suspicion), and despite the emperor's objurgations, he kills himself. And as a crowning confusion, the *Ratio*, eliminated at the moment of the irreparable, is restored *after the fact*: dead, the victim is paradoxically extracted from the funereal universe, introduced into a trial where death is not certain: Nero would have pardoned him, he says, if he had lived; or again, the victim is given a choice of demise; or yet again, the suicide's corpse is strangled so that his estate may be confiscated.

Since dying is a protocol, the victim is always shown in the decor of life: one dreaming on a promontory, another at table, another in his garden, another in his bath. Once death is presented, it is suspended a moment: we perform our toilet, we

[2] Vetus, his mother-in-law, and his daughter: "Then, in the same chamber, with the same weapon, they sundered their veins and hurried into a bath, covered each, as delicacy required, with a single garment . . ." (XVI.11).

visit our pyre, we recite verses, we add a codicil to our will: this is the complimentary interval of last words, the interval in which death utters itself. When the act occurs, it is always absorbed into an object: it is death's object which is there, death is *praxis, technē*, its mode is instrumental: dagger, sword, cudgel, noose, razor for opening veins, poisoned feather for tickling the throat, wadding chewed by the man dying of hunger, blankets for smothering, cliff from which the victim is thrown, ceiling which falls in (Agrippina), garbage cart in which escape is vain (Messalina)—death always employs the mild substance of life: wood, metal, cloth, innocent tools. In order to be destroyed, the body makes contact, exposes itself, seeks out the object's murderous function hidden under its instrumental surface: this world of terrorism is a world which has no need of the scaffold: it is the object which momentarily abandons its vocation, lends itself to death, supports it.

To die, in Tacitus, is to perceive life. Whence "the fashionable manner": to open the veins or have them opened, to make death liquid, in other words, to convert it to duration and purification: one sprinkles the gods and the bystanders with blood, death is a libation; it is suspended, procrastinated, and one exerts a capricious freedom over it at the very heart of its final fatality—like Petronius opening and closing his veins at will; like Paulina, Seneca's wife, rescued on Nero's orders and retaining for years, in the pallor of her drained face, the very sign of a communication with the void. For this world of dying signifies that death is both easy and resistant: it is ubiquitous and yet eludes; no one escapes it and yet it must be wrestled with, its means must be accumulated, hemlock added to bloodletting and the steam bath, the act ceaselessly retraced, like a drawing consisting of several lines whose final beauty derives both from the multiplication and the rectitude of the essential outline.

For perhaps that is what the baroque is: the torment of a finality in profusion. Tacitean death is an open system, subject at once to a structure and a contestation, to a repetition and a direction; it seems to proliferate on all sides and yet remains imprisoned in a great moral and existential intention. Here again, it is the vegetable image which substantiates the baroque: the deaths correspond, but their symmetry is false. Spread out in time, subject to a movement, like that of sprouts on the same stalk: the regularity is a delusion, life directs the funerary system, terrorism is not bookkeeping but vegetation: everything is reproduced and yet nothing is repeated; such is perhaps the meaning of this Tacitean universe, in which the brilliant description of the phoenix (VI.28) seems to construe death symbolically as the purest moment of life.

1959

PART TWO

from *On Racine*

1. THE STRUCTURE

THERE are three Mediterraneans in Racine: Classical, Hebrew, and Byzantine. But poetically, these three spaces form only a single complex of water, dust, and fire. The great tragic sites are arid lands, squeezed between the sea and the desert, shade and sun raised to the absolute state. One need merely visit Greece today to understand the violence of limitation, and how much Racinian tragedy, by its "constrained" nature, corresponds to these sites Racine had never seen: Thebes, Buthrotum, Troezen—these capitals of tragedy are villages. Troezen, where Phaedra dies, is a scorched knoll fortified by rubble. The sun produces a landscape that is pure, distinct, depopulated; life is without shade, which is simultaneously repose, secrecy, exchange, and flaw. Even outside the house, there is no real breath of air: there is the scrub, the desert, an unorganized space. The Racinian habitat knows only one dream of flight: the sea, the ships; in *Iphigénie*, a whole people remains imprisoned by the tragedy because the wind fails to rise.

On Racine, translated by Richard Howard (New York: Hill and Wang, 1964).

The Chamber

This geography sustains a special relation between the house and its exterior, between the Racinian palace and its hinterland. Although there is only one setting, according to the rules, one might say that there are three tragic sites. There is first of all the Chamber: vestige of the mythic cave, it is the invisible and dreadful place where Power lurks: Nero's throne room, Ahasuerus' palace, the Holy of Holies where the God of the Jews lives. This cavern has a frequent substitute: the King's exile, portentous because no one ever knows if the King is living or dead (Amurath, Mithridates, Theseus). The characters speak of this undefined site only with respect and terror, they scarcely dare enter it, they pass before it with anxiety. The Chamber is both the abode of Power and its essence, for Power is only a secret: its form exhausts its function, it kills by being invisible. In *Bajazet* it is the mutes and black Orcan who deal out death, extend by silence and darkness the terrible inertia of the hidden Power.[1]

The Chamber is contiguous to the second tragic site, which is the Antechamber, the eternal space of all subjections, since it is here that one *waits*. The Antechamber (the stage proper) is a medium of transmission; it partakes of both interior and exterior, of Power and Event, of the concealed and the exposed. Fixed between the world, a place of action, and the Chamber, a place of silence, the Antechamber is the site of language: it is here that tragic man, lost between the letter and

---

[1] The function of the throne room, the Royal Chamber, is well expressed in these lines from *Esther*:

Au fond de leur palais leur majesté terrible
Affecte à leurs sujets de se rendre invisible;
Et la mort est le prix de tout audacieux.
Qui sans être appelé se présente à leurs yeux. (I,3)

Their dread majesty elects to remain deep within their palace, invisible to their subjects; and death is the reward of any intruder who is seen there without being summoned.

the meaning of things, utters his reasons. The tragic stage is therefore not strictly secret;[2] it is rather a blind alley, the anxious passage from secrecy to effusion, from immediate fear to fear expressed. It is a trap suspected, which is why the posture the tragic character must adopt within it is always of an extreme mobility (in Greek tragedy, it is the chorus that waits, that moves in the circular space, or orchestra, in front of the palace).

Between the Chamber and the Antechamber stands a tragic object which menacingly expresses both contiguity and exchange, the tangency of hunter and prey: the Door. Here one waits, here one trembles; to enter it is a temptation and a transgression: Agrippina stakes all her power at Nero's door. The Door has an active substitute, necessary when the Power wants to spy on the Antechamber or paralyze the character within it, and this is the Veil (*Britannicus, Esther, Athalie*). The Veil (or the Wall that has ears) is not an inert substance intended to conceal, it is an eyelid, symbol of the masked gaze, so that the Antechamber is a site-object encircled by a space-subject. The Racinian stage is thus a spectacle twice over: to the eyes of the Invisible and to the eyes of the spectator (the site that best expresses this tragic contradiction is the Seraglio of *Bajazet*).

The third tragic site is the Exterior. Between Antechamber and Exterior, there is no transition; they are joined as immediately as the Antechamber and the Chamber. This contiguity is expressed poetically by the "linear" nature of the tragic enclosure: the palace walls plunge down into the sea, the stairs lead to the ships ready to sail, the ramparts are a balcony above the battle itself, and if there are hidden passages, they no longer constitute part of the tragedy, they are already Flight. Thus the line that separates tragedy from its negation is

---

[2] On the enclosure of the Racinian site, see Bernard Dort, *Huis clos racinien*.

thin, almost abstract; what is involved is a *limit*, in the ritual sense of the word: the tragedy is simultaneously prison and protection against impurity, against all that is not itself.

The three exterior spaces: death, escape, event

The Exterior is in fact the site of non-tragedy; it contains three kinds of space: that of death, that of escape, that of the event. Physical death never belongs to tragic space: this is reputedly for reasons of propriety;[3] but what propriety rejects in carnal death is an element alien to tragedy, an "impurity," the density of a reality scandalous because it no longer proceeds from the order of language, which is the only tragic order: in tragedy one never dies because one is always talking. And conversely, for the hero, to leave the stage is to die, one way or another. Roxanne's *Go!*'s to Bajazet are death sentences, and this movement is the model of a whole series of exits in which it is enough for the executioner to dismiss or banish his prey to cause death, as if the mere contact with the outer air was enough to dissolve or blast: how many Racinian victims die because they are no longer protected by this tragic site which nonetheless, they said, made them suffer mortally (Britannicus, Bajazet, Hippolytus). The essential image of this exterior death, in which the victim slowly suffocates out of the tragic air, is the Berenician Orient, which interminably summons the heroes into non-tragedy. More generally, transplanted outside the tragic space, Racinian man *languishes* (*s'ennuie*): he experiences all real space as a succession of chains (Orestes, Antiochus, Hippolytus): here suffering is evidently a substitute for death: all behavior that suspends language causes life to stop.

The second exterior space is that of escape: but escape is never named except by the inferior caste of friends and ser-

---

[3] Atalide *kills herself* on stage but *expires* off. Nothing illustrates better the disjunction of gesture and reality.

vants; the confidants and minor figures (Acomat, Zares) constantly recommend escape to the hero on one of those countless ships that cruise in front of every Racinian tragedy,
representing how immediate and how easy its negation is[4]
(there is only one ship-prison in Racine, the one on which the
captive Eriphyle falls in love with her ravisher). The Exterior,
moreover, is a space ritually transmitted, that is, entrusted and
assigned to all the non-tragic personnel, like a kind of reverse
ghetto, since it is the amplitude of space that is taboo here,
confinement that is a privilege: it is to and from the Exterior
that this race of confidants, servants, messengers, matrons,
and guards come and go, responsible for feeding tragedy with
events: their entrances and exits are tasks, not signs or acts. In
that infinite (and infinitely sterile) conclave which is every
tragedy, they are the officious secretaries who preserve the
hero from profane contact with reality, spare him what might
be called the trivial kitchenry of *doing*, and transmit the event
to him only when it is pared down, reduced to the state of pure
cause. This is the third function of exterior space: to keep
action in a kind of quarantine accessible only to a neutral
population responsible for sifting events, extracting the tragic
essence from each and bringing on stage only fragments of the
external world, distilled as *news*, ennobled as *narratives* (battles, suicides, returns, murders, feasts, miracles). Confronting
this exclusive order of language which is tragedy, action is
impurity itself.

    Moreover, nothing indicates better the physical disparity of
the two kinds of space, internal and external, than a curious
phenomenon of temporal distortion that Racine has described

---

[4] *Nos vaisseaux sont tout prêts et le vent nous appelle . . . (And.* III,1)
Our ships are ready and the wind favorable . . .
Des vaisseaux dans Ostie armés en diligence . . . (Bér. I,3)
Ships hastily armed in Ostia . . .
Déjà sur un vaisseau dans le port préparé . . . (Baj. III,2)
Already on a ship made ready in the harbor . . .

typically in *Bajazet*: between exterior time and confined time occurs the time the message takes, so that one is never certain the event reported is the same as the event produced. The external event is actually never *finite*, it does not complete its transformation into pure cause. Confined in the Antechamber, receiving from the world outside only the nourishment brought to him by the confidant, the hero lives in an irremediable uncertainty: he *misses* the event. There is always too much time, the time of space itself. This quite Einsteinian problem constitutes most of the tragic action.[5] In short, Racinian topography is convergent; everything leads to the tragic site, but everything is locked there. The tragic site is *stupefied,* caught between two fears, two hallucinations: that of extent and that of depth.

The horde

This, then, is a first definition of the tragic hero: he is a man confined, a man who cannot *get out* without dying; his limit is his privilege, captivity his distinction. Take away the servant class, paradoxically defined by its very freedom, and what is left in the tragic site? A caste glorious in proportion to its immobility. Where does it come from?

---

[5] *Mais, comme vous savez, malgré ma diligence,*
Un long chemin sépare et le camp et Byzance;
Mille obstacles divers m'ont même traversé,
Et je puis ignorer tout ce qui s'est passé. (Baj. I,1)

But, as you know, for all my haste, the road between the camp and Byzantium is a long one; a thousand different obstacles lay in my path, and I may know nothing of all that has occurred.

Ce combat doit, dit-on, fixer nos destinées;
Et même, si d'Osmin je compte les journées,
Le Ciel en a déjà réglé l'événement,
Et le Sultan triomphe ou fuit en ce moment. (Baj. I,2)

This battle is supposed to settle our fate; and even if I number Osmin's days, Heaven has already settled the outcome, and the Sultan triumphs or flees at this moment.

Darwin, Atkinson, and later Freud (in *Totem and Taboo*) have suggested that in the earliest period of our history, men lived in savage hordes. Each horde was subject to the most powerful male, who possessed women, children, and property without distinction. The sons were dispossessed of everything, for the father's strength prevented them from obtaining the sisters or mothers whom they coveted. If the sons happened to provoke the father's jealousy, they were pitilessly killed, castrated, or driven out. Hence, according to these authors, the sons ultimately banded together to kill the father and take his place. Once the father was out of the way, discord broke out among the sons; they quarreled bitterly over his inheritance, and it was only after a long period of fratricidal struggles that they managed to establish a rational alliance among themselves: each renounced his desire for his mother or sisters: the incest taboo was instituted.

Such a history, even if it is only a "romance," is the whole of Racine's theater. If we make one essential tragedy out of eleven, if we arrange in a kind of exemplary constellation this tribe of some fifty tragic characters who inhabit Racinian tragedy, we shall discover the figures and the actions of the primeval horde: the father, unconditional master of the sons' lives (Amurath, Mithridates, Agamemnon, Theseus, Mordecai, Jehoiada, even Agrippina); the women, simultaneously mothers, sisters, and mistresses, always coveted, rarely obtained (Andromache, Junia, Atalide, Monimia); the brothers, always enemies because they are quarreling over the inheritance of a father who is not quite dead and who returns to punish them (Eteocles and Polynices, Nero and Britannicus, Pharnaces and Xiphares); lastly, the son, mortally torn between terror of the father and the necessity of destroying him (Pyrrhus, Nero, Titus, Pharnaces, Athaliah). Incest, rivalry among the brothers, murder of the father, overthrow of the sons—these are the fundamental actions of the Racinian theater.

We are not certain just what is being represented here. Is it, as in Darwin's hypothesis, an extremely early folklore theme, the virtually asocial state of humanity? Is it, as in Freud's hypothesis, the primal history of the psyche, reproduced in the childhood of every man? I merely observe that the Racinian theater finds its coherence only on the level of this ancient fable, situated far beyond history or the human psyche:[6] the purity of the language, the grace of the alexandrines, the precision of the "psychology," the conformism of the metaphysics are very slight protections; the archaic bedrock is there, close at hand. This original action is not performed by *characters*, in the modern sense of the word; Racine, with the age, called them much more appositely *actors*; we are dealing, essentially, with masks, with figures that differ from each other not according to their public status but according to their place in the general configuration that keeps them confined; sometimes it is their function that distinguishes them (father opposed to son, for instance), sometimes it is their degree of emancipation with regard to the most regressive figure of their lineage (Pyrrhus represents a more independent son than Nero, Pharnaces than Xiphares, Titus than Antiochus; Hermione represents a fidelity less supple than Andromache's). Thus the Racinian discourse affords great masses of undifferentiated language, as if, through different speeches, a single person were expressing himself; in relation to such profound utterance, the extremely pure contour of the Racinian language functions as a veritable command; here language is aphoristic, not realistic; it is expressly intended for quotation.

---

[6] "Racine paints a man for us not as he is, but somewhat beneath and beside himself, at the moment when the other members of his family, the doctor, and the magistrates would in fact begin to be concerned, if it were not just a play." (Charles Mauron, *L'Inconscient dans l'œuvre et la vie de Racine.*)

The double Eros

The tragic unit is thus not the individual but the figure, or, better still, the function which defines that figure. In the primeval horde, human relations fall into two chief categories: the relation of lust and the relation of authority; it is these that recur obsessively in Racine.

The Racinian Eros is double. The first Eros is born between lovers who share a very early community of existence: they have been raised together, love each other (or one loves the other) from childhood (Britannicus and Junia, Antiochus and Berenice, Bajazet and Atalide); here love is generated by duration, a gradual maturation process; there is, then, a mediation between the two partners, a mediation of time, of the past, in short, of legality: it is the parents themselves who have established the legitimacy of this love. The beloved woman is a sister for whom lust is authorized and consequently appeased; such love might be called the sororal Eros; its future is tranquil, for it is thwarted only by what is outside itself; its success appears to derive from its very origin: because it has consented to start from a mediation, misfortune is not fatal to it.

The other Eros, on the contrary, is an immediate one; it is born abruptly; its generation admits of no latency, it appears in the manner of an absolute Event, which is usually expressed by a brutal *passé défini* (*je le vis, elle me plut,* etc.). This Eros-Event is the one that attaches Nero to Junia, Berenice to Titus, Roxanne to Bajazet, Eriphyle to Achilles, Phaedra to Hippolytus. The hero is seized by it, bound as in a rape, and this capture is always of a visual order (we shall return to this matter): to love is to see. This double Eros is incompatible, one cannot proceed from one to the other, from love-as-rape (which is always condemned) to love-as-duration (which is always coveted), and this impossibility constitutes one of the

fundamental forms of Racinian failure. Of course, the unsuc-
cessful lover can always try to replace the immediate Eros
by a substitute; he can, for instance, enumerate the reasons to
which he is appealing;[7] he can try to introduce a mediation
into this relation, can appeal to causality; he can suppose that
merely by seeing him often enough, his beloved will come to
love him, that coexistence, the basis of sororal love, will ultimately produce that love. But these are, precisely, *reasons*—
that is, a language destined to mask an inevitable failure. The
sororal Eros is actually given as a utopia, far in the past or in
the future, whose institutional version will be marriage (so
important for Racine). The true Eros, the one that is *painted*,
in other words immobilized in the tragic tableau, is the immediate Eros. And precisely because this is a predatory Eros, it
supposes an entire physics, or strictly speaking an *optics* of the
image.

We know nothing of the age or the beauty of the Racinian
lovers. Periodically, critics debate whether Phaedra is very
young, if Nero is an adolescent, if Berenice is middle-aged, if
Mithridates is still attractive. We know of course the norms of
the period; we know that "one could declare one's love to a
girl of fourteen without her being rightly offended thereby,"
and that "a woman is ugly after she has lived thirty years."
But this matters little. Racinian beauty is abstract in that it is
always *named*: Racine says that Bajazet is lovable, that
Berenice has beautiful hands; the concept somehow gets rid of

---

[7] *Ouvrez les yeux, Seigneur, et songeons entre nous
Par combien de raisons Bérénice est à vous.* (*Bér.* III,2)

Open your eyes, my lord, and consider here the reasons why Berenice belongs
to you.

*Quoi! Madame, les soins qu'il a pris pour vous plaire,
Ce que vous avez fait, ce que vous pouvez faire,
Ses périls, ses respects, et surtout vos appas,
Tout cela de son cœur ne vous répond-il pas?* (*Baj.* I,3)

But, my lady, think of all he has done to please you, and all you have done,
all you can do still, his dangers, his respect, and most of all your own
beauty—does all this not answer for his heart?

the thing.[8] We might say that here beauty is a propriety, a class characteristic, not an anatomical disposition: no effort is made toward what might be called the body's *adjectivity*.

Yet the Racinian Eros (at least the immediate Eros, which will henceforth be our concern here) is never sublimated; emerging fully armed, entirely *finished*, from pure vision, it is immobilized in the perpetual fascination of the adverse body, it constantly reproduces the original scene that has formed it (Berenice, Phaedra, Eriphyle, Nero *relive* the birth of their love[9]); the recital these heroes make of it to their confidant is obviously not a matter of information but a veritable obsessive protocol. Moreover it is because love, in Racine, is a pure ordeal of fascination that it is so difficult to distinguish from hate; hate is openly physical, it is the acute sense of the other body. Like love, it is born from sight, feeds on it, and like love it produces a current of joy. Racine has given us the theory of this carnal hatred in his first play, *La Thébaïde*.[10]

What Racine expresses immediately, then, is alienation, not desire. This is evident if we examine Racinian sexuality, which is a sexuality of situation rather than of Nature. In Racine, sex itself is subject to the fundamental situation of the tragic figures among themselves, which is a relation of force. There

---

[8] *Cette fière princesse a percé son beau sein . . . (Théb.* V,5)
This proud princess has stabbed her lovely breast . . .

J'ai senti son beau corps tout froid entre mes bras . . . (V,5)
I felt his splendid body turn cold in my arms . . .

On sait qu'elle est charmante, et de si belles mains
Semblent vous demander l'empire des humains (Bér. II,2)
We know she is charming, and such beautiful hands seem to ask you for the throne

Bajazet est aimable; il vit que son salut . . . (Baj. I,2)
Bajazet is appealing; he saw that his survival . . .

[9] More generally, such narratives are not at all the dead wood of the tragedy; quite the contrary, they are the hallucinatory—that is, in a sense, the most profound—part.

[10] The theory of physical hatred is given in *La Thébaïde*, IV,1. The feudal system had sublimated the Eros of the adversaries by subjecting the duel to a knightly ritual. We find a trace of this sublimation in *Alexandre* (the conflict between Alexander and Porus); Alexander is chivalrous—but he is, precisely, outside the tragedy.

are no characters in the Racinian theater (which is why it is
quite futile to argue about the individuality of the *dramatis
personae*, to wonder whether Andromache is coquettish or
Bajazet virile); there are only situations, in the almost formal
sense of the word: everything derives its being from its place
in the general constellation of strengths and weaknesses. The
division of the Racinian world into strong and weak, into
tyrants and captives, covers in a sense the division of the
sexes: it is their situation in the relation of force that orches-
trates some characters as virile and others as feminine, without
concern for their biological sex. There are viriloid women
(they need merely participate in Power: Axiane, Agrippina,
Roxanne, Athaliah). There are feminoid men, not by character but by situation: Taxiles, whose cowardice is softness, accessibility to Alexander's strength; Bajazet, both captive and
coveted, doomed by a strictly Racinian alternative to murder
or to rape; Hippolytus, who is in Phaedra's power, desired by
her and a virgin as well (Racine tried to "defeminize" Hippolytus by making him Aricia's lover, but without success, as
the judgment of his contemporaries attests—the initial situation was too strong); lastly Britannicus, hated by Nero, is
nonetheless in a certain erotic relation with him, for it is
enough that hate coincide with Power for sex to be ambiguous;
Nero delights in Britannicus' suffering as in that of a woman
loved and tortured.[11] Here we find a first sketch of Racinian
fatality: a simple relation, in origin purely circumstantial
(captivity or tyranny), is converted into a biological datum;
situation is converted into sex, chance into essence.

The constellations change little in Racinian tragedy, and
sexuality is generally immobile. But if, by exception, the relation of force yields, if the tyranny weakens, sex itself tends to

---

[11] The erotic relation between Nero and Britannicus is explicit in Tacitus. As
for Hippolytus, Racine has made him Aricia's lover to keep the public from
taking him for an invert.

be modified, inverted. It is enough for Athaliah, the most virile of Racine's women, to become sensitive to Joash's "charm" and relax her power for her sexuality to be disturbed: once the constellation appears to be modified, a new division affects the character's being, a new sex appears, and Athaliah *becomes* a woman.[12] Inversely, those who are by condition outside any relation of force (that is, outside the tragedy) have no sex. Confidants, servants, advisers (Burrhus, for instance, is scornfully excluded from Eros by Nero[13]), never accede to sexual existence. And it is obviously in the most manifestly asexualized characters, matron (Oenone) or eunuch (Acomat), that the spirit most contrary to tragedy declares itself, the spirit of viability: only the absence of sex can authorize a definition of life not as a critical relation of forces, but as duration, and this duration as value. Sex is a tragic privilege insofar as it is the first attribute of the original conflict: it is not the sexes that create the conflict, it is the conflict that defines the sexes.

Disorder

Thus it is alienation that constitutes the Racinian Eros. As a consequence, the human body is not treated in plastic, but in magical terms. As we have seen, neither age nor beauty has any specificity here: the body is never given as an Apollonian object (for Racine, Apollonism is a canonical attribute of death, in which the body becomes a statue, that is, a glorified,

---

[12] *Ami, depuis deux jours, je ne la connais plus.*
Ce n'est plus cette reine éclairée, intrépide,
Elevée au-dessus de son sexe timide . . .
Elle flotte, elle hésite; en un mot, elle est femme. (*Ath.* III,3)

Friend, for the last two days I no longer recognize her. She is no longer that enlightened, fearless queen, raised above her timid sex. . . . She wavers, she hesitates; in a word, she is a woman.

[13] *Mais, croyez-moi, l'amour est une autre science,*
Burrhus; et je ferais quelque difficulté
D'abaisser jusque-là votre sévérité (*Brit.* III,1)

But love, believe me, is knowledge of another kind, Burrhus; and I should find it hard to reduce your severity to its level.

arranged past). The Racinian body is essentially disturbance, defection, disorder. Garments—which as we know extend the body in an equivocal way, both masking and flaunting it—are responsible for dramatizing the state of the body: they *weigh down* in transgression, they *come undone* in agitation; the implicit gesture, here, is *disrobing* (Phaedra, Berenice, Junia),[14] the simultaneous token of transgression and attraction, for in Racine carnal disorder is always a kind of blackmail, an attempt to compel pity (sometimes carried to the point of sadistic provocation).[15] This is the implicit function of all the physical disturbances so abundantly recorded by Racine: blushing, blanching, the abrupt succession of one and then the other, sighs, and finally tears, whose erotic power is so familiar. Here reality is always ambiguous, both expression and act, escape and blackmail: in short, the Racinian disorder is essentially a *sign*, that is, a signal and a commination.

The most spectacular agitation, that is, the one best suited to tragedy, is the kind that attacks Racinian man at his vital center, his language.[16] Suspension of speech, whose sexual nature has been suggested by certain authors, is very frequent in the Racinian hero; it perfectly expresses the sterility of the

---

[14] *Belle, sans ornements, dans le simple appareil*
D'une beauté qu'on vient d'arracher au sommeil. (Brit. II,2)
Lovely, unadorned, clad simply in her beauty torn from sleep.

Laissez-moi relever ces voiles détachés,
Et ces cheveux épars dont vos yeux sont cachés. (Bér. IV,2)
Let me bind these loosened veils, and smooth the hair that hides your eyes.

Que ces vains ornements, que ces voiles me pèsent! (Phèd. I,3)
How these vain adornments, how these veils weigh me down!

[15] *Laisse, laisse, Phénice, il verra son ouvrage . . . (Bér. IV,2)*
Leave me as I am, Phenice, he will see what he has done . . .

[16] Among others:
J'ai voulu lui parler, et ma voix s'est perdue . . . (Brit. II,2)
I tried to speak to her, and my voice failed . . .

Et dès le premier mot, ma langue embarrassée
Dans ma bouche vingt fois a demeuré glacée. (Bér. II,2)
And at the first word, my tongue froze in my mouth, however often I tried to speak.

Mes yeux ne voyaient plus, je ne pouvais parler . . . (Phèd. I,3)
My eyes went blind, I could not speak . . .

erotic relation, its immobility. To be able to break with Berenice, Titus turns aphasiac, in one and the same movement withdraws and apologizes. Here "I love you too much" and "I don't love you enough" find, economically enough, a common sign. To avoid speech is to avoid the relation of force, to avoid tragedy: only the extreme heroes can attain this limit (Nero, Titus, Phaedra), from which their tragic partner leads them back as quickly as possible, *constraining* them in a sense to recover a language (Agrippina, Berenice, Oenone). Muteness has a gestural analogy: the swoon, or at least its noble version, immobility. This is always a kind of bilingual act: as escape, such paralysis tends to deny the tragic order; as blackmail, it still participates in the relation of force. Each time a Racinian hero resorts to bodily disorder, we have the indication of a tragic bad faith: the hero *feints* with tragedy. All such behavior tends, in effect, to a frustration of tragic reality, being a rejection (an ambiguous one, moreover, since to reject tragedy may be to rediscover the world), a simulation of death, a paradoxical, even a useful death, since one comes back to life. Naturally, disorder is a privilege of the tragic hero, for he alone is engaged in a relation of force. The confidants may share the master's agitation—more often they attempt to calm it—but they never employ the ritual language of disorder: a handmaid does not faint. For example, the tragic hero cannot sleep (except if he is a monster, like Nero, whose sleep is wicked). Archas sleeps; Agamemnon lies awake, or better still, indulging in a noble—because tormented—form of repose, he dreams.

In short, the Racinian Eros brings bodies into confrontation only to destroy them. The sight of the adverse body disorders language,[17] troubles it, whether by exaggerating it (in the

---

[17] Naturally, the fascination of the adverse body also occurs in situations of hatred. Here is how Nero describes his relation to Agrippina:

Éloigné de ses yeux, j'ordonne, je menace . . .
Mais (je t'expose ici mon âme toute nue)

excessively rationalized harangues) or by silencing it. The Racinian hero never achieves *adequate* behavior toward the adverse body: real frequentation is always a failure. Then is there no moment when the Racinian Eros is happy? Yes, precisely when it is unreal. The adverse body confers happiness only when it is an image; the successful moments of Racinian Eros are always memories.

. . .

1960

Sitôt que mon malheur me ramène à sa vue,
Soit que je n'ose encor démentir le pouvoir
De ces yeux où j'ai lu si longtemps mon devoir . . .
Mais enfin mes efforts ne me servent de rien;
Mon génie étonné tremble, devant le sien. (*Brit.* II,2)

When she cannot see me, I threaten, command . . . But (I am showing you my heart laid bare) as soon as I am unlucky enough to be in her presence, I dare not dispute the power of those eyes that for so long defined my duty . . . All my efforts are futile: my awed spirit trembles before hers.

Authors and Writers

WHO speaks? Who writes? We still lack a sociology of language. What we know is that language is a power and that, from public body to social class, a group of men is sufficiently defined if it possesses, to various degrees, the national language. Now, for a very long time—probably for the entire classical capitalist period, i.e., from the sixteenth to the nineteenth century, in France—the uncontested owners of the language, and they alone, were authors; if we except preachers and jurists (enclosed moreover in functional languages), no one else spoke, and this "monopoly" of the language produced, paradoxically, a rigid order, an order less of producers than of production: it was not the literary profession which was structured (it has developed greatly in three hundred years, from the domestic poet to the businessman-writer), but the very substance of this literary discourse, subjected to rules of use, genre, and composition, more or less immutable from Marot to Verlaine, from Montaigne to Gide. Contrary to so-called primitive societies, in which there is witchcraft only through the agency of a witch doctor, as Mauss has shown, the literary institution transcended the literary functions, and

From *Critical Essays*.

within this institution, its essential raw material, language. Institutionally, the literature of France is its language, a half-linguistic, half-aesthetic system which has not lacked a mythic dimension as well, that of its clarity.

When, in France, did the author cease being the only one to speak? Doubtless at the time of the Revolution, when there first appear men who appropriate the authors' language for political ends. The institution remains in place: it is still a matter of that great French language, whose lexicon and euphony are respectfully preserved throughout the greatest paroxysm of French history; but the functions change, the personnel is increased for the next hundred years; the authors themselves, from Chateaubriand or Maistre to Hugo or Zola, help broaden the literary function, transform this institution-alized language of which they are still the acknowledged owners into the instrument of a new action; and alongside these authors in the strict sense of the word, a new group is constituted and develops, a new custodian of the public language. Intellectuals? The word has a complex resonance;[1] I prefer calling them here *writers*. And since the present may be that fragile moment in history where the two functions coexist, I should like to sketch a comparative typology of the author and the writer with reference to the substance they share: language.

The author performs a function, the writer an activity. Not that the author is a pure essence: he acts, but his action is immanent in its object, it is performed paradoxically on its own instrument: language; the author is the man who *labors*, who works up his utterance (even if he is inspired) and functionally absorbs himself in this labor, this work. His activity involves two kinds of norm: technical (of composition, genre, style) and artisanal (of patience, correctness, perfection). The

---

[1] Apparently the word *intellectual*, in the sense we give it today, was born at the time of the Dreyfus affair, obviously applied by the anti-Dreyfusards to the Dreyfusards.

paradox is that, the raw material becoming in a sense its own end, literature is at bottom a tautological activity, like that of those cybernetic machines constructed for themselves (Ashby's homeostat): the author is a man who radically absorbs the world's *why* in a *how to write*. And the miracle, so to speak, is that this narcissistic activity has always provoked an interrogation of the world: by enclosing himself in the *how to write*, the author ultimately discovers the open question par excellence: why the world? What is the meaning of things? In short, it is precisely when the author's work becomes its own end that it regains a mediating character: the author conceives of literature as an end, the world restores it to him as a means: and it is in this perpetual inconclusiveness that the author rediscovers the world, an alien world moreover, since literature represents it as a question—never, finally, as an answer.

Language is neither an instrument nor a vehicle: it is a structure, as we increasingly suspect; but the author is the only man, by definition, to lose his own structure and that of the world in the structure of language. Yet this language is an (infinitely) labored substance; it is a little like a superlanguage —reality is never anything but a pretext for it (for the author, *to write* is an intransitive verb); hence it can never explain the world, or at least, when it claims to explain the world, it does so only the better to conceal its ambiguity: once the explanation is fixed in a work, it immediately becomes an ambiguous product of the real, to which it is linked by perspective; in short, literature is always unrealistic, but its very unreality permits it to question the world—though these questions can never be direct: starting from a theocratic explanation of the world, Balzac finally does nothing but interrogate. Thus the author existentially forbids himself two kinds of language, whatever the intelligence or the sincerity of his enterprise: first, *doctrine*, since he converts despite himself, by his very project, every explanation into a spectacle: he is always an inductor of ambiguity;[2] second, *evidence*, since he has consigned himself to language, the author cannot have a naïve consciousness, cannot "work up" a protest without his message finally bearing much more on the working-up than on the protest: by identifying himself with language, the author loses all claim to truth, for language is precisely that structure whose very goal (at least historically, since the Sophists), once it is no longer rigorously transitive, is to neutralize the true and the false.[3] But what he obviously gains is the power to disturb the world, to afford it the dizzying spectacle of *praxis* without sanction. This is why it is absurd to ask an author for "commitment": a "committed" author claims simultaneous participation in two structures, inevitably a source of deception. What we can ask of an author is that he be responsible; again, let there be no mistake: whether or not an author is responsible for his opinions is unimportant; whether or not an author assumes, more or less intelligently, the ideological implications of his work is also secondary; an author's true responsibility is to support literature as a failed commitment, as a Mosaic glance at the Promised Land of the real (this is Kafka's responsibility, for example).

Naturally, literature is not a grace, it is the body of the projects and decisions which lead a man to fulfill himself (that is, in a sense, to essentialize himself) in language alone: an author is a man who wants to be an author. Naturally too, society, which consumes the author, transforms project into vocation, labor into talent, and technique into art: thus is born the myth of fine writing: the author is a salaried priest, he is the half-respectable, half-ridiculous guardian of the sanctuary

[2] An author can produce a system, but it will never be consumed as such.
[3] Structure of reality and structure of language: no better indication of the difficulty of a coincidence between the two than the constant failure of dialectic, once it becomes discourse: for language is not dialectic, it can only say "we must be dialectical," but it cannot be so itself: language is a representation without perspective, except precisely for the author's; but the author dialecticizes himself, he does not dialecticize the world.

of the great French language, a kind of national treasure, a sacred merchandise, produced, taught, consumed, and exported in the context of a sublime economy of values. This sacralization of the author's struggle with form has great consequences, and not merely formal ones: it permits society—or Society—to distance the work's content when it risks becoming an embarrassment, to convert it into pure spectacle, to which it is entitled to apply a liberal (i.e., an indifferent) judgment, to neutralize the revolt of passion, the subversion of criticism (which forces the "committed" author into an incessant and impotent provocation)—in short, to recuperate the author: every author is eventually digested by the literary institution, unless he scuttles himself, i.e., unless he ceases to identify his being with that of language: this is why so few authors renounce writing, for that is literally to kill themselves, to die to the being they have chosen; and if there are such authors, their silence echoes like an inexplicable conversion (Rimbaud).[4]

The *writer*, on the other hand, is a "transitive" man, he posits a goal (to give evidence, to explain, to instruct), of which language is merely a means; for him language supports a *praxis,* it does not constitute one. Thus language is restored to the nature of an instrument of communication, a vehicle of "thought." Even if the writer pays some attention to style, this concern is never ontological. The writer performs no essential technical action upon language; he employs an utterance common to all writers, a *koinē* in which we can of course distinguish certain dialects (Marxist, for example, or Christian, or existentialist), but very rarely styles. For what defines the writer is the fact that his project of communication is *naïve*: he does not admit that his message is reflexive, that it

---

[4] These are the modern elements of the problem. We know that on the contrary Racine's contemporaries were not at all surprised when he suddenly stopped writing tragedies and became a royal functionary.

closes over itself, and that we can read in it, diacritically, anything else but what he means: what writer would tolerate a psychoanalysis of his language? He considers that his work resolves an ambiguity, institutes an irreversible explanation (even if he regards himself as a modest instructor); whereas for the author, as we have seen, it is just the other way around: he knows that his language, intransitive by choice and by labor, inaugurates an ambiguity, even if it appears to be peremptory, that it offers itself, paradoxically, as a monumental silence to be deciphered, that it can have no other motto but Jacques Rigaut's profound remark: *and even when I affirm, I am still questioning.*

The author participates in the priest's role, the writer in the clerk's; the author's language is an intransitive act (hence, in a sense, a gesture), the writer's an activity. The paradox is that society consumes a transitive language with many more reservations than an intransitive one: the writer's status, even today when writers abound, is much more problematic than the author's. This is primarily the consequence of a material circumstance: the author's language is a merchandise offered through traditional channels, it is the unique object of an institution created only for literature; the writer's language, on the contrary, can be produced and consumed only in the shadow of institutions which have, originally, an entirely different function than to focus on language: the university, scientific and scholarly research, politics, etc. Then, too, the writer's language is dependent in another way: because it is (or considers itself) no more than a simple vehicle, its nature as merchandise is transferred to the project of which it is the instrument: we are presumed to sell "thought" exclusive of any art; now the chief mythic attribute of "pure" thought (it would be better to say "unapplied" thought) is precisely that it is produced outside the channel of money: contrary to form (which costs a lot, as Valéry said), thought costs nothing, but it also does not sell itself, it gives itself—generously. This points up at least two new differences between author and writer. First, the writer's production always has a free but also a somewhat "insistent" character: the writer offers society what society does not always ask of him: situated on the margin of institutions and transactions, his language appears paradoxically more individual, at least in its motifs, than the author's language: *the writer's function is to say at once and on every occasion what he thinks*;[5] and this function suffices, he thinks, to justify him; whence the critical, urgent aspect of the writer's language: it always seems to indicate a conflict between thought's irrepressible character and the inertia of a society reluctant to consume a merchandise which no specific institution normalizes. Thus we see *a contrario*—and this is the second difference—that the social function of literary language (that of the author) is precisely *to transform thought* (or consciousness, or protest) *into merchandise*; society wages a kind of vital warfare to appropriate, to acclimatize, to institutionalize the risk of thought, and it is language, that model institution, which affords it the means to do so: the paradox here is that "provocative" *language* is readily accommodated by the literary institution: the scandals of language, from Rimbaud to Ionesco, are rapidly and perfectly integrated; whereas "provocative" *thought*, insofar as it is to be immediate (without mediation), can only exhaust itself in the no man's land of form: the scandal is never total.

I am describing here a contradiction which, in fact, is rarely pure: everyone today moves more or less openly between the two postulations, the author's and the writer's; it is doubtless the responsibility of history which has brought us into the

---

[5] This function of *immediate manifestation* is the very opposite of the author's: (1) the author hoards, he publishes at a rhythm which is not that of his consciousness; (2) he mediatizes what he thinks by a laborious and "regular" form; (3) he permits a free interrogation of his work, he is anything but dogmatic.

world too late to be complacent authors and too soon (?) to be heeded writers. Today, each member of the intelligentsia harbors both roles in himself, one or the other of which he "retracts" more or less well: authors occasionally have the impulses, the impatiences of writers; writers sometimes gain access to the theater of language. We want *to write something,* and at the same time *we write* (intransitively). In short, our age produces a bastard type: the author-writer. His function is inevitably paradoxical: he provokes and exorcises at the same time; formally, his language is free, screened from the institution of literary language, and yet, enclosed in this very freedom, it secretes its own rules in the form of a common style; having emerged from the club of men-of-letters, the author-writer finds another club, that of the intelligentsia. On the scale of society as a whole, this new group has a complementary function: the intellectual's style functions as the paradoxical sign of a non-language, it permits society to experience the dream of a communication without system (without institution): to write without "style," to communicate "pure thought" without such communication developing any parasitical message—that is the model which the author-writer creates for society. It is a model at once distant and necessary, with which society plays something of a cat-and-mouse game: it acknowledges the author-writer by buying his books (however few), recognizing their public character; and at the same time it keeps him at a distance, obliging him to support himself by means of the subsidiary institutions it controls (the university, for instance), constantly accusing him of intellectualism, i.e., in terms of myth, sterility (a reproach the author never incurs). In short, from an anthropological viewpoint, the author-writer is an excluded figure integrated by his very exclusion, a remote descendant of the accursed: his function in society as a whole is perhaps related to the one Lévi-Strauss attributes to the witch doctor: a function of complementarity, both witch doctor and intellectual in a sense stabilizing a disease which is necessary to the collective economy of health. And naturally it is not surprising that such a conflict (or such a contract, if you prefer) should be joined on the level of language; for language is this paradox: the institutionalization of subjectivity.

1960

The Photographic Message

THE press photograph is a message. Considered overall this message is formed by a source of emission, a channel of transmission and a point of reception. The source of emission is the staff of the newspaper, the group of technicians certain of whom take the photo, some of whom choose, compose, and treat it, while others, finally, give it a title, a caption, and a commentary. The point of reception is the public which reads the paper. As for the channel of transmission, this is the newspaper itself, or, more precisely, a complex of concurrent messages with the photograph as center and surrounds constituted by the text, the title, the caption, the layout and, in a more abstract but no less "informative" way, by the very name of the paper (this name represents a knowledge that can heavily orientate the reading of the message strictly speaking: a photograph can change its meaning as it passes from the very conservative *L'Aurore* to the Communist *L'Humanité*). These observations are not without their importance for it can readily be seen that in the case of the press photograph the three traditional parts of the message do not call for the same

From *Image-Music-Text*, translated by Stephen Heath (New York: Hill and Wang, 1978).

method of investigation. The emission and the reception of the message both lie within the field of a sociology: it is a matter of studying human groups, of defining motives and attitudes, and of trying to link the behavior of these groups to the social totality of which they are a part. For the message itself, however, the method is inevitably different: whatever the origin and the destination of the message, the photograph is not simply a product or a channel but also an object endowed with a structural autonomy. Without in any way intending to divorce this object from its use, it is necessary to provide for a specific method prior to sociological analysis and which can only be the immanent analysis of the unique structure that a photograph constitutes.

Naturally, even from the perspective of a purely immanent analysis, the structure of the photograph is not an isolated structure; it is in communication with at least one other structure, namely the text—title, caption, or article—accompanying every press photograph. The totality of the information is thus carried by two different structures (one of which is linguistic). These two structures are cooperative but, since their units are heterogeneous, necessarily remain separate from one another: here (in the text) the substance of the message is made up of words; there (in the photograph) of lines, surfaces, shades. Moreover, the two structures of the message each occupy their own defined spaces, these being contiguous but not "homogenized," as they are for example in the rebus, which fuses words and images in a single line of reading. Hence, although a press photograph is never without a written commentary, the analysis must first of all bear on each separate structure; it is only when the study of each structure has been exhausted that it will be possible to understand the manner in which they complement one another. Of the two structures, one is already familiar, that of language (but not, it is true, that of the "literature" formed by the language use of the newspaper; an enormous amount of work is still to be done in this connection), while almost nothing is known about the other, that of the photograph. What follows will be limited to the definition of the initial difficulties in providing a structural analysis of the photographic message.

THE PHOTOGRAPHIC PARADOX

What is the content of the photographic message? What does the photograph transmit? By definition, the scene itself, the literal reality. From the object to its image there is of course a reduction—in proportion, perspective, color—but at no time is this reduction a *transformation* (in the mathematical sense of the term). In order to move from the reality to its photograph it is in no way necessary to divide up this reality into units and to constitute these units as signs, substantially different from the object they communicate; there is no necessity to set up a relay, that is to say a code, between the object and its image. Certainly the image is not the reality but at least it is its perfect *analogon* and it is exactly this analogical perfection which, to common sense, defines the photograph. Thus can be seen the special status of the photographic image: *it is a message without a code*; from which proposition an important corollary must immediately be drawn: the photographic message is a continuous message.

Are there other messages without a code? At first sight, yes: precisely the whole range of analogical reproductions of reality —drawings, paintings, cinema, theater. In fact, however, each of those messages develops in an immediate and obvious way a supplementary message, in addition to the analogical content itself (scene, object, landscape), which is what is commonly called the *style* of the reproduction; second meaning, whose signifier is a certain "treatment" of the image (result of the action of the creator) and whose signified, whether aesthetic or ideological, refers to a certain "culture" of the society receiving the message. In short, all these "imitative" arts comprise two messages: a *denoted* message, which is the *analogon* itself, and a *connoted* message, which is the manner in which the society to a certain extent communicates what it thinks of it. This duality of messages is evident in all reproductions other than photographic ones: there is no drawing, no matter how exact, whose very exactitude is not turned into a style (the style of "verism"); no filmed scene whose objectivity is not finally read as the very sign of objectivity. Here again, the study of these connoted messages has still to be carried out (in particular it has to be decided whether what is called a work of art can be reduced to a system of significations); one can only anticipate that for all these imitative arts—when common— the code of the connoted system is very likely constituted either by a universal symbolic order or by a period rhetoric, in short by a stock of stereotypes (schemes, colors, graphisms, gestures, expressions, arrangements of elements).

When we come to the photograph, however, we find in principle nothing of the kind, at any rate as regards the press photograph (which is never an "artistic" photograph). The photograph professing to be a mechanical analogue of reality, its first-order message in some sort completely fills its substance and leaves no place for the development of a second-order message. Of all the structures of information,[1] the photograph appears as the only one that is exclusively constituted and occupied by a "denoted" message, a message which totally exhausts its mode of existence. In front of a photograph, the feeling of "denotation," or, if one prefers, of analogical plenitude, is so great that the description of a photograph is literally

---

[1] It is a question, of course, of "cultural" or culturalized structures, not of operational structures. Mathematics, for example, constitutes a denoted structure without any connotation at all; should mass society seize on it, however, setting out for instance an algebraic formula in an article on Einstein, this originally purely mathematical message now takes on a very heavy connotation, since it *signifies* science.

impossible; *to describe* consists precisely in joining to the denoted message a relay or second-order message derived from a code which is that of language and constituting in relation to the photographic analogue, however much care one takes to be exact, a connotation: to describe is thus not simply to be imprecise or incomplete, it is to change structures, to signify something different from what is shown.[2]

This purely "denotative" status of the photograph, the perfection and plenitude of its analogy, in short its "objectivity," has every chance of being mythical (these are the characteristics that common sense attributes to the photograph). In actual fact, there is a strong probability (and this will be a working hypothesis) that the photographic message too—at least in the press—is connoted. Connotation is not necessarily immediately graspable at the level of the message itself (it is, one could say, at once invisible and active, clear and implicit) but it can already be inferred from certain phenomena which occur at the levels of the production and reception of the message: on the one hand, the press photograph is an object that has been worked on, chosen, composed, constructed, treated according to professional, aesthetic, or ideological norms which are so many factors of connotation; while on the other, this same photograph is not only perceived, received, it is *read*, connected more or less consciously by the public that consumes it to a traditional stock of signs. Since every sign supposes a code, it is this code (of connotation) that one should try to establish. The photographic paradox can then be seen as the co-existence of two messages, the one without a code (the photographic analogue), the other with a code (the "art," or the treatment, or the "writing," or the rhetoric, of the photograph); structurally, the paradox is clearly not the collu-

---

[2] The description of a drawing is easier, involving, finally, the description of a structure that is already connoted, fashioned with a *coded* signification in view. It is for this reason perhaps that psychological texts use a great many drawings and very few photographs.

sion of a denoted message and a connoted message (which is the—probably inevitable—status of all the forms of mass communication), it is that here the connoted (or coded) message develops on the basis of a message *without a code*. This structural paradox coincides with an ethical paradox: when one wants to be "neutral," "objective," one strives to copy reality meticulously, as though the analogical were a factor of resistance against the investment of values (such at least is the definition of aesthetic "realism"); how then can the photograph be at once "objective" and "invested," natural and cultural? It is through an understanding of the mode of imbrication of denoted and connoted messages that it may one day be possible to reply to that question. In order to undertake this work, however, it must be remembered that since the denoted message in the photograph is absolutely analogical, which is to say *continuous*, outside of any recourse to a code, there is no need to look for the signifying units of the first-order message; the connoted message on the contrary does comprise a plane of expression and a plane of content, thus necessitating a veritable decipherment. Such a decipherment would as yet be premature, for in order to isolate the signifying units and the signified themes (or values) one would have to carry out (perhaps using tests) directed readings, artificially varying certain elements of a photograph to see if the variations of forms led to variations in meaning. What can at least be done now is to forecast the main planes of analysis of photographic connotation.

CONNOTATION PROCEDURES

Connotation, the imposition of second meaning on the photographic message proper, is realized at the different levels of the production of the photograph (choice, technical treatment, framing, layout) and represents, finally, a coding of the photographic analogue. It is thus possible to separate out various connotation procedures, bearing in mind however that these procedures are in no way units of signification such as a subsequent analysis of a semantic kind may one day manage to define; they are not strictly speaking part of the photographic structure. The procedures in question are familiar and no more will be attempted here than to translate them into structural terms. To be fully exact, the first three (trick effects, pose, objects) should be distinguished from the last three (photogenia, aestheticism, syntax), since in the former the connotation is produced by a modification of the reality itself, of, that is, the denoted message (such preparation is obviously not peculiar to the photograph). If they are nevertheless included among the connotation procedures, it is because they too benefit from the prestige of the denotation: the photograph allows the photographer to *conceal elusively* the preparation to which he subjects the scene to be recorded. Yet the fact still remains that there is no certainty from the point of view of a subsequent structural analysis that it will be possible to take into account the material they provide.

1. *Trick effects*. A photograph given wide circulation in the American press in 1951 is reputed to have cost Senator Millard Tydings his seat; it showed the Senator in conversation with the Communist leader Earl Browder. In fact, the photograph had been faked, created by the artificial bringing together of the two faces. The methodological interest of trick effects is that they intervene without warning in the plane of denotation; they utilize the special credibility of the photograph—this, as was seen, being simply its exceptional power of denotation—in order to pass off as merely denoted a message which is in reality heavily connoted; in no other treatment does connotation assume so completely the "objective" mask of denotation. Naturally, signification is only possible to the extent that there is a stock of signs, the beginnings of a code. The signifier here is the conversational attitude of the two

figures and it will be noted that this attitude becomes a sign only for a certain society, only given certain values. What makes the speakers' attitude the sign of a reprehensible familiarity is the tetchy anti-Communism of the American electorate; which is to say that the code of connotation is neither artificial (as in a true language) nor natural, but historical.

2. *Pose*. Consider a press photograph of President Kennedy widely distributed at the time of the 1960 election: a half-length profile shot, eyes looking upward, hands joined together. Here it is the very pose of the subject which prepares the reading of the signifieds of connotation: youthfulness, spirituality, purity. The photograph clearly only signifies because of the existence of a store of stereotyped attitudes which form ready-made elements of signification (eyes raised heavenward, hands clasped). A "historical grammar" of iconographic connotation ought thus to look for its material in painting, theater, associations of ideas, stock metaphors, etc., that is to say, precisely in "culture." As has been said, pose is not a specifically photographic procedure, but it is difficult not to mention it insofar as it derives its effect from the analogical principle at the basis of the photograph. The message in the present instance is not "the pose" but "Kennedy praying": the reader receives as a simple denotation what is in actual fact a double structure—denoted-connoted.

3. *Objects*. Special importance must be accorded to what could be called the posing of objects, where the meaning comes from the objects photographed (either because these objects have, if the photographer had the time, been artificially arranged in front of the camera or because the person responsible for layout chooses a photograph of this or that object). The interest lies in the fact that the objects are accepted inducers of associations of ideas (bookcase = intellectual) or, in a more obscure way, are veritable symbols (the door of the gas chamber for Chessman's execution with its reference to the

funeral gates of ancient mythologies). Such objects constitute excellent elements of signification: on the one hand they are discontinuous and complete in themselves, a physical qualification for a sign, while on the other they refer to clear, familiar signifieds. They are thus the elements of a veritable lexicon, stable to a degree which allows them to be readily constituted into syntax. Here, for example, is a "composition" of objects: a window opening on to vineyards and tiled roofs; in front of the window a photograph album, a magnifying glass, a vase of flowers. Consequently, we are in the country, south of the Loire (vines and tiles), in a bourgeois house (flowers on the table) whose owner, advanced in years (the magnifying glass), is reliving his memories (the photograph album)—François Mauriac in Malagar (photo in *Paris-Match*). The connotation somehow "emerges" from all these signifying units which are nevertheless "captured" as though the scene were immediate and spontaneous, that is to say, without signification. The text renders the connotation explicit, developing the theme of Mauriac's ties with the land. Objects no longer perhaps possess a *power*, but they certainly possess meanings.

4. *Photogenia*. The theory of photogenia has already been developed (by Edgar Morin in *Le Cinéma ou l'homme imaginaire*) and this is not the place to take up again the subject of the general signification of that procedure; it will suffice to define photogenia in terms of informational structure. In photogenia the connoted message is the image itself, "embellished" (which is to say, in general sublimated) by techniques of lighting, exposure, and printing. An inventory needs to be made of these techniques, but only insofar as each of them has a corresponding signified of connotation sufficiently constant to allow its incorporation in a cultural lexicon of technical "effects" (as for instance the "blurring of movement" or "flowingness" launched by Dr. Steinert and his team to signify

space-time). Such an inventory would be an excellent opportunity for distinguishing aesthetic effects from signifying effects
—unless perhaps it be recognized that in photography, contrary to the intentions of exhibition photographers, there is
never *art* but always *meaning*; which precisely would at last
provide an exact criterion for the opposition between good
painting, even if strongly representational, and photography.

5. *Aestheticism.* For if one can talk of aestheticism in photography, it is seemingly in an ambiguous fashion: when photography turns painting, composition, or visual substance
treated with deliberation in its very material "texture," it is
either so as to signify itself as "art" (which was the case with
the "pictorialism" of the beginning of the century) or to impose a generally more subtle and complex signified than would
be possible with other connotation procedures. Thus Cartier-
Bresson constructed Cardinal Pacelli's reception by the faithful of Lisieux like a painting by an early master. The resulting
photograph, however, is in no way a painting: on the one
hand, its display of aestheticism refers (damagingly) to the
very idea of a painting (which is contrary to any true painting); while on the other, the composition signifies in a declared manner a certain ecstatic spirituality translated precisely in terms of an objective spectacle. One can see here the
difference between photograph and painting: in a picture by a
Primitive, "spirituality" is not a signified but, as it were, the
very being of the image. Certainly there may be coded elements in some paintings, rhetorical figures, period symbols,
but no signifying unit refers to spirituality, which is a mode of
being and not the object of a structured message. ·

6. *Syntax.* We have already considered a discursive reading
of object-signs within a single photograph. Naturally, several
photographs can come together to form a sequence (this is
commonly the case in illustrated magazines); the signifier of
connotation is then no longer to be found at the level of any

one of the fragments of the sequence but at that—what the linguists would call the suprasegmental level—of the concatenation. Consider for example four snaps of a presidential shoot at Rambouillet: in each, the illustrious sportsman (Vincent Auriol) is pointing his rifle in some unlikely direction, to the great peril of the keepers who run away or fling themselves to the ground. The sequence (and the sequence alone) offers an effect of comedy which emerges, according to a familiar procedure, from the repetition and variation of the attitudes. It can be noted in this connection that the single photograph, contrary to the drawing, is very rarely (that is, only with much difficulty) comic; the comic requires movement, which is to say repetition (easy in film) or typification (possible in drawing), both these "connotations" being prohibited to the photograph.

TEXT AND IMAGE

Such are the main connotation procedures of the photographic image (once again, it is a question of techniques, not of units). To these may invariably be added the text which accompanies the press photograph. Three remarks should be made in this context.

Firstly, the text constitutes a parasitic message designed to connote the image, to "quicken" it with one or more second-order signifieds. In other words, and this is an important historical reversal, the image no longer *illustrates* the words; it is now the words which, structurally, are parasitic on the image. The reversal is at a cost: in the traditional modes of illustration the image functioned as an episodic return to denotation from a principal message (the text) which was experienced as connoted since, precisely, it needed an illustration; in the relationship that now holds, it is not the image which comes to elucidate or "realize" the text, but the latter which comes to sublimate, patheticize, or rationalize the image. As however this operation is carried out accessorily, the new informational totality appears to be chiefly founded on an objective (denoted) message in relation to which the text is only a kind of secondary vibration, almost without consequence. Formerly, the image illustrated the text (made it clearer); today, the text loads the image, burdening it with a culture, a moral, an imagination. Formerly, there was reduction from text to image; today, there is amplification from the one to the other. The connotation is now experienced only as the natural resonance of the fundamental denotation constituted by the photographic analogy and we are thus confronted with a typical process of naturalization of the cultural.

Secondly, the effect of connotation probably differs according to the way in which the text is presented. The closer the text to the image, the less it seems to connote it; caught as it were in the iconographic message, the verbal message seems to share in its objectivity, the connotation of language is "innocented" through the photograph's denotation. It is true that there is never a real incorporation since the substances of the two structures (graphic and iconic) are irreducible, but there are most likely degrees of amalgamation. The caption probably has a less obvious effect of connotation than the headline or accompanying article: headline and article are palpably separate from the image, the former by its emphasis, the latter by its distance; the first because it breaks, the other because it distances the content of the image. The caption, on the contrary, by its very disposition, by its average measure of reading, appears to duplicate the image, that is, to be included in its denotation.

It is impossible however (and this will be the final remark here concerning the text) that the words "duplicate" the image; in the movement from one structure to the other second signifieds are inevitably developed. What is the relationship of these signifieds of connotation to the image? To all appearances, it is one of making explicit, of providing a stress; the text most often simply amplifying a set of connotations already given in the photograph. Sometimes, however, the text produces (invents) an entirely new signified which is retroactively projected into the image, so much so as to appear denoted there. *"They were near to death, their faces prove it,"* reads the headline to a photograph showing Elizabeth and Philip leaving a plane—but at the moment of the photograph the two still knew nothing of the accident they had just escaped. Sometimes, too, the text can even contradict the image so as to produce a compensatory connotation. An analysis by Gerbner (*The Social Anatomy of the Romance Confession Cover Girl*) demonstrated that in certain romance magazines the verbal message of the headlines, gloomy and anguished, on the cover always accompanied the image of a radiant cover girl; here the two messages enter into a compromise, the connotation having a regulating function, preserving the irrational movement of projection-identification.

PHOTOGRAPHIC INSIGNIFICANCE

We saw that the code of connotation was in all likelihood neither "natural" nor "artificial" but historical, or, if it be preferred, "cultural." Its signs are gestures, attitudes, expressions, colors, or effects, endowed with certain meanings by virtue of the practice of a certain society: the link between signifier and signified remains, if not unmotivated, at least entirely historical. Hence it is wrong to say that modern man projects into reading photographs feelings and values which are characterial or "eternal" (infra- or trans-historical), unless it be firmly specified that *signification* is always developed by a given society and history. Signification, in short, is the dialectical movement which resolves the contradiction between cultural and natural man.

Thanks to its code of connotation the reading of the photograph is thus always historical; it depends on the reader's "knowledge" just as though it were a matter of a real language [*langue*], intelligible only if one has learned the signs. All things considered, the photographic "language" ["*langage*"] is not unlike certain ideographic languages which mix analogical and specifying units, the difference being that the ideogram is experienced as a sign whereas the photographic "copy" is taken as the pure and simple denotation of reality. To find this code of connotation would thus be to isolate, inventoriate, and structure all the "historical" elements of the photograph, all the parts of the photographic surface which derive their very discontinuity from a certain knowledge on the reader's part, or, if one prefers, from the reader's cultural situation.

This task will perhaps take us a very long way indeed. Nothing tells us that the photograph contains "neutral" parts, or at least it may be that complete insignificance in the photograph is quite exceptional. To resolve the problem, we would first of all need to elucidate fully the mechanisms of reading (in the physical, and no longer the semantic, sense of the term), of the perception of the photograph. But on this point we know very little. How do we read a photograph? What do we perceive? In what order, according to what progression? If, as is suggested by certain hypotheses of Bruner and Piaget, there is no perception without immediate categorization, then the photograph is verbalized in the very moment it is perceived; better, it is only perceived verbalized (if there is a delay in verbalization, there is disorder in perception, questioning, anguish for the subject, traumatism, following G. Cohen-Séat's hypothesis with regard to filmic perception). From this point of view, the image—grasped immediately by an inner metalanguage, language itself—in actual fact has no denoted state, is immersed for its very social existence in at least an initial layer of connotation, that of the categories of language. We know that every language takes up a position with regard to things, that it connotes reality, if only in dividing it up; the connotations of the photograph would thus coincide, *grosso modo*, with the overall connotative planes of language.

In addition to "perceptive" connotation, hypothetical but possible, one then encounters other, more particular, modes of connotation, and firstly a "cognitive" connotation whose signifiers are picked out, localized, in certain parts of the analogon. Faced with such and such a townscape, I *know* that this is a North African country because on the left I can see a sign in Arabic script, in the center a man wearing a gandoura, and so on. Here the reading closely depends on my culture, on my knowledge of the world, and it is probable that a good press photograph (and they are all good, being selected) makes ready play with the supposed knowledge of its readers, those prints being chosen which comprise the greatest possible quantity of information of this kind in such a way as to render the reading fully satisfying. If one photographs Agadir in ruins, it is better to have a few signs of "Arabness" at one's disposal, even though "Arabness" has nothing to do with the disaster itself; connotation drawn from knowledge is always a reassuring force—man likes signs and likes them clear.

Perceptive connotation, cognitive connotation; there remains the problem of ideological (in the very wide sense of the term) or ethical connotation, that which introduces reasons or values into the reading of the image. This is a strong connotation requiring a highly elaborated signifier of a readily syntactical order: conjunction of people (as was seen in the discussion of trick effects), development of attitudes, constellation of objects. A son has just been born to the Shah of Iran and in a photograph we have: royalty (cot worshipped by a crowd of servants gathering round), wealth (several nursemaids), hygiene (white coats, cot covered in Plexiglas), the nevertheless human condition of kings (the baby is crying)—

all the elements, that is, of the myth of princely birth as it is consumed today. In this instance the values are apolitical and their lexicon is abundant and clear. It is possible (but this is only a hypothesis) that political connotation is generally entrusted to the text, insofar as political choices are always, as it were, in bad faith: for a particular photograph I can give a right-wing reading or a left-wing reading (see in this connection an IFOP survey published by *Les Temps Modernes* in 1955). Denotation, or the appearance of denotation, is powerless to alter political opinions: no photograph has ever convinced or refuted anyone (but the photograph can "confirm") insofar as political consciousness is perhaps nonexistent outside the *logos*: politics is what allows *all* languages.

These few remarks sketch a kind of differential table of photographic connotations, showing, if nothing else, that connotation extends a long way. Is this to say that a pure denotation, a *this-side of language*, is impossible? If such a denotation exists, it is perhaps not at the level of what ordinary language calls the insignificant, the neutral, the objective, but, on the contrary, at the level of absolutely traumatic images. The trauma is a suspension of language, a blocking of meaning. Certainly situations which are normally traumatic can be seized in a process of photographic signification but then precisely they are indicated via a rhetorical code which distances, sublimates and pacifies them. Truly traumatic photographs are rare, for in photography the trauma is wholly dependent on the certainty that the scene "really" happened: *the photographer had to be there* (the mystical definition of denotation). Assuming this (which, in fact, is already a connotation), the traumatic photograph (fires, shipwrecks, catastrophes, violent deaths, all captured "from life as lived") is the photograph about which there is nothing to say; the shock photo is by structure insignificant: no value, no knowledge, at the limit no verbal categorization can have a hold on the process instituting the signification. One could imagine a kind of law: the more direct the trauma, the more difficult is connotation; or again, the "mythological" effect of a photograph is inversely proportional to its traumatic effect.

Why? Doubtless because photographic connotation, like every well-structured signification, is an institutional activity; in relation to society overall, its function is to integrate man, to reassure him. Every code is at once arbitrary and rational; recourse to a code is thus always an opportunity for man to prove himself, to test himself through a reason and a liberty. In this sense, the analysis of codes perhaps allows an easier and surer historical definition of a society than the analysis of its signifieds, for the latter can often appear as trans-historical, belonging more to an anthropological base than to a proper history. Hegel gave a better definition of the ancient Greeks by outlining the manner in which they made nature signify than by describing the totality of their "feelings and beliefs" on the subject. Similarly, we can perhaps do better than to take stock directly of the ideological contents of our age; by trying to reconstitute in its specific structure the code of connotation of a mode of communication as important as the press photograph we may hope to find, in their very subtlety, the forms our society uses to ensure its peace of mind and to grasp thereby the magnitude, the detours, and the underlying function of that activity. The prospect is the more appealing in that, as was said at the beginning, it develops with regard to the photograph in the form of a paradox—that which makes of an inert object a language and which transforms the unculture of a "mechanical" art into the most social of institutions.

1961

The Imagination of the Sign

Every sign includes or implies three relations. To start with, an interior relation which unites its signifier to its signified; then two exterior relations: a virtual one that unites the sign to a specific reservoir of other signs it may be drawn from in order to be inserted in discourse; and an actual one that unites the sign to other signs in the discourse preceding or succeeding it. The first type of relation appears clearly in what is commonly called a *symbol*; for instance, the Cross "symbolizes" Christianity, red "symbolizes" a prohibition to advance; we shall call this first relation, then, a *symbolic* relation, though we encounter it not only in symbols but also in signs (which are, roughly speaking, purely conventional symbols). The second type of relation implies the existence, for each sign, of a reservoir or organized "memory" of forms from which it is distinguished by the smallest difference necessary and sufficient to effect a change of meaning; in *lupum*, the element *-um* (which is a sign, and more precisely a morpheme) affords its meaning of "accusative case" only insofar as it is opposed to the (virtual) remainder of the declension (*-us, -i, -o,* etc.); red signifies prohibition only insofar as it is *systematically* opposed

From *Critical Essays.*

to green and yellow (of course, if there were no other color but red, red would still be opposed to the absence of color); this second type of relation is therefore that of the system, sometimes called paradigm; we shall therefore call it a *paradigmatic* relation. According to the third type of relation, the sign is no longer situated with regard to its (virtual) "brothers," but with regard to its (actual) "neighbors"; in *homo homini lupus, lupus* maintains certain connections with *homo* and with *homini*; in garment systems, the elements of an outfit are associated according to certain rules: to wear a sweater and a leather jacket is to create, between these two garments, a temporary but signifying association, analogous to the one uniting the words of a sentence; this level of association is the level of the syntagm, and we shall call the third relation the *syntagmatic relation*.

Now it seems that when we consider the signifying phenomenon (and this interest may proceed from very different horizons), we are obliged to focus on one of these three relations more than on the other two; sometimes we "see" the sign in its symbolic aspect, sometimes in its systematic aspect, sometimes in its syntagmatic aspect; this is occasionally the result of mere ignorance of the other relations: symbolism has long been blind to the formal relations of the sign; but even when the three relations have been defined (for example, in linguistics), each school tends to base its analysis on one of the sign's dimensions: one vision overflows the whole of the signifying phenomenon, so that we may speak, apparently, of different semiological consciousnesses (I refer, of course, to the consciousness of the analyst, not of the user, of the sign). Now, on the one hand, the choice of a dominant relation implies a certain ideology; and, on the other hand, one might say that each consciousness of the sign (symbolic, paradigmatic, and syntagmatic) corresponds to a certain moment of reflection, either individual or collective: structuralism, in particular, can be defined historically as the passage from symbolic consciousness to paradigmatic consciousness: there is a history of the sign, which is the history of its "consciousnesses."

The symbolic consciousness sees the sign in its profound, one might almost say its geological, dimension, since for the symbolic consciousness it is the tiered arrangement of signifier and signified which constitutes the symbol; there is a consciousness of a kind of vertical relation between the Cross and Christianity: Christianity is *under* the Cross, as a profound mass of beliefs, values, practices, more or less disciplined on the level of its form. The verticality of the relation involves two consequences: on the one hand, the vertical relation tends to seem solitary: the symbol seems to stand by itself in the world, and even when we assert that it is abundant, it is abundant in the fashion of a "forest"—i.e., by an anarchic juxtaposition of profound relations which communicate, so to speak, only by their roots (by what is signified); and on the other hand, this vertical relation necessarily appears to be an analogical relation: to some degree the form resembles the content, as if it were actually produced by it, so that the symbolic consciousness may sometimes mask an unacknowledged determinism: thus there is a massive privilege of resemblance (even when we emphasize the inadequate character of the sign). The symbolic consciousness has dominated the sociology of symbols and of course a share of psychoanalysis in its early stages, though Freud himself acknowledged the inexplicable (nonanalogical) character of certain symbols; this moreover was the period when the very word *symbol* prevailed; during all this time, the symbol possessed a mythic prestige, the glamor of "richness": the symbol was rich, hence it could not be reduced to a "simple sign" (today we may doubt the sign's "simplicity"): its form was constantly exceeded by the power and the movement of its content; indeed, for the symbolic consciousness, the symbol is much less a (codified) form of communication than an (affective) instrument of participation. The word *symbol* has now gone a little stale; we readily replace it by *sign* or *signification*. This terminological shift expresses a certain crumbling of the symbolic consciousness, notably with regard to the analogical character of signifier and signified; nonetheless the symbolic consciousness remains typical, insofar as its analytical consideration is not interested in the formal relations of signs, for the symbolic consciousness is essentially the rejection of form; what interests it in the sign is the signified: the signifier is always a determined element.

Once the forms of two signs are compared, or at least perceived in a somewhat comparative manner, a certain paradigmatic consciousness appears; even on the level of the classical symbol, the least subtle of signs, if there is some occasion to perceive the variation of two symbolic forms, the other dimensions of the sign are immediately discovered; as in the case, for instance, of the opposition between *Red Cross* and *Red Crescent*: on the one hand, *Cross* and *Crescent* cease to entertain a "solitary" relation with what they respectively signify (Christianity and Islam), they are included in a stereotyped syntagm; and, on the other hand, they form between themselves an interplay of distinctive terms, each of which corresponds to a different signified: the paradigm is born. The paradigmatic consciousness therefore defines meaning not as the simple encounter of signifier and signified, but, according to Merleau-Ponty's splendid expression, as a veritable "modulation of co-existence"; it substitutes for the bilateral relation of the symbolic consciousness a quadrilateral or more precisely a homological relation. It is the paradigmatic consciousness which permitted Lévi-Strauss to reconceive the problem of totemism: whereas the symbolic consciousness vainly seeks the "dimensional," more or less analogical characters which unite a signifier (the totem) to a signified (the clan), the paradigmatic consciousness establishes a homology (as Lévi-Strauss calls it) between the relation of two totems and that of two clans. Naturally, by retaining in the signified only its demonstrative role (it designates the signifier and makes it possible to locate the terms of the opposition), the paradigmatic consciousness tends to empty it: but it does not thereby empty the signification. It is obviously the paradigmatic consciousness which has permitted (or expressed) the extraordinary development of phonology, a science of exemplary paradigms (*marked/nonmarked*): it is the paradigmatic consciousness which, through the work of Lévi-Strauss, defines the structuralist threshold.

The syntagmatic consciousness is a consciousness of the relations which unite signs on the level of discourse itself, i.e., essentially a consciousness of the constraints, tolerances, and liberties of the sign's associations. This consciousness has marked the linguistic endeavors of the Yale school and, outside linguistics, the investigations of the Russian formalist school, notably those of Propp in the domain of the Slavic folk tale (hence we may expect that it will eventually illuminate analysis of the major contemporary "narratives," from the *fait-divers* to the popular novel). But this is not the only orientation of the syntagmatic consciousness; of the three, it is certainly the syntagmatic consciousness which most readily renounces the signified: it is more a structural consciousness than a semantic one, which is why it comes closest to practice: it is the syntagmatic consciousness which best permits us to imagine operational groups, "dispatchings," complex classifications: the paradigmatic consciousness permits the fruitful return from decimalism to binarism; but it is the syntagmatic consciousness which actually permits us to conceive cybernetic "programs," just as it has permitted Propp and Lévi-Strauss to reconstruct the myth "series."

Perhaps we shall someday be able to return to the description of these semantic consciousnesses, attempt to link them to a history; perhaps we shall someday be able to create a semiology of the semiologists, a structural analysis of the structuralists. All we are endeavoring to say here is that there is probably a genuine imagination of the sign; the sign is not only the object of a particular knowledge, but also the object of a vision, analogous to the vision of the celestial spheres in Cicero's *Somnium Scipionis* or related to the molecular representations used by chemists; the semiologist *sees* the sign moving in the field of signification, he enumerates its valences, traces their configuration: the sign is, for him, a sensuous idea. Of the three (still fairly technical) consciousnesses discussed here, we must presume an extension toward much wider types of imagination, which we may find mobilized in many other objects than the sign.

The symbolic consciousness implies an imagination of depth; it experiences the world as the relation of a superficial form and a many-sided, massive, powerful *Abgrund*, and the image is reinforced by a very intense dynamics: the relation of form and content is ceaselessly renewed by time (history), the superstructure overwhelmed by the infrastructure, without our ever being able to grasp the structure itself. The paradigmatic consciousness, on the contrary, is a formal imagination; it *sees* the signifier linked, as if in profile, to several virtual signifiers which it is at once close to and distinct from: it no longer sees the sign in its depth, it sees it in its perspective; thus the dynamics attached to this vision is that of a summons: the sign is chosen from a finite organized reservoir, and this summons is the sovereign act of signification: imagination of the surveyor, the geometrician, the owner of the world who finds himself at his ease on his property, since man, in order to signify, has merely to choose from what is presented to him already prestructured either by his brain (in the binarist hypothesis), or by the material finitude of forms. The syntagmatic imagination no longer sees the sign in its perspective, it *foresees* it in its extension: its antecedent or consequent links, the bridges it extends to other signs; this is a "stemmatous" imagination of the chain or the network; hence the dynamics of the image here is that of an arrangement of mobile, substitutive parts, whose combination produces meaning, or more generally a new object; it is, then, a strictly fabricative or even *functional* imagination (the word is conveniently ambiguous, since it refers both to the notion of a variable relation and to that of a usage).

Such are (perhaps) the three imaginations of the sign. We may doubtless attach to each of them a certain number of different creations, in the most diverse realms, for nothing constructed in the world today escapes meaning. To remain in the realm of recent intellectual creation, among the works of the profound (symbolic) imagination, we may cite biographical or historical criticism, the sociology of "visions," the realist or introspective novel, and in a general way, the "expressive" arts or languages, postulating the signified as sovereign, extracted either from an interiority or from a history. The formal (or paradigmatic) imagination implies an acute attention to the *variation* of several recurrent elements; thus this type of imagination accommodates the dream and oneiric narratives, powerfully thematic works and those whose aesthetic implies the interplay of certain commutations (Robbe-Grillet's novels, for example). The functional (or syntagmatic) imagination nourishes, lastly, all those works whose fabrication, by arrangement of discontinuous and mobile elements, constitutes the spectacle itself: poetry, epic theater, serial music, and structural compositions, from Mondrian to Butor.

1962

The Plates of
the *Encyclopedia*

OUR literature has taken a long time to discover the object;
we must wait till Balzac for the novel to be the space not only
of pure human relations but also of substances and usages
called upon to play their part in the story of passions: could
Grandet have been a miser (literarily speaking) without his
candle ends, his lumps of sugar, and his gold crucifix? Long
before literature, the *Encyclopedia*, particularly in its plates,
practices what we might call a certain philosophy of the object, i.e., reflects on its being, produces at once an inventory
and a definition; technological purpose no doubt compelled the
description of objects; but by separating image from text, the
Encyclopedia committed itself to an autonomous iconography
of the object whose power we enjoy today, since we no longer
look at these illustrations with mere information in mind.

The plates of the *Encyclopedia* present the object, and this
presentation already adds to the illustration's didactic purpose
a more gratuitous justification, of an aesthetic or oneiric
order: the imagery of the *Encyclopedia* can best be compared

From *New Critical Essays*, translated by Richard Howard (New York:
Hill and Wang, 1980).

with one of those Great Expositions held the world over in the
last century or so, and of which, in its period, the Encyclopedic illustration was a kind of ancestor: in both cases, we are
concerned with a census and a spectacle: we consult the plates
of the *Encyclopedia* as we would visit today's World's Fair in
Brussels or New York. The objects presented are literally encyclopedic, i.e., they cover the entire sphere of substances
shaped by man: clothes, vehicles, tools, weapons, instruments,
furniture, all that man makes out of wood, metal, glass, or
fiber is catalogued here, from the chisel to the statue, from the
artificial flower to the ship. This Encyclopedic object is ordinarily apprehended by the image on three levels: anthological,
since the object, isolated from any context, is presented *in
itself*; anecdotic, when it is "naturalized" by its insertion into a
large-scale *tableau vivant* (which is what we call a vignette);
genetic, when the image offers us the trajectory from raw substance to finished object: genesis, essence, praxis, the object is
thus accounted for in all its categories: sometimes it *is*, sometimes it is *made*, sometimes it even *makes*. Of these three
states, assigned here and there to the object-as-image, one is
certainly favored by the *Encyclopedia*: that of birth: it is good
to be able to show how we can produce things from their very
nonexistence and thus to credit man with an extraordinary
power of creation: here is a countryside; the plenitude of Nature (meadows, hills, trees) constitutes a kind of human void
from which we cannot see what will emerge; yet the image
moves, objects are born, precursors of humanity: lines are
drawn on the earth, stakes are pounded in, holes dug; a cross-
section shows us, beneath a desert Nature, the powerful network of galleries and lodes: a mine is born. This is a kind of
symbol: Encyclopedic man *mines* all Nature with human
signs; in the Encyclopedic landscape, we are never alone;
however strong the elements, there is always a fraternal

product of man: the object is the world's human signature.

We know that a simple substance can make a whole story legible: Brecht has rediscovered the wretched essence of the Thirty Years' War by the radical treatment of fabrics, wicker, and wood. The Encyclopedic object emerges from general substances which are still those of the artisanal era. If we visit a World's Fair today, we perceive in all the objects exhibited two or three dominant substances, glass, metal, plastic no doubt; the substance of the Encyclopedic object is of a more vegetal age: it is wood which dominates in this great catalogue; it produces a world of objects easy on the eyes, already human by their substance, resistant but not brittle, constructible but not plastic. Nothing shows wood's humanizing power better than the *Encyclopedia*'s machines; in this world of technology (which is still artisanal, for the industrial is as yet unborn), the machine is obviously a capital object; now most of the *Encyclopedia*'s machines are made out of wood; they are enormous, highly complicated scaffoldings in which metal frequently supplies only notched wheels. The wood which constitutes them keeps them subservient to a certain notion of *play*: these machines are (for us) like big toys; contrary to modern images, man, always present in some corner of the machine, does not accompany it in a simple relation of surveillance; turning a crank, pressing a pedal, spinning a thread, he participates in the machine in a manner that is both active and delicate; the engraver represents him for the most part dressed neatly as a gentleman; this is not a worker but a little lord who plays on a kind of technological organ, all of whose gears and wheels are exposed; what is striking about the Encyclopedic machine is its absence of secrecy; in it there is no hidden place (spring or housing) which would magically conceal energy, as is the case with our modern machines (it is the myth of electricity to be a self-generated, hence enclosed, power); the energy here is essentially transmission, amplification of a simple human movement; the Encyclopedic machine is never anything but an enormous relay; man is at one term, the object at the other; between the two, an architectural milieu, consisting of beams, ropes, and gears, through which, like a light, human strength is simultaneously developed, refined, focused, and enlarged: hence, in the gauze-loom, a little man in a jacket, sitting at the keyboard of a huge wooden machine, produces an extremely fine web, as if he were playing music; elsewhere, in a completely bare room, containing only a maze of wood and tarred ropes, a young woman sitting on a bench turns a crank, while her other hand rests gently on her knee. a *simpler* idea of technology is inconceivable.

An almost naïve simplicity, a kind of Golden Legend of artisanry (for there is no trace of social distress): the *Encyclopedia* identifies the simple, the elementary, the essential, and the causal. Encyclopedic technology is simple because it is reduced to a two-term space: the causal trajectory which proceeds from substance to object; hence all the plates which involve some technological operation (of transformation) mobilize an aesthetic of bareness: huge, empty, well-lighted rooms, in which man cohabits alone with his work: a space without parasites, walls bare, tables cleared; the simple, here, is nothing but the vital; this is made explicit in the bakery; as a primary element, bread implies an austere site; on the other hand, pastry, belonging to the order of the superfluous, proliferates in instruments, operations, products, whose fussy ensemble constitutes a certain *baroque*. In a general way, the object's *production* sweeps the image toward an almost sacred simplicity; its *use*, on the other hand (represented at the moment of sale, in the shop), authorizes an embellishment of the vignette, abounding in instruments, accessories, and attitudes: austerity of creation, luxury of commerce, such is the double regime of the Encyclopedic object: the density of the image and its ornamental charge always signifies that we are shifting from production to consumption.

Of course, the object's pre-eminence in this world derives from an inventorying effort, but inventory is never a neutral idea; to catalogue is not merely to ascertain, as it appears at first glance, but also to appropriate. The *Encyclopedia* is a huge ledger of ownership; Bernard Groetheuysen has noted an opposition between the *orbis pictus* of the Renaissance, animated by the spirit of an adventurous knowledge, and the encyclopedism of the eighteenth century, based on a learning of appropriation. Formally (this is apparent in the plates), ownership depends on a certain dividing up of things: to appropriate is to fragment the world, to divide it into finite objects subject to man in proportion to their very discontinuity: for we cannot separate without finally naming and classifying, and at that moment, property is born. In mythic terms, possession of the world began not with Genesis but at the Flood, when man was obliged to name each kind of animal and to house it, i.e., to separate it from its next of species; the *Encyclopedia*, moreover, takes an essentially pragmatic view of Noah's ark; for it, the ark is not a ship—an object always more or less *oneiric*—but a long floating crate, a goods locker; the only problem it appears to offer the *Encyclopedia* is certainly not theological: it is the problem of its construction, or even, in more technical terms, as is only right, of its framing, and even more specifically, of its fenestration, since each of its windows corresponds to a typical pair of animals, thus divided, named, domesticated (docilely sticking their heads out the opening).

Encyclopedic nomenclature, whatever its technological esotericism on occasion, actually establishes a familiar possession. This is remarkable, for nothing logically obliges the object to be invariably friendly to man. The object, quite the contrary, is humanly a very ambiguous thing; we have noted that for a long time our literature did not acknowledge it; later (which is to say, on the whole, today), the object has been endowed with an unfortunate opacity; assimilated to an inhuman state of nature, its proliferation cannot be noted without a sentiment of apocalypse or of alienation: the modern object is either asphyxiation (Ionesco) or nausea (Sartre). The Encyclopedic object is on the contrary subjugated (we might say that it is precisely pure *object* in the etymological sense of the term), for a very simple and constant reason: it is on each occasion *signed* by man; the image is the privileged means of this human presence, for it permits discreetly locating a permanent man on the object's horizon; the plates of the *Encyclopedia* are always populated (they afford thereby a close relationship with another "progressive" or, to be more precise, bourgeois iconography: seventeenth-century Dutch painting); you can imagine the most naturally solitary, "savage" object; be sure that man will nonetheless appear in a corner of the image; he will be considering the object, or measuring it, or surveying it, using it at least as a spectacle; take the Giant's Causeway, that mass of terrifying basalt composed by Nature at Antrim, in Ireland; this inhuman landscape is, one might say, stuffed with humanity; gentlemen in tricornes, lovely ladies contemplate the horrible landscape, chatting familiarly; farther on, men are fishing, scientists are weighing the mineral substance: analyzed into functions (spectacle, fishing, science), the basalt is *reduced*, tamed, familiarized, because it is *divided*; what is striking in the entire *Encyclopedia* (and especially in its images) is that it proposes a *world without fear* (we shall see in a moment that the monstrous is not excluded, but in a category much more "surrealist" than terrifying). We can even specify more clearly what the man of the Encyclopedic image is reduced to—what is, in some sense, the very essence of his humanity: his hands. In many plates (and not the least beautiful), hands, severed from any body, flutter around the work (for their lightness is extreme); these hands are doubtless the symbol of an artisanal world (again we are concerned with traditional, virtually unmechanized trades, the steam engine is kept out of sight), as is seen by the importance of the tables (huge, flat, well lighted, often encircled by hands); but beyond artisanship, the hands are inevitably the inductive sign of the human essence: do we not see even today, in a less obvious fashion, that our advertising constantly returns to this mysterious motif, at once natural and supernatural, as if man could not get over having hands? It is not easy to be done with a civilization of the hand.

Hence in the immediate state of its representations, the *Encyclopedia* is constantly concerned to familiarize the world of objects (which is its primary substance) by adding to it the obsessive cipher of man. Yet beyond the letter of the image, this humanization implies an intellectual system of an extreme subtlety: the Encyclopedic image is human not only because man is represented in it but also because it constitutes a structure of *information*. This structure, though iconographic, is articulated in most instances like real language (the one which, in fact, we call *articulate*), whose two dimensions as revealed by structural linguistics it reproduces: we know, in fact, that all discourse involves signifying units and that these units are ordered according to two axes, one of substitution (paradigmatic), the other of contiguity (syntagmatic); each unit can thereby *vary* (potentially) with its parents, and *link* (in reality) with its neighbors. This is what happens, *grosso modo*, in an *Encyclopedia* plate. The majority of these plates are formed of two parts; in the lower part, the tool or the gesture (the object of the demonstration), isolated from any real context, is shown in its essence; it constitutes the informative unit, and this unit is generally *varied*: its aspects, elements, kinds are detailed; this part of the plate has the role of *declining* the object, of manifesting its paradigm; on the contrary, in the upper part or vignette, this same object (and its varieties) is apprehended in a lively scene (generally a scene of sale or manufacture, shop or workroom), linked to other objects within a real situation: here we rediscover the syntagmatic dimension of the message; and just as in oral discourse the system of the language, perceptible chiefly on the paradigmatic level, is somehow *hidden* behind the living stream of words, in the same way the Encyclopedic plate plays simultaneously on intellectual demonstration (by its objects) and on fictive life (by its scenes). Here is a trade plate (the pastrycook): down below, the ensemble of various instruments necessary to the profession; in this paradigmatic state, the instrument has no life: inert, frozen in its essence, it is merely a demonstrative schema, analogous to the quasi-academic form of a verbal or nominal paradigm; up above, on the contrary, the chopping board, the whisk (the pastrycooks were making *pâtés en croûte*), the sieve, the molds are arranged, linked together, "enacted" in a *tableau vivant*, exactly as the "cases" distinguished by grammar are ordinarily given without our thinking of them in real discourse, with this difference, that the Encyclopedic syntagm is of an extreme density of meaning; in informational language, we would say that the scene involves little "noise" (see, for instance, the workshop in which the chief operations of engraving are gathered together).

Most of the objects from the lower paradigm are therefore reassembled in the vignette under the heading of signs; whereas the figured nomenclature of the instruments, utensils, products, and gestures involves by definition no secrecy, the vignette, charged with a disseminated meaning, always presents itself a little like a riddle: we must decipher it, locate in it the informative units. The vignette has the riddle's actual density: *all* the information must turn up in the experienced scene (whence, upon scrutiny, a certain exploration of meaning); in the plate devoted to cotton, a certain number of accidents must necessarily refer to the exoticism of the vegetal realm: the palm, the stubble, the island, the Chinaman's shaved head, his long pipe (impractical, it would seem, for working with cotton but which evokes the image of opium), none of this information is innocent: the image is crammed with demonstrative significations; analogously, Demosthenes' lantern is admirable *because* two men are discussing it and pointing to it; it is an antiquity *because* it adjoins a ruin; it is situated in Greece *because* there is the sea, a boat; we contemplate its present state *because* a band of men are dancing in a ring nearby, performing something like the *bouzouki*. Of this kind of cryptographic vocation of the image, there is no better symbol than the two plates dedicated to the hemispheres; a sphere, enclosed by a fine network of lines, makes legible the outline of its continents; but these lines and these contours are only a light transparency behind which float, like a meaning *from behind*, the figures of the constellations (the Wagoner, the Dolphin, the Scales, the Dog).

However, the vignette, a condensate of meaning, also offers a resistance to meaning, and we might say that it is in this resistance, paradoxically, that the plate's language becomes a complete, an adult language. It is, as a matter of fact, apparent that for a reader of the period the scene itself often involves very little new information: who had not seen a pastrycook's shop, a tilled field, a river fishery? The vignette's function is therefore elsewhere: the syntagm (since it is with it that we are concerned) tells us here, once again, that language (and *a fortiori*, iconic language) is not pure intellectual communication: meaning is completed only when it is somehow naturalized in a complete action of man; for the *Encyclopedia*, too, there is a message only *in situation*, whereby we see how ambiguous, finally, the *Encyclopedia*'s didacticism is: very strong in the lower (paradigmatic) part of the plate, it is diluted at its syntagmatic level, to join (without actually being lost) what we must, in fact, call the fictive truth of any human action. At its demonstrative stage, the Encyclopedic plate constitutes a *radical language*, consisting of pure concepts, with neither word tools nor syntax; at the higher stage, this radical language becomes a human *langue*, it deliberately loses in intelligibility what it gains in experience.

The vignette does not have only an existential function, but also, one might say, an *epic* one; it is entrusted to represent the glorious term of a great trajectory, that of substance, transformed, sublimated by man, through a series of episodes and stations: this is symbolized perfectly by the cross-section of the mill, where we see the grain proceed from story to story to be resolved into flour. The demonstration becomes even stronger when it is deliberately artificial: through the weapon shop's open door, we see two men dueling out in the street: the scene is unlikely, though logical if one wants to show the ultimate term of the operation (subject of the plate), which is small-arms supply: there is a trajectory of the object which must be honored to the end. This trajectory is often paradoxical (whence the interest in showing the terms clearly); an enormous mass of wood and cordage produces a delicate flowered carpet: the finished object, so different from the apparatus which has given birth to it, is placed in view; the effect and the cause, juxtaposed, form a figure of meaning by contiguity (what is called metonymy): the framing of the loom finally *signifies* the carpet. The paradox reaches its (delicious) apogee when we can no longer perceive any relation of substance between the initial substance and the object arrived at: at the card-maker's, the playing cards are generated out of a

void, the hole in the cardboard; in the workshop of the arti-
ficial-flower maker, not only does nothing recall the flower, but
even the operations which lead to it are constantly antipathetic
to the idea of the flower: these are stampings, stencilings,
hammer taps, punch-outs: what relation between such shows
of strength and the anemone's fragile efflorescence? Precisely a
human relation, the relation of the omnipotent praxis of man,
which out of nothing can make everything.

Thus the *Encyclopedia* constantly testifies to a certain epic
of substance, but this epic is also in a sense that of the mind:
the trajectory of substance is nothing, for the Encyclopedist,
but the progress of reason: the image has a logical function *as
well*. Diderot says as much explicitly apropos of the machine
for making stockings, whose image will reproduce structure:
*"We may regard it as a single and unique reasoning of which
the work's fabrication is the conclusion; therefore there reigns
among its parts so great a dependence that were we to remove
even a single one, or to alter the form of those regarded as
least important, we should destroy the entire mechanism."*
Here we find prophetically formulated the very principle of
cybernetic ensembles; the plate, image of the machine, is indeed in its way a brain; we introduce substance into it and set
up the "program": the vignette (the syntagm) serves as a
conclusion. This logical character of the image has another
model, that of dialectics: the image analyzes, first enumerating
the scattered elements of the object or of the operation and
flinging them as on a table before the reader's eyes, then re-
composing them, even adding to them the density of the scene,
i.e., of life. The Encyclopedic mounting is based on reason: it
descends into analysis as deeply as is necessary in order to
"perceive the elements without confusion" (according to another phrase of Diderot's, precisely apropos of the drawings,
results of investigations on the spot made by draughtsmen in

the workshops): the image is a kind of rational synopsis: it illustrates not only the object or its trajectory but also the very mind which conceives it; this double movement corresponds to a double reading: if you read the plate from bottom to top, you obtain in a sense an experiential reading, you relive the object's epic trajectory, its flowering in the complex world of consumers; you proceed from Nature to sociality; but if you read the image from top to bottom, starting from the vignette, it is the progress of the analytic mind that you are reproducing; the world gives you the usual, the evident (the scene); with the Encyclopedist, you descend gradually to causes, to substances, to primary elements, you proceed from the experiential to the causal, you intellectualize the object. The privilege of the image—opposed in this to writing, which is linear —is to compel our reading to have no specific meaning: an image is always deprived of a logical vector (as certain modern experiences tend to prove); those of the *Encyclopedia* possess a precious circularity: we can read them starting from the experiential or, on the contrary, from the intelligible: the real world is not reduced, it is suspended between two great orders of reality, in truth, irreducible orders.

Such is the informative system of the Encyclopedic image. Yet the information does not end with what the image could say to the reader of its period: the modern reader also receives from this old image certain information which the Encyclopedist could not foresee: historical information, first of all: it is quite evident that the plates of the *Encyclopedia* are a mine of precious data as to the civilization of the eighteenth century (at least of its first half); oneiric information, if one may put it so, subsequently: the period object stirs in us certain strictly modern analogies; here is a phenomenon of connotation (connotation, a specific linguistic notion, is constituted by the development of a second meaning) which profoundly justifies the new edition of the old documents. Take, for example, the Lyons diligence; the *Encyclopedia* could aim at nothing but the objective—matte, one might say—reproduction of a certain means of transport; now it happens that this massive and closed trunk immediately wakens in us what we might call memories of the imagination: stories of bandits, kidnappings, ransoms, nocturnal transfers of mysterious prisoners, and, even closer to us, Westerns, the whole heroic and sinister myth of the mail coach is there, in this black object, innocently given, as a photograph of the period might have given it to us. There is a *depth* in the Encyclopedic image, the very depth of time which transforms the object into myth.

This leads to what we must call the Poetics of the Encyclopedic image, if we agree to define Poetics as the sphere of the infinite vibrations of meaning, at the center of which is placed the literal object. We can say that there is not one plate of the *Encyclopedia* which fails to vibrate well beyond its demonstrative intent. This singular vibration is above all an astonishment. Of course, the Encyclopedic image is always clear; but in a deeper region of ourselves, beyond the intellect, or at least in its profile, certain questions are born and exceed us. Consider the astonishing image of man reduced to his network of veins; here anatomical boldness unites with the great poetic and philosophic interrogation: *What is it?* What name to give it? How give a name? A thousand names rise up, dislodging each other: a tree, a bear, a monster, a hair shirt, a fabric, everything which overflows the human silhouette, distends it, draws it toward regions remote from itself, makes it overstep the divisions of Nature; yet, just as in the sketch of a master, the swarm of pencil strokes finally resolves into a pure and exact form, perfectly signifying, so here all the vibrations of meaning concur to impose upon us a certain idea of the object; in this initially human, then animal, then vegetal form we still recognize a kind of unique matter—vein, hair, or

thread—and we accede to that great undifferentiated substance of which verbal or pictorial poetry is the mode of knowledge: confronting the man of the *Encyclopedia* we must
say *the fibrous*, as the ancient Greeks said *the moist* or *the
warm* or *the round*: a certain essence of substance is here
affirmed.

As a matter of fact, there cannot be anarchic poetry. The
iconography of the *Encyclopedia* is poetic because its overflows of meaning always have a certain unity, suggest an ultimate meaning transcending all the *essays* of meaning. For
example: the image of the womb is actually quite enigmatic;
yet its metaphoric vibrations (as if it were a flayed ox, the
interior of a body which dissolves and floats away) do not
contradict the original traumatism attached to this object.
There is a certain horror and a certain fascination common
to some objects, which precisely establishes them in a homogeneous *class*, whose unity and identity is affirmed by Poetics.
It is this profound order of metaphor which justifies—poetically—the recourse to a certain category of the *monstrous* (at
least, according to the law of connotation, this is what we
perceive in the presence of certain plates): anatomical monsters, as in the case of the enigmatic womb or that of the bust
with the arms cut off, the breast opened, the face thrown back
(meant to show the arteries of the thorax); surrealist monsters
(those equestrian statues sheathed in wax and cords), huge
and incomprehensible objects (halfway between the stocking
and the wallet and which are neither one nor the other, in the
stocking loom), subtler monsters (plates of poison with sharp,
black crystals); all these transgressions of Nature make us
understand that the poetic (for the monstrous can only be the
poetic) is never established except by a displacement of the
level of perception: it is one of the *Encyclopedia*'s great gifts
to *vary* (in the musical sense of the term) the level on which
one and the same object can be perceived, thereby liberating

the very secrets of form: seen through the microscope, the flea becomes a horrible monster, caparisoned with plates of bronze, armed with steel spines, with the head of a wicked bird, and this monster achieves the strange sublimity of mythological dragons; elsewhere, and in another key, the snowflake, enlarged, becomes a complicated and harmonious flower. Is poetry not a certain power of *disproportion*, as Baudelaire saw so well, describing the effects of reduction and focusing that hashish induces?

Another exemplary category of the poetic (alongside the monstrous): a certain *immobility*. We always praise the movement of a drawing. Yet, by an inevitable paradox, the *image* of movement can only be arrested; in order to signify itself, movement must be immobilized at the extreme point of its course; it is this incredible, untenable repose that Baudelaire called the emphatic truth of gesture and that we find in demonstrative painting—that of Gros, for instance; to this suspended, oversignifying gesture we might give the name *numen*, for it is indeed the gesture of a god who silently creates man's fate, i.e., meaning. In the *Encyclopedia*, numinous gestures abound, for what man makes cannot be insignificant. In the chemical laboratory, for example, each character offers us *slightly* impossible actions, for in truth an action cannot be simultaneously effective and significant, a gesture cannot be altogether an action: the boy washing the pans, oddly, is not looking at what he is doing; his face, turned toward us, grants the operation he is performing a kind of demonstrative solitude; and if the two chemists are having a discussion, it is necessary that one of them raise a finger to signify by this emphatic gesture the learned character of the conversation. Similarly, in the drawing academy, the students are *caught* at the most improbable moment of their agitation. There is, in fact, a physical order in which Zeno's paradox is true, when the arrow flies and yet does not, flies by not flying, and this order is that of painting (here, of drawing).

As we see, Encyclopedic poetics are always defined as a certain unrealism. It is the *Encyclopedia*'s wager (in its plates) to be both a didactic work, based consequently on a severe demand for objectivity (for "reality"), and a poetic work in which the real is constantly overcome by *some other thing* (the *other* is the sign of all mysteries). By purely graphic means, which never resort to the noble alibi of *art*, Encyclopedic drawing explodes the exact world it takes as its subject. We may specify the meaning of this subversion which affects not only ideology (and in this the *Encyclopedia*'s plates singularly enlarge the dimensions of the enterprise) but also, in a much more serious manner, human rationality. In its very order (described here in the form of the syntagm and the paradigm, the vignette and the bottom of the page), the Encyclopedic plate accomplishes this *risk* of reason. The vignette, a realistic representation of a simple, familiar world (shops, workshops, landscapes) is linked to a certain tranquil evidence of the world: the vignette is calm, reassuring; what can be more deliciously domestic than the kitchen garden with its enclosing walls, its espaliers in the sun? What can be happier, more docile, than the fisherman at his line, the tailor sitting at his window, the feather vendors and the child talking to them? In this Encyclopedic heaven (the upper part of the plates), evil is infrequent; scarcely a trace of discomfort over the hard labors of the glassworkers, armed with pathetic tools, poorly protected against the terrible heat; and when Nature darkens, there always remains a man somewhere to reassure us: a fisherman with a torch beside the night sea, a scientist discoursing before the black basalts of Antrim, the surgeon's light hand resting on the body he is cutting open, figures of knowledge inserted into the heart of the storm (in the engraving of waterspouts). Yet as soon as we leave the vignette for the more analytic plates or images, the world's peaceful order gives way to a certain *violence*. All the forces of reason and unreason concur in this poetic disquiet; first of all metaphor itself makes an infinitely ambiguous object out of a simple, literal object: the sea urchin is *also* a sun, a monstrance: the named world is never certain, constantly fascinated by divined and inaccessible essences; and then, above all (and this is the final interrogation raised by these plates), the analytic mind itself, armed with triumphant reason, can only double the explained world by a new world *to be explained*, according to a process of infinite circularity which is that of the dictionary itself, wherein the world can be defined only by other words; by "entering" into details, by displacing the levels of perception, by revealing the hidden, by isolating the elements from their practical context, by giving objects an abstract essence, in short by "opening up" nature, the Encyclopedic image can only, at a certain moment, transcend Nature, attaining to a supernature: it is by dint of didacticism that a kind of wild surrealism is generated here (a phenomenon which we also find in an ambiguous mode in the disturbing encyclopedia Flaubert gives us in *Bouvard and Pécuchet*): do we want to show how equestrian statues are cast? We must wrap them in an extravagant apparatus of wax, tapes, and supports: what madness could attain to this *limit* (not to mention the violent demystification which reduces a warrior Louis XIV to this monstrous doll)? In a general way, the *Encyclopedia* is fascinated, at reason's instance, by the *wrong side* of things: it cross-sections, it amputates, it turns inside out, it tries to get *behind* Nature. Now any "wrong side" is disturbing: science and parascience are mixed, above all on the level of the image. The *Encyclopedia* constantly proceeds to an impious fragmentation of the world, but what it finds at the term of this fracture is not the fundamental state of pure causes; in most cases the image obliges it to recompose an object that is strictly *unreasonable*; once the first nature is dissolved, another nature appears, quite as formed as the first. In a word, the fracture of the world is impossible: a glance suffices—ours—for the world to be eternally complete.

1964

The Eiffel Tower

MAUPASSANT often lunched at the restaurant in the Tower, though he didn't care much for the food: *It's the only place in Paris,* he used to say, *where I don't have to see it.* And it's true that you must take endless precautions, in Paris, not to see the Eiffel Tower; whatever the season, through mist and cloud, on overcast days or in sunshine, in rain—wherever you are, whatever the landscape of roofs, domes, or branches separating you from it, *the Tower is there*; incorporated into daily life until you can no longer grant it any specific attribute, determined merely to persist, like a rock or the river, it is as literal as a phenomenon of Nature whose meaning can be questioned to infinity but whose existence is incontestable. There is virtually no Parisian glance it fails to *touch* at some time of day; at the moment I begin writing these lines about it, the Tower is there, in front of me, framed by my window; and at the very moment the January night blurs it, apparently trying to make it invisible, to deny its presence, two little lights come on, winking gently as they revolve at its very tip: all this night, too, it will be there, connecting me above Paris to each of my friends that I know are seeing it: with it we all comprise

From *The Eiffel Tower and Other Mythologies.*

a shifting figure of which it is the steady center: the Tower is friendly.

The Tower is also present to the entire world. First of all as a universal symbol of Paris, it is everywhere on the globe where Paris is to be stated as an image; from the Midwest to Australia, there is no journey to France which isn't made, somehow, in the Tower's name, no schoolbook, poster, or film about France which fails to propose it as the major sign of a people and of a place: it belongs to the universal language of travel. Further: beyond its strictly Parisian statement, it touches the most general human image-repertoire: its simple, primary shape confers upon it the vocation of an infinite cipher: in turn and according to the appeals of our imagination, the symbol of Paris, of modernity, of communication, of science or of the nineteenth century, rocket, stem, derrick, phallus, lightning rod or insect, confronting the great itineraries of our dreams, it is the inevitable sign; just as there is no Parisian glance which is not compelled to encounter it, there is no fantasy which fails, sooner or later, to acknowledge its form and to be nourished by it; pick up a pencil and let your hand, in other words your thoughts, wander, and it is often the Tower which will appear, reduced to that simple line whose sole mythic function is to join, as the poet says, *base and summit*, or again, *earth and heaven*.

This pure—virtually empty—sign—is ineluctable, *because it means everything*. In order to negate the Eiffel Tower (though the temptation to do so is rare, for this symbol offends nothing in us), you must, like Maupassant, get up on it and, so to speak, identify yourself with it. Like man himself, who is the only one not to know his own glance, the Tower is the only blind point of the total optical system of which it is the center and Paris the circumference. But in this movement which seems to limit it, the Tower acquires a new power: an object when we look at it, it becomes a lookout in its turn when we visit it, and now constitutes as an object, simultaneously extended and collected beneath it, that Paris which just now was looking at it. The Tower is an object which sees, a glance which is seen; it is a complete verb, both active and passive, in which no function, no *voice* (as we say in grammar, with a piquant ambiguity) is defective. This dialectic is not in the least banal, it makes the Tower a singular monument; for the world ordinarily produces either purely functional organisms (camera or eye) intended to see things but which then afford nothing to sight, what *sees* being mythically linked to what remains *hidden* (this is the theme of the voyeur), or else spectacles which themselves are blind and are left in the pure passivity of the visible. The Tower (and this is one of its mythic powers) transgresses this separation, this habitual divorce of *seeing* and *being seen*; it achieves a sovereign circulation between the two functions; it is a complete object which has, if one may say so, both sexes of sight. This radiant position in the order of perception gives it a prodigious propensity to meaning: the Tower attracts meaning, the way a lightning rod attracts thunderbolts; for all lovers of signification, it plays a glamorous part, that of a pure signifier, i.e., of a form in which men unceasingly put *meaning* (which they extract at will from their knowledge, their dreams, their history), without this meaning thereby ever being finite and fixed: who can say what the Tower will be for humanity tomorrow? But there can be no doubt it will always be something, and something of humanity itself. Glance, object, symbol, such is the infinite circuit of functions which permits it always to be something other and something much more than the Eiffel Tower.

In order to satisfy this great oneiric function, which makes it into a kind of total monument, the Tower must escape reason. The first condition of this victorious flight is that the Tower be an utterly *useless* monument. The Tower's inutility has always been obscurely felt to be a scandal, i.e., a truth, one that is precious and inadmissible. Even before it was built, it was blamed for being useless, which, it was believed at the time, was sufficient to condemn it; it was not in the spirit of a period commonly dedicated to rationality and to the empiricism of great bourgeois enterprises to endure the notion of a useless object (unless it was declaratively an *objet d'art*, which was also unthinkable in relation to the Tower); hence Gustave Eiffel, in his own defense of his project in reply to the Artists' Petition, scrupulously lists all the future uses of the Tower: they are all, as we might expect of an engineer, scientific uses: aerodynamic measurements, studies of the resistance of substances, physiology of the climber, radio-electric research, problems of telecommunication, meteorological observations, etc. These uses are doubtless incontestable, but they seem quite ridiculous alongside the overwhelming myth of the Tower, of the human meaning which it has assumed throughout the world. This is because here the utilitarian excuses, however ennobled they may be by the myth of Science, are nothing in comparison to the great imaginary function which enables men to be strictly human. Yet, as always, the gratuitous meaning of the work is never avowed directly: it is rationalized under the rubric of *use*: Eiffel saw his Tower in the form of a serious object, rational, useful; men return it to him in the form of a great baroque dream which quite naturally touches on the borders of the irrational.

This double movement is a profound one: architecture is always dream and function, expression of a utopia and instrument of a convenience. Even before the Tower's birth, the nineteenth century (especially in America and in England) had often dreamed of structures whose height would be astonishing, for the century was given to technological feats, and the conquest of the sky once again preyed upon humanity. In 1881, shortly before the Tower, a French architect had elaborated the project of a sun tower; now this project, quite mad technologically, since it relied on masonry and not on steel, also put itself under the warrant of a thoroughly empirical utility; on the one hand, a bonfire placed on top of the structure was to illuminate the darkness of every nook and cranny in Paris by a system of mirrors (a system that was undoubtedly a complex one!), and on the other, the last story of this sun tower (about 1,000 feet, like the Eiffel Tower) was to be reserved for a kind of sunroom, in which invalids would benefit from an air "as pure as in the mountains." And yet, here as in the case of the Tower, the naïve utilitarianism of the enterprise is not separate from the oneiric, infinitely powerful function which, actually, inspires its creation: use never does anything but shelter meaning. Hence we might speak, among men, of a true Babel complex: Babel was supposed to *serve* to communicate with God, and yet Babel is a dream which touches much greater depths than that of the theological project; and just as this great ascensional dream, released from its utilitarian prop, is finally what remains in the countless Babels represented by the painters, as if the function of art were to reveal the profound uselessness of objects, just so the Tower, almost immediately disengaged from the scientific considerations which had authorized its birth (it matters very little here that the Tower should be in fact useful), has arisen from a great human dream in which movable and infinite meanings are mingled: it has reconquered the basic uselessness which makes it live in men's imagination. At first, it was sought—so paradoxical is the notion of an empty monument—to make it into a "temple of Science"; but this is only a metaphor; as a matter of fact, the Tower is *nothing*, it achieves a kind of zero degree of the monument; it participates in no rite, in no cult, not even in Art; you cannot visit the Tower as a museum: there is nothing to see *inside* the Tower. This empty monument nevertheless receives each year twice as many visitors as the Louvre and considerably more than the largest movie house in Paris.

Then why do we visit the Eiffel Tower? No doubt in order to participate in a dream of which it is (and this is its originality) much more the crystallizer than the true object. The Tower is not a usual spectacle; to enter the Tower, to scale it, to run around its courses, is, in a manner both more elementary and more profound, to accede to a *view* and to explore the interior of an object (though an openwork one), to transform the touristic rite into an adventure of sight and of the intelligence. It is this double function I should like to speak of briefly, before passing in conclusion to the major symbolic function of the Tower, which is its final meaning.

The Tower looks at Paris. To visit the Tower is to get oneself up onto the balcony in order to perceive, comprehend, and savor a certain essence of Paris. And here again, the Tower is an original monument. Habitually, belvederes are outlooks upon Nature, whose elements—waters, valleys, forests—they assemble beneath them, so that the tourism of the "fine view" infallibly implies a naturist mythology. Whereas the Tower overlooks not Nature but the city; and yet, by its very position of a visited outlook, the Tower makes the city into a kind of Nature; it constitutes the swarming of men into a landscape, it adds to the frequently grim urban myth a romantic dimension, a harmony, a mitigation; by it, starting from it, the city joins up with the great natural themes which are offered to the curiosity of men: the ocean, the storm, the mountains, the snow, the rivers. To visit the Tower, then, is to enter into contact not with a historical Sacred, as is the case for the majority of monuments, but rather with a new Nature, that of human space: the Tower is not a trace, a souvenir, in short a culture; but rather an immediate consumption of a humanity made natural by that glance which transforms it into space.

One might say that for this reason the Tower materializes an imagination which has had its first expression in literature (it is frequently the function of the great books to achieve in advance what technology will merely put into execution). The nineteenth century, fifty years before the Tower, produced indeed two works in which the (perhaps very old) fantasy of a panoramic vision received the guarantee of a major poetic writing (*écriture*): these are, on the one hand, the chapter of *Notre-Dame de Paris* (*The Hunchback of Notre Dame*) devoted to a bird's-eye view of Paris, and on the other, Michelet's *Tableau chronologique*. Now, what is admirable in these two great inclusive visions, one of Paris, the other of France, is that Hugo and Michelet clearly understood that to the marvelous mitigation of altitude the panoramic vision added an incomparable power of *intellection*: the bird's-eye view, which each visitor to the Tower can assume in an instant for his own, gives us the world to *read* and not only to perceive; this is why it corresponds to a new sensibility of vision; in the past, to travel (we may recall certain—admirable, moreover—promenades of Rousseau) was to be thrust into the midst of sensation, to perceive only a kind of tidal wave of things; the bird's-eye view, on the contrary, represented by our romantic writers as if they had anticipated both the construction of the Tower and the birth of aviation, permits us to transcend sensation and to see things *in their structure*. Hence it is the advent of a new perception, of an intellectualist mode, which these literatures and these architectures of vision mark out (born in the same century and probably from the same history): Paris and France become under Hugo's pen and Michelet's (and under the glance of the Tower) intelligible objects, yet without—and this is what is new—losing anything of their materiality; a new category appears, that of concrete abstraction; this, moreover, is the meaning which we can give today to the word *structure*: a corpus of intelligent forms.

Like Monsieur Jourdain confronted with prose, every visitor to the Tower makes structuralism without knowing it (which does not keep prose and structure from existing all the same); in Paris spread out beneath him, he spontaneously distinguishes separate—because known—points—and yet does not stop linking them, perceiving them within a great functional space; in short, he separates and groups; Paris offers itself to him as an object virtually *prepared*, exposed to the intelligence, but which he must himself construct by a final activity of the mind: nothing less passive than the *overall view* the Tower gives to Paris. This activity of the mind, conveyed by the tourist's modest glance, has a name: decipherment.

What, in fact, is a panorama? An image we attempt to decipher, in which we try to recognize known sites, to identify landmarks. Take some view of Paris taken from the Eiffel Tower; here you make out the hill sloping down from Chaillot, there the Bois de Boulogne; but where is the Arc de Triomphe? You don't see it, and this absence compels you to inspect the panorama once again, to look for this point which is missing in your structure; your knowledge (the knowledge you may have of Parisian topography) struggles with your perception, and in a sense, that is what intelligence is: to *reconstitute*, to make memory and sensation cooperate so as to produce in your mind a simulacrum of Paris, of which the elements are in front of you, real, ancestral, but nonetheless disoriented by the total space in which they are given to you, for this space was unknown to you. Hence we approach the complex, dialectical nature of all panoramic vision; on the one hand, it is a euphoric vision, for it can slide slowly, lightly the entire length of a continuous image of Paris, and initially no "accident" manages to interrupt this great layer of mineral and vegetal strata, perceived in the distance in the bliss of altitude; but, on the other hand, this very continuity engages the mind in a certain struggle, it seeks to be deciphered, we must find *signs* within it, a familiarity proceeding from history and from myth; this is why a panorama can never be consumed as a work of art, the aesthetic interest of a painting ceasing once we try to *recognize* in it particular points derived from our knowledge; to say that there is a beauty to Paris stretched out at the feet of the Tower is doubtless to acknowledge this euphoria of aerial vision which recognizes nothing other than a nicely connected space; but it is also to mask the quite intellectual effort of the eye before an object which requires to be divided up, identified, reattached to memory; for the bliss of sensation (nothing happier than a lofty outlook) does not suffice to elude the questioning nature of the mind before any image.

This generally intellectual character of the panoramic vision is further attested by the following phenomenon, which Hugo and Michelet had moreover made into the mainspring of their bird's-eye views: to perceive Paris from above is infallibly to imagine a history; from the top of the Tower, the mind finds itself dreaming of the mutation of the landscape which it has before its eyes; through the astonishment of space, it plunges into the mystery of time, lets itself be affected by a kind of spontaneous anamnesis: it is duration itself which becomes panoramic. Let us put ourselves back (no difficult task) at the level of an average knowledge, an ordinary question put to the panorama of Paris; four great moments immediately leap out to our vision, i.e., to our consciousness. The first is that of prehistory; Paris was then covered by a layer of water, out of which barely emerged a few solid points; set on the Tower's first floor, the visitor would have had his nose level with the waves and would have seen only some scattered islets, the Etoile, the Pantheon, a wooded island which was Montmartre and two blue stakes in the distance, the towers of Notre-Dame, then to his left, bordering this huge lake, the slopes of Mont Valérien; and conversely, the traveler who chooses to put himself today on the heights of this eminence, in foggy weather, would see emerging the two upper stories of the Tower from a liquid base; this prehistoric relation of the Tower and the water has been, so to speak, symbolically maintained down to our own days, for the Tower is partly built on a thin arm of the Seine filled in (up to the rue de l'Université) and it still seems to rise from a gesture of the river whose bridges it guards. The second history which lies before the Tower's gaze is the Middle Ages; Cocteau once said that the Tower was the Notre-Dame of the Left Bank; though the cathedral of Paris is not the highest of the city's monuments (the Invalides, the Pantheon, Sacré-Coeur are higher), it forms with the Tower a pair, a symbolic couple, recognized, so to speak, by Tourist folklore, which readily reduces Paris to its Tower and its Cathedral: a symbol articulated on the opposition of the past (the Middle Ages always represent a dense time) and the present, of stone, old as the world, and metal, sign of modernity. The third moment that can be read from the Tower is that of a broad history, undifferentiated since it proceeds from the Monarchy to the Empire, from the Invalides to the Arc de Triomphe: this is strictly the History of France, as it is experienced by French schoolchildren, and of which many episodes, present in every schoolboy memory, touch Paris. Finally, the Tower surveys a fourth history of Paris, the one which is being made now; certain modern monuments (UNESCO, the Radio-Télévision building) are beginning to set signs of the future within its space; the Tower permits harmonizing these unaccommodated substances (glass, metal), these new forms, with the stones and domes of the past; Paris, in its duration, under the Tower's gaze, composes itself like an abstract canvas in which dark oblongs (derived from a very old past) are contiguous with the white rectangles of modern architecture.

Once these points of history and of space are established by the eye, from the top of the Tower, the imagination continues filling out the Parisian panorama, giving it its structure; but what then intervenes are certain human functions; like the devil Asmodeus, by rising above Paris, the visitor to the Tower has the illusion of raising the enormous lid which covers the private life of millions of human beings; the city then becomes an intimacy whose functions, i.e., whose connections he deciphers; on the great polar axis, perpendicular to the horizontal curve of the river, three zones stacked one after the other, as though along a prone body, three functions of human life: at the top, at the foot of Montmartre, pleasure; at the center, around the Opéra, materiality, business, commerce; toward the bottom, at the foot of the Pantheon, knowledge, study; then, to the right and left, enveloping this vital axis like two protective muffs, two large zones of habitation, one residential, the other blue-collar; still farther, two wooded strips, Boulogne and Vincennes. It has been observed that a kind of very old law incites cities to develop toward the west, in the direction of the setting sun; it is on this side that the wealth of the fine neighborhoods proceeds, the east remaining the site of poverty; the Tower, by its very implantation, seems to follow this movement discreetly; one might say that it accompanies Paris in this westward shift, which our capital does not escape, and that it even invites the city toward its pole of development, to the south and to the west, where the sun is warmer, thereby participating in that great mythic function which makes every city into a living being: neither brain nor organ, situated a little apart from its vital zones, the Tower is merely the witness, the gaze which discreetly fixes, with its slender signal, the whole structure—geographical, historical, and social—of Paris space. This deciphering of Paris, performed by the Tower's gaze, is not only an act of the mind, it is also an initiation. To climb the Tower in order to contemplate Paris from it is the equivalent of that first journey, by which the young man from the provinces went up to Paris, in order to conquer the city. At the age of twelve, young Eiffel himself took the diligence from Dijon with his mother and discovered the "magic" of Paris. The city, a kind of superlative capital, summons up that movement of accession to a superior order of pleasures, of values, of arts and luxuries; it is a kind of precious world of which knowledge makes the man, marks an entrance into a true life of passions and responsibilities; it is this myth—no doubt a very old one—which the trip to the Tower still allows us to suggest; for the tourist who climbs the Tower, however mild he may be, Paris laid out before his eyes by an individual and deliberate act of contemplation is still something of the Paris confronted, defied, possessed by Rastignac. Hence, of all the sites visited by the foreigner or the provincial, the Tower is the first obligatory monument; it is a Gateway, it marks the transition to a knowledge: one must sacrifice to the Tower by a rite of inclusion from which, precisely, the Parisian alone can excuse himself: the Tower is indeed the site which allows one to be incorporated into a race, and when it regards Paris, it is the very essence of the capital it gathers up and proffers to the foreigner who has paid to it his initiational tribute.

From Paris contemplated, we must now work our way back toward the Tower itself: the Tower which will live its life as an object (before being mobilized as a symbol). Ordinarily, for the tourist, every object is first of all an *inside*, for there is no visit without the exploration of an enclosed space: to visit a church, a museum, a palace is first of all to shut oneself up, to "make the rounds" of an interior, a little in the manner of an owner: every exploration is an appropriation; this tour of the *inside* corresponds, moreover, to the question raised by the *outside*: the monument is a riddle, to enter it is to solve, to possess it; here we recognize in the tourist visit that initiational function we have just invoked apropos of the trip to the Tower; the cohort of visitors which is enclosed by a monument and processionally follows its internal meanders before coming back outside is quite like the neophyte who, in order to accede to the initiate's status, is obliged to traverse a dark and unfamiliar route within the initiatory edifice. In the religious protocol as in the tourist enterprise, being enclosed is therefore a function of the rite. Here, too, the Tower is a paradoxical object: one cannot be shut up within it since what defines the Tower is its longilineal form and its open structure: How can you be enclosed within emptiness, how can you visit a line? Yet incontestably the Tower is visited: we linger within it, before using it as an observatory. What is happening? What becomes of the great exploratory function of the *inside* when it is applied to this empty and depthless monument which might be said to consist entirely of an exterior substance?

In order to understand how the modern visitor adapts himself to the paradoxical monument which is offered to his imagination, we need merely observe what the Tower gives him, insofar as one sees in it an object and no longer a lookout. On this point, the Tower's provisions are of two kinds. The first is of a technical order; the Tower offers for consumption a certain number of performances, or, if one prefers, of paradoxes, and the visitor then becomes an engineer by proxy; these are, first of all, the four bases, and especially (for enormity does not astonish) the exaggeratedly oblique insertion of the metal pillars in the mineral mass; this obliquity is curious insofar as it gives birth to an upright form, whose very verticality absorbs its departure in slanting forms, and here there is a kind of agreeable challenge for the visitor; then come the elevators, quite surprising by their obliquity, for the ordinary imagination requires that what rises mechanically slide along a vertical axis; and for anyone who takes the stairs, there is the enlarged spectacle of all the details, plates, beams, bolts, which *make* the Tower, the surprise of seeing how this rectilinear form, which is consumed in every corner of Paris as a pure line, is composed of countless segments, interlinked, crossed, divergent: an operation of reducing an appearance (the straight line) to its contrary reality (a lacework of broken substances), a kind of demystification provided by simple enlargement of the level of perception, as in those photographs in which the curve of a face, by enlargement, appears to be formed of a thousand tiny squares variously illuminated. Thus the Tower-as-object furnishes its observer, provided he insinuates himself into it, a whole series of paradoxes, the delectable contraction of an appearance and of its contrary reality.

The Tower's second provision, as an object, is that, despite its technical singularity, it constitutes a familiar "little world"; from the ground level, a whole humble commerce accompanies its departure: vendors of postcards, souvenirs, knick-knacks, balloons, toys, sunglasses, herald a commercial life which we rediscover thoroughly installed on the first platform. Now any commerce has a space-taming function; selling, buying, exchanging—it is by these simple gestures that men truly dominate the wildest sites, the most sacred constructions. The myth of the moneylenders driven out of the Temple is actually an ambiguous one, for such commerce testifies to a kind of affectionate familiarity with regard to a monument whose singularity no longer intimidates, and it is by a Christian sentiment (hence to a certain degree a special one) that the spiritual excludes the familiar; in Antiquity, a great religious festival as well as a theatrical representation, a veritable sacred ceremony, in no way prevented the revelation of the most everyday gestures, such as eating or drinking: all pleasures proceeded simultaneously, not by some heedless permissiveness but because the ceremonial was never savage and certainly offered no contradiction to the quotidian. The Tower is

not a sacred monument, and no taboo can forbid a commonplace life to develop there, but there can be no question, nonetheless, of a trivial phenomenon here; the installation of a
restaurant on the Tower, for instance (food being the object of
the most symbolic of trades), is a phenomenon corresponding
to a whole meaning of leisure; man always seems disposed—if
no constraints appear to stand in his way—to seek out a kind
of counterpoint in his pleasures: this is what is called comfort.
The Eiffel Tower is a comfortable object, and moreover, it is
in this that it is an object either very old (analogous, for
instance, to the ancient Circus) or very modern (analogous to
certain American institutions such as the drive-in movie, in
which one can simultaneously enjoy the film, the car, the food,
and the freshness of the night air). Further, by affording its
visitor a whole polyphony of pleasures, from technological
wonder to haute cuisine, including the panorama, the Tower
ultimately reunites with the essential function of all major
human sites: autarchy; the Tower can live on itself: one can
dream there, eat there, observe there, understand there, marvel
there, shop there; as on an ocean liner (another mythic object
that sets children dreaming), one can feel oneself cut off from
the world and yet the owner of a world.

1964

Introduction to the
Structural Analysis of Narratives

THE narratives of the world are numberless. Narrative is first and foremost a prodigious variety of genres, themselves distributed amongst different substances—as though any material were fit to receive man's stories. Able to be carried by articulated language, spoken or written, fixed or moving images, gestures, and the ordered mixture of all these substances; narrative is present in myth, legend, fable, tale, novella, epic, history, tragedy, drama, comedy, mime, painting (think of Carpaccio's *Saint Ursula*), stained-glass windows, cinema, comics, news item, conversation. Moreover, under this almost infinite diversity of forms, narrative is present in every age, in every place, in every society; it begins with the very history of mankind and there nowhere is nor has been a people without narrative. All classes, all human groups, have their narratives, enjoyment of which is very often shared by men with different, even opposing,[1] cultural backgrounds. Caring nothing for the division between good and bad literature, narrative is interna-

From *Image-Music-Text*.

[1] It must be remembered that this is not the case with either poetry or the essay, both of which are dependent on the cultural level of their consumers.

tional, transhistorical, transcultural: it is simply there, like life itself.

Must we conclude from this universality that narrative is insignificant? Is it so general that we can have nothing to say about it except for the modest description of a few highly individualized varieties, something literary history occasionally undertakes? But then how are we to master even these varieties, how are we to justify our right to differentiate and identify them? How is novel to be set against novella, tale against myth, drama against tragedy (as has been done a thousand times) without reference to a common model? Such a model is implied by every proposition relating to the most individual, the most historical, of narrative forms. It is thus legitimate that, far from the abandoning of any idea of dealing with narrative on the grounds of its universality, there should have been (from Aristotle on) a periodic interest in narrative form and it is normal that the newly developing structuralism should make this form one of its first concerns—is not structuralism's constant aim to master the infinity of utterances [*paroles*] by describing the "language" ["*langue*"] of which they are the products and from which they can be generated. Faced with the infinity of narratives, the multiplicity of standpoints—historical, psychological, sociological, ethnological, aesthetic, etc.—from which they can be studied, the analyst finds himself in more or less the same situation as Saussure confronted by the heterogeneity of language [*langage*] and seeking to extract a principle of classification and a central focus for description from the apparent confusion of the individual messages. Keeping simply to modern times, the Russian formalists, Propp, and Lévi-Strauss have taught us to recognize the following dilemma: either a narrative is merely a rambling collection of events, in which case nothing can be said about it other than by referring back to the storyteller's (the author's) art, talent, or genius—all mythical forms of chance[2]—or else it shares with other narratives a common structure which is open to analysis, no matter how much patience its formulation requires. There is a world of difference between the most complex randomness and the most elementary combinatory scheme, and it is impossible to combine (to produce) a narrative without reference to an implicit system of units and rules.

Where then are we to look for the structures of narrative? Doubtless, in narratives themselves. *Each and every* narrative? Many commentators who accept the idea of a narrative structure are nevertheless unable to resign themselves to dissociating literary analysis from the example of the experimental sciences; nothing daunted, they ask that a purely inductive method be applied to narrative and that one start by studying all the narratives within a genre, a period, a society. This commonsense view is utopian. Linguistics itself, with only some three thousand languages to embrace, cannot manage such a program and has wisely turned deductive, a step which in fact marked its veritable constitution as a science and the beginning of its spectacular progress, it even succeeding in anticipating facts prior to their discovery.[3] So what of narrative analysis, faced as it is with millions of narratives? Of necessity, it is condemned to a deductive procedure, obliged first to devise a hypothetical model of description (what American linguists call a "theory") and then gradually to work down from this model toward the different narrative

[2] There does, of course, exist an "art" of the storyteller, which is the ability to generate narratives (messages) from the structure (the code). This art corresponds to the notion of *performance* in Chomsky and is far removed from the "genius" of the author, romantically conceived as some barely explicable personal secret.

[3] See the history of the Hittite *a*, postulated by Saussure and actually discovered fifty years later, as given in Emile Benveniste, *Problèmes de linguistique générale.*

species which at once conform to and depart from the model. It is only at the level of these conformities and departures that analysis will be able to come back to, but now equipped with a single descriptive tool, the plurality of narratives, to their historical, geographical and cultural diversity.[4]

Thus, in order to describe and classify the infinite number of narratives, a "Theory" (in this pragmatic sense) is needed and the immediate task is that of finding it, of starting to define it. Its development can be greatly facilitated if one begins from a model able to provide it with its initial terms and principles. In the current state of research, it seems reasonable[5] that the structural analysis of narrative be given linguistics itself as founding model.

I. THE LANGUAGE OF NARRATIVE

1. Beyond the sentence

As we know, linguistics stops at the sentence, the last unit which it considers to fall within its scope. If the sentence, being an order and not a series, cannot be reduced to the sum of the words which compose it and constitutes thereby a specific unit, a piece of discourse, on the contrary, is no more than the succession of the sentences composing it. From the

[4] Let us bear in mind the present conditions of linguistic description: ". . . linguistic 'structure' is always relative not just to the data or corpus but also to the grammatical theory describing the data," E. Bach, *An Introduction to Transformational Grammars*; "it has been recognized that language must be described as a formal structure, but that the description first of all necessitates specification of adequate procedures and criteria and that, finally, the reality of the object is inseparable from the method given for its description," Benveniste.

[5] But not imperative: see Claude Bremond, "La logique des possibles narratifs," *Communications* 8, 1966, which is more logical than linguistic. [Bremond's various studies in this field have now been collected in a volume entitled, precisely, *Logique du récit*; his work consists in the analysis of narrative according to the pattern of possible alternatives, each narrative moment—or function—giving rise to a set of different possible resolutions, the actualization of any one of which in turn produces a new set of alternatives.]

point of view of linguistics, there is nothing in discourse that is not to be found in the sentence: "The sentence," writes Martinet, "is the smallest segment that is perfectly and wholly representative of discourse."[6] Hence there can be no question of linguistics setting itself an object superior to the sentence, since beyond the sentence are only more sentences—having described the flower, the botanist is not to get involved in describing the bouquet.

And yet it is evident that discourse itself (as a set of sentences) is organized and that, through this organization, it can be seen as the message of another language, one operating at a higher level than the language of the linguists.[7] Discourse has its units, its rules, its "grammar": beyond the sentence, and though consisting solely of sentences, it must naturally form the object of a second linguistics. For a long time indeed, such a linguistics of discourse bore a glorious name, that of Rhetoric. As a result of a complex historical movement, however, in which Rhetoric went over to belles-lettres and the latter was divorced from the study of language, it has recently become necessary to take up the problem afresh. The new linguistics of discourse has still to be developed, but at least it is being postulated, and by the linguists themselves.[8] This last fact is not without significance, for, although constituting an autonomous object, discourse must be studied from the basis of linguistics. If a working hypothesis is needed for an analysis whose task is immense and whose materials infinite, then the most reasonable thing is to posit a homological relation between sentence and discourse insofar as it is likely that a similar formal organization orders all semiotic systems, whatever

[6] André Martinet, "Réflexions sur la phrase," in *Language and Society*.
[7] It goes without saying, as Jakobson has noted, that between the sentence and what lies beyond the sentence there are transitions; coordination, for instance, can work over the limit of the sentence.
[8] See especially: Benveniste, op. cit., Chapter 10; Z. S. Harris, "Discourse Analysis," *Language* 28, 1952; N. Ruwet, "Analyse structurale d'un poème français," *Linguistics* 3, 1964.

their substances and dimensions. A discourse is a long "sentence" (the units of which are not necessarily sentences), just as a sentence, allowing for certain specifications, is a short "discourse." This hypothesis accords well with a number of propositions put forward in contemporary anthropology. Jakobson and Lévi-Strauss have pointed out that mankind can be defined by the ability to create secondary—"self-multiplying"—systems (tools for the manufacture of other tools, double articulation of language, incest taboo permitting the fanning out of families) while the Soviet linguist Ianov supposes that artificial languages can only have been acquired after natural language: what is important for men is to have the use of several systems of meaning and natural language helps in the elaboration of artificial languages. It is therefore legitimate to posit a "secondary" relation between sentence and discourse—a relation which will be referred to as homological, in order to respect the purely formal nature of the correspondences.

The general language [*langue*] of narrative is one (and clearly only one) of the idioms apt for consideration by the linguistics of discourse[9] and it accordingly comes under the homological hypothesis. Structurally, narrative shares the characteristics of the sentence without ever being reducible to the simple sum of its sentences: a narrative is a long sentence, just as every constative sentence is in a way the rough outline of a short narrative. Although there provided with different signifiers (often extremely complex), one does find in narrative, expanded and transformed proportionately, the principal verbal categories: tenses, aspects, moods, persons. Moreover the "subjects" themselves, as opposed to the verbal predicates, readily yield to the sentence model; the actantial typology pro-

[9] One of the tasks of such a linguistics would be precisely that of establishing a typology of forms of discourse. Three broad types can be recognized provisionally: metonymic (narrative), metaphoric (lyric, poetry, sapiential discourse), enthymematic (intellectual discourse).

posed by A. J. Greimas[10] discovers in the multitude of narrative characters the elementary functions of grammatical analysis. Nor does the homology suggested here have merely a
heuristic value: it implies an identity between language and
literature (inasmuch as the latter can be seen as a sort of
privileged vehicle of narrative). It is hardly possible any
longer to conceive of literature as an art that abandons all
further relation with language the moment it has used it as an
instrument to express ideas, passion, or beauty: language
never ceases to accompany discourse, holding up to it the
mirror of its own structure—does not literature, particularly
today, make a language of the very conditions of language?[11]

2. Levels of meaning

From the outset, linguistics furnishes the structural analysis
of narrative with a concept which is decisive in that, making
explicit immediately what is essential in every system of meaning, namely its organization, it allows us both to show how a
narrative is not a simple sum of propositions and to classify
the enormous mass of elements which go to make up a narrative. This concept is that of *level of description*.[12]

A sentence can be described, linguistically, on several levels
(phonetic, phonological, grammatical, contextual) and these
levels are in a hierarchical relationship with one another, for,
while all have their own units and correlations (whence the
necessity for a separate description of each of them), no level

[10] See below III.1. Greimas's own account can be found in *Sémantique
structurale*.

[11] Remember Mallarmé's insight at the time when he was contemplating a
work of linguistics: "Language appeared to him the instrument of fiction: he
will follow the method of language (determine it). Language self-reflecting.
So fiction seems to him the very process of the human mind—it is this that
sets in play all method, and man is reduced to will." It will be recalled
that for Mallarmé "Fiction" and "Poetry" are taken synonymously.

[12] "Linguistic descriptions are not, so to speak, monovalent. A description is
not simply 'right' or 'wrong' in itself . . . it is better thought of as more
useful or less," M. A. K. Halliday, "General linguistics and its application
to language teaching," *Patterns of Language*.

on its own can produce meaning. A unit belonging to a particular level only takes on meaning if it can be integrated in a
higher level; a phoneme, though perfectly describable, means
nothing in itself: it participates in meaning only when integrated in a word, and the word itself must in turn be integrated
in a sentence.[13] The theory of levels (as set out by Benveniste) gives two types of relations: distributional (if the
relations are situated on the same level) and integrational (if
they are grasped from one level to the next); consequently,
distributional relations alone are not sufficient to account for
meaning. In order to conduct a structural analysis, it is thus
first of all necessary to distinguish several levels or instances of
description and to place these instances within a hierarchical
(integrationary) perspective.

The levels are operations.[14] It is therefore normal that, as it
progresses, linguistics should tend to multiply them. Discourse
analysis, however, is as yet only able to work on rudimentary
levels. In its own way, rhetoric had assigned at least two
planes of description to discourse: *dispositio* and *elocutio*.[15]
Today, in his analysis of the structure of myth, Lévi-Strauss
has already indicated that the constituent units of mythical
discourse (mythemes) acquire meaning only because they are
grouped in bundles and because these bundles themselves
combine together.[16] As too, Tzvetan Todorov, reviving the
distinction made by the Russian formalists, proposes working
on two major levels, themselves subdivided: *story* (the argu-

[13] The levels of integration were postulated by the Prague School (vid. J.
Vachek, *A Prague School Reader in Linguistics*, Bloomington 1964, p. 468)
and have been adopted since by many linguists. It is Benveniste who, in my
opinion, has given the most illuminating analysis in this respect; op. cit.,
Chapter 10.

[14] "In somewhat vague terms, a level may be considered as a system of
symbols, rules, and so on, to be used for representing utterances," Bach,
op. cit.

[15] The third part of rhetoric, *inventio*, did not concern language—it had to
do with *res*, not with *verba*.

[16] *Structural Anthropology*.

ment), comprising a logic of actions and a "syntax" of characters, and *discourse*, comprising the tenses, aspects, and modes of the narrative.[17] But however many levels are proposed and whatever definition they are given, there can be no doubt that narrative is a hierarchy of instances. To understand a narrative is not merely to follow the unfolding of the story, it is also to recognize its construction in "stories," to project the horizontal concatenations of the narrative "thread" onto an implicitly vertical axis; to read (to listen to) a narrative is not merely to move from one word to the next, it is also to move from one level to the next. Perhaps I may be allowed to offer a kind of apologue in this connection. In "The Purloined Letter," Poe gives an acute analysis of the failure of the chief commissioner of the Paris police, powerless to find the letter. His investigations, says Poe, were perfect *"within the sphere of his specialty"*;[18] he searched everywhere, saturated entirely the level of the "police search," but in order to find the letter, protected by its conspicuousness, it was necessary to shift to another level, to substitute the concealer's principle of relevance for that of the policeman. Similarly, the "search" carried out over a horizontal set of narrative relations may well be as thorough as possible but must still, to be effective, also operate "vertically": meaning is not "at the end" of the narrative, it runs across it; just as conspicuous as the purloined letter, meaning eludes all unilateral investigation.

A great deal of tentative effort is still required before it will be possible to ascertain precisely the levels of narrative. Those that are suggested in what follows constitute a provisional profile whose merit remains almost exclusively didactic; they

---

[17] See T. Todorov "Les catégories du récit littéraire," *Communications* 8, 1966 [Todorov's work on narrative is now most easily accessible in two books, *Littérature et signification; poétique de la prose*. For a short account in English, see "Structural analysis of narrative," *Novel* I, 3, 1969.]

[18] [This in accordance with the Baudelaire version of the Poe story from which Barthes quotes; Poe's original reads: "so far as his labors extended."]

enable us to locate and group together the different problems, and this without, I think, being at variance with the few analyses so far.[19] It is proposed to distinguish three levels of description in the narrative work: the level of *"functions"* (in the sense this word has in Propp and Bremond), the level of *"actions"* (in the sense this word has in Greimas when he talks of characters as actants) and the level of *"narration"* (which is roughly the level of "discourse" in Todorov). These three levels are bound together according to a mode of progressive integration: a function only has meaning insofar as it occupies a place in the general action of an actant, and this action in turn receives its final meaning from the fact that it is narrated, entrusted to a discourse which possesses its own code.

II. FUNCTIONS

1. The determination of the units

Any system being the combination of units of known classes, the first task is to divide up narrative and determine the segments of narrative discourse that can be distributed into a limited number of classes. In a word, we have to define the smallest narrative units.

Given the integrational perspective described above, the analysis cannot rest satisfied with a purely distributional definition of the units. From the start, meaning must be the criterion of the unit: it is the functional nature of certain segments of the story that makes them units—hence the name "functions" immediately attributed to these first units. Since the Russian formalists,[20] a unit has been taken as any segment of the story which can be seen as the term of a correla-

---

[19] I have been concerned in this introduction to impede research in progress as little as possible.

[20] See especially B. Tomachevski, "Thématique" (1925), in *Théorie de la littérature*, ed. T. Todorov. A little later, Propp in *Morphology of the Folktale* defined the function as "an act of a character, defined from the point of view of its significance for the course of the action."

tion. The essence of a function is, so to speak, the seed that it sows in the narrative, planting an element that will come to fruition later—either on the same level or elsewhere, on another level. If in *Un Cœur simple* Flaubert at one point tells the reader, seemingly without emphasis, that the daughters of the Sous-Préfet of Pont-l'Evêque owned a parrot, it is because this parrot is subsequently to have a great importance in Félicité's life; the statement of this detail (whatever its linguistic form) thus constitutes a function, or narrative unit.

Is everything in a narrative functional? Does everything, down to the slightest detail, have a meaning? Can narrative be divided up entirely into functional units? We shall see in a moment that there are several kinds of functions, there being several kinds of correlations, but this does not alter the fact that a narrative is never made up of anything other than functions: in differing degrees, everything in it signifies. This is not a matter of art (on the part of the narrator), but of structure; in the realm of discourse, what is noted is by definition notable. Even were a detail to appear irretrievably insignificant, resistant to all functionality, it would nonetheless end up with precisely the meaning of absurdity or uselessness: everything has a meaning, or nothing has. To put it another way, one could say that art is without noise (as that term is employed in information theory):[21] art is a system which is pure, no unit ever goes wasted,[22] however long, however loose, however tenuous may be the thread connecting it to one of the levels of the story.[23]

---

[21] This is what separates art from "life," the latter knowing only "fuzzy" or "blurred" communications. "Fuzziness" (that beyond which it is impossible to see) can exist in art, but it does so as coded element (in Watteau for example). Even then, such "fuzziness" is unknown to the written code: writing is inescapably distinct.

[22] At least in literature, where the freedom of notation (in consequence of the abstract nature of articulated language) leads to a much greater responsibility than in the "analogical" arts such as cinema.

[23] The functionality of a narrative unit is more or less immediate (and hence apparent) according to the level on which it operates: when the units are

262 ප A BARTHES READER

From the linguistic point of view, the function is clearly a unit of content: it is "what it says" that makes of a statement a functional unit,[24] not the manner in which it is said. This constitutive signified may have a number of different signifiers, often very intricate. If I am told (in *Goldfinger*) that *Bond saw a man of about fifty*, the piece of information holds simultaneously two functions of unequal pressure: on the one hand, the character's age fits into a certain description of the man (the "usefulness" of which for the rest of the story is not nil, but diffuse, delayed); while on the other, the immediate signified of the statement is that Bond is unacquainted with his future interlocutor, the unit thus implying a very strong correlation (initiation of a threat and the need to establish the man's identity). In order to determine the initial narrative units, it is therefore vital never to lose sight of the functional nature of the segments under consideration and to recognize in advance that they will not necessarily coincide with the forms into which we traditionally cast the various parts of narrative discourse (actions, scenes, paragraphs, dialogues, interior monologues, etc.) still less with "psychological" divisions (modes of behavior, feelings, intentions, motivations, rationalizations of characters).

In the same way, since the "language" ["*langue*"] of narrative is not the language [*langue*] of articulated language [*langage articulé*]—though very often vehicled by it—narrative units will be substantially independent of linguistic units; they may indeed coincide with the latter, but occasionally, not systematically. Functions will be represented sometimes by units higher than the sentence (groups of sentences of varying

---

situated on the same level (as for instance in the case of suspense), the functionality is very clear; it is much less so when the function is saturated on the narrational level—a modern text, weakly signifying on the plane of the anecdote, only finds a full force of meaning on the plane of the writing.
[24] "Syntactical units beyond the sentence are in fact units of content," A. J. Greimas, *Cours de sémantique structurale*, 1964. The exploration of the functional level is thus part of general semantics.

lengths, up to the work in its entirety) and sometimes by lower ones (syntagm, word, and even, within the word, certain literary elements only[25]). When we are told that—the telephone ringing during night duty at Secret Service headquarters—*Bond picked up one of the four receivers*, the moneme *four* in itself constitutes a functional unit, referring as it does to a concept necessary to the story (that of a highly developed bureaucratic technology). In fact, the narrative unit in this case is not the linguistic unit (the word) but only its connoted value (linguistically, the word /four/ never means "four"); which explains how certain functional units can be shorter than the sentence without ceasing to belong to the order of discourse: such units then extend not beyond the sentence, than which they remain materially shorter, but beyond the level of denotation, which, like the sentence, is the province of linguistics properly speaking.

2. Classes of units

The functional units must be distributed into a small number of classes. If these classes are to be determined without recourse to the substance of content (psychological substance for example), it is again necessary to consider the different levels of meaning: some units have as correlates units on the same level, while the saturation of others requires a change of levels; hence, straightaway, two major classes of functions, distributional and integrational. The former correspond to what Propp and subsequently Bremond (in particular) take as functions but they will be treated here in a much more detailed way than is the case in their work. The term *"functions"* will be reserved for these units (though the other units are also functional), the model of description for which has become

---

[25] "The word must not be treated as an indivisible element of literary art, like a brick in building. It can be broken down into much finer 'verbal elements.' " J. Tynianov, quoted T. Todorov in *Langages* 6, 1971.

classic since Tomachevski's analysis: the purchase of a re-
volver has for correlate the moment when it will be used (and
if not used, the notation is reversed into a sign of indecision,
etc.); picking up the telephone has for correlate the moment
when it will be put down; the intrusion of the parrot into
Félicité's home has for correlate the episode of the stuffing,
the worshipping of the parrot, etc. As for the latter, the integrational units, these comprise all the *"indices"* (in the very
broad sense of the word[26]), the unit now referring not to a
complementary and consequential act but to a more or less
diffuse concept which is nevertheless necessary to the meaning
of the story: psychological indices concerning the characters,
data regarding their identity, notations of "atmosphere," and
so on. The relation between the unit and its correlate is now
no longer distributional (often several indices refer to the
same signified and the order of their occurrence in the discourse is not necessarily pertinent) but integrational. In order
to understand what an indicial notation "is for," one must
move to a higher level (characters' actions or narration), for
only there is the indice clarified: the power of the administra-
tive machine behind Bond, indexed by the number of tele-
phones, has no bearing on the sequence of actions in which
Bond is involved by answering the call; it finds its meaning
only on the level of a general typology of the actants (Bond is
on the side of order). Indices, because of the, in some sort,
vertical nature of their relations, are truly semantic units: unlike "functions" (in the strict sense), they refer to a signified,
not to an "operation." The ratification of indices is "higher
up," sometimes even remaining virtual, outside any explicit
syntagm (the "character" of a narrative agent may very well
never be explicitly named while yet being constantly indexed),
is a paradigmatic ratification. That of functions, by contrast, is

---

[26] These designations, like those that follow, may all be provisional.

always "further on," is a syntagmatic ratification.[27] *Functions* and *indices* thus overlay another classic distinction: functions involve metonymic relata, indices metaphoric relata; the former correspond to a functionality of doing, the latter to a functionality of being.[28]

These two main classes of units, functions and indices, should already allow a certain classification of narratives. Some narratives are heavily functional (such as folk tales), while others on the contrary are heavily indicial (such as "psychological" novels); between these two poles lies a whole series of intermediary forms, dependent on history, society, genre. But we can go further. Within each of the two main classes it is immediately possible to determine two subclasses of narrative units. Returning to the class of functions, its units are not all of the same "importance": some constitute real hinge points of the narrative (or of a fragment of the narrative); others merely "fill in" the narrative space separating the hinge functions. Let us call the former *cardinal functions* (or *nuclei*) and the latter, having regard to their complementary nature, *catalyzers*. For a function to be cardinal, it is enough that the action to which it refers open (or continue, or close) an alternative that is of direct consequence for the subsequent development of the story, in short that it inaugurate or conclude an uncertainty. If, in a fragment of narrative, *the telephone rings*, it is equally possible to answer or not answer, two acts which will unfailingly carry the narrative along different paths. Between two cardinal functions however, it is always possible to set out subsidiary notations which cluster around one or other nucleus without modifying its alternative nature:

[27] Which does not mean that the syntagmatic setting out of functions may not *finally* hold paradigmatic relations between separate functions, as is recognized since Lévi-Strauss and Greimas.
[28] Functions cannot be reduced to actions (verbs), nor indices to qualities (adjectives), for there are actions that are indicial, being "signs" of a character, an atmosphere, etc.

the space separating *the telephone rang* from *Bond answered* can be saturated with a host of trivial incidents or descriptions —*Bond moved toward the desk, picked up one of the receivers, put down his cigarette*, etc. These catalyzers are still functional, insofar as they enter into correlation with a nucleus, but their functionality is attenuated, unilateral, parasitic; it is a question of a purely chronological functionality (what is described is what separates two moments of the story), whereas the tie between two cardinal functions is invested with a double functionality, at once chronological and logical. Catalyzers are only consecutive units, cardinal functions are both consecutive and consequential. Everything suggests, indeed, that the mainspring of narrative is precisely the confusion of consecution and consequence, what comes *after* being read in narrative as what is *caused by*; in which case narrative would be a systematic application of the logical fallacy denounced by Scholasticism in the formula *post hoc, ergo propter hoc*—a good motto for Destiny, of which narrative all things considered is no more than the "language."

It is the structural framework of cardinal functions which accomplishes this "telescoping" of logic and temporality. At first sight, such functions may appear extremely insignificant; what defines them is not their spectacularity (importance, volume, unusualness or force of the narrated action), but, so to speak, the risk they entail: cardinal functions are the risky moments of a narrative. Between these points of alternative, these "dispatchers," the catalyzers lay out areas of safety, rests, luxuries. Luxuries which are not, however, useless: it must be stressed again that from the point of view of the story a catalyzer's functionality may be weak but not nil. Were a catalyzer purely redundant (in relation to its nucleus), it would nonetheless participate in the economy of the message; in fact, an apparently merely expletive notation always has a discursive function: it accelerates, delays, gives fresh impetus to the discourse, it summarizes, anticipates and sometimes even leads astray.[29] Since what is noted always appears as being notable, the catalyzer ceaselessly revives the semantic tension of the discourse, says ceaselessly that there has been, that there is going to be, meaning. Thus, in the final analysis, the catalyzer has a constant function which is, to use Jakobson's term, a phatic one:[30] it maintains the contact between narrator and addressee. A nucleus cannot be deleted without altering the story, but neither can a catalyst without altering the discourse.

As for the other main class of units, the indices, an integrational class, its units have in common that they can only be saturated (completed) on the level of characters or on the level of narration. They are thus part of a *parametrical* relation[31] whose second—implicit—term is continuous, extended over an episode, a character or the whole work. A distinction can be made, however, between *indices* proper, referring to the character of a narrative agent, a feeling, an atmosphere (for example suspicion) or a philosophy, and *informants*, serving to identify, to locate in time and space. To say that through the window of the office where Bond is on duty the moon can be seen half-hidden by thick billowing clouds, is to index a stormy summer night, this deduction in turn forming an index of atmosphere with reference to the heavy, anguish-laden climate of an action as yet unknown to the reader. Indices always have implicit signifieds. Informants, however, do not, at least on the level of the story: they are pure data with immediate signification. Indices involve an activity of de-

[29] Valéry spoke of "dilatory signs." The detective novel makes abundant use of such "confusing" units.
[30] [For the scheme of the six factors of verbal communication and their corresponding linguistic functions—emotive, conative, referential, phatic, metalinguistic, and poetic—see R. Jakobson, "Linguistics and Poetics" in *Style in Language*, ed. T. A. Sebeok.]
[31] N. Ruwet calls "parametrical" an element which remains constant for the whole duration of a piece of music (for instance, the tempo in a Bach allegro or the monodic character of a solo).

ciphering, the reader is to learn to know a character or an atmosphere; informants bring ready-made knowledge, their functionality, like that of catalyzers, is thus weak without being nil. Whatever its "flatness" in relation to the rest of the story, the informant (for example, the exact age of a character) always serves to authenticate the reality of the referent, to embed fiction in the real world. Informants are realist operators and as such possess an undeniable functionality not on the level of the story but on that of the discourse.[32]

Nuclei and catalyzers, indices and informants (again, the names are of little importance), these, it seems, are the initial classes into which the functional level units can be divided. This classification must be completed by two remarks. Firstly, a unit can at the same time belong to two different classes: to drink a whiskey (in an airport lounge) is an action which can act as a catalyzer to the (cardinal) notation of *waiting*, but it is also, and simultaneously, the indice of a certain atmosphere (modernity, relaxation, reminiscence, etc.). In other words, certain units can be mixed, giving a play of possibilities in the narrative economy. In the novel *Goldfinger*, Bond, having to search his adversary's bedroom, is given a master key by his associate: the notation is a pure (cardinal) function. In the film, this detail is altered and Bond laughingly takes a set of keys from a willing chambermaid: the notation is no longer simply functional but also indicial, referring to Bond's character (his easy charm and success with women). Secondly, it should be noted (this will be taken up again later) that the four classes just described can be distributed in a different way which is moreover closer to the linguistic model. Catalyzers,

---

[32] In "Frontières du récit," *Communications* 8, 1966 [reprinted in *Figures II*], Gérard Genette distinguishes two types of description: ornamental and significant. The second clearly relates to the level of the story; the first to that of the discourse, which explains why for a long time it formed a perfectly coded rhetorical "piece": *descriptio* or *ekphrasis*, a very highly valued exercise in neo-rhetoric.

indices, and informants have a common characteristic: in relation to nuclei, they are *expansions*. Nuclei (as will be seen in a moment) form finite sets grouping a small number of terms, are governed by a logic, are at once necessary and sufficient. Once the framework they provide is given, the other units fill it out according to a mode of proliferation in principle infinite. As we know, this is what happens in the case of the sentence, which is made up of simple propositions endlessly complicated with duplications, paddings, embeddings, and so on. So great an importance did Mallarmé attach to this type of structure that from it he constructed *Jamais un coup de dés*, a poem which with its "nodes" and "loops," its "nucleus words" and its "lace words," can well be regarded as the emblem of every narrative—of every language.

3. Functional syntax

How, according to what "grammar," are the different units strung together along the narrative syntagm? What are the rules of the functional combinatory system? Informants and indices can combine freely together: as for example in the portrait which readily juxtaposes data concerning civil status and traits of character. Catalyzers and nuclei are linked by a simple relation of implication: a catalyzer necessarily implies the existence of a cardinal function to which it can connect, but not vice versa. As for cardinal functions, they are bound together by a relation of solidarity: a function of this type calls for another function of the same type and reciprocally. It is this last relation which needs to be considered further for a moment—first, because it defines the very framework of the narrative (expansions can be deleted, nuclei cannot); second, because it is the main concern of those trying to work toward a structure of narrative.

It has already been pointed out that structurally narrative institutes a confusion between consecution and consequence, temporality and logic. This ambiguity forms the central problem of narrative syntax. Is there an atemporal logic lying behind the temporality of narrative? Researchers were still quite recently divided on this point. Propp, whose analytic study of the folk tale paved the way for the work going on today, is totally committed to the idea of the irreducibility of the chronological order: he sees time as reality and for this reason is convinced of the necessity for rooting the tale in temporality. Yet Aristotle himself, in his contrast between tragedy (defined by the unity of action) and historical narrative (defined by the plurality of actions and the unity of time), was already giving primacy to the logical over the chronological.[33] As do all contemporary researchers (Lévi-Strauss, Greimas, Bremond, Todorov), all of whom (while differing on other points) could subscribe to Lévi-Strauss's proposition that "the order of chronological succession is absorbed in an atemporal matrix structure."[34] Analysis today tends to "dechronologize" the narrative continuum and to "relogicize" it, to make it dependent on what Mallarmé called with regard to the French language "*the primitive thunderbolts of logic*"; or rather, more exactly (such at least is our wish), the task is to succeed in giving a structural description of the chronological illusion—it is for narrative logic to account for narrative time. To put it another way, one could say that temporality is only a structural category of narrative (of discourse), just as in language [*langue*] temporality only exists in the form of a system; from the point of view of narrative, what we call time does not exist, or at least only exists functionally, as an element of a semiotic system. Time belongs not to discourse strictly speak-

---

[33] *Poetics.*

[34] Quoted by Claude Bremond, "Le message narratif," *Communications* 4, 1964 [Claude Lévi-Strauss, "La structure et la forme," *Cahiers de l'Institut de Science Economique Appliquée* 99, March 1960.]

ing but to the referent; both narrative and language know only a semiotic time, "true" time being a "realist," referential illusion, as Propp's commentary shows. It is as such that structural analysis must deal with it.[35]

What then is the logic which regulates the principal narrative functions? It is this that current work is actively trying to establish and that has so far been the major focus of debate. Three main directions of research can be seen. The first (Bremond) is more properly logical in approach: it aims to reconstitute the syntax of human behavior utilized in narrative, to retrace the course of the "choices" which inevitably face[36] the individual character at every point in the story and so to bring out what could be called an energetic logic,[37] since it grasps the characters at the moment when they choose to act. The second (Lévi-Strauss, Jakobson) is linguistic: its essential concern is to demonstrate paradigmatic oppositions in the functions, oppositions which, in accordance with the Jakobsonian definition of the "poetic,"[38] are "extended" along the line of the narrative (new developments in Greimas's work correct or complete the conception of the paradigmatic nature of functions).[39] The third (Todorov) is somewhat different in

[35] In his own way—as always perspicacious but left undeveloped—Valéry well expressed the status of narrative time: "The belief in time as agent and guiding thread is based on *the mechanism of memory and on that of combinatory discourse,*" *Tel Quel* (my italics); the illusion is precisely produced by the discourse itself.

[36] This idea recalls Aristotle: *proairesis,* the rational choice of actions to be undertaken, is the foundation of *praxis,* the practical science which, contrary to *poiesis,* produces no object-work distinct from its agent. Using these terms, one can say that the analyst tries to reconstitute the praxis inherent in narrative.

[37] Such a logic, based on alternatives (*doing this or that*), has the merit of accounting for the process of dramatization for which narrative is usually the occasion.

[38] ["The poetic function projects the principle of equivalence of the axis of selection on to the axis of combination." Jakobson, "Linguistics and Poetics."]

[39] See A. J. Greimas, "Eléments pour une théorie de l'interprétation du récit mythique," *Communications* 8, 1966.

that it sets the analysis at the level of the "actions" (that is to say, of the characters), attempting to determine the rules by which narrative combines, varies, and transforms a certain number of basic predicates.

There is no question of choosing between these working hypotheses; they are not competitive but concurrent, and at present moreover are in the throes of elaboration. The only complement we will attempt to give them here concerns the dimensions of the analysis. Even leaving aside the indices, informants, and catalyzers, there still remains in a narrative (especially if it is a novel and no longer a tale) a very large number of cardinal functions and many of these cannot be mastered by the analyses just mentioned, which until now have worked on the major articulations of narrative. Provision needs to be made, however, for a description sufficiently close as to account for *all* the narrative units, for the smallest narrative segments. We must remember that cardinal functions cannot be determined by their "importance," only by the (doubly implicative) nature of their relations. A "telephone call," no matter how futile it may seem, on the one hand itself comprises some few cardinal functions (telephone ringing, picking up the receiver, speaking, putting down the receiver), while on the other, taken as a whole, it must be linkable—at the very least proceeding step by step—to the major articulations of the anecdote. The functional covering of the narrative necessitates an organization of relays the basic unit of which can only be a small group of functions, hereafter referred to (following Bremond) as a *sequence*.

A sequence is a logical succession of nuclei bound together by a relation of solidarity:[40] the sequence opens when one of its terms has no solidary antecedent and closes when another

[40] In the Hjelmslevian sense of double implication: two terms presuppose one another.

of its terms has no consequent. To take a deliberately trivial example, the different functions order a drink, obtain it, drink it, pay for it, constitute an obviously closed sequence, it being impossible to put anything before the order or after the payment without moving out of the homogeneous group *"Having a drink."* The sequence indeed is always nameable. Determining the major functions of the folk tale, Propp and subsequently Bremond have been led to name them (*Fraud, Betrayal, Struggle, Contract, Seduction*, etc.); the naming operation is equally inevitable in the case of trivial sequences, the "micro-sequences" which often form the finest grain of the narrative tissue. Are these namings solely the province of the analyst? In other words, are they purely metalinguistic? No doubt they are, dealing as they do with the code of narrative. Yet at the same time they can be imagined as forming part of an inner metalanguage for the reader (or listener) who can grasp every logical succession of actions as a nominal whole: to read is to name; to listen is not only to perceive a language, it is also to construct it. Sequence titles are similar enough to the *cover words* of translation machines which acceptably cover a wide variety of meanings and shades of meaning. The narrative language [*la langue du récit*] within us comprises from the start these essential headings: the closing logic which structures a sequence is inextricably linked to its name; any function which initiates a *seduction* prescribes from the moment it appears, in the name to which it gives rise, the entire process of seduction such as we have learned it from all the narratives which have fashioned in us the language of narrative.

However minimal its importance, a sequence, since it is made up of a small number of nuclei (that is to say, in fact, of "dispatchers"), always involves moments of risk and it is this which justifies analyzing it. It might seem futile to constitute

into a sequence the logical succession of trifling acts which go
to make up the offer of a cigarette (*offering, accepting, lighting, smoking*), but precisely, at every one of these points, an
alternative—and hence a freedom of meaning—is possible. Du
Pont, Bond's future partner, offers him a light from his lighter
but Bond refuses; the meaning of this bifurcation is that Bond
instinctively fears a booby-trapped gadget.[41] A sequence is
thus, one can say, a *threatened logical unit*, this being its
justification *a minimo*. It is also founded *a maximo*: enclosed
on its function, subsumed under a name, the sequence itself
constitutes a new unit, ready to function as a simple term in
another, more extensive sequence. Here, for example, is a
micro-sequence: *hand held out, hand shaken, hand released*.
This *Greeting* then becomes a simple function: on the one
hand, it assumes the role of an indice (flabbiness of Du Pont,
Bond's distaste); on the other, it forms globally a term in a
larger sequence, with the name *Meeting*, whose other terms
(*approach, halt, interpellation, sitting down*) can themselves
be micro-sequences. A whole network of subrogations structures the narrative in this way, from the smallest matrices to
the largest functions. What is in question here, of course, is a
hierarchy that remains within the functional level: it is only
when it has been possible to widen the narrative out step by
step, from Du Pont's cigarette to Bond's battle against Goldfinger, that functional analysis is over—the pyramid of functions then touches the next level (that of the Actions). There
is both a syntax within the sequences and a (subrogating)
syntax between the sequences together. The first episode of
Goldfinger thus takes on a "stemmatic" aspect:

[41] It is quite possible to identify even at this infinitesimal level an opposition
of paradigmatic types, if not between two terms, at least between two poles
of the sequence: the sequence *Offer of a cigarette* spreads out, by suspending
it, the paradigm *Danger/Safety* (demonstrated by Cheglov in his analysis of
the Sherlock Holmes cycle), *Suspicion/Protection, Aggressiveness/Friend-
liness*.

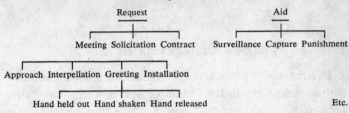

Obviously this representation is analytical; the reader perceives a linear succession of terms. What needs to be noted, however, is that the terms from several sequences can easily be imbricated in one another: a sequence is not yet completed when already, cutting in, the first term of a new sequence may appear. Sequences move in counterpoint;[42] functionally, the structure of narrative is fugued: thus it is this that narrative at once "holds" and "pulls on." Within the single work, the imbrication of sequences can indeed only be allowed to come to a halt with a radical break if the sealed-off blocks which then compose it are in some sort recuperated at the higher level of the Actions (of the characters). *Goldfinger* is composed of three functionally independent episodes, their functional stemmas twice ceasing to intercommunicate: there is no sequential relation between the swimming-pool episode and the Fort Knox episode; but there remains an actantial relation, for the characters (and consequently the structure of their relations) are the same. One can recognize here the epic pattern (a "whole made of multiple fables"): the epic is a narrative broken at the functional level but unitary at the actantial level (something which can be verified in the *Odyssey* or in Brecht's plays). The level of functions (which provides the major part of the narrative syntagm) must thus be capped by a higher level from which, step by step, the first level units draw their meaning, the level of actions.

[42] This counterpoint was recognized by the Russian formalists, who outlined its typology; it is not without recalling the principal "intricate" structures of the sentence (see below V.1).

III. ACTIONS

1. Toward a structural status of characters

In Aristotelian poetics, the notion of character is secondary, entirely subsidiary to the notion of action: there may be actions without "characters," says Aristotle, but not characters without an action; a view taken over by classical theoreticians (Vossius). Later the character, who until then had been only a name, the agent of an action,[43] acquired a psychological consistency, became an individual, a "person," in short a fully constituted "being," even should he do nothing and of course even before acting.[44] Characters stopped being subordinate to the action, embodied immediately psychological essences; which essences could be drawn up into lists, as can be seen in its purest form in the list of "character parts" in bourgeois theater (the coquette, the noble father, etc.). From its very outset, structural analysis has shown the utmost reluctance to treat the character as an essence, even merely for purposes of classification; Tomachevski went so far as to deny the character any narrative importance, a point of view he subsequently modified. Without leaving characters out of the analysis altogether, Propp reduced them to a simple typology based not on psychology but on the unity of the actions assigned them by the narrative (*Donor of a magical agent*, *Helper*, *Villain*, etc.).

Since Propp, the character has constantly set the structural analysis of narrative the same problem. On the one hand, the characters (whatever one calls them—*dramatis personae* or *actants*) form a necessary plane of description, outside of which the slightest reported "actions" cease to be intelligible;

---

[43] It must not be forgotten that classical tragedy as yet knows only "actors," not "characters."

[44] The "character-person" reigns in the bourgeois novel; in *War and Peace*, Nikolai Rostov is from the start a good fellow, loyal, courageous, and passionate, Prince Andrei a disillusioned individual of noble birth, etc. What happens illustrates them, it does not form them.

so that it can be said that there is not a single narrative in the world without "characters,"[45] or at least without agents. Yet on the other hand, these—extremely numerous—"agents" can be neither described nor classified in terms of "persons"— whether the "person" be considered as a purely historical form, limited to certain genres (those most familiar to us it is true), in which case it is necessary to leave out of account the very large number of narratives (popular tales, modern texts) comprising agents but not persons, or whether the "person" is declared to be no more than a critical rationalization foisted by our age on pure narrative agents. Structural analysis, much concerned not to define characters in terms of psychological essences, has so far striven, using various hypotheses, to define a character not as a "being" but as a "participant." For Bremond, every character (even secondary) can be the agent of sequences, of actions which belong to him (*Fraud, Seduction*); when a single sequence involves two characters (as is usual), it comprises two perspectives, two names (what is *Fraud* for the one is *Gullibility* for the other); in short, every character (even secondary) is the hero of his own sequence. Todorov, analyzing a "psychological" novel (*Les Liaisons dangereuses*), starts not from the character-persons but from the three major relationships in which they can engage and which he calls base predicates (love, communication, help). The analysis brings these relationships under two sorts of rules: rules of *derivation*, when it is a question of accounting for other relationships, and rules of *action*, when it is a question of describing the transformation of the major relationships in the course of the story. There are many characters in

[45] If one section of contemporary literature has attacked the "character," it is not in order to destroy it (which is impossible) but to depersonalize it, which is quite different. A novel seemingly devoid of characters, such as *Drame* by Philippe Sollers, gets rid of the person to the benefit of language but nonetheless retains a fundamental play of actants confronting the very action of discourse. There is still a "subject" in this literature, but that "subject" is henceforth that of language.

Les Liaisons dangereuses but "what is said of them" (their predicates) can be classified. Finally, Greimas has proposed to describe and classify the characters of narrative not according to what they are but according to what they do (whence the name *actants*), inasmuch as they participate in three main semantic axes (also to be found in the sentence: subject, object, indirect object, adjunct) which are communication, desire (or quest), and ordeal.[46] Since this participation is ordered in couples, the infinite world of characters is, it too, bound by a paradigmatic structure (*Subject/Object*, *Donor/Receiver*, *Helper/Opponent*) which is projected along the narrative; and since an actant defines a class, it can be filled by different actors, mobilized according to rules of multiplication, substitution, or replacement.

These three conceptions have many points in common. The most important, it must be stressed again, is the definition of the character according to participation in a sphere of actions, these spheres being few in number, typical, and classifiable; which is why this second level of description, despite its being that of the characters, has here been called the level of Actions: the word *actions* is not to be understood in the sense of the trifling acts which form the tissue of the first level but in that of the major articulations of *praxis* (desire, communication, struggle).

2. *The problem of the subject*

The problems raised by a classification of the characters of narrative are not as yet satisfactorily resolved. Certainly there is ready agreement on the fact that the innumerable characters of narrative can be brought under rules of substitution and that, even within the one work, a single figure can absorb different characters.[47] Again, the actantial model proposed by

[46] *Sémantique structurale.*
[47] Psychoanalysis has widely accredited these operations of condensation.

Greimas (and adopted by Todorov in another perspective) seems to stand the test of a large number of narratives. Like any structural model, its value lies less in its canonic form (a matrix of six actants) than in the regulated transformations (replacements, confusions, duplications, substitutions) to which it lends itself, thus holding out the hope of an actantial typology of narratives.[48] A difficulty, however, is that when the matrix has a high classificational power (as is the case with Greimas's actants) it fails adequately to account for the multiplicity of participations as soon as these are analyzed in terms of perspectives and that when these perspectives are respected (as in Bremond's description) the system of characters remains too fragmented. The reduction proposed by Todorov avoids both pitfalls but has so far only been applied to one narrative. All this, it seems, can be quickly and harmoniously resolved. The real difficulty posed by the classification of characters is the place (and hence the existence) of the *subject* in any actantial matrix, whatever its formulation. *Who* is the subject (the hero) of a narrative? Is there—or not—a privileged class of actors? The novel has accustomed us to emphasize in one way or another—sometimes in a devious (negative) way—one character in particular. But such privileging is far from extending over the whole of narrative literature. Many narratives, for example, set two adversaries in conflict over some stake; the subject is then truly double, not reducible further by substitution. Indeed, this is even perhaps a common archaic form, as though narrative, after the fashion of certain languages, had also known a *dual* of persons. This

---

Mallarmé was saying already, writing of *Hamlet*: "Supernumeraries, necessarily! for in the ideal painting of the stage, everything moves according to a symbolic reciprocity of types amongst themselves or relatively to a single figure." *Crayonné au théâtre*.

[48] For example: narratives where object and subject are confounded in a single character, that is, narratives of the search for oneself, for one's own identity (*The Golden Ass*); narratives where the subject pursues successive objects (*Madame Bovary*), etc.

dual is all the more interesting in that it relates narrative to the structures of certain (very modern) games in which two equal opponents try to gain possession of an object put into circulation by a referee; a schema which recalls the actantial matrix proposed by Greimas, and there is nothing surprising in this if one is willing to allow that a game, being a language, depends on the same symbolic structure as is to be found in language and narrative: a game too is a sentence.[49] If therefore a privileged class of actors is retained (the subject of the quest, of the desire, of the action), it needs at least to be made more flexible by bringing that actant under the very categories of the grammatical (and not psychological) person. Once again, it will be necessary to look toward linguistics for the possibility of describing and classifying the personal (*je/tu*, first person/ second person) or apersonal (*il*, third person), singular, dual, or plural, instance of the action. It will—perhaps—be the grammatical categories of the person (accessible in our pronouns) which will provide the key to the actional level; but since these categories can only be defined in relation to the instance of discourse, not to that of reality,[50] characters, as units of the actional level, find their meaning (their intelligibility) only if integrated in the third level of description, here called the level of Narration (as opposed to Functions and Actions).

IV. NARRATION

1. Narrative communication

Just as there is within narrative a major function of exchange (set out between a donor and a beneficiary), so, homo-

---

[49] Umberto Eco's analysis of the James Bond cycle ("James Bond: une combinatoire narrative," *Communications* 8, 1966) refers more to game than to language.

[50] See the analysis of person given by Benveniste in *Problèmes de linguistique générale*.

logically, narrative as object is the point of a communication: there is a donor of the narrative and a receiver of the narrative. In linguistic communication, *je* and *tu* (*I* and *you*) are absolutely presupposed by one another; similarly, there can be no narrative without a narrator and a listener (or reader). Banal perhaps, but still little developed. Certainly the role of the sender has been abundantly enlarged upon (much study of the "author" of a novel, though without any consideration of whether he really is the "narrator"); when it comes to the reader, however, literary theory is much more modest. In fact, the problem is not to introspect the motives of the narrator or the effects the narration produces on the reader, it is to describe the code by which narrator and reader are signified throughout the narrative itself. At first sight, the signs of the narrator appear more evident and more numerous than those of the reader (a narrative more frequently says *I* than *you*); in actual fact, the latter are simply more oblique than the former. Thus, each time the narrator stops "representing" and reports details which he knows perfectly well but which are unknown to the reader, there occurs, by signifying failure, a sign of reading, for there would be no sense in the narrator giving himself a piece of information. *Leo was the owner of the joint*,[51] we are told in a first-person novel: a sign of the reader, close to what Jakobson calls the conative function of communication. Lacking an inventory however, we shall leave aside for the moment these signs of reception (though they are of equal importance) and say a few words concerning the signs of narration.[52]

Who is the donor of the narrative? So far, three conceptions

---

[51] *Double Bang à Bangkok* [secret agent thriller by Jean Bruce, 1959]. The sentence functions as a "wink" to the reader, as if he was being turned toward. By contrast, the statement *"So Leo had just left"* is a sign of the narrator, part of a process of reasoning conducted by a "person."

[52] In "Les catégories du récit littéraire" Todorov deals with the images of narrator and reader.

seem to have been formulated. The first holds that a narrative emanates from a person (in the fully psychological sense of the term). This person has a name, the author, in whom there is an endless exchange between the "personality" and the "art" of a perfectly identified individual who periodically takes up his pen to write a story: the narrative (notably the novel) then being simply the expression of an *I* external to it. The second conception regards the narrator as a sort of omniscient, apparently impersonal, consciousness that tells the story from a superior point of view, that of God:[53] the narrator is at once inside his characters (since he knows everything that goes on in them) and outside them (since he never identifies with any one more than another). The third and most recent conception (Henry James, Sartre) decrees that the narrator must limit his narrative to what the characters can observe or know, everything proceeding as if each of the characters in turn were the sender of the narrative. All three conceptions are equally difficult in that they seem to consider narrator and characters as real—"living"—people (the unfailing power of this literary myth is well known), as though a narrative were originally determined at its referential level (it is a matter of equally "realist" conceptions). Narrator and characters, however, at least from our perspective, are essentially "paper beings"; the (material) author of a narrative is in no way to be confused with the narrator of that narrative.[54] The signs of the narrator are immanent to the narrative and hence readily accessible to a semiological analysis; but in order to conclude that the author himself (whether declared, hidden or withdrawn) has "signs" at his disposal which he sprinkles through his work, it is necessary to assume the existence between this

[53] "When will someone write from the point of view of a *superior joke*, that is as God sees things from above?" Flaubert, *Letters*.

[54] A distinction all the more necessary, given the scale at which we are working, in that historically a large mass of narratives are without authors (oral narratives, folk tales, epics entrusted to bards, reciters, etc.).

"person" and his language of a straight descriptive relation which makes the author a full subject and the narrative the instrumental expression of that fullness. Structural analysis is unwilling to accept such an assumption: *who speaks* (in the narrative) is not *who writes* (in real life) and *who writes* is not *who is*.[55]

In fact, narration strictly speaking (the code of the narrator), like language, knows only two systems of signs: personal and apersonal. These two narrational systems do not necessarily present the linguistic marks attached to person (*I*) and non-person (*he*): there are narratives or at least narrative episodes, for example, which though written in the third person nevertheless have as their true instance the first person. How can we tell? It suffices to rewrite the narrative (or the passage) from *he* to *I*: so long as the rewriting entails no alteration of the discourse other than this change of the grammatical pronouns, we can be sure that we are dealing with a personal system. The whole of the beginning of *Goldfinger*, though written in the third person, is in fact "spoken" by James Bond. For the instance to change, rewriting must become impossible; thus the sentence "he saw a man in his fifties, still young-looking . . ." is perfectly personal despite the *he* ("I, James Bond, saw . . ."), but the narrative statement "the tinkling of the ice against the glass appeared to give Bond a sudden inspiration" cannot be personal on account of the verb "appeared," it (and not the *he*) becoming a sign of the apersonal. There is no doubt that the apersonal is the traditional mode of narrative, language having developed a whole tense system peculiar to narrative (based on the aorist[56]), designed to wipe out the present of the speaker. As Benveniste puts it: "In narrative, no one speaks." The personal instance

[55] J. Lacan: "Is the subject I speak of when I speak the same as the subject who speaks?"
[56] E. Benveniste, op. cit. [especially Chapter XIX].

(under more or less disguised forms) has, however, gradually invaded narrative, the narration being referred to the *hic et nunc* of the locutionary act (which is the definition of the personal system). Thus it is that today many narratives are to be found (and of the most common kinds) which mix together in extremely rapid succession, often within the limits of a single sentence, the personal and the apersonal; as for instance this sentence from *Goldfinger*:

His eyes,	*personal*
gray-blue,	*apersonal*
looked into those of Mr. Du Pont, who did	
not know what face to put on,	*personal*
for this look held a mixture of candor,	
irony, and self-deprecation.	*personal*

The mixing of the systems is clearly felt as a facility and this facility can go as far as trick effects. A detective novel by Agatha Christie (*The Sittaford Mystery*) only keeps the enigma going by cheating on the person of the narration: a character is described from within when he is already the murderer[57]—as if in a single person there were the consciousness of a witness, immanent to the discourse, and the consciousness of a murderer, immanent to the referent, with the dishonest tourniquet of the two systems alone producing the enigma. Hence it is understandable that at the other pole of literature the choice of a rigorous system should have been made a necessary condition of a work—without it always being easy fully to meet that condition.

Rigor of this kind—the aim of certain contemporary writers —is not necessarily an aesthetic imperative. What is called the psychological novel usually shows a mixture of the two sys-

[57] Personal mode: "It even seemed to Burnaby that nothing looked changed . . ." The device is still more blatant in *The Murder of Roger Ackroyd*, since there the murderer actually says *I*.

tems, successively mobilizing the signs of non-person and those of person; "psychology," that is, paradoxically, cannot accommodate itself to a pure system, for by bringing the whole narrative down to the sole instance of the discourse—or, if one prefers, to the locutionary act—it is the very content of the person which is threatened: the psychological person (of referential order) bears no relation to the linguistic person, the latter never defined by states of mind, intentions or traits of character but only by its (coded) place in discourse. It is this formal person that writers today are attempting to speak and such an attempt represents an important subversion (the public moreover has the impression that "novels" are no longer being written) for it aims to transpose narrative from the purely constative plane, which it has occupied until now, to the performative plane, whereby the meaning of an utterance is the very act by which it is uttered:[58] today, writing is not "telling" but saying that one is telling and assigning all the referent ("what one says") to this act of locution; which is why part of contemporary literature is no longer descriptive, but transitive, striving to accomplish so pure a present in its language that the whole of the discourse is identified with the act of its delivery, the whole *logos* being brought down—or extended—to a *lexis*.[59]

2. Narrative situation

The narrational level is thus occupied by the signs of narrativity, the set of operators which reintegrate functions and actions in the narrative communication articulated on its donor and its addressee. Some of these signs have already

[58] On the performative, see Todorov's "Les catégories du récit littéraire." The classic example of a performative is the statement *I declare war* which neither "constates" nor "describes" anything but exhausts its meaning in the act of its utterance (by contrast to the statement *the king declared war*, which constates, describes).

[59] For the opposition logos/lexis, see Genette, "Frontières du récit."

received study; we are familiar in oral literatures with certain codes of recitation (metrical formulas, conventional presentation protocols) and we know that here the "author" is not the person who invents the finest stories but the person who best masters the code which is practiced equally by his listeners: in such literatures the narrational level is so clearly defined, its rules so binding, that it is difficult to conceive of a "tale" devoid of the coded signs of narrative (*"once upon a time,"* etc.). In our written literatures, the "forms of discourse" (which are in fact signs of narrativity) were early identified: classification of the modes of authorial intervention (outlined by Plato and developed by Diomedes[60]), coding of the beginnings and endings of narratives, definition of the different styles of representation (*oratio directa, oratio indirecta* with its *inquit, oratio tecta*),[61] study of "points of view," and so on. All these elements form part of the narrational level, to which must obviously be added the writing as a whole, its role being not to "transmit" the narrative but to display it.

It is indeed precisely in a display of the narrative that the units of the lower levels find integration: the ultimate form of the narrative, as narrative, transcends its contents and its strictly narrative forms (functions and actions). This explains why the narrational code should be the final level attainable by our analysis, other than by going outside of the narrative object, other, that is, than by transgressing the rule of immanence on which the analysis is based. Narration can only receive its meaning from the world which makes use of it: beyond the narrational level begins the world, other systems (social, economic, ideological) whose terms are no longer simply narratives but elements of a different substance (historical facts,

---

[60] *Genus activum vel imitativum* (no intervention of the narrator in the discourse: as for example theater); *genus ennarativum* (the poet alone speaks: sententiae, didactic poems); *genus commune* (mixture of the two kinds: epic poems).

[61] H. Sorensen in *Language and Society.*

determinations, behaviors, etc.). Just as linguistics stops at the sentence, so narrative analysis stops at discourse—from there it is necessary to shift to another semiotics. Linguistics is acquainted with such boundaries which it has already postulated —if not explored—under the name of *situations*. Halliday defines the "situation" (in relation to a sentence) as "the associated non-linguistic factors,"[62] Prieto as "the set of facts known by the receiver at the moment of the semic act and independently of this act."[63] In the same way, one can say that every narrative is dependent on a "narrative situation," the set of protocols according to which the narrative is "consumed." In so-called archaic societies, the narrative situation is heavily coded;[64] nowadays, avant-garde literature alone still dreams of reading protocols—spectacular in the case of Mallarmé, who wanted the book to be recited in public according to a precise combinatory scheme, typographical in that of Butor, who tries to provide the book with its own specific signs. Generally, however, our society takes the greatest pains to conjure away the coding of the narrative situation: there is no counting the number of narrational devices which seek to naturalize the subsequent narrative by feigning to make it the outcome of some natural circumstance and thus, as it were, "disinaugurating" it: epistolary novels, supposedly rediscovered manuscripts, author who met the narrator, films which begin the story before the credits. The reluctance to declare its codes characterizes bourgeois society and the mass culture issuing from it: both demand signs which do not look like signs. Yet this is only, so to speak, a structural epiphenomenon: however familiar, however casual may today be the act of opening a novel or a newspaper or of turning on the television, nothing can prevent that humble act from installing in us,

[62] M. A. K. Halliday, op. cit.
[63] *Principes de noologie.*
[64] A tale, as Lucien Sebag stressed, can be told anywhere anytime, but not a mythical narrative.

all at once and in its entirety, the narrative code we are going to need. Hence the narrational level has an ambiguous role: contiguous to the narrative situation (and sometimes even including it), it gives on to the world in which the narrative is undone (consumed), while at the same time, capping the preceding levels, it closes the narrative, constitutes it definitively as utterance of a language [*langue*] which provides for and bears along its own metalanguage.

V. THE SYSTEM OF NARRATIVE

Language [*langue*] proper can be defined by the concurrence of two fundamental processes: articulation, or segmentation, which produces units (this being what Benveniste calls *form*), and integration, which gathers these units into units of a higher rank (this being *meaning*). This dual process can be found in the language of narrative [*la langue du récit*] which also has an articulation and an integration, a form and a meaning.

1. Distortion and expansion

The form of narrative is essentially characterized by two powers: that of distending its signs over the length of the story and that of inserting unforeseeable expansions into these distortions. The two powers appear to be points of freedom but the nature of narrative is precisely to include these "deviations" within its language.[65]

The distortion of signs exists in linguistic language [*langue*] and was studied by Bally with reference to French and German.[66] Dystaxia occurs when the signs (of a message) are no longer simply juxtaposed, when the (logical) linearity is disturbed (predicate before subject for example). A notable form

---

[65] Valéry: "Formally the novel is close to the dream; both can be defined by consideration of this curious property: *all their deviations form part of them.*"

[66] *Linguistique générale et linguistique française.*

of dystaxia is found when the parts of one sign are separated by other signs along the chain of the message (for instance, the negative *ne jamais* and the verb *a pardonné* in *elle ne nous a jamais pardonné*): the sign split into fractional parts, its signified is shared out among several signifiers, distant from one another and not comprehensible on their own. This, as was seen in connection with the functional level, is exactly what happens in narrative: the units of a sequence, although forming a whole at the level of that very sequence, may be separated from one another by the insertion of units from other sequences—as was said, the structure of the functional level is fugued.[67] According to Bally's terminology, which opposes synthetic languages where dystaxia is predominant (such as German) and analytic languages with a greater respect for logical linearity and monosemy (such as French), narrative would be a highly synthetic language, essentially founded on a syntax of embedding and enveloping: each part of the narrative radiates in several directions at once. When Bond orders a whiskey while waiting for his plane, the whiskey as indice has a polysemic value, is a kind of symbolic node grouping several signifieds (modernity, wealth, leisure); as a functional unit, however, the ordering of the whiskey has to run step by step through numerous relays (consumption, waiting, departure, etc.) in order to find its final meaning: the unit is "taken" by the whole narrative at the same time that the narrative only "holds" by the distortion and irradiation of its units.

This generalized distortion is what gives the language of narrative its special character. A purely logical phenomenon, since founded on an often distant relation and mobilizing a sort of confidence in intellective memory, it ceaselessly substi-

---

[67] Cf. Lévi-Strauss: "Relations pertaining to the same bundle may appear diachronically at remote intervals," *Structural Anthropology*. A. J. Greimas has emphasized the spacing out of functions.

tutes meaning for the straightforward copy of the events recounted. On meeting in "life," it is most unlikely that the
invitation to take a seat would not immediately be followed by
the act of sitting down; in narrative these two units, contiguous
from a mimetic point of view, may be separated by a long
series of insertions belonging to quite different functional
spheres. Thus is established a kind of *logical time* which has
very little connection with real time, the apparent pulverization of units always being firmly held in place by the logic that
binds together the nuclei of the sequence. "Suspense" is clearly
only a privileged—or "exacerbated"—form of distortion: on
the one hand, by keeping a sequence open (through emphatic
procedures of delay and renewal), it reinforces the contact
with the reader (the listener), has a manifestly phatic function; while on the other, it offers the threat of an uncompleted
sequence, of an open paradigm (if, as we believe, every sequence has two poles), that is to say, of a logical disturbance,
it being this disturbance which is consumed with anxiety and
pleasure (all the more so because it is always made right in the
end). "Suspense," therefore, is a game with structure, designed to endanger and glorify it, constituting a veritable
"thrilling" of intelligibility: by representing order (and no
longer series) in its fragility, "suspense" accomplishes the very
idea of language: what seems the most pathetic is also the
most intellectual—"suspense" grips you in the "mind," not in
the "guts."[68]

What can be separated can also be filled. Distended, the
functional nuclei furnish intercalating spaces which can be
packed out almost infinitely; the interstices can be filled in
with a very large number of catalyzers. Here, however, a new
typology comes in, for the freedom to catalyze can be regu-

[68] J. P. Faye, writing of Klossowski's *Baphomet*: "Rarely has fiction (or
narrative) so clearly revealed what it always is, necessarily: an experimentation
of thought on life." *Tel Quel* 22.

lated according both to the content of the functions (certain functions are more apt than others for catalyzing—as for example *Waiting*[69]) and to the substance of the narrative (writing contains possibilities of diaeresis—and so of catalyzing—far superior to those of film: a gesture related linguistically can be "cut up" much more easily than the same gesture visualized[70]). The catalystic power of narrative has for corollary its elliptic power. Firstly, a function (*he had a good meal*) can economize on all the potential catalyzers it covers over (the details of the meal)[71]; secondly, it is possible to reduce a sequence to its nuclei and a hierarchy of sequences to its higher terms without altering the meaning of the story: a narrative can be identified even if its total syntagm be reduced to its actants and its main functions as these result from the progressive upward integration of its functional units.[72] In other words, narrative lends itself to *summary* (what used to be called the *argument*). At first sight this is true of any discourse, but each discourse has its own kind of summary. A lyric poem, for example, is simply the vast metaphor of a single signified[73] and to summarize it is thus to give this signified, an operation so drastic that it eliminates the poem's identity (summarized, lyric poems come down to the signifieds *Love* and *Death*)—hence the conviction that poems cannot be

---

[69] Logically *Waiting* has only two nuclei: 1. the wait established 2. the wait rewarded or disappointed; the first, however, can be extensively catalyzed, occasionally even indefinitely (*Waiting for Godot*): yet another game—this time extreme—with structure.

[70] Valéry: "Proust divides up—and gives us the feeling of being able to divide up indefinitely—what other writers are in the habit of passing over."

[71] Here again, there are qualifications according to substance: literature has an unrivaled elliptic power—which cinema lacks.

[72] This reduction does not necessarily correspond to the division of the book into chapters; on the contrary, it seems that increasingly chapters have the role of introducing breaks, points of suspense (serial technique).

[73] N. Ruwet: "A poem can be understood as the outcome of a series of transformations applied to the proposition 'I love you.'" "Analyse structurale d'un poème français," *Linguistics* 3, 1964. Ruwet here refers precisely to the analysis of paranoiac delirium given by Freud in connection with President Schreber ("Psychoanalytic Notes on an Autobiographical Account of a Case of Paranoia").

summarized. By contrast, the summary of a narrative (if conducted according to structural criteria) preserves the individuality of the message; narrative, in other words, is *translatable* without fundamental damage. What is untranslatable is determined only at the last, narrational, level. The signifiers of narrativity, for instance, are not readily transferable from novel to film, the latter utilizing the personal mode of treatment only very exceptionally;[74] while the last layer of the narrational level, namely the writing, resists transference from one language to another (or transfers very badly). The translatability of narrative is a result of the structure of its language, so that it would be possible, proceeding in reverse, to determine this structure by identifying and classifying the (varyingly) translatable and untranslatable elements of a narrative. The existence (now) of different and concurrent semiotics (literature, cinema, comics, radio/television) would greatly facilitate this kind of analysis.

2. *Mimesis and meaning*

The second important process in the language of narrative is integration: what has been disjoined at a certain level (a sequence for example) is most often joined again at a higher level (a hierarchically important sequence, the global signified of a number of scattered indices, the action of a class of characters). The complexity of a narrative can be compared to that of an organization profile chart, capable of integrating backward and forward movements; or, more accurately, it is integration in various forms which compensates for the seemingly unmasterable complexity of units on a particular level. Integration guides the understanding of the discontinuous elements, simultaneously contiguous and heterogeneous (it is

[74] Once again, there is no relation between the grammatical "person" of the narrator and the "personality" (or subjectivity) that a film director puts into his way of presenting a story: the *camera-I* (continuously identified with the vision of a particular character) is exceptional in the history of cinema.

thus that they appear in the syntagm which knows only one dimension—that of succession). If, with Greimas, we call *isotopy* the unity of meaning (that, for instance, which impregnates a sign and its context), then we can say that integration is a factor of isotopy: each (integrational) level gives its isotopy to the units of the level below, prevents the meaning from "dangling"—inevitable if the staggering of levels were not perceived. Narrative integration, however, does not present itself in a serenely regular manner like some fine architectural style leading by symmetrical chicaneries from an infinite variety of simple elements to a few complex masses. Very often a single unit will have two correlates, one on one level (function of a sequence), the other on another (indice with reference to an actant). Narrative thus appears as a succession of tightly interlocking mediate and immediate elements; dystaxia determines a "horizontal" reading, while integration superimposes a "vertical" reading: there is a sort of structural "limping," an incessant play of potentials whose varying falls give the narrative its dynamism or energy: each unit is perceived at once in its surfacing and in its depth and it is thus that the narrative "works"; through the concourse of these two movements the structure ramifies, proliferates, uncovers itself—and recovers itself, pulls itself together: the new never fails in its regularity. There is, of course, a freedom of narrative (just as there is a freedom for every speaker with regard to his or her language), but this freedom is limited, literally *hemmed in*: between the powerful code of language [*langue*] and the powerful code of narrative a hollow is set up—the sentence. If one attempts to embrace the whole of a written narrative, one finds that it starts from the most highly coded (the phonematic, or even the merismatic, level), gradually relaxes until it reaches the sentence, the farthest point of combinatorial freedom, and then begins to tighten up again, moving progressively from small groups of sentences (micro-sequences), which are still very free, until it comes to the main actions, which form a strong and restricted code. The creativity of narrative (at least under its mythical appearance of "life") is thus situated *between two codes*, the linguistic and the translinguistic. That is why it can be said paradoxically that *art* (in the Romantic sense of the term) is a matter of statements of detail, whereas *imagination* is mastery of the code: "It will be found in fact," wrote Poe, "that the ingenious are always fanciful, and the *truly* imaginative never otherwise than analytic . . .[75]

Claims concerning the "realism" of narrative are therefore to be discounted. When a telephone call comes through in the office where he is on duty, Bond, so the author tells us, reflects that "Communications with Hong Kong are as bad as they always were and just as difficult to obtain." Neither Bond's "reflection" nor the poor quality of the telephone call is the real piece of information; this contingency perhaps gives things more "life" but the true information, which will come to fruition later, is the localization of the telephone call, Hong Kong. In all narrative imitation remains contingent.[76] The function of narrative is not to "represent," it is to constitute a spectacle still very enigmatic for us but in any case not of a mimetic order. The "reality" of a sequence lies not in the "natural" succession of the actions composing it but in the logic there exposed, risked, and satisfied. Putting it another way, one could say that the origin of a sequence is not the observation of reality, but the need to vary and transcend the first *form* given man, namely repetition: a sequence is essentially a whole within which nothing is repeated. Logic has here an emancipatory value—and with it the entire narrative. It

[75] "The Murders in the Rue Morgue."
[76] G. Genette rightly reduces *mimesis* to passages of directly reported dialogue (cf. "Frontières du récit"); yet even dialogue always contains a function of intelligibility, not of mimesis.

may be that men ceaselessly reinject into narrative what they have known, what they have experienced; but if they do, at least it is in a form which has vanquished repetition and instituted the model of a process of becoming. Narrative does not show, does not imitate; the passion which may excite us in reading a novel is not that of a "vision" (in actual fact, we do not "see" anything). Rather, it is that of meaning, that of a higher order of relation which also has its emotions, its hopes, its dangers, its triumphs. "What takes place" in a narrative is from the referential (reality) point of view literally *nothing*;[77] "what happens" is language alone, the adventure of language, the unceasing celebration of its coming. Although we know scarcely more about the origins of narrative than we do about the origins of language, it can reasonably be suggested that narrative is contemporaneous with monologue, a creation seemingly posterior to that of dialogue. At all events, without wanting to strain the phylogenetic hypothesis, it may be significant that it is at the same moment (around the age of three) that the little human "invents" at once sentence, narrative, and the Oedipus.

1966

---

[77] Mallarmé: "A dramatic work displays the succession of exteriors of the act without any moment retaining reality and, in the end, anything happening." *Crayonné au théâtre.*

Flaubert and the Sentence

LONG before Flaubert, writers had experienced—and expressed—the arduous labor of style, the exhaustion of incessant corrections, the sad necessity of endless hours committed to an infinitesimal output.[1] Yet in Flaubert, the dimension of this agony is altogether different; the labor of style is for him an unspeakable suffering (even if he speaks it quite often), an almost expiatory ordeal for which he acknowledges no compensation of a magical (i.e., aleatory) order, as the sentiment of inspiration might be for many writers: style, for Flaubert, is absolute suffering, infinite suffering, useless suffering. Writing is disproportionately slow (*"four pages this week," "five days for a page," "two days to reach the end of two lines"*); it requires an "irrevocable farewell to life," a pitiless sequestration; we may note in this regard that Flaubert's sequestration occurs uniquely for the sake of style, while Proust's, equally famous, has for its object a total recuperation of the work:

From *New Critical Essays.*

[1] Here are several examples from Antoine Albalat's book, *Le Travail du style, enseigné par les corrections manuscrites des grands écrivains* (1903): Pascal rewrote the 18th Provincial Letter thirteen times; Rousseau worked on *Émile* for three years; Buffon worked more than ten hours a day; Chateaubriand would spend twelve to fifteen hours at a time rewriting, erasing, etc.

Proust retires from the world because he has a great deal to say and because he is pressed by death, Flaubert because he has an infinite correction to perform; once sequestered, Proust adds endlessly (his famous *"paperolles"*), Flaubert subtracts, erases, constantly returns to zero, begins over again. Flaubertian sequestration has for its center (and its symbol) a piece of furniture which is not the desk but the divan: when the depths of agony are plumbed, Flaubert throws himself on his sofa[2]: this is his "marinade," an ambiguous situation, in fact, for the sign of failure is also the site of fantasy, whence the work will gradually resume, giving Flaubert a new substance which he can erase anew. Flaubert qualifies this Sisyphean circuit by a very strong word, *"Atrocious,"*[3] the sole recompense he receives for his life's sacrifice.[4]

Apparently, then, style engages the writer's entire existence, and for this reason it would be better to call it henceforth a *writing*: to write is to live (*"A book has always been for me,"* Flaubert says, *"a particular way of living"*), writing is the book's goal, not publication.[5] This precellence, attested—or purchased—by the very sacrifice of a life, somewhat modifies the traditional conceptions of "writing well," ordinarily given as the final garment (the ornament) of ideas or passions. First of all, according to Flaubert, the very opposition of form and content vanishes[6]: to write and to think are but one action, writing is a total being. Then comes, so to speak, the reversion

[2] "Sometimes when I feel empty, when expression is refractory, when after having scribbled many pages I discover I haven't made a single sentence, I fall on my couch and lie there stupefied in an inner marsh of ennui" (1852).

[3] "One achieves style only by atrocious labor, a fanatic and dedicated stubbornness" (1846).

[4] "I have spent my life depriving my heart of its most legitimate nourishment. I have led a laborious and austere existence. And now I can bear no more, I am at the end of my tether" (1875).

[5] ". . . I don't want to publish anything . . . I work with an absolute disinterestedness and without ulterior motive, without external preoccupation . . ." (1846).

[6] "For me, insofar as you have not separated form from content in a given sentence, I maintain that these are actually two words devoid of meaning" (1846).

of the merits of poetry over prose: poetry holds up to prose
the mirror of its constraints, the image of a close-set, sure
code: this model exerts an ambiguous fascination upon Flaubert, since prose must at once rejoin verse and exceed it, equal
it, and absorb it. Finally, there is a special distribution of
technical tasks required by the elaboration of a novel; classical
rhetoric focused on the problems of *dispositio*, or order of the
parts of discourse (which we must not confuse with *com-
positio*, or order of the internal elements of the sentence);
Flaubert seems not to be interested in this; he does not neglect
the tasks proper to narration,[7] but these tasks, evidently, have
only a loose link with his essential project: to compose his
work or any of its episodes is not "atrocious" but simply
"wearisome."[8]

As an odyssey, Flaubertian writing (and how active a meaning we should like to give this word) thus confines itself to
what we commonly call corrections of style. These corrections
are not in any way rhetorical accidents; they affect the primary
code, that of the language; they commit the writer to experiencing the structure of the language as a passion. Here we
must prepare what we might call a linguistics (and not a stylistics) of corrections, somewhat symmetrical to what Henri Frei
has called the grammar of mistakes.

The corrections writers make on their manuscripts may be
readily classified according to the two axes of the paper on
which they write; on the vertical axis are made the substitutions of words (these are the crossings out or "hesitations");
on the horizontal axis, the suppressions or additions of syntagms (these are the "recastings"). Now the axes of the paper

---

[7] See notably the account of the pages concerning various episodes of
Madame Bovary: "I already have 260 pages which contain only preparations
for action, more or less disguised expositions of characters (it is true that
they are graduated), landscapes, places . . ."
[8] "I have a narration to compose; now the story is something which is very
wearisome for me. I have to send my heroine to a ball" (1852).

are the very same thing as the axes of the language. The first corrections are substitutive, metaphorical; they tend to replace the sign initially inscribed by another sign chosen from a paradigm of affinitary and different elements; these corrections can then bear on the monemes (Hugo substituting *modest* for *charming* in *"Eden wakened, charming and nude"*) or on the phonemes, when it is a matter of prohibiting certain assonances (which classical prose does not tolerate) or over-insistent homophonies held to be absurd (in French the sound of *Après cet essai fait: cétécéfé*). The secondary corrections (corresponding to the horizontal order of the page) are associative, metonymic; they affect the syntagmatic chain of the message, modifying its volume by diminution or enlargement according to two rhetorical models: ellipsis and catalysis.

In short, the writer possesses three main types of corrections: substitutive, diminutive, and augmentative: he can work by permutation, subtraction, or expansion. Now these three types have not altogether the same status, and moreover they have not had the same fortune. Substitution and ellipsis bear on limited groups. The paradigm is closed by the constraints of distribution (which oblige the writer, in principle, to permute only terms of the same class) and by those of meaning, which require him to exchange affinitary terms.[9] As we cannot replace a sign by just any other sign, we also cannot reduce a sentence indefinitely; the diminutive correction (ellipsis) eventually comes up against the irreducible cell of any sentence, the subject-predicate group (it will be understood that *in practical terms* the limits of ellipsis are often reached much sooner, by reason of various cultural constraints, such as eurhythmy, symmetry, etc.): ellipsis is limited by the structure of the language. This very structure permits us, on the contrary, to give

[9] We must not limit affinity to a purely analogical relation, and it would be wrong to suppose that writers permute only synonymous terms: a classical writer like Bossuet can substitute *laugh* for *weep*: the antonymous relation constitutes part of the affinity.

free rein, without limit, to augmentative corrections; on the one hand, the parts of speech can be indefinitely multiplied (if only by digression), and on the other (this is what particularly interests us here), the sentence may be indefinitely furnished with interpolations and expansions: the catalytic work is theoretically infinite; even if the structure of the sentence is actually governed and limited by literary models (in the manner of poetical meter) or by physical constraints (the limits of human memory, relative moreover, since classical literature admits the *period*, virtually unknown to ordinary speech), it remains nonetheless true that the writer, confronting the sentence, experiences the infinite freedom of speech, as it is inscribed within the very structure of language. Hence what is involved is a problem of freedom, and we must note that the three types of corrections of which we have just spoken have not had the same fortune; according to the classical ideal of style, the writer is required to rework his substitutions and his ellipses tirelessly, by virtue of the correlative myths of the "exact word" and of "concision," both guarantees of "clarity,"[10] while he is discouraged from any labor of expansion; in classical manuscripts, permutations and crossings out abound, but we find virtually no augmentative corrections except in Rousseau and above all in Stendhal, whose subversive attitude with regard to "fine style" is well known.

To return to Flaubert: the corrections he made on his manuscripts are doubtless varied, but if we abide by what he himself asserted and commented, the "atrocity" of style is concentrated in two points, which are the writer's two crosses. The first cross is the repetition of words; it is a matter of substitutive correction here, since it is the (phonic) form of the word

---

[10] It is a classical paradox—which in my opinion should be explored—that clarity should be given as the natural product of concision (see Mme Necker's remark, given in Brunot's *Histoire de la langue française*: "The shortest sentence is always preferable when it is also clear, *for it necessarily becomes more so*").

whose too-immediate return must be avoided, while retaining
the content; as we have said, the possibilities of correction are
limited here, which should lighten the writer's responsibility all
the more; yet here Flaubert manages to introduce the vertigo
of an infinite correction: the difficulty, for him, is not correction itself (actually limited), but discernment of the place
where it is necessary: certain repetitions appear, which had
not been noticed the day before, so that nothing can guarantee
that the next day new "mistakes" will not be discovered;[11]
thus, there develops an anxious insecurity, for it always seems
possible to *bear* new repetitions:[12] the text, even when it
has been meticulously worked over, is somehow *mined* with
risks of repetition: limited and consequently reassured in its
act, substitution again becomes free and consequently agonizing by the infinity of its possible emplacements: the paradigm
is of course closed, but since it functions with each significa-
tive unit, it is seized again by the infinity of the syntagm. The
second cross of Flaubertian writing is the transitions (or articulations) of the discourse.[13] As we might expect of a writer
who has continuously absorbed content in form—or more precisely contested this very antinomy—the linking of ideas is not
experienced directly as a logical constraint but must be defined
in terms of the signifier; what is to be obtained is fluidity, the
optimal rhythm of the course of speech, in a word *sequence*,
that *flumen orationis* already demanded by the classical
rhetoricians. Here Flaubert comes up against the problem of
syntagmatic corrections once more: the good syntagm is an

[11] Apropos of three pages of *Madame Bovary* (1853): "I will doubtless
discover in them a thousand repetitions of words which I'll have to get
rid of. At this moment, late as it is, I can see virtually none."
[12] This audition of a language within language (however erroneous) recalls
another audition quite as vertiginous: that which permitted Saussure to hear
a second, anagrammatic message in most verses of Greek, Latin, and Vedic
poetry.
[13] "What is atrociously difficult is the linking of ideas, so that they derive
naturally from each other" (1852). ". . . And then the transitions, the
sequence—what an entanglement!" (1853).

equilibrium between excessive forces of constriction and of dilatation; but whereas ellipsis is normally limited by the very structure of the sentential unit, Flaubert reintroduces an infinite freedom into it: once acquired, he turns it back and reorients it toward a new expansion: a matter of constantly "unscrewing" what is too tight: ellipsis now acquires the vertigo of expansion.[14]

For it is indeed a matter of vertigo: correction is infinite, it has no sure sanction. The corrective protocols are perfectly systematic—and in this they might be reassuring—but since their points of application are endless, no appeasement is possible:[15] they are groups at once structured and floating. Yet this vertigo does not have as its motif the infinity of discourse, the traditional field of rhetoric; it is linked to a linguistic object, known of course to rhetoric, at least from the moment when, with Dionysus of Halicarnassus and the anonymous author of *On the Sublime*, rhetoric had discovered "style," but to which Flaubert has given a technical and even metaphysical existence of an incomparable force, and which is *the sentence*.

For Flaubert, the sentence is at once a unit of style, a unit of work, and a unit of life; it attracts the essential quality of his confidences as his work as a writer.[16] If we rid the expression of any metaphorical resonance, we might say that Flau-

---

[14] "Each paragraph is good in itself, and there are pages I am certain are perfect. But just because of this, *it doesn't work*. It's a series of well-turned paragraphs which do not lead into each other. I'm going to have to unscrew them, loosen the joints" (1853).
[15] "I ended by leaving off the corrections; I had reached the point where I understood nothing—pressing too hard on a piece of work, it dazzles you; what seems to be wrong now in five minutes seems perfectly all right" (1853).
[16] "I'd rather die like a dog than rush my sentence through, before it's ripe" (1852).—"I only want to write three more pages . . . and find four or five sentences that I've been searching for, nearly a month now" (1853).—"My work is going very slowly; sometimes I suffer real tortures to write the simplest sentence" (1852).—"I can't stop myself, even swimming, I test my sentences, despite myself" (1876).—And especially this, which might serve as an epigraph for what has just been said about the sentence in Flaubert: "I'm going on again, then, with my dull and simple life, poor wretched thing, in which the sentences are adventures . . ." (1857).

bert has spent his life "making sentences"; the sentence is, so to speak, the work's double *reflection*, it is on the level of the fabrication of sentences that the writer has created the history of this work: the odyssey of the sentence and the novel of Flaubert's novels. Thus, the sentence becomes, in our literature, a new object: not only *de jure*, in Flaubert's numerous declarations in this regard, but *de facto*: a sentence by Flaubert is immediately identifiable, not by its "air," its "color," or some turn of phrase habitual to the writer—which we might say of any author—but because it always presents itself as a separate, finite object, which we might almost call transportable, though it never joins the aphoristic model, for its unit does not abide by the closure of its content, but by the evident project which has established it as an object: Flaubert's sentence is a *thing*.

As we have seen apropos of Flaubert's corrections, this thing has a history, and this history, issuing from the very structure of the language, is inscribed in every sentence by Flaubert. His drama (his confidences authorize us to use so novelistic a word) in confronting the sentence can be articulated as follows: the sentence is an object, in it a finitude fascinates, analogous to that finitude which governs the metrical maturation of verse; but at the same time, by the very mechanism of expansion, every sentence is unsaturable, there is no structural reason to stop it here rather than there. *Let us work in order to end the sentence* (in the fashion of a line of verse), Flaubert implicitly says at each moment of his labor, of his life, while contradictorily he is obliged to exclaim unceasingly (as he notes in 1853): *It's never finished.*[17] The Flaubertian sentence is the very trace of this contradiction, experienced intensely by the writer during the countless hours when he shuts himself up with it: it is like the gratuitous arrest

[17] "Ah! What discouragements sometimes, what a Sisyphean labor style is, and prose especially! *It's never finished!*" (1853).

of an infinite freedom, in it is inscribed a kind of metaphysical contradiction: because the sentence is free, the writer is condemned not to search for the *best* sentence, but to assume *every* sentence: no god, even the god of art, can establish it in its place.

As we know, this situation was not experienced in the same way during the entire classical period. Confronting the freedom of language, rhetoric had constructed a system of surveillance (promulgating since Aristotle the metrical rules of the "period" and determining the field of corrections, where the freedom is limited by the very nature of language, i.e., on the level of substitutions and ellipses), and this system granted the writer a slight freedom by limiting his choices. This rhetorical code—or secondary code, since it transforms the freedoms of language into constraints of expression—grows moribund by the middle of the nineteenth century; rhetoric withdraws and in a sense exposes the fundamental linguistic unit, the sentence. This new object—in which the writer's freedom is henceforth directly invested—Flaubert discovers with anguish. A writer appears a little later who will make the sentence into the site of a demonstration at once poetic and linguistic: Mallarmé's *Un coup de dés* is explicitly based on the infinite possibility of sentential expansion, whose freedom, so burdensome for Flaubert, becomes for Mallarmé the very meaning— a blank meaning—of *the book to come*. Henceforth the writer's brother and guide will no longer be the master of rhetoric but of linguistics, the one who reveals no longer figures of discourse but the fundamental categories of language.

1967

Lesson in Writing

THE puppets of Bunraku theater are from three to five feet in height. They are little men or women with movable limbs, hands, and mouth. Each puppet is worked by three men who remain in view, surrounding, supporting, and accompanying it. The principal operator controls the upper part of the doll and its right arm; his face is visible, smooth, clear, impassive, cold like "a white onion freshly washed."[1] The two assistants are clad in black, their faces hidden by a piece of cloth; the first, gloved but with thumb exposed, holds a large scissors mechanism with which he operates the doll's left arm and hand; the second, crawling along on his knees, supports the body, makes it walk. These men move about along a low trench which leaves them unconcealed. The scenery is behind them, as at the theater. To the side, there is a dais for the musicians and the narrators whose role is to *express* the text (a little as one presses out the juice of a fruit); this text is half-spoken, half-sung, and, punctuated with great plectrum strokes by the sami-

From *Image-Music-Text*.

[1] Haiku by Basho:
*A white onion
freshly washed.
Feeling of cold.*

sen players, is at once measured and thrown off, given with violence and artifice. Sweating and motionless, the mouth-pieces sit behind little lecterns on which rests the writing they must vocalize, its vertical characters glimpsed from afar when they turn a page of their libretto; a triangle of stiff canvas fixed to their shoulders like a kite frames their faces, faces in throes to all the torments of the voice.

Antithesis is a privileged figure of our culture, doubtless because it corresponds well to our vision of good and evil and to that inveterate emblematism which has us turn every word into a watchword against its opposite (creativity versus intelligence, spontaneity versus reflection, truth versus appearance, etc.). Bunraku cares nothing for these contraries, for this antonymy that regulates our whole morality of discourse; concerned with a fundamental antilogy, that of the *animate/inanimate*, it disturbs it, dissipates it to the advantage of neither of the terms. With us, the marionette (Punch, for example) is there to hold up to the actor the mirror of his opposite, animating the inanimate but so as the better to reveal its degradation, the abjectness of its inertia; a caricature of "life," it affirms precisely thereby life's *moral* limits and serves to confine beauty, truth, and emotion in the living body of the actor—he who nevertheless makes of that body a lie. Bunraku on the other hand does not ape the actor, it rids us of him. How? Exactly by a certain reflection on the human body here conducted by inanimate matter with infinitely more rigor and excitement than by the animate body (endowed with a "soul"). The (naturalistic) Western actor is never beautiful, his body is intended as essentially physiological and not plastic; it is a collection of organs, a musculature of passions, whose every resource (voice, facial expressions, gestures) is subject to a kind of gymnastic drill. By a reversal that is specifically bourgeois, the actor's body, although built on a division of the essences of passion, then borrows from physiology the alibi of an organic unity, the unity of "life." In this way it is the actor who is a marionette and this despite the smooth flow of his acting, the model for which is not the caress but only the visceral "truth."

Thus, beneath a "living" and "natural" outward appearance, the Western actor maintains the division of his body and, consequently, the food of our fantasies. Voice, look, figure are in turn eroticized, like so many pieces of the body, like so many fetishes. The Western marionette too (as is evident in Punch) is a by-product of fantasy: as reduction, a grating reflection with an adherence to the human order ceaselessly recalled by a caricatural simulation, it lives not as a total body, totally vibrating, but as a rigid portion of the actor of whom it is an emanation; as automaton, it is again a fragment of movement, a start, a jolt, essence of discontinuity, fractured projection of bodily gestures; as doll finally, a reminiscence of the bit of material, of the genital swathe, it is indeed the phallic "little thing" (*das Kleine*), fallen from the body to become a fetish.

It may well be that the Japanese marionette retains something of this fantasy origin; the art of Bunraku, however, endows it with a different meaning. Bunraku does not aim at "animating" an inanimate object in such a way as to bring to life a piece of the body, a scrap of man, while preserving its vocation as "part"; it is not the simulation of the body that it is after, but, as it were, its concrete abstraction. Everything which we attribute to the total body and which is refused to our actors under pretense of a "living" organic unity is taken up and stated without any falsehood by the Bunraku puppet: fragility, discretion, sumptuousness, extraordinary nuance, abandonment of all triviality, melodic phrasing of gestures, in short those very qualities that the dreams of the old theology granted to the glorified body, namely impassiveness, clarity, agility, subtlety. This is what Bunraku accomplishes, this is how it converts the body fetish into a lovable body, this is how it refuses the antinomy of *animate/inanimate* and dismisses the concept hiding behind all *animation* of matter, that, quite simply, of "the soul."

Another opposition destroyed is that of *inner/outer*. Consider the Western theater of the last few centuries. Its function is essentially to reveal what is reputed to be secret ("feelings," "situations," "conflicts") while concealing the very artifice of the process of revelation (machinery, painting, makeup, sources of light). The Italian stage is the space of this deceit, everything there taking place in a room surreptitiously thrown open, surprised, spied on, and relished by a hidden spectator; a theological space, that of the moral failing: on the one side, under a light of which he pretends to be unaware, the actor, that is to say, gesture and speech; on the other, in the darkness, the public, that is to say, consciousness and conscience. Bunraku does not directly subvert the relation between stage and auditorium (any more than did Brecht), though Japanese theaters are infinitely less confined, less suffocating, less ponderous than ours. What it changes, more profoundly, is the driving link between character and actor which is always conceived by us as the expressive channel of an interiority. It has to be remembered that the agents of the spectacle in Bunraku are both visible and impassive. The men in black busy themselves around the doll but without any affectation of skill or discretion, without any promotional demagogy: silent, rapid, elegant, their actions are eminently transitive, operational, colored by that mixture of strength and subtlety that characterizes Japanese gestuality and that can be seen as the aesthetic envelope of efficacy. As for the master, it has already been said that his head is left uncovered, smooth and bare, without makeup, this conferring on him a *civic* (and not a theatrical) appearance; his face is offered to the spectator for reading, but what is so carefully and so preciously given to be read is that there is nothing to be read—here we find that exemption from meaning which does indeed illumine so many works of the East and which we are scarcely able to comprehend, since for us to attack meaning is to conceal or oppose it, never to absent it. With Bunraku, the sources of the theater are exposed in their void. What is expelled from the stage is hysteria, that is theater itself, and what is put in its place is the action necessary for the production of the spectacle—work is substituted for interiority.

It is thus futile to ask oneself as do certain Europeans (Claudel among them) whether or not the spectator can forget the presence of the manipulators. Bunraku practices neither the dissimulation nor the emphatic disclosure of its various mechanisms, hence ridding the animation of the actor of any suggestion of the sacred and abolishing the metaphysical bond that the West cannot stop itself from setting up between soul and body, cause and effect, motor and machine, agent and actor, Fate and man. God and creature:[2] if the manipulator is not hidden, then why and how turn him into a God? In Bunraku, the puppet is held by no thread; without a thread, there is no longer any metaphor, any Fate; puppet no longer aping creature, man is no longer a puppet in the hands of the deity, the *inner* no longer controls the *outer*.

Finally, a still more radical undertaking, Bunraku attacks the writing of the spectacle. With us, such writing involves an illusion of totality. "We find nothing more difficult," says Brecht, "than to break with the habit of considering an artistic production *as a whole*."[3] No doubt it is for this reason that periodically, from the Greek *choréia* to the bourgeois opera, we conceive of lyric art as the simultaneity of several modes of

[2] "Bunraku . . . is, quite simply, metaphysical theater . . . The puppet is man. The manipulator is God. The assistants are the messengers of Fate." J.-L. Barrault, "Le Bunraku," in *Cahiers Renaud-Barrault* 31, November 1960.
[3] Bertolt Brecht, "Alienation Effects in Chinese Acting," *Brecht on Theatre*—with somewhat different wording.

expression (acted, sung, mimed) with a sole, indivisible, origin. This origin is the body and the required totality has for its model organic unity. Western spectacle is anthropomorphous:[4] gesture and speech (not to mention song) form but a single tissue, conglomerate and lubrificated like a unique muscle that sets expression going without ever dividing it: the unity of movement and voice produces *the one* who acts; in other words, it is in this unity that is constituted the person of the personage, that is, the actor. In Bunraku, however, no one is on stage, or, more precisely, no person has taken up position there. The (personal) corporal illusion disappears, not because the actors are made of wood and cloth (we saw that Bunraku designates on the contrary a certain *lovableness* of the human body) but because the codes of expression are detached from one another, pulled free from the sticky organicism in which they are held by Western theater.

In fact then, Bunraku practices three separate writings which are given for reading simultaneously in three areas of the spectacle: the marionette, the manipulator, the vociferator; the effected gesture, the effective gesture, the vocal gesture. The voice is what is really at stake in modernity, the voice as specific substance of language everywhere triumphantly pushed forward. Modern society (as has been repeated often enough) believes itself to be ushering in a civilization of the image, but what it actually establishes overall, and particularly in its leisure activities which are massively spoken, is a civilization of speech. In complete contrast, Bunraku has a *limited* conception of the voice; not suppressing it, it assigns it a clearly defined function that is essentially trivial. The narrator's voice gathers together extravagant declamation, tremulous quiver, shrill feminine tones, broken intonations, tears, paroxysms of anger and lamentation, supplication and aston-

[4] Aristotle: "The action . . . being one and whole like a living being," *Poetics* 1459a.

ishment, indecent pathos, the whole concoction of emotion openly prepared at the level of this visceral, inner body of which the larynx is the mediating muscle. Even then, such excess is only presented in terms of the very code of the excessive: the voice moves only through a few discontinuous signs of fury; expelled from a body that remains motionless, mounted in the triangle of the costume, linked to the book which guides it from the lectern, studded sharply by the slightly off-phased (and so non-pertinent) strokes of the samisen player, the vocal substance stays written, discontinued, obedient to an irony (if one accepts the word free from any sense of a caustic humor). Thus what the voice exteriorizes finally is not what it carries in it ("feelings") but itself, its own prostitution; while pretending to deliver over contents (anecdotes, passions), the signifier artfully does nothing but turn itself inside out, like a glove.

Hence the voice, without being eliminated (which would be a way of censuring it, that is, of indicating its importance), is set aside (theatrically, the narrators occupy a lateral dais). Bunraku gives the voice a counterbalance, or better, a countermarch, that of gesture. Gesture here is twofold: emotive gesture with the marionette (people cry at the suicide of the doll-lover); transitive action with the manipulators. In our theatrical art the actor pretends to engage in action but his actions are never anything but gestures: on stage, nothing but theater, and yet a theater that is ashamed. Bunraku (this is its definition) separates the act from the gesture: it exhibits the gesture, it allows the act to be seen; it exposes at once the art and the work, keeping for each its own particular writing. The voice (and there is then no risk in letting it run the gamut of its excesses) is folded into an immense volume of silence in which other traits, other writings, are inscribed with so much finesse. It is here that an extraordinary effect occurs: far from the voice and almost without mimicry, these silent writings—

the one transitive, the other gestural—produce an exaltation as special, perhaps, as the intellectual hyperaesthesia attributed to certain drugs. Speech being not purified (Bunraku knows no ascetic ambition) but, as it were, *massed* on the side, the tackily clinging substances of Western theater are dissolved: emotion no longer submerges everything in its flood but becomes matter for reading; the stereotypes disappear without however the spectacle falling into originality, the "stroke of genius." All of which has an evident kinship with the distancing effect recommended by Brecht, who was, as perhaps needs recalling, the first to understand and state the critical importance of Oriental theater. This distance, reputed by us to be impossible, useless or derisory and speedily abandoned, despite its being placed by Brecht very precisely at the center of revolutionary dramatic art (the latter doubtless explains the former), is what Bunraku shows—shows how it can function: by the discontinuity of codes, by the cæsura imposed in the different traits of the representation, so that the *copy* elaborated on the stage is not destroyed but shattered, scored, freed from the metonymical contagion of voice and gesture, soul and body, which entangles our actors.

A total spectacle, but divided, Bunraku evidently excludes improvisation, doubtless aware that the return to spontaneity is the return to all those stereotypes which go to make up our "inner depths." Here we have, as Brecht saw in connection with the Oriental actor whose lesson he wished to receive and propagate on this point too, the reign of the *quotation*,[5] the pinch of writing, the fragment of code, none of the promoters of the action being able to take responsibility in his own person for what he is never alone in writing. As in the modern

[5] "He limits himself from the start to simply quoting the character played. But with what art he does this! He only needs a minimum of illusion. What he has to show is worth seeing even for a man in his right mind." And elsewhere: "Once the idea of total transformation is given up, the actor speaks his part not as if he were improvising it himself but like a quotation."

text, the stressing of codes, references, discontinuous observations, anthological gestures, multiplies the written line, and this not by virtue of some metaphysical appeal but by the play of a combinatory set which opens in the entire space of the theater: what is started by the one is continued by the other, unendingly.

1968

PART THREE

The Third Meaning

RESEARCH NOTES ON SOME EISENSTEIN STILLS

Here is an image from *Ivan the Terrible* (I): two courtiers, two adjuvants, two supernumeraries (it matters little if I am unable to remember the details of the story exactly) are raining down gold over the young czar's head. I think it possible to distinguish three levels of meaning in this scene:

1) An informational level, which gathers together everything I can learn from the setting, the costumes, the characters, their relations, their insertion in an anecdote with which I am (even if vaguely) familiar. This level is that of communication. Were it necessary to find a mode of analysis for it, I should turn to the first semiotics (that of the "message"); this level, this semiotics, however, will be of no further concern here.

2) A symbolic level, which is the downpour of gold and which is itself stratified. There is the referential symbolism: the imperial ritual of baptism by gold. Then there is the diegetic symbolism: the theme of gold, of wealth, in *Ivan the Terrible* (supposing such a theme to exist), which makes a significant intervention in this scene. Then again there is the Eisensteinian symbolism—if by chance a critic should decide to demonstrate that the gold or the raining down or the curtain

From *Image-Music-Text*.

317

or the disfiguration can be seen as held in a network of displacements and substitutions peculiar to S. M. Eisenstein. Finally, there is a historical symbolism, if, in a manner even more widely embracing than the previous ones, it can be shown that the gold brings in a (theatrical) playing, a scenography of exchange, locatable both psychoanalytically and economically, that is to say semiologically. Taken in its entirety, this second level is that of *signification*. Its mode of analysis would be a semiotics more highly developed than the first, a second or neo-semiotics, open no longer to the science of the message but to the sciences of the symbol (psychoanalysis, economy, dramaturgy).

3) Is that all? No, for I am still held by the image. I read, I receive (and probably even first and foremost) a third meaning[1]—evident, erratic, obstinate. I do not know what its signified is, at least I am unable to give it a name, but I can see clearly the traits, the signifying accidents of which this—consequently incomplete—sign is composed: a certain compactness of the courtiers' make-up, thick and insistent for the one, smooth and distinguished for the other; the former's "stupid" nose, the latter's finely traced eyebrows, his lank blondness, his faded, pale complexion, the affected flatness of his hairstyle suggestive of a wig, the touching up with chalky foundation talc, with face powder. I am not sure if the reading of this third meaning is justified—if it can be generalized—but already it seems to me that its signifier (the traits to which I have tried to give words, if not to describe) possesses a theoretical individuality. On the one hand, it cannot be conflated with the

---

[1] In the classical paradigm of the five senses, the third sense is hearing (first in importance in the Middle Ages). This is a happy coincidence, since what is here in question is indeed *listening*: firstly, because the remarks by Eisenstein to which reference will be made are taken from a consideration of the coming of sound in film; second, because listening (no reference to the *phoné* alone) bears within it that metaphor best suited to the "textual": orchestration (SME's own word), counterpoint, stereophony.

I

II

III

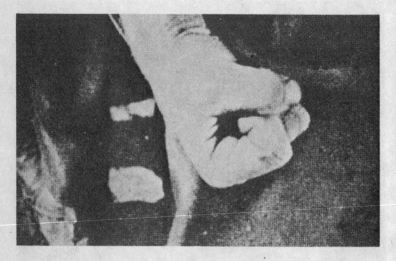

IV

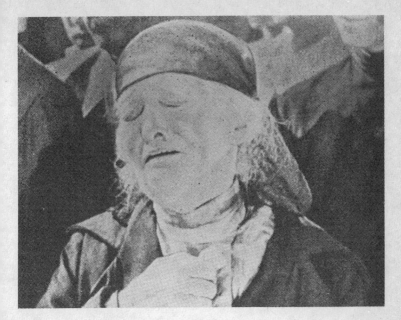

V

VI

VII

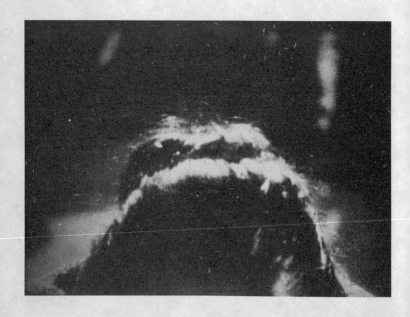

VIII

IX

X

XI

XII

XIII

XIV

XV

XVI

simple *existence* of the scene, it exceeds the copy of the referential motif, it compels an interrogative reading (interrogation bears precisely on the signifier not on the signified, on reading not on intellection: it is a "poetical" grasp); on the other, neither can it be conflated with the dramatic meaning of the episode: to say that these traits refer to a significant "attitude" of the courtiers, this one detached and bored, that one diligent (*"They are simply doing their job as courtiers"*), does not leave me fully satisfied; something in the two faces exceeds psychology, anecdote, function, exceeds meaning without, however, coming down to the obstinacy in presence shown by any human body. By contrast with the first two levels, communication and signification, this third level—even if the reading of it is still hazardous—is that of *signifiance*, a word which has the advantage of referring to the field of the signifier (and not of signification) and of linking up with, via the path opened by Julia Kristeva who proposed the term, a semiotics of the text.

My concern here lies not with communication but with signification and *signifiance*. I must therefore name as economically as possible the second and third meanings. The symbolic meaning (the shower of gold, the power of wealth, the imperial rite) forces itself upon me by a double determination: it is intentional (it is what the author wanted to say) and it is taken from a kind of common, general lexicon of symbols; it is a meaning which seeks me out, me, the recipient of the message, the subject of the reading, a meaning which starts with SME and which goes on *ahead of me;* evident certainly (so too is the other), but *closed* in its evidence, held in a complete system of destination. I propose to call this complete sign *the obvious meaning. Obvious* means *which comes ahead* and this is exactly the case with this meaning, which comes to seek me out. In theology, we are told, the obvious meaning is that "which presents itself quite naturally to the mind" and this again is the case here: the symbolics of the raining down of gold appears to me as forever having been endowed with a "natural" clarity. As for the other meaning, the third, the one "too many," the supplement that my intellection cannot succeed in absorbing, at once persistent and fleeting, smooth and elusive, I propose to call it *the obtuse meaning*. The word springs readily to mind and, miracle, when its etymology is unfolded, it already provides us with a theory of the supplementary meaning. *Obtusus* means *that which is blunted, rounded in form*. Are not the traits which I indicated (the make-up, the whiteness, the wig, etc.) just like the blunting of a meaning too clear, too violent? Do they not give the obvious signified a kind of difficulty prehensible roundness, cause my reading to slip? An obtuse angle is greater than a right angle: *an obtuse angle of 100°*, says the dictionary; the third meaning also seems to me greater than the pure, upright, secant, legal perpendicular of the narrative, it seems to open the field of meaning totally, that is infinitely. I even accept for the obtuse meaning the word's pejorative connotation: the obtuse meaning appears to extend outside culture, knowledge, information; analytically, it has something derisory about it: opening out into the infinity of language, it can come through as limited in the eyes of analytic reason; it belongs to the family of pun, buffoonery, useless expenditure. Indifferent to moral or aesthetic categories (the trivial, the futile, the false, the pastiche), it is on the side of the carnival. *Obtuse* is thus very suitable.

THE OBVIOUS MEANING

A few words with regard to the obvious meaning, even though it is not the object of this study. Here are two images in which it can be seen in its pure state. The four figures in II "symbolize" three ages of life and the unanimity of mourning (Vak-ulinchuk's funeral). The clenched fist in IV, given in full "detail," signifies indignation, anger mastered and channeled, the determination of the struggle; metonymically joined to the whole Potemkin story, it "symbolizes" the working class in all its resolute strength, for, by a miracle of semantic intelligence, this fist which is *seen wrong way up*, kept by its owner in a sort of clandestinity (it is the hand which *first of all* hangs down naturally along the trouser leg and which *then* closes, hardens, *thinks* at once its future struggle, its patience and its prudence), cannot be read as the fist of some hoodlum, of some fascist: it is *immediately* a proletarian fist. Which shows that Eisenstein's "art" is not polysemous: it chooses the meaning, imposes it, hammers it home (if the signification is overrun by the obtuse meaning, this is not to say that it is thereby denied or blurred): the Eisensteinian meaning devastates ambiguity. How? By the addition of an aesthetic value, emphasis. Eisenstein's "decorativism" has an economic function: it proffers the truth. Look at III: in extremely classic fashion, grief comes from the bowed heads, the expressions of suffering, the hand over the mouth stifling a sob, but when once all this has been said, very adequately, a decorative trait says it again: the superimposition of the two hands aesthetically arranged in a delicate, maternal, floral ascension toward the face bowing down. Within the general detail (the two women), another detail is mirroringly inscribed; derived from a pictorial order as a quotation of the gestures to be found in icons and *pietà*, it does not distract but accentuates the meaning. This accentuation (characteristic of all realist art) has some connection with the "truth" of *Potemkin*. Baudelaire spoke of *"the emphatic truth of gesture in the important moments of life"*; here it is the truth of the "important proletarian moment" which requires emphasis. The Eisensteinian aesthetic does not constitute an independent level: it is part of the obvious meaning, and the obvious meaning is always, in Eisenstein, the revolution.

THE OBTUSE MEANING

I first had the conviction of the obtuse meaning with image V. A question forced itself upon me: what is it in this tearful old woman that poses for me the question of the signifier? I quickly convinced myself that, although perfect, it was neither the facial expression nor the gestural figuration of grief (the closed eyelids, the taut mouth, the hand clasped on the breast): all that belongs to the full signification, to the obvious meaning of the image, to Eisensteinian realism and decorativism. I felt that the penetrating trait—disturbing like a guest who obstinately sits on saying nothing when one has no use for him— must be situated somewhere in the region of the forehead: the coif, the headscarf holding in the hair, had something to do with it. In image VI, however, the obtuse meaning vanishes, leaving only a message of grief. It was then I understood that the scandal, supplement or drift imposed on this classic representation of grief came very precisely from a tenuous relationship: that of the low headscarf, the closed eyes and the convex mouth; or rather, to use the distinction made by SME himself between "the shadows of the cathedral" and "the enshadowed cathedral," from a relation between the "lowness" of the line of the headscarf, pulled down abnormally close to the eyebrows as in those disguises intended to create a facetious, simpleton look, the upward circumflex of the faded eyebrows, faint and old, the excessive curve of the eyelids, lowered but brought together as though squinting, and the bar of the half-opened mouth, corresponding to the bar of the headscarf and to that of the eyebrows, metaphorically speaking "like a fish out of water." All these traits (the funny headdress, the old woman, the squinting eyelids, the fish) have as their vague reference a somewhat low language, the language of a rather pitiful disguise. In connection with the noble grief of the obvious meaning, they form a dialogism so tenuous that there is no guarantee of its intentionality. The characteristic of this third meaning is indeed—at least in SME—to blur the limit separating expression from disguise, but also to allow that oscillation succinct demonstration—an elliptic emphasis, if one can put it like that, a complex and extremely artful disposition (for it involves a temporality of signification), perfectly described by Eisenstein himself when he jubilantly quotes the golden rule of the old Gillette: "*Just short of the cutting edge.*"

The obtuse meaning, then, has something to do with disguise. Look at Ivan's beard raised to obtuse meaning, in my opinion, in image VII; it declares its artifice but without in so doing abandoning the "good faith" of its referent (the historical figure of the czar): an actor disguised twice over (once as actor in the anecdote, once as actor in the dramaturgy) without one disguise destroying the other; a multi-layering of meanings which always lets the previous meaning continue, as in a geological formation, saying the opposite without giving up the contrary—a (two-term) dramatic dialectic that Brecht would have liked. The Eisensteinian "artifice" is at once falsification of itself—pastiche—and derisory fetish, since it shows its fissure and its suture: what can be seen in image VII is the join and thus the initial disjoin of the beard perpendicular to the chin. That the top of a head (the most "obtuse" part of the human person), that a single bun of hair (in image VIII) can be the *expression* of grief, that is what is derisory—for the expression, not for the grief. Hence no parody, no trace of burlesque; there is no aping of grief (the obvious meaning must remain revolutionary, the general mourning which accompanies Vakulinchuk's death has a historical meaning), and yet, "embodied" in the bun, it has a cut-off, a refusal of contamination; the populism of the woollen shawl (obvious meaning) stops at the bun; here begins the fetish—the hair—and a kind of *non-negating derision* of the expression. The whole of the obtuse meaning (its disruptive force) is staked on the excessive mass of the hair. Look at another bun (that of the woman in image IX): it contradicts the tiny raised fist, atrophies it without the reduction having the slightest symbolic (intellectual) value; prolonged by small curls, pulling the face in toward an ovine model, it gives the woman something *touching* (in the way that a certain generous foolishness can be) or *sensitive*—these antiquated words, mystified words if ever there were, with little that is revolutionary or political about them, must nevertheless be assumed. I believe that the obtuse meaning carries a certain *emotion*. Caught up in the disguise, such emotion is never sticky, it is an emotion which simply *designates* what one loves, what one wants to defend: an emotion value, an evaluation. Everyone will agree, I think, that SME's proletarian ethnography fragmented the length of Vakulinchuk's funeral, is constantly informed by something loving (using the word regardless of any specification as to age or sex). Maternal, cordial, virile, "sympathetic" without any recourse to stereotypes, the Eisensteinian people is essentially *lovable*. We savor, we love the two round-capped heads in image X, we enter into complicity, into an understanding with them. Doubtless beauty can work as an obtuse meaning; this is the case in image XI, where the extremely dense obvious meaning (Ivan's attitude, young Vladimir's half-wit foolishness) is anchored and/or set adrift by Basmanov's beauty. But the eroticism included in the obtuse meaning (or rather: the eroticism which this meaning picks up) is no respector of the aesthetic: Euphrosyne is ugly, "obtuse" (images XII and XIII), like the monk (image XIV), but this obtuseness exceeds the anecdote, becomes a blunting of meaning, its drifting. There is in the obtuse meaning an eroticism which includes the con-

trary of the beautiful, as also what falls outside such con-
trariety, its limit—inversion, unease, and perhaps sadism.
Look at the flabby innocence of the "Children in the Fiery
Furnace" (image XV), the schoolboyish ridicule of their
mufflers dutifully tucked up to the chin, the curds-and-whey
skin (of their eyes, of their mouths set in the skin) which
Fellini seems to have remembered in the hermaphrodite of his
Satyricon—the very same mentioned by Georges Bataille,
notably in that text in *Documents* which situates for me one
of the possible regions of obtuse meaning, "The Big Toe."[2]

Let us continue (if these examples will suffice to lead on to
one or two more theoretical remarks). The obtuse meaning is
not in the language-system (even that of symbols). Take away
the obtuse meaning and communication and signification still
remain, still circulate, still come through: without it, I can still
state and read. No more, however, is it to be located in language use. It may be that there is a certain constant in Eisensteinian obtuse meaning, but in that case it is already a thematic language, an idiolect, this idiolect being provisional
(simply decided by a critic writing a book on SME). Obtuse
meanings are to be found not everywhere (the signifier is rare,
a future figure) but *somewhere*: in other *authors* of films (perhaps), in a certain manner of reading "life" and so "reality"
itself (the word is simply used here in opposition to the deliberately fictive). In image XVI from *Ordinary Fascism* (by
Mikhail Romm), a documentary image, I can easily read an
obvious meaning, that of fascism (aesthetics and symbolics of
power, the theatrical hunt), but I can also read an obtuse
meaning: the (again) disguised, blond silliness of the young
quiver-bearer, the flabbiness of his hands and mouth (I cannot
manage to describe, only to designate a location), Goering's
thick nails, his trashy ring (this already on the brink of obvious
meaning, like the treacly platitude of the imbecile smile of the

[2] [Georges Bataille, "Le gros orteil," *Documents*, Paris 1968, pp. 75–82.]

bespectacled man in the background—visibly an "arse-licker"). In other words, the obtuse meaning is not situated structurally, a semantologist would not agree as to its objective existence (but then what is an objective reading?); and if to me it is clear (to me), that is *still* perhaps (for the moment) by the same "aberration" which compelled the lone and unhappy Saussure to hear in ancient poetry the enigmatic voice of anagram, unoriginated and obsessive. Same uncertainty when it is a matter of *describing* the obtuse meaning (of giving an idea of where it is going, where it goes away). The obtuse meaning is a signifier without a signified, hence the difficulty in naming it. My reading remains suspended between the image and its description, between definition and approximation. If the obtuse meaning cannot be described, that is because, in contrast to the obvious meaning, it does not copy anything—how do you describe something that does not represent anything? The pictorial "rendering" of words is here impossible, with the consequence that if, in front of these images, we remain, you and I, at the level of articulated language—at the level, that is, of my own text—the obtuse meaning will not succeed in existing, in entering the critic's metalanguage. Which means that the obtuse meaning is outside (articulated) language while nevertheless within interlocution. For if you look at the images I am discussing, you can see this meaning, we can agree on it "over the shoulder" or "on the back" of articulated language. Thanks to the image (fixed, it is true; a factor which will be taken up later) or much rather thanks to what, in the image, is purely image (which is in fact very little), we do without language yet never cease to understand one another.

In short, what the obtuse meaning disturbs, sterilizes, is metalanguage (criticism). A number of reasons can be given for this. First and foremost, obtuse meaning is discontinuous, indifferent to the story and to the obvious meaning (as signification of the story). This dissociation has a de-naturing or at least a distancing effect with regard to the referent (to "reality" as nature, the realist instance). Eisenstein would probably have acknowledged this incongruity, this im-pertinence of the signifier, Eisenstein who tells us concerning sound and color: "Art begins the moment the creaking of a boot on the sound track occurs against a different visual shot and thus gives rise to corresponding associations. It is the same with color: color begins where it no longer corresponds to natural coloration . . ." Then, the signifier (the third meaning) is not filled out, it keeps a permanent state of *depletion* (a word from linguistics which designates empty, all-purpose verbs, as for example the French verb *faire*). We could also say on the contrary—and it would be just as correct—that this same signifier is not empty (cannot empty itself), that it maintains a state of perpetual erethism, desire not finding issue in that spasm of the signified which normally brings the subject voluptuously back into the peace of nominations. Finally, the obtuse meaning can be seen as an *accent*, the very form of an emergence, of a fold (a crease even) marking the heavy layer of informations and significations. If it could be described (a contradiction in terms), it would have exactly the nature of the Japanese *haiku*—anaphoric gesture without significant content, a sort of gash rased of meaning (of desire for meaning). Thus in image V:

Mouth drawn, eyes shut squinting,
Headscarf low over forehead,
She weeps.

This accent—the simultaneously emphatic and elliptic character of which has already been mentioned—is not directed toward meaning (as in hysteria), does not theatricalize (Eisensteinian decorativism belongs to another level), does not even indicate an *elsewhere* of meaning (another content, added to the obvious meaning); it outplays meaning—subverts not the content but the whole practice of meaning. A new—rare—practice affirmed against a majority practice (that of signification), obtuse meaning appears necessarily as a luxury, an expenditure with no exchange. This luxury does not *yet* belong to today's politics but nevertheless *already* to tomorrow's.

Something has still to be said concerning the syntagmatic responsibility of the third meaning: what is its place in the movement of the anecdote, in the logico-temporal system without which, so it seems, it is impossible to communicate a narrative to the "mass" of readers and spectators? It is clear that the obtuse meaning is the epitome of a counter-narrative; disseminated, reversible, set to its own temporality, it inevitably determines (if one follows it) a quite different analytical segmentation to that in shots, sequences and syntagms (technical or narrative)—an extraordinary segmentation: counter-logical and yet "true." Imagine "following" not Euphrosyne's schemings, nor even the character (as diegetic entity or symbolic figure), nor even, again, the face of the Wicked Mother, but merely, in this face, this attitude, this black veil, the heavy, ugly flatness—you will then have a different time-scale, neither diegetic nor oneiric, a different film. A theme with neither variations nor development (the obvious meaning is fully thematic: there is a theme of the Funeral), the obtuse meaning can only come and go, appearing–disappearing. The play of presence/absence undermines the character, making of it a simple nub of facets; a disjunction expressed in another connection by SME himself: *"What is characteristic is that the different positions of one and the same czar . . . are given without link between one position and the next."*

Precisely. The *indifference* or freedom of position of the supplementary signifier in relation to the narrative allows us to situate with some exactitude the historical, political, theoretical task accomplished by Eisenstein. In his work, the story (the diegetic, anecdotal representation) is not destroyed—quite the contrary: what finer story than that of *Ivan* or *Potemkin*? This importance given to the narrative is necessary in order *to be understood* in a society which, unable to resolve the contradictions of history without a long political transaction, draws support (provisionally?) from mythical (narrative) solutions. The *contemporary* problem is not to destroy the narrative but to subvert it; today's task is to dissociate subversion from destruction. It seems to me that SME operates such a distinction: the presence of an obtuse, supplementary, third meaning—if only in a few images, but then as an imperishable signature, as a seal endorsing the whole of the work (and the whole of his work)—radically recasts the theoretical status of the anecdote: the story (the diegesis) is no longer just a strong system (the millennial system of narrative) but also and contradictorily a simple space, a field of permanences and permutations. It becomes that configuration, that stage, whose false limits multiply the signifier's permutational play, that vast trace which, by difference, compels what SME himself calls a *vertical* reading, that *false* order which permits the turning of the pure series, the aleatory combination (chance is crude, a signifier on the cheap) and the attainment of a structuration *which slips away from the inside*. It can thus be said that with SME we have to reverse the cliché according to which the more gratuitous a meaning, the more it will appear as a mere parasite of the story being narrated; on the contrary, it is this story which here finds itself in some sort parametric to the signifier for which it is now merely the field of displacement, the constitutive negativity, or, again, the fellow-traveler.

In other words, the third meaning structures the film *differently* without—at least in SME—subverting the story and for this reason, perhaps, it is at the level of the third meaning, and at that level alone, that the "filmic" finally emerges. The filmic is that in the film which cannot be described, the representation which cannot be represented. The filmic begins only where language and metalanguage end. Everything that can be *said* about *Ivan* or *Potemkin* can be said of a written text (entitled *Ivan the Terrible* or *Battleship Potemkin*) except this, the obtuse meaning; I can gloss everything in Euphrosyne, except the obtuse quality of her face. The filmic, then, lies precisely here, in that region where articulated language is no longer more than approximative and where another language begins (whose science, therefore, cannot be linguistics, soon discarded like a booster rocket). The third meaning—theoretically locatable but not describable—can now be seen as the *passage* from language to *significance* and the founding act of the filmic itself. Forced to develop in a civilization of the signified, it is not surprising that (despite the incalculable number of films in the world) the filmic should still be rare (a few flashes in SME, perhaps elsewhere?), so much so that it could be said that as yet the film does not exist (any more than does the text); there is only "cinema," language, narrative, poetry, sometimes extremely "modern," "translated" into "images" said to be "animated." Nor is it surprising that the filmic can only be located after having—analytically—gone across the "essential," the "depth" and the "complexity" of the cinematic work; all those riches which are merely those of articulated language, with which we constitute the work and believe we exhaust it. The filmic is not the same as the film, is as far removed from the film as the novelistic is from the novel (I can write in the novelistic without ever writing novels).

THE STILL

Which is why to a certain extent (the extent of our theoretical fumblings) the filmic, very paradoxically, cannot be grasped in the film "in situation," "in movement," "in its natural state," but only in that major artefact, the still. For a long time, I have been intrigued by the phenomenon of being interested and even fascinated by photos from a film (outside a cinema, in the pages of *Cahiers du cinéma*) and of then losing everything of those photos (not just the captivation but the memory of the image) when once inside the viewing room— a change which can even result in a complete reversal of values. I at first ascribed this taste for stills to my lack of cinematic culture, to my resistance to film; I thought of myself as like those children who prefer the pictures to the text, or like those clients who, unable to attain the adult possession of objects (because too expensive), are content to derive pleasure from looking at a choice of samples or a department store catalogue. Such an explanation does no more than reproduce the common opinion with regard to stills which sees them as a remote subproduct of the film, a sample, a means of drawing in custom, a pornographic extract, and, technically, a reduction of the work by the immobilization of what is taken to be the sacred essence of cinema—the movement of the images.

If, however, the specific filmic (the filmic of the future) lies not in movement, but in an inarticulable third meaning that neither the simple photograph nor figurative painting can assume since they lack the diegetic horizon, the possibility of configuration mentioned earlier,[3] then the "movement" regarded as the essence of film is not animation, flux, mobility,

---

[3] There are other "arts" which combine still (or at least drawing) and story, diegesis—namely, the photo-novel and the comic strip. I am convinced that these "arts," born in the lower depths of high culture, possess theoretical qualifications and present a new signifier (related to the obtuse meaning). This is acknowledged as regards the comic strip but I myself experience this slight trauma of *significance* faced with certain photo-novels: *"their stupidity touches me"* (which could be a certain definition of obtuse meaning). There may thus be a future—or a very ancient past—truth in these derisory, vulgar, foolish, dialogical forms of consumer subculture. And there is an autonomous "art" (a "text"), that of the *pictogram* ("anecdotalized" images, obtuse meanings placed in a diegetic space); this art taking across historically and culturally heteroclite productions: ethnographic pictograms, stained-glass windows, Carpaccio's *Legend of Saint Ursula, images d'Epinal*, photo-novels, comic strips. The innovation represented by the still (in comparison with these other pictograms) would be that the filmic (which it constitutes) is *doubled* by another text, the film.

"life," copy, but simply the framework of a permutational unfolding and a theory of the still becomes necessary, a theory
whose possible points of departure must be given briefly here
in conclusion.

The still offers us the *inside* of the fragment. In this connection we would need to take up—displacing them—Eisenstein's own formulations when envisaging the new possibilities
of audio-visual montage: ". . . the basic center of gravity . . .
is transferred to *inside* the fragment, into the elements included
in the image itself. *And the center of gravity is no longer the
element 'between shots'—the shock—but the element 'inside
the shot'—the accentuation within the fragment . . .*" Of
course, there is no audio-visual montage in the still, but SME's
formula is general insofar as it establishes a right to the syntagmatic disjunction of images and calls for a *vertical* reading
of the articulation. Moreover, the still is not a sample (an idea
that supposes a sort of homogeneous, statistical nature of the
film elements) but a quotation (we know how much importance
presently accrues to this concept in the theory of the text): at
once parodic and disseminatory. It is not a specimen chemically
extracted from the substance of the film, but rather the trace of
a superior *distribution* of traits of which the film as experienced
in its animated flow would give no more than one text among
others. The still, then, is the fragment of a second text *whose
existence never exceeds the fragment*; film and still find themselves in a palimpsest relationship without it being possible to
say that one is *on top of* the other or that one is *extracted* from
the other. Finally, the still throws off the constraint of filmic
time; which constraint is extremely powerful, continuing to
form an obstacle to what might be called the adult birth of film
(born technically, occasionally even aesthetically, film has still
to be born theoretically). For written texts, unless they are
very conventional, totally committed to logico-temporal order,
reading time is free; for film, this is not so, since the image

cannot go faster or slower without losing its perceptual figure. The still, by instituting a reading that is at once instantaneous and vertical, scorns logical time (which is only an operational time); it teaches us how to dissociate the technical constraint from what is the specific filmic and which is the "indescribable" meaning. Perhaps it was the reading of *this other text* (here in stills) that SME called for when he said that a film is not simply to be seen and heard but to be scrutinized and listened to attentively. This seeing and this hearing are obviously not the postulation of some simple need to apply the mind (that would be banal, a pious wish) but rather a veritable mutation of reading and its object, text or film—which is a crucial problem of our time.

1970

Fourier

BEGINNINGS

I

ONE DAY I was invited to eat a couscous with rancid butter;
the rancid butter was customary; in certain regions it is an
integral part of the couscous code. However, be it prejudice,
or unfamiliarity, or digestive intolerance, I don't like rancidity.
What to do? Eat it, of course, so as not to offend my host, but
gingerly, in order not to offend the conscience of my disgust
(since for disgust *per se* one needs some stoicism). In this
difficult meal, Fourier would have helped me. On the one
hand, intellectually, he would have persuaded me of three
things: the first is that the rancidness of couscous is in no way
an idle, futile, or trivial question, and that debating it is no
more futile than debating Transubstantiation;[1] the second is
that by forcing me to lie about my likes (or dislikes), society
is manifesting its *falseness*, i.e., not only its hypocrisy (which
is banal) but also the vice of the social mechanism whose
gearing is faulty; the third, that this same society cannot rest
until it has guaranteed (how? Fourier has clearly explained it,

From *Sade/Fourier/Loyola*, translated by Richard Miller (New York:
Hill and Wang, 1976).

[1] "First we will deal with the puerility of these battles over the superiority
of sweet cream or little pies; we might reply that the debate will be no
more ridiculous than our Religious Wars over Transubstantiation" (VII, 346).

but it must be admitted that it hasn't worked) the exercise of my manias, whether "bizarre" or "minor," like those of people who like old chickens, the eater of horrid things (like the astronomer Lalande, who liked to eat live spiders), the fanatics about butter, pears, bergamots, Ankles, or "Baby Dolls."[2] On the other hand, practically, Fourier would at once have put an end to my embarrassment (being torn between my good manners and my lack of taste for rancid things) by taking me from my meal (where, in addition, I was stuck for hours, a barely tolerable situation against which Fourier protested) and sending me to the Anti-Rancid group, where I would be allowed to eat fresh couscous as I liked without bothering anyone—which would not have kept me from preserving the best of relations with the Rancid group, whom I would henceforth consider as not at all "ethnic," foreign, strange, at for example a great couscous tournament, at which couscous would be the "theme," and where a jury of gastrosophers would decide on the superiority of rancid over fresh (I almost said: *normal*, but for Fourier, and this is his victory, there is no normality).[3]

[2] "Ankles" are men who like to scratch their mistress's ankle (VII, 335); the "Baby Doll" is a sixty-year-old man who, desirous of being treated like a spoiled child, wants the soubrette to punish him by "gently patting his patriarchal buttocks" (VII, 334).

[3] Fourier would, I am sure, have been enraptured at my friend Abd el Kebir's entry into the couscous tournament, in defense of the Rancid side, in a letter I received from him:

"I am not a Rancist either. I prefer couscous with pumpkin, and a light sprinkling of raisins—well blended, of course—and that produces: an insubordination of the expression.

"The apparent instability of the Moroccan peasant's culinary system proceeds, dear friend, from the fact that rancid butter is made in a strange underground hearth at the intersection of cosmic time and the time of consumption. Rancid butter is a kind of decomposed property, pleasing to interior monologue.

"Dug out in handfuls, rancid butter is worked in the following circular rite: a huge and magnificent ball of couscous is ejaculated into the throat to such an extent that the rancidity is neutralized. Fourier would call it a double-focus ellipse.

"This is why the peasant works to get rid of it: the parabole means a surplus, since the earth belongs to God. He inters the fresh butter, then extracts it when the time is ripe. However, the female is the one, the

II

Fourier likes compotes, fine weather, perfect melons, the little spiced pastries known as *mirlitons*, and the company of lesbians. Society and Nature hinder these tastes a bit: sugar is (or was) expensive (more expensive than bread), the French climate is insupportable except in May, September, and October, we know no sure method of detecting a melon's quality, in Civilization little pastries bring on indigestion, lesbians are proscribed and, blind for a long time as far as he himself was concerned, Fourier did not know until very late in life that he liked them. Thus the world must be remade for my pleasure: my pleasure will be simultaneously the ends and the means: in organizing it, in distributing it, I shall overwhelm it.

III

Everywhere we travel, on every occasion on which we feel a desire, a longing, a lassitude, a vexation, it is possible to ask Fourier, to wonder: What would he have said about it? What would he make of this place, this adventure? Here am I one evening in a southern Moroccan hotel: some hundred meters outside the populous, tattered, dusty town, a park filled with rare scents, a blue pool, flowers, quiet bungalows, hordes of discreet servants. In Harmony, what would that give? First of all, this: there would come to this place all who have this strange liking, this low mania for dim lights in the woods,

---

squatter, always squatting down, who carries out the operation from above. Slow and painstaking preparation, making my couscous taste rather androgynous.

"Thus, I agree to act within its limits: the rancid is an imperative fantasy. The pleasure is in eating with the group.

"Relating this manner of conserving butter underground to a traditional practice of mental healing, the frenzied madman is buried for a day or two, left almost naked, without food. When he is brought out, he is often reborn or really dies. Between heaven and earth there are signs to be seen for those who know.

"The high price put on couscous—a truly enigmatic material—obliges me to sign off and to send you my friendly wishes."

candlelit dinners, a staff of native servants, night frogs, and a camel in a meadow beneath the window. Then this rectification: the Harmonians would scarcely have need of this place, luxurious owing to its temperature (spring in mid-winter), because, by acting on the atmosphere, by modifying the polar cap, this exotic climate could be transported to Jouy-en-Josas or Gif-sur-Yvette. Finally, this compromise: at certain times during the year, hordes of people, driven by a taste for travel and adventure, would descend upon the idyllic motel and there hold their councils of love and gastronomy (it would be just the place for our couscous investigations). From which, once again, it emerges: that Fourierist pleasure is the end of the tablecloth: pull the slightest futile incident, provided it concerns your happiness, and all the rest of the world will follow: its organization, its limits, its values; this sequence, this fatal induction which ties the most tenuous inflection of our desire to the broadest sociality, this unique space in which fantasy and the social combinative are trapped, this is very precisely *systematics* (but not, as we shall see, the system); with Fourier, impossible to relax without constructing a theory about it. And this: in Fourier's day none of the Fourierist system had been achieved, but today? Caravans, crowds, the collective search for fine climate, pleasure trips, exist: in a derisory and rather atrocious form, the organized tour, the planting of a vacation club (with its classed population, its planned pleasures) is there in some fairy-tale site; in the Fourierist utopia there is a twofold reality, realized as a farce by mass society: *tourism*—the just ransom of a fantasmatic system which has "forgotten" politics, whereas politics pays it back by "forgetting" no less systematically to "calculate" for our pleasure. It is in the grip of these two forgettings, whose confrontation determines total futility, insupportable emptiness, that we are still floundering.

THE CALCULATION OF PLEASURE

The motive behind all Fourierist construction (all combination) is not justice, equality, liberty, etc., it is pleasure. Fourierism is not a radical eudaemonism. Fourierist pleasure (*positive happiness*) is very easy to define: it is sensual pleasure: "amorous freedom, good food, insouciance, and the other delights that the Civilized do not even dream of coveting because philosophy has taught them to treat the desire for true pleasures as vice."[4] Fourierist sensuality is, above all, oral. Of course, the two major sources of pleasure are equally Love and Food, always in tandem; however, although Fourier pushes the claims of erotic freedom, he does not describe it sensually; whereas food is lovingly fantasized in detail (compotes, *mirlitons*, melons, pears, lemonades); and Fourier's speech itself is sensual, it progresses in effusiveness, enthusiasm, throngs of words, verbal gourmandise (neologism is an erotic act, which is why he never fails to arouse the censure of pedants).

This Fourierist pleasure is commodious, *it stands out*: easily isolated from the heteroclite hotchpotch of causes, effects, values, protocols, habits, alibis, it appears throughout in its sovereign purity: mania (the ankle scratcher, the filth eater, the "Baby Doll") is never captured save through the pleasure it procures for its partners, and this pleasure is never encumbered with other images (absurdities, inconveniences, difficulties); in short, there is no metonymy attached to it: pleasure is what it is, nothing more. The emblematic ceremony of this

[4] Let us briefly recall that in the Fourierist lexicon, *Civilization* has a precise (numbered) meaning: the word designates the 5th period of the 1st phase (Infancy of Mankind), which comes between the period of the federal patriarchate (the birth of large agriculture and manufacturing industry) and that of guaranteeism or demi-association (industry by association). Whence a broader meaning: in Fourier, *Civilization* is synonymous with wretched barbarism and designates the state of his own day (and ours); it contrasts with universal Harmony (2nd and 3rd phases of mankind). Fourier believed himself to be at the axis of Barbaric Civilization and Harmony.

isolation of essence would be a *museum orgy*: it consists of a simple exposition of the desirable, "a séance wherein notable lovers lay bare the most remarkable thing they have. A woman whose only beautiful feature is her bosom exposes only the bosom and is covered elsewhere ; . ." (we refrain from commenting on the fetishist character of this framework, evident enough; his intention not analytical but merely ethical, Fourier would not deign to take fetishism into a symbolic, reductive system: that would be merely a mania *along with* others, and not inferior or superior to them).

Fourierist pleasure is free from evil: it does not include vexation, in the Sadean manner, but on the contrary dissipates it; his discourse is one of "general well-being": for example, in the war of love (game and theater), out of delicacy, in order not to disturb, no flags or leaders are captured. If, however, in Harmony, one chances to suffer, the entire society will attempt to divert you: have you had some failure in love, have you been turned down, the Bacchantes, Adventuresses, and other pleasure corporations will surround you and lead you off, instantly efface the harm that has befallen you (they exercise, Fourier says, philanthropy). But if someone has a mania to harass? Should they be allowed? The pleasure of harassing is due to a congestion; Harmony will decongest the passions, sadism will be reabsorbed: Dame Strogonoff had the unpleasant habit of harassing her beautiful slave by piercing her breast with pins; in fact, it was counterpassion: Dame Strogonoff was in love with her victim without knowing it: Harmony, by authorizing and favoring Sapphic loves, would have relieved her of her sadism. Yet a final threat: satiety: how to *sustain* pleasure? "How act so as to have a continually renewed appetite? Here lies the secret of Harmonian politics." This secret is twofold: on the one hand, change the race and, through the overall benefits of the societal diet (based on meats and fruits, with very little bread), form physiologically stronger men, fit for the renewal of pleasures, capable of digesting more quickly, of being hungry more frequently; and on the other hand, vary pleasures incessantly (never more than two hours at the same task), and from all these successive pleasures make one sole continual pleasure.

Here we have pleasure alone and triumphant, it reigns over all. Pleasure cannot be measured, it is not subject to quantification, its nature is the *overmuch* ("Our fault is not, as has been believed, to desire *overmuch*, but to desire *too little* . . ."); it is itself the measurement: "feeling" depends on pleasure: "The privation of the sensual need degrades feeling," and "full satisfaction in material things is the only way to elevate the feelings": counter-Freudianism: "feeling" is not the sublimating transformation of a lack, but on the contrary the panic effusion of an acme of satiety. Pleasure overcomes Death (pleasures will be sensual in the afterlife), it is the Federator, what operates the solidarity of the living and the dead· (the happiness of the defunct will begin only with that of the living, they having in a way to *await* the others: no happy dead so long as on earth the living are not happy; a view of a generosity, a "charity" that no religious eschatology has dared). Pleasure is, lastly, the everlasting principle of social organization: whether, negatively, it induces a condemnation of all society, however progressive, that neglects it (such as Owen's experiment at New Lamarck, denounced as "too severe" because the societaries went barefoot), whether, positively, pleasures are made *affairs of State* (*pleasures* and not *leisure*: this is what separates—fortunately—the Fourierist Harmony from the modern State, where the pious organization of leisure time corresponds to a relentless censure of pleasure); pleasure results, in fact, from a *calculation*, an operation that for Fourier is the highest form of social organization and mastery; this calculation is the same as that of all societal theory, whose practice is to transform work into pleasure (and not to suspend work for the sake of leisure time): the barrier that separates work from pleasure in Civilization crumbles, there is a paradigmatic fall, philosophical conversion of the unpleasant into the attractive (taxes will be paid "as readily as the busy mother sees to those foul but attractive duties her infant demands"), and pleasure itself becomes an exchange value, since Harmony recognizes and honors, by the name of *Angelicate*, collective prostitution: it is in a way the monad of energy which in its thrust and scope ensures the advance of society.

Since pleasure is the Unique, to reveal pleasure is itself a unique duty: Fourier stands alone against everyone (especially against all the Philosophers, against all Libraries), he alone is right, and being right is the desirable thing: "Is it not to be desired that I alone am right, against everyone?" From the Unique derives the incendiary character of pleasure: it burns, shocks, frightens to speak of it: how many are the statements about the mortal shock brought on by the overabrupt revelation of pleasure! What precautions, what preparations of writing! Fourier experiences a kind of prophylactic obligation for dispassion (poorly observed, by the way: he imagines his "calculations" are boring and that reassures him, whereas they are delightful); whence an incessant restraint of the discourse: "fearing to allow you to glimpse the vastness of these pleasures, I have only dissertated on . . ." etc.: Fourier's discourse is never just propaedeutic, so blazing with splendor is its object, its center:[5] articulated on pleasure, the sectarian world is *dazzling*.

The area of Need is *Politics*, the area of Desire is what

---

[5] "If we could suddenly see this arranged Order, this work of God as it will be seen in its full functioning . . . it is not to be doubted that many of the Civilized would be struck dead by the violence of their ecstasy. The description [of the 8th Society] alone could inspire in many of them, the women in particular, an enthusiasm that would approach frenzy; it could render them indifferent to amusements, unsuited to the labors of Civilization" (I, 65).

Fourier calls *Domestics*. Fourier has chosen Domestics over Politics, he has constructed a domestic utopia (but can a utopia be otherwise? can a utopia ever be political? isn't politics: *every language less one*, that of Desire? In May 1968, there was a proposal to one of the groups that were spontaneously formed at the Sorbonne to study *Domestic Utopia*— they were obviously thinking of Fourier; to which the reply was made that the expression was too "studied," *ergo* "bourgeois"; politics is what forecloses desire, save to achieve it in the form of neurosis: political neurosis or, more exactly: the neurosis of politicizing).

MONEY CREATES HAPPINESS

In Harmony, not only is wealth redeemed, but it is also magnified, it participates in a play of felicitous metaphors, lending the Fourierist demonstrations either the ceremonial brio of jewels ("the diamond star in a radiant triangle," the decoration of amatory sainthood, i.e., widespread prostitution) or the modesty of the sou ("20 sous to Racine for his tragedy *Phèdre*": multiplied, true, by all the cantons that have chosen to honor the poet); the operations connected with money are themselves motifs in a delectable game: in the game of love, that of the redemption (repurchase) of captives. Money participates in the brilliance of pleasure ("The senses cannot have their full indirect scope without the intervention of money"): money is desirable, as in the best days of civilized corruption, beyond which it perpetuates itself by virtue of a splendid and "incorruptible" fantasy.

Curiously detached from commerce, from exchange, from the economy, Fourierist money is an analogic (poetic) metal, the sum of happiness. Its exaltation is obviously a countermeasure: it is because all (civilized) Philosophy has condemned money that Fourier, destroyer of Philosophy and critic of Civilization, rehabilitates it: *the love of wealth* being a pejorative *topos* (at the price of a constant hypocrisy: Seneca, the man who possessed 80 million sesterces, declared that one must instantly rid oneself of wealth), Fourier turns contempt into praise:[6] marriage, for example, is a ridiculous cere-mony,[7] save "when a man marries a very rich woman; then there is occasion for rejoicing"; everything, where money is concerned, seems to be conceived in view of this counterdis-course, frankly scandalous in relation to the literary con-straints of the admonition: "Search out the tangible wealth, gold, silver, precious metals, jewels, and objects of luxury de-spised by philosophers."[8]

However, this fact of discourse is not rhetorical: it has that energy of language that in writing makes the discourse waver, it forms the basis for the major transgression against which *everyone*—Christians, Marxists, Freudians—for whom money continues to be an accursed matter, fetish, excrement, has spoken out: who would dare defend money? There is *no discourse* with which money can be compatible. Because it is completely solitary (Fourier does not find on this point among his colleagues, "literary agitators," any co-maniac), Fourierist transgression lays bare the most secret area of the Civilized conscience. Fourier exalted money because for him the image of happiness was properly furnished with the mode of life of

[6] "Whence a conclusion that may seem facetious but that will nonetheless be rigorously demonstrated; in the 18 societies of Combined Order, the most basic quality for the triumph of truth is the love of wealth" (I, 70). "Glory and science are truly desirable, of course, but quite insufficient when unaccompanied by fortune. Fame, trophies, and other illusions do not lead to happiness, which consists first of all in the possession of wealth . . ." (I, 14).

[7] "One must be born in Civilization to tolerate the sight of those indecent customs known as marriages, where one sees the simultaneous coincidence of magistrate and priest with the fools and drunks of the neighborhood" (I, 174).

[8] Since the coming of Harmony was imminent, Fourier counseled the Civilized to profit at once from the few goods of Civilization; this is the age-old theme (reversed, i.e., positive): Live to the full now, tomorrow is another day, it is futile to save, to keep, to transmit.

the wealthy: a shocking view today, in the eyes of the contestants themselves, who condemn all pleasure induced from the bourgeois model. We know that metonymy (contagion) is the purview of Error (of religion); Fourier's radical materialism stems from his constant, vigilant refusal of any metonymy. For him, money is not a conductor of sickness but merely the dry, pure element in a combinative to be reordered.

INVENTOR, NOT WRITER

To remake the world (including Nature), Fourier mobilized: an intolerance (for Civilization), a form (classification), a standard (pleasure), an imagination (the "scene"), a discourse (his book). All of which pretty well defines the action of the signifier—or the signifier in action. This action continually makes visible on the page a glaring lack, that of science and politics, that is, of the signified.[9] What Fourier lacks (for that matter voluntarily) points in return to what we ourselves lack when we reject Fourier: to be ironic about Fourier is always—even from the scientific point of view—to censure the signifier. Political and Domestic (the name of Fourier's system),[10] science and utopia, Marxism and Fourierism, are like two nets whose meshes are of different sizes. On the one hand, Fourier allows to pass through all the science that Marx collects and develops; from the political point of view (and above all since Marxism has given an indelible name to its shortcomings), Fourier is completely *off to one side*, unrealistic and immoral. However, the other, facing, net

[9] ". . . seek the good only in operations having no relationship with the administration or with the priesthood, that rest solely on industrial or domestic measures and that are compatible with any government, without having need of their intervention" (I, 5).

[10] ". . . to demonstrate the extreme facility of exiting from the civilized labyrinth, without political upheaval, without scientific effort, but by a purely domestic operation" (I, 126).

allows pleasure, which Fourier collects, to pass through.[11] Desire and Need pass through, as though the two nets were alternatively superimposed, playing at topping hands. However, the relationship of Desire and Need is not *complementary* (were they fitted one into the other, everything would be perfect), but *supplementary*: each is the *excess* of the other. The *excess*: what does not pass through. For example, seen from today (i.e., *after* Marx), politics is a necessary purge; Fourier is the child who avoids the purge, who vomits it up.

The vomiting of politics is what Fourier calls Invention. Fourierist invention ("For me, I am an inventor, and not an orator") addresses the absolutely new, that about which nothing has yet been said. The rule of invention is a rule of refusal: to doubt absolutely (more than did Descartes, who, Fourier thought, never made more than a partial and misplaced use of doubt), to be in opposition with everything being done, to treat only of what has not been treated, to stand apart from "literary agitators," Book People, to preach what Opinion holds to be *impossible*. It is in sum for this purely structural reason (*old/new*) and through a simple constraint of the discourse (to speak only where there has not yet been speech) that Fourier is silent about politics. Fourierist invention is a fact of writing, a deploying of the signifier. These words should be understood in the modern sense: Fourier repudiates *the writer*, i.e., the certified manager of good writing, of literature, he who guarantees decorative union and thus the fundamental separation of substance and form; in calling himself an inventor ("I am not a writer, but an inventor"), he places himself at the limit of meaning, what we today call Text. Perhaps, following Fourier, we should henceforth call *inventor*

[11] ". . . sophists deceive us about their incompetency in calculations of amatory or petty politics, and occupy us exclusively with ambitious or major politics . . ." (IV, 51).

(and not *writer* or *philosopher*) he who proposes new formulae and thereby invests, by fragments, *immensely and in detail*, the space of the signifier.

THE META-BOOK

The meta-book is the book that talks about the book. Fourier spends his time talking about his book in such a way that the work of Fourier that we read, indissolubly blending the two discourses, finally forms an autonomous book, in which form incessantly states form.

Fourier escorts his book a long way. For example, he imagines a dialogue between bookseller and client. Or elsewhere, knowing his book will be brought into court, he establishes a whole institutional system of defense (judge, jury, lawyers) and diffusion (the rich reader who wants to clear up some doubts for himself will call in the author to give lessons, as in sciences and the arts: "a kind of relationship without consequences, as with a merchant from whom one buys": after all, it is something like what a writer does today, going off on lecture tours to repeat words he has stated in writing).

As for the book itself, he posits rhetoric, i.e., the adaptation of types of discourse to types of readers: the *exposition* is addressed to the "Curious" (that is, to studious men); the *descriptions* (insights into the delights of private Destinies) are addressed to Voluptuaries or Sybarites; the *confirmation*, pointing up the blunders of the Civilized in thrall to the Spirit of Commerce, is addressed to the Critics. We can distinguish bits of *perspective* and bits of *theory* (I, 160); there will be *insights* (abstract), *summaries* (half-concrete), *elaborate dissertations* (bodies of doctrine). It follows that the book (a somewhat Mallarméan view) is not only pieced out, articulated (a banal structure), but, further, mobile, subject to a rule of *intermittent* actualization: the chapters will be inverted, the reading will be speeded up (expedited movement) or slowed down, according to the class of readers we want to reach; at its limit, the book is composed of nothing but jumps, full of holes like Fourier's manuscripts (especially *Le Nouveau Monde amoureux*), whose words are constantly missing, eaten by mice, and which therefore have the dimensions of an infinite cryptogram whose key will be given later.

This reminds us of reading in the Middle Ages, based on the work's legal discontinuity: not only was the ancient text (subject of medieval reading) *broken up* and its fragments then capable of being diversely combined, but, further, it was normal to conduct on any subject two independent and concurrent discourses, shamelessly put in a redundant relationship: Donatus's *ars minor* (abridged) and *ars major* (extended), the Modistes' *modi minores* and *modi majores*; this is the Fourierist opposition of insight-abridgment and dissertation. Yet the effect of this doubling up is twisted, paradoxical. We would expect that like any redundancy it would completely cover the subject, fill it out and end it (what can be added to a discourse that essentializes its purpose in résumé form and develops it in the form of an elaborate dissertation?). Now the contrary: the duplicity of the discourse produces an *interstice* through which the subject leaks away; Fourier spends his time in withholding the decisive utterance of his doctrine, concerning it he gives us only examples, seductions, "appetizers"; the message of his book is the announcement of a forthcoming message: *wait a little longer, I will tell you the essential very soon*. This method of writing could be called *counter-paralypse* (the paralypse is the rhetorical figure that consists in stating what one is not going to say and thus stating what one pretends not to say: *I shall not speak of . . .* followed by three pages). The paralypse implies the conviction that the indirect is a profitable mode of language; however, Fourier's countermarch, other than that it obviously translates the neurotic fear of failure (like that of a man afraid to jump—which Fourier,

transferring to the reader, utters as the mortal fear of pleasure), points out the vacuum of language: caught in the toils of
the meta-book, his book is *without subject*: its signified is
dilatory, incessantly withdrawn further away: only the signifier
remains, stretching out of sight, *in the book's future*.

THE OLD SHOE ABLAZE

Somewhere, Fourier speaks of "nocturnal furnishings."
What do I care that this expression is the trace of an earth-
shaking transport? I am carried away, dazzled, convinced by a
kind of *charm* in the expression, which is its delight. Fourier is
crammed full of these delights: no discourse was ever *happier*.
With Fourier, the expression derives its felicity (and ours)
from a kind of upheaval: it is excentric, displaced, it lives on
its own, outside its context (the context, the semanticists'
puzzler, has all the ingratitude of law: it reduces polysemy,
clips the wings of the signifier: doesn't all poetry consist in
liberating the word from its context? doesn't all philosophy
consist in putting it back?). I do not resist these pleasures,
they seem "true" to me: I have been "taken in" by the form.

Of what do these charms consist: of a counter-rhetoric, that
is, a way of contriving figures by introducing into their code a
"grain" (of sand, of madness). Let us here, once again (after
many centuries of rhetorical classification), distinguish tropes
(or simple metaboles) and figures (or ornaments that act
upon an entire syntagm). Fourier's metaphorical vein is the
path of truth; it supplies him with simple metaphors of a definitive precision ("from delivery vans we derive *fatigue dress*,
the gray cloak and trousers"), it clarifies meaning (monological function), but at the same time and contradictorily it clarifies *ad infinitum* (poetical function), not only because the
metaphor is drawn out, orchestrated ("Nocturnal furnishings
will be considerably assorted and composed of our vivid and
variously colored moons, next to which Phoebe will appear as

what she is, a pale ghost, a sepulchral lamp, a Swiss cheese. One would have to have as bad taste as the Civilized do to admire this pallid mummy"), but further and above all because the Fourierist syntagm simultaneously produces a sonorous pleasure and a logical vertigo. Fourier's enumerations (for his verbal "delirium," based on calculation, is basically enumerative) always contain a preposterous point, a twist, a wrinkle: ". . . the ostrich, the deer, the jerboa . . .": why the jerboa, unless for the sonorous flourish at the end, for the sound? "And what can Hell in its fury invent worse than the rattlesnake, the bug, the legion of insects and reptiles, the sea monsters, poisons, plague, rabies, leprosy, venereal disease, gout, and all the morbiferous virulences?": the bug and the sea monster? Rattlesnakes and venereal disease? This string of nonsense derives a final savor from the *morbiferous*, plump and brilliant, more alimentary than funereal, both sensual and ridiculous (Molièresque), that crowns it; for the enumerative *cumulus*, in Fourier, is as abrupt as the movement of the head of an animal, a bird, a child who has heard "something else": "There will remain only the useful strains, like the whiting, the herring, the mackerel, sole, tuna, tortoise, in short, all those that do not attack swimmers . . .": what charms us is not the content (after all, there is no question that these fish are beneficent), but a certain turn that makes the affirmation vibrate toward its opposite region: mischievously, through an irresistible metonymy seizing the words, a vague image becomes detached which, across the denegation, reveals the whiting and the mackerel in the process of attacking a swimmer . . . (a properly surrealist mechanism). Paradoxical, for it is always in the name of the "concrete" that Civilization claims to teach the "mad," it is always through the "concrete" that Fourier becomes absurd and charming at once: the "concrete" is constructed in a scene, the substance calls upon the practices metonymically attached to it; the coffee break refers to the whole of civilized bureaucracy: "Isn't it shocking to see thirty-year-old athletes crouched over desks and transporting a cup of coffee with their hairy arms, as though there weren't women and children to attend to the finicky functioning of offices and households?" This vivid representation provokes laughter because it is out of proportion with its signified; hypotypose usually serves to illustrate intense and noble passions (Racine: "Imagine, Céphise . . ."); in Fourier, it is demonstrative; a kind of anacoluthon intervenes between the domestic detail of the example and the scope of the utopian plan. This is the secret of these amusing syntagms frequent in Fourier (in Sade too) that join in a single sentence a very ambitious thought and a very futile object; starting from the notion of the culinary contests in Harmony ("thesis meals"), Fourier continues to concoct strange and delicious, ridiculous and decisive syntagms, in which the tiny pastries (which he so liked, *mirlitons*) are associated with highly abstract terms ("the 44 systems of tiny pastries," "the batches of tiny pastries anathemized by the council," "the tiny pastries adopted by the Council of Babylon," etc.). Very precisely, this is what we can now call *paragrammatics*: namely, the superimpression (in dual hearing) of two languages that are ordinarily foreclosed to each other, the braid formed by two classes of words whose traditional hierarchy is not annulled, balanced, but—what is more subversive—disoriented: Council and System lend their nobility to tiny pastries; tiny pastries lend their futility to Anathema, a sudden contagion *deranges* the institution of language.

The transgression Fourier commits goes even further. The frivolous object he promotes to demonstrative rank is very often a *base* object. This conversion is justified because Harmony recuperates what Civilization disdains and transforms it into a delightful good ("If the Vaucluse phalanstery harvests 50,000 melons or watermelons, almost 10,000 of them will be set aside for its own consumption, 30,000 for exportation, and 10,000 will be of inferior grade and divided among horses, cats, and for fertilizer": here we find that art of enumerative cadence we have just mentioned: Fourierist enumeration is always reverse conundrum: what is the difference between a horse, a cat, and fertilizer? None, for the function of all three is to reabsorb inferior-grade melons). Thus a poetics of rubbish is constructed, magnified by the societary economy (e.g., the old marinated chickens). Fourier knows this poetics well: he knows the emblems of rubbish, the old shoe, the rag, the sewer: an entire episode in *Le Nouveau Monde amoureux* (VII, 362 *et seq.*) hymns the exploits of the new crusaders, dealers in old shoes and boot cleaners, whose arrival at the Euphrates crossing is greeted by a magnificent display of fireworks "ending with an old shoe ablaze, beneath which is the legend: Long live pious cobblers."

Naturally, Fourier was aware of the "ridiculousness" of his demonstrative objects (of his rhetoric);[12] he was well aware that the bourgeoisie is devoted to the hierarchical division of languages, objects, and usages as strongly as it is to those of class, that nothing is worse in their eyes than the crime of lèse-language, and that one has only to join a noble (abstract) word and a base (denoting a sensual or repulsive object) term to be sure of loosing their zeal as proprietors (of "fine" language); he knew that people made fun of his faithful melons, of the triumph of his leathery fowl, of the English debt paid off in hens' eggs. Yet he assumed the incongruity of his demonstrations with a certain martyred air (the martyrdom of the inventor). Thus to the paragrammaticism of his examples (in-

[12] "This respectable convoy of cobblers marches after them in pomp and the finest boat is loaded with their baggage and this is the arm upon which they learn to win the palms of true glory. Bah! glory in old shoes, our Civilized will say; I was expecting this stupid response. And what fruit have they gleaned from the trophies of St. Louis and Bonaparte who have led immense armies vast distances only to have them drown in their trophies after having ravaged the country and been execrated by it?" (VII, 364).

terweaving two exclusive languages, one noble, one outcast),
must be added a final, infinitely dizzier, ambiguity: that of
their utterance. Where is Fourier? in the invention of the example (old marinated chickens)? in the indignation he feels at
the laughter of others? In our reading, which simultaneously
encompasses the ridicule and his defense? The loss of the
subject in the writing has never been more complete (the subject becoming totally irreparable) than in these utterances
where the disconnection of the utterance occurs *ad infinitum*,
without a brake, on the model of the game of topping hands or
the game of "rock, scissors, paper": texts whose "ridiculousness" or "stupidity" is based on no certain utterance and over
which, consequently, the reader can never gain any advantage
(Fourier, Flaubert). "God," Fourier says, "displays a subtle
and judicious irony in creating certain products that are enigmatic in quality, like the melon, made for the innocent mystification of banquets ill suited to divine methods, without in any
way deceiving the gastronomes who cleave to the divine or
societary diet" [allusion to the difficulty that exists in choosing
a good melon, "such a perfidious fruit for the Civilized"]. "I
do not mean to say that God created the melon solely for the
sake of this jest, but it is part of that fruit's many uses. Irony is
never overlooked in the calculations of nature. . . . The melon
has among its properties that of *ironic harmony* . . ." (in short,
the melon is an element of a *writing*). What reader can hope
to *dominate* such an utterance—adopt it as a laughable or a
critical object, *dictate to it*, in a word?—in the name of *what
other language*?

HIEROGLYPHICS

Fourier wants to decipher the world in order to remake it
(for how remake it without deciphering it?).

Fourierist deciphering starts from the most difficult of situations, which is not so much the latency of signs as their con-

tent. There is a saying of Voltaire that Fourier refers to in this regard: "But what obscure night still enveileth nature?"; now, in this veil finally there is less the notion of mask than of a cloth. Once again, the task of the logothete, of the founder of language, is an endless cutting up of the text: the primary operation is to "grab" the cloth in order then to pull on it (to pull it off).

We must therefore in some measure make a distinction between deciphering and cutting up. Deciphering refers to a pregnant depth, to an area of relationships, to a distribution. In Fourier, deciphering is postulated, but in a completely minor way: it concerns the lies and pretenses of the Civilized classes: thus the "secret principles" of the bourgeois "who begins by debiting a hundred lies in his shop by virtue of the principles of free trade. Hence a bourgeois goes to hear Mass and returns to debit three to four hundred lies, to trick and steal from thirty or so buyers in line with the secret principle of businessmen: we are not working for glory, we want money" (VII, 246). Quite another thing, and of quite another order of importance, is cutting up—or systematization (putting to a system); this reading, an essential part of the Fourier-ist task, concerns all of Nature (societies, sentiments, forms, natural kingdoms) as it represents the total space of Harmony —Fourier's man being totally incorporated into the universe, including the stars; this is no longer a denunciatory, reductive reading (limited to the moral falsehoods of the bourgeoisie), but an exalting, integrating, restorative reading, extended to the plethora of universal forms.

Is the "real" the object of this second reading? We are accustomed to considering the "real" and the residue as identical: the "unreal," the fantasmatic, the ideological, the verbal, the proliferating, in short, the "marvelous," may conceal from us the "real," rational, infrastructural, schematic; from real to unreal there may be the (self-seeking) production of a screen of arabesques, whereas from unreal to real there may be critical reduction, an alethic, scientific movement, as though the real were at once more meager and more essential than the superstructures with which we have covered it. Obviously, Fourier is working on a conceptual material whose constitution denies this contrast and which is that of the *marvelous real*. This marvelous real is contrasted with the marvelous ideal of novels; it corresponds to what we might call, contrasting it directly with the novel, the novelesque. This marvelous real very precisely is the signifier, or if one prefers, "reality," characterized, relative to the scientific real, by its fantasmatic train. Now, the category under which this novelesque begins to be read is the *hieroglyphic*, different from the symbol as the signifier can be from the full, mystified sign.

The hieroglyph (the theory of which is set forth principally in the *Théorie des Quatre Mouvements*, I, 31 *et seq.* and 286 *et seq.*) postulates a formal and arbitrary correspondence (it depends on Fourier's free will: it is an idiolectal concept) between the various realms of the universe, for example between forms (circle, ellipse, parabola, hyperbola), colors, musical notes, passions (friendship, love, parental, ambition), the races of animals, the stars, and the periods of societal phylogenesis. The arbitrary obviously resides in the attribution: why is the ellipse the geometric hieroglyph for love? The parabola for parenthood? Yet this arbitrary is just as relative as is that of linguistic signs: we believe there to be an arbitrary correspondence between the signifier /pear tree/ and the signified "pear tree," between some Melanesian tribe and its totem (bear, god), because we spontaneously (i.e., by virtue of historical, ideological determinations) imagine the world in substitute, paradigmatic, analogical terms, and not in serial, associative, homological—in short, poetic—terms. Fourier has this second imagination; for him, the basis of meaning is not substitution, equivalence, but the proportional series; just as the

signifier /pear tree/ or the signifier *bear* is *relatively* motivated
if taken in the series *pear tree–plum tree–apple tree* or in the
series *bear–dog–tiger*, so Fourierist hieroglyphics, detached
from any univocity, accede to language, i.e., to a system both
conventional and reasonable. The hieroglyphic, in fact, implies
a complete theory of meaning (whereas only too often, relying
on the presence of the dictionary, we reduce meaning to a
substitution): hieroglyphics, says Fourier, can be explained in
three ways: (1) *by contrast* (beehive/wasp's nest, elephant/
rhinoceros): this is the paradigm: the beehive is *marked* with
productivity, a characteristic absent in the wasp's nest; the ele-
phant is marked with lengthy defenses, a trait reduced to a
short horn in the rhinoceros; (2) *by alliance* (the dog and the
sheep, the pig and the truffle, the donkey and the thistle): this
is the syntagm, metonymy: these elements usually go together;
(3) lastly, *by progression* (branches: giraffe, stag, buck, roe-
buck, reindeer, etc.): this, foreign to linguistic classification, is
the *series*, a kind of extended paradigm, consisting of differences and proximities, out of which Fourier creates the very
principle of societal organization, which basically consists in
putting in a phalanstery contrasting groups of individuals, each
group linked by an affinity: for example, the sectine of Flower-
lets, amateurs of small, varied flowers, contrasted to but coex-
isting with the Rosist sectine: it might be said that the series is
an actualized, syntagmatized paradigm, by virtue of the number of its terms, not only *livable* (whereas the semantic paradigm is subject to the law of rival, inexpiable opposites, which
cannot cohabit), but even *felicitous*. Progression (the series)
is undoubtedly what Fourier adds to meaning (as linguists
describe it for us), and consequently, what frustrates its arbitrary nature. Why, for example, in Association, is the giraffe
the hieroglyph for Truth (I, 286)? A farfetched notion and
assuredly unjustifiable if we try, desperately, to discover some
affinitive or even contrasting trait shared by Truth and this

huge mammiferous ungulant. The explanation is that the giraffe is caught up in a system of homologies: Association having the beaver as its practical hieroglyph (because of its associative and constructive abilities) and the peacock as its visual hieroglyph (because of the spread of its nuances), we need, across from but yet in the same series, that of animals, a properly unfunctional element, a kind of neuter, a zero degree of zoological symbolism: this is the giraffe, as useless as the Truth is in Civilization; whence a counter-giraffe (complex term of contrast): this is the Reindeer, from which we derive every imaginable service (in the societary order there will even be a new animal created, even more ecumenical than the Reindeer: the Anti-Giraffe).

So replaced in the history of the sign, the Fourierist construction posits the rights of a baroque semantics, i.e., open to the proliferation of the signifier, infinite and yet structured.

LIBERAL?

The combination of differences implies the respecting of the individuation of each term: there is no attempt to redress, to correct, to annul taste, whatever it may be (however "bizarre" it may be); quite the contrary, it is affirmed, it is emphasized, it is recognized, it is legalized, it is reinforced by associating everyone who wishes to indulge it: taste being thus incorporated, it is allowed to act in opposition to other tastes at once affinitive and different: a competitive game (of intrigue, but *coded*) is initiated between the amateurs of bergamot pears and the amateurs of butter pears: to the satisfaction of a simple taste (a liking for pears) is then added the exercise of other, formal, combinative passions: for example, *cabalistics*, or the passion for intrigues, and *butterfly*, if there are unstable Harmonians who take pleasure in switching from the bergamot pear to the butter pear.

From this semantic construction of the world it follows that, in Fourier's eyes, "association" is not a "humanist" principle: it is not a matter of bringing together everyone with the same mania ("co-maniacs") so that they can be comfortable together and can enchant each other by narcissistically gazing at one another; on the contrary, it is a matter of associating to combine, to contrast. The Fourierist coexistence of passions is not based on a liberal principle. There is no noble demand to "understand," to "admit" the passions of others (or to ignore them, indeed). The goal of Harmony is neither to further the conflict (by associating through similitude), nor to reduce it (by sublimating, sweetening, or normalizing the passions), nor yet to transcend it (by "understanding" the other person), but to exploit it for the greatest pleasure of all and without hindrance to anyone. How? By playing at it: by making a text of the conflictual.

PASSIONS

Passion (character, taste, mania) is the irreducible unity of the Fourierist combinative, the absolute grapheme of the utopian text. Passion is *natural* (nothing to be corrected about it, unless to produce a *contra-naturam*, which is what occurs in Civilization). Passion is *clean* (its being is pure, strong, shapely: only Civilized philosophy advises flaccid, apathetic passions, controls, and compromises). Passion is *happy* ("Happiness . . . consists in having many passions and ample means to satisfy them," I, 92).

Passion is not the idealized form of feeling, mania is not the monstrous form of passion. Mania (and even whim) is the very being of passion, the unit from which Attraction (attractive and attracting) is determined. Passion is neither deformable, nor transformable, nor reducible, nor measurable, nor substitutable: it is not a force, it is a number: there can be neither decomposition nor amalgamation of this happy, frank, natural monad, but only combination, up to the reunion of the *integral soul*, the trans-individual body of 1,620 characters.

THE TREE OF HAPPINESS

The passions (810 for each sex) spring, like the branches of a tree (the classifier's fetish tree) from three main trunks: *lustful-ness*, which includes the passions of feeling (one for each of the five senses), *group-ness* (four basic passions: honor, friendship, love, and family), and *serial-ness* (three distributive passions). The entire combinative stems from these twelve passions (whose pre-eminence is not moral, merely structural).

The first nine passions are derived from classical psychology, but the latter, formal, three are a Fourierist invention. The Dissident (or Cabalistic) is a reflective enthusiasm, a passion for intrigue, a calculating mania, an art of exploiting differences, rivalries, conflicts (here there is no difficulty in recognizing the paranoid texture); it is the delight of courtesans, women, and philosophers (intellectuals), which is why it can also be called the Speculative. The Composite (actually less well defined than its fellows) is the passion for excess, for (sensual or sublime) exaltation, for multiplication; it can be called the Romantic. The Variating (or Alternating or Butterfly) is a need for periodic variety (changing occupation or pleasure every two hours); we might say that it is the disposition of the subject who does not devote himself to the "good object" in a stable manner: a passion whose mythical prototype is Don Juan: individuals who constantly change occupation, manias, affections, desires, "cruisers" who are incorrigible, unfaithful, renegade, subject to "moods," etc.: a passion disdained in Civilization, but one Fourier places very high: the one that permits ranging through many passions at once, and like an agile hand on a multiple keyboard, creating a *harmoni-*

ous (appropriately put) vibration throughout the integral soul; an agent of universal transition, it animates that type of happiness that is attributed to Parisian sybarites, *the art of living well and fast, the variety and interconnection of pleasures*, rapidity of movement (we recall that for Fourier the mode of life of the possessing class is the very model of happiness).

These three passions are formal: included in the classification, they ensure its functioning ("mechanics"), or more precisely still: its game. If we compare the aggregate of the passions to a deck of cards or a chess set (as did Fourier), the three distributive passions are in sum the rules of this game; they state how to conciliate, balance, set in motion, and permit the transformation of the other passions, each of which would be nugatory in isolation, into a series of "brilliant and countless combinations." These rules of the game (these formal, distributive passions) are precisely the ones society rejects: they produce (the very sign of their excellence) "the characters accused of corruption, called libertines, profligates, etc.": as in Sade, it is syntax and syntax alone that produces the supreme immorality.

Thus the twelve radical passions (like the twelve notes in the scale). Naturally, there is a thirteenth (every good classifier knows he must have a supernumber in his chart and that he must make adjustments for the outcome of his system), which is the very trunk of the tree of passions: Unity-ness (or Harmonism). Unity-ness is the passion for unity, "the individual's tendency to reconcile his happiness with that of everything around him, and with every human type"; this supplementary passion produces the Originals, people who appear to be ill at ease in this world and who cannot accommodate themselves to the ways of Civilization; it is thus the passion of Fourier himself. Unity-ness is in no way a moral, recommendable passion (*love each other, unite with each other*), since the societal unit is a combinative, a structural game of differences; Unity-ness is in direct contrast to simplism, the vice of the Civilized spirit, "the use of the mind without the marvelous, or of the marvelous without the mind"; simplism "made Newton miss out on the discovery of the system of Nature and Bonaparte on the conquest of the world." Simplism (or totalitarianism, or monologism) would today be either the censure of Need or the censure of Desire; which, in Harmony (in Utopia), would be answered by the combined science of one and the other.

NUMBERS

Fourier's authority, the Reference, the Citation, the Science, the Anterior Discourse that enables him to speak and to have personal authority concerning the "carelessness of 25 learned centuries that failed to conceive of it," is *calculation* (as for us today it is formalization). This calculation need not be extensive or complicated: it is a *petty calculation*. Why petty? Because although important (the happiness of mankind depends upon it), this calculation is simple. Further, pettiness includes the notion of a certain affectionate complacence: Fourier's petty calculation is the simple lever that opens up the fantasmagory of adorable detail.

Everything occurs as though Fourier were searching for the very notion of detail, as though he had found it in a numeration or frantic subdivision of every object that came into his mind, as though this object instantly released in him a number or a classification: it is like a conditioned reflex that comes into play apropos a whole crazy total: "In Rome in the time of Varro there were 278 contradictory opinions concerning true happiness." A question of illicit liaisons (in Civilization)? They exist for Fourier only if he enumerates them: "During the twelve years of bachelorhood, man forms on the average 12 liaisons of illicit love, around 6 of fornication and 6 adulterous, etc." Everything is a pretext for numbering, from the age of the world (80,000 years) to the number of characters in it (1,620).

The Fourierist number is not rounded off, and in fact this is what gives it its insanity (a minor sociological problem: why does our society consider a decimal number "normal" and an intradecimal number "irrational"? At what point does normality occur?). This insanity is often justified by the even more insane reasons Fourier gives in denying the arbitrary constants in his accounts, or, which is even crazier still, displaces this arbitrary by justifying not the number given, but the standard for it: the height of societary man will be 84 thumbs or 7 feet; why? we will never know, but the unit of measurement is pompously justified: "I am not being arbitrary in indicating the foot of the King of Paris as a natural measurement; it has this property because it is equal to the 32nd part of the water level in suction pumps" (here we find that sudden twisting of the syntagm, the anacoluthon, the audacious metonymy that makes Fourier's "charm": in the space of a few words, we have suction pumps mingled with the height of societary man). The number exalts, it is an operator of glory, as is the triangular number of the Trinity in the Jesuit mode, not because it enlarges (which would destroy the fascination with detail), but because it demultiplies: "Consequently, if we divide by 810 the number of 36 million which the population of France has attained, we will find that in this Empire there exist 45,000 capable of equaling Homer, 45,000 capable of equaling Demosthenes, etc." Fourier is like a child (or an adult: the author of these lines, never having studied mathematics, has been very late in experiencing this feeling) discovering with enchantment the exorbitant power of combinatory analysis or geometrical progression. In the end, the number itself is not needed for this exaltation; one need only subdivide a class in order triumphantly to achieve this paradox: detail (literally: *minutia*) magnifies, like joy. It is a fury of expansion, of possession, and, in a word, of orgasm, by number, by classification: scarcely does an object appear than Fourier taxinomizes (we are tempted to say: sodomizes) it: is the husband unhappy in Civilized marriage? It is *immediately* for eight reasons (risk of unhappiness, expense, vigilance, monotony, sterility, widowhood, union, ignorance of his wife's infidelity). Does the word "harem" arise *currente calamo* into the sentence? *Immediately*, there are three classes of odalisks: honest women, petites bourgeoises, and courtesans. What happens to women over eighteen years of age in Harmony? nothing, save to be *classified: Wives* (themselves subdivided into *constant, doubtful,* and *unfaithful*), *Misses* or *Demi-dames* (they change protectors, but successively, having only one at a time), and *Galantes* (both further subdivided); for both terms in the series, two taxinomic embellishments: *Damsels* and *Independents*. Wealth? there are not only Rich and Poor, there are: the poor, those who scrape by, those who have just enough, the comfortable, and the rich. Of course, for anyone. with the contrary mania, tolerant neither of number nor of classification nor of system (numerous in Civilization, jealous of "spontaneity," of "life," of "imagination," etc.), the Fourierist Harmony would be hell itself: at thesis meals (contest meals), every course would have two labels, written in large letters, visible from afar and set on pivots, in both directions, "so that one can be read from across the table and the other the length of the table" (the present author has experienced a minor hell of this sort—but the system came from a French brain: in the American college where he took his meals, in order that the students might converse profitably while eating, and that they might benefit equally from the professor's lively discourse, each diner was supposed to advance one place at each meal, moving closer to the professorial sun, "in a clockwise direction," as the rule stated; there is little need to say that no "conversation" resulted from this astral movement).

Perhaps the *imagination of detail* is what specifically defines Utopia (opposed to political science); this would be logical, since detail is fantasmatic and thereby achieves the very pleasure of Desire. In Fourier, the number is rarely statistical (designed to assert averages, probabilities); it is, through the apparent finesse of its precision, essentially quantitative. Nuance, the game being stalked in this taxinomic hunting expedition, is a guarantee of pleasure (of fulfillment), since it determines a *just* combinative (knowing with' whom to group ourselves in order to achieve complementarity with our own differences). Harmony must thus admit the operators of nuances, just as a tapestry workshop has specialists who are detailed to knot the threads. These nuance makers are: either operations (in Fourierist erotics, the "simple salute" is a preambular bacchanalia, a scrimmage enabling the partners to test each other before making a choice; during it, "trial caresses or reconnoiterings of the terrain" are practiced; this takes about eight minutes), or they are agents: there are: either "confessors" (these confessors do not hear any Fault: they "psychoanalyze" in order to elicit sympathies, often hidden by the subjects' appearance and ignorance: they are the decipherers of complementary nuances) or "dissolvents" (dissolvents, introjected into a group that has not yet found its just combinative, its "harmony," produce tremendous effects on it: they undo erroneous couplings by revealing to each his passions, they are transferers, mutators: thus lesbians and pederasts, who, thrown into the scrimmage, first accost the "champions of their own ilk," "recognize their own kind and sunder a good number of couples whom chance had united").

Nuance, the acme of number and of classification, has the *integral soul* as its total field, a human space defined by its amplitude, since it is the combinative dimension within which meaning is possible; no man is self-sufficient, no one his own integral soul: we need 810 characters of both sexes, or 1,620, to which are added the omnititles (the complex degree of contrasts) and the infinitesimal nuances of passion. The integral soul, a tapestry in which each nuance finds utterance, is the great sentence being sung by the universe: it is, in sum, the language of which each of us is but a word. The Language is immortal: "At the era of the planet's death, its great soul, and consequently ours, inherent in it, will pass on to another, new sphere, to a planet which will be implaned, concentrated, saturated . . ."

THE NECTARINE

In any classification of Fourier, there is always a portion that is reserved. This portion has various names: passage, composite, transition, neuter, triviality, ambiguity (we might call it: *supplement*); naturally, it has a number: it is the ⅛ of any collection. First, this ⅛ has a function, familiar to scientists: it is the legal margin of error. ("Calculations of attraction and Social Mobility are all subject to the ⅛ exception . . . it will always be understood.") Only, since in Fourier it is always a question of the *calculation of happiness*, error is at once ethical: when (abhorrent) Civilization "makes a mistake" (in its own system), it produces happiness: in Civilization, the ⅛ thus represents happy people. It is easy from this example to see that for Fourier the ⅛ portion does not derive from a liberal or statistical concession, from the vague recognition of a possible *deviation*, from a "human" failing in the system (to be taken philosophically); quite the contrary, it is a question of an important structural function, of a code constraint. Which one?

As a classifier (a taxinomist), what Fourier needs most are passages, special terms that permit making transitions (meshing) from one class to another,[13] the kind of lubricator the

---

[13] "Transitions are to passionate equilibrium what bolts and joints are to a framework."

combinatory apparatus must use so as not to creak; the reserved portion is thus that of Transitions or Neuters (the neuter is what comes *between* the mark and the non-mark, this sort of buffer, damper, whose role is to muffle, to soften, to fluidify the semantic *tick-tock*, that metronome-like noise the paradigmatic alternative obsessively produces: *yes/no, yes/no, yes/no*, etc.). The nectarine, which is one of these Transitions, damps the opposition of prune and peach, as the quince damps that of pear and apple: they belong to the ⅛ of fruits. This portion (⅛) is shocking because it is contradictory: it is the class in which everything that attempts to escape classification is swallowed up; however, this portion is also superior: the space of the Neuter, of the *supplement of classification*, it joins realms, passions, characters; the art of employing Transitions is the major art of Harmonian calculation: the neuter principle is controlled by mathematics, the pure language of the combinative, of the composed, the very badge of the *game*.

There are ambiguities in every series: the sensitive, the bat, the flying fish, the amphibians, the zoophytes, sapphism, pederasty, incest, Chinese society (half-barbaric, half-civilized, with harems and courts of law and etiquette), lime (fire and water), the nervous system (body and soul), twilights, coffee (ignominiously ignored for Mocha for 4,000 years, then suddenly the subject of a mercantile craze, passing from abjection to the highest rank), children (the third passionate sex, neither men nor women). Transition (mixed, Ambiguous, Neuter) is everything that is contrary duplicity, junction of extremes, and hence it takes as its emblematic form the ellipse, which has a double focus.

In Harmony, Transitions have a beneficent role; for example, they prevent monotony in love, despotism in politics: the distributive passions (composite, cabalistic, and butterfly) have a transitional role (they "mesh," ensure changes of "objects"); Fourier always reasoned contrariwise, what is beneficent in Harmony necessarily proceeds from what is discredited or rejected in Civilization: thus Transitions are "trivialities," ignored by civilized scholars as unworthy subjects: the bat, the albino, ugly ambiguous race, the taste for feathered fowl. The prime example of Trivial Transition is Death: transition ascending between Harmonian life and the happiness of the other life (sensual happiness), it "will shed all its odiousness when philosophy deigns to consent to study the transitions it proscribes as trivial." Everything rejected in Civilization, from pederasty to Death, has in Harmony a value that is eminent (but not pre-eminent: nothing dominates anything else, everything combines, meshes, alternates, revolves). This functional *justness* (this *justice*) is ensured by the ⅛ error. Thus, the *Neuter* is in opposition to the *Median*; the latter is a quantitative, not a structural, notion; it is the amount of the oppression to which the large number subjects the small number; caught in a statistical calculation, the intermediate swells up and engulfs the system (thus the *middle* class: the neuter, on the other hand, is a purely qualitative, structural notion; it is what *confuses* meaning, the norm, normality. To enjoy the *neuter* is perforce to be disgusted by the *average*.

SYSTEM/SYSTEMATICS

". . . that the real content of these systems is hardly to be found in their systematic form is best proved by the orthodox Fourierists . . . who, despite their orthodoxy, are the exact antipodes of Fourier: doctrinaire bourgeois."—MARX AND ENGELS, *German Ideology*

Fourier perhaps enables us to restate the following opposition (which we lately stated by distinguishing the novelistic from the novel, poetry from the poem, the essay from the dissertation, the writing from the style, production from the product, structuration from the structure[14]): the *system* is a

[14] *S/Z.*

body of doctrine within which the elements (principles, facts, consequences) develop logically, i.e., from the point of view of the discourse, rhetorically. The system being a closed (or monosemic) one, it is always theological, dogmatic; it is nourished by illusions: an illusion of transparency (the language employed to express it is purportedly purely instrumental, it is not a writing) and an illusion of reality (the goal of the system is to be *applied*, i.e., that it leave the language in order to found a reality that is incorrectly defined as the exteriority of language); it is a strictly paranoid insanity whose path of transmission is insistence, repetition, cathechism, orthodoxy. Fourier's work does not constitute a *system*; only when we have tried to "realize" this work (in phalansteries) has it become, retrospectively, a "system" doomed to instant fiasco; system, in the terminology of Marx and Engels, is the "systematic form," i.e., pure ideology, ideological reflection; *systematics* is the play of the system; it is language that is open, infinite, free from any referential illusion (pretension); its mode of appearance, its constituency, is not "development" but pulverization, dissemination (the gold dust of the signifier); it is a discourse without "object" (it only speaks of a thing obliquely, by approaching it indirectly: thus Civilization in Fourier) and without "subject" (in writing, the author does not allow himself to be involved in the imaginary subject, for he "performs" his enunciatory role in such a manner that we cannot decide whether it is serious or parody). It is a vast madness which does not end, but which permutates. In contrast to the system, monological, systematics is dialogical (it is the operation of ambiguities, it does not suffer contradictions); it is a writing, it has the latter's eternity (the perpetual permutation of meanings throughout History); systematics is not concerned with application (save as purist imagining, a theater of the discourse), but with transmission, (significant) circulation; further, it is transmittable only on condition it is *de-*

formed (by the reader); in the terminology of Marx and Engels, systematics would be the *real contents* (of Fourier). Here, we are not explaining Fourier's system (that portion of his systematics that plays with the system in an image-making way), we are talking solely about the several sites in his discourse that belong to systematics.

(Fourier puts the system to flight—cuts it adrift—by two operations: first, by incessantly delaying the definitive exposé until later: the doctrine is simultaneously highhanded and dilatory; next, by inscribing the system in the systematics, as dubious parody, shadow, game. For example, Fourier attacks the civilized [repressive] "system," he calls for an integral freedom [of tastes, passions, manias, whims]; thus, we would expect a spontaneistic philosophy, but we get quite the opposite: a wild system, whose very excess, whose fantastic tension, goes beyond system and attains systematics, i.e., writing: liberty is never the opposite of order, it is *order paragrammatized*: the writing must simultaneously mobilize an image and its opposite.)

THE PARTY

What is a "party"? (1) *a partitioning*, isolating one group from another, (2) an orgy, or *partouze*, as we say in French, wherein the participants are linked erotically, and (3) a hand, or *partie*, the regulated moment in a game, a collective diversion. In Sade, in Fourier, the party, the highest form of societary or Sadean happiness, has this threefold character: it is a worldly ceremony, an erotic practice, a social act.

Fourierist life is one immense party. At three-thirty in the morning on the summer solstice (little sleep is needed in Harmony), societary man is ready for the world: engaged in a succession of "roles" (each one being the naked affirmation of a passion) and subject to the combinative (meshing) rules of these roles: this very exactly is the definition of mundanity, which functions like a language: the mundane man is someone who spends his time *citing* (and *weaving* what he cites). The citations Fourier employs in blissfully describing the worldly life of societary man are drawn paradoxically (paragrammatically) from the repressive lexicons of the Civilized regime: the Church, State, Army, Stock Exchange, Salons, the penitentiary colony, and Scouting furnish the Fourierist party with its most felicitous images.[15]

All mundanity is dissociative: it is a matter of isolating oneself in order to retreat and to trace out the area within which the rules of the game can function. The Fourierist party has two traditional enclosures, that of time and that of place.

The topography of the phalanstery traces an original site which is broadly that of palaces, monasteries, manors, and great blocks of buildings in which are mingled an organization of the building and an organization of territory, so that (a very modern viewpoint) architecture and urbanism reciprocally withdraw in favor of an overall science of human space, the primary characteristic of which is no longer protection, but movement: the phalanstery is a retreat within which one moves (however, trips are taken outside the phalanstery: great mass excursions, ambulatory "parties"). Obviously, this space is functionalized, as shown in the following reconstruction (very approximate, since Fourierist discourse, like all writing, is irreducible).

The greatest concern of this organization is communication. Like the adolescent groups who live together during their summer vacations with constant pleasure and regretfully return home in the evenings, the societaries have only a tem-

[15] Innumerable locutions, such as: "Saints and Patrons beatified and canonized in the council of the Spheric Hierarchy." "Every pivotal sin is liable to a sevenfold reparation" (VII, 191)—true, that this reparation is hardly penitential, consisting as it does of making love seven times with seven different people. "The Official Journal of Gastronomic Transactions of the Army of the Euphrates" (VII, 378), etc.

porary place for undressing and sleeping, warmed only by a brazier. In contrast, Fourier describes with great predilection and insistence the covered, heated, ventilated galleries, sanded basements, and corridors raised on columns that connect the palaces or manors of neighboring Tribes. A private place is allowed solely for lovemaking, and even this is only so that the unions made during the bacchanalias, get-togethers, or meetings for the purpose of selecting a companion, can be consummated—or "sealed."

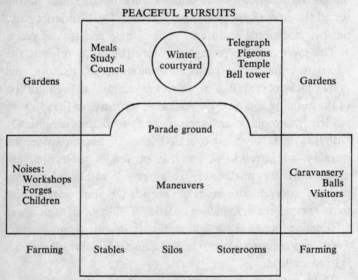

There are three stories, children on mezzanine

Corresponding to topographical delimitation is this apparatus for temporal enclosure called *timing*; since a passion (for investments, for objects) must be changed every two hours, the optimal time is a divided time (the function of *timing* is to demultiply duration, to superproduce time and thereby to augment life power: "The day will never be long enough for the intrigues and merry reunions produced by the new order": we might be listening to an adolescent who, on vacation, has discovered his "group"); for example, in the combined Order there are five meals (at 5 a.m., the matutinal or "eye opener," at 8 a.m., lunch, dinner at 1, snack at 6, and supper at 9), and two collations (at 10 and 4): reminiscent of the schedule in an old-fashioned sanatorium. Harmonian man—physiologically regenerated by a diet of happiness—sleeps only from 11 in the evening to 3:30 in the morning; he never makes love at night, a detestable Civilized habit.

Love (erotic happiness, including the sentimental *eros*) is the main business of the long Harmonian day: "In Harmony, where no one is poor and where everyone is acceptable for lovemaking until a very advanced age, everyone devotes a set part of the day to this passion and love thus becomes a principal business: it has its code, its tribunals [we already know that the penalties consist in new loves], its court, and its institutions." Like the Sadean *eros*, Fourier's is a classifier, a distributor: the population is divided into amorous classes. In Sade, there are storytellers, fuckers, etc.; in Fourier there are troops of Vestals, Youths and Favorites of both sexes, Genitors, etc. From Sade to Fourier, only the *ethos* of the discourse changes: here jubilant, there euphoric. For the erotic fantasy remains the same; it is that of *availability*: that every love demand *at once* find a subject-object to be *at its disposal*, either by constraint or by association; this is the province of the ideal orgy, or in French, *partouze*, a fantasmatic site, contra-civilized, where no one refuses himself to anyone, the purpose not being to multiply partners (not a quantitative problem!) but to abolish the wound of denial; the abundance of erotic material, precisely because it is a matter of Desire and not of Need, is not intended to constitute a "consumer society" of love, but, paradox, truly utopian scandal, to make Desire function in its contradiction, namely: to fulfill *perpetu-*

ally (*perpetually* meaning simultaneously *always* and *never*
fulfilled; or: *never and always*: that depends on the degree of
enthusiasm or bitterness in which the fantasy is concluded).
This is the sense of the supreme amorous institution of Fourierist society: the Angelicate (another ecclesiastical citation): in
Harmony, the Angelicate is this handsome couple who,
through "philanthropy," properly give themselves to any man
or woman desiring them (including the deformed). The Angelicate has an additional function, not philanthropic but
mediatory: it *conducts* desire: as though, left on his own,
every man were incapable of knowing whom to desire, as
though he were blind, powerless to invest his desire, as though
it were always up to others to show us *where the desirable is*
(clearly not the principal function of so-called erotic representations in mass culture: conduction, not substitution); the An-
gelic couple is the apex of the amorous triangle: it is the
vanishing point without which there can be no erotic *perspective*.[16]

The party, a ritual common in Sade and in Fourier, has as
its "proof" a fact of the discourse which is to be found in
both: the amorous practice cannot be uttered save in the form
of a "scene," a "scenario," a "tableau vivant" (a strictly fantasmatic disposition): the Sadean "séances" which often even
have a "setting": gardens, woods, colored veils, garlands of
flowers, in Fourier the Cnidian novel. In fact, they are part of
the very force of fantasy, of the destructive power it has over
cultural models by using them *disrespectfully*, of "representing"
the erotic scene in the most insipid colors and with the
"proper" tone of petit-bourgeois art: Sade's most shocking

---

[16] Can a more Sadean classification be imagined than the following: the
Angelicate is organized along three degrees of novitiate: (1) *cherubic* (the
postulant must sacrifice an entire day to each member of the venerable
choir); (2) *seraphic* (the sacrifice lasts several days and is offered to both
sexes); (3) *sayidic* (the sacrifice is offered up to a chorus of patriarchs:
probably even older!).

scenes, Fourier's pro-sapphic ravings, occur in a Folies-Bergère setting: a carnival-like conjunction of transgression and opera, the sober site of mad acts, where the *subject is swallowed up in its culture,* a decision that simultaneously sweeps away art and sex, denies transgression itself any gravity, prohibits its ritualization (by providing for widespread prostitution the stage setting of *The Pearl Fishers*), the headlong flight of the signified across the shifting of aesthetics or sex, which ordinary language tries to achieve in its fashion when it speaks (in French) of *ballets roses* and *ballets bleus* ("performances" by girls [pink] or boys [blue] "danced" before older men).

COMPOTES

An Eastern book says there is no better remedy for thirst than a little cold compote, well sweetened, followed by a few swallows of cool water. Fourier would have been doubly enchanted at this advice: first, because of the conjunction of solid and liquid (the exemplar of a Transition, a Mix, a Neuter, a Passage, a Twilight); next, because of its promotion of compotes to the status of a philosophical food (the *Compound*, not the Simple, slakes thirst, desire).

Harmony will be sweet. Why? For many reasons, constructed in superdetermination (the likely index of a fantasy). First because sugar is an *anti-bread*; since bread is a mystic object of Civilization, the symbol of labor and bitterness, the emblem of Need, Harmony will invert the use of bread and turn it into the colophon of Desire; bread will become a luxury food ("one of the most costly and most husbanded victuals"); in contrast, sugar will become wheat.[17] Next, because sugar, hereby promoted, mixed with fruit in a compote, will form the

---

[17] "Then Africa will cheaply furnish the commodities of its hot climate, cane sugar, which, pound for pound, will have the value of wheat, when it is cultivated by 70 million Africans and all the peoples of the Torrid Zone" (II, 14).

bread of Harmony, the basic nourishment of those who have become wealthy and happy.[18] In a way, all Harmony has grown out of Fourier's taste for compotes, as a man's desire can grow out of a child's dream (here the dream of Candyland, of lakes of jam, of chocolate mountains): the opus turns the far-off fantasy into sense: an entire construct with immense, subtle ramifications (the societary regime, the cosmogony of the new world) grows out of the etymological metaphor: the compote (*composita*) being a composite, a euphoric system of the Mixed is built up; for example: is a hyperglycemic diet dangerous to health? Fourier is quick to invent a countersugar, itself often highly sugared: "There will be no drawbacks to this abundance of sweets when we can counterbalance sugar's wormy influence with a great abundance of alcoholic wines for men, white wines for women and children, acid beverages like lemonade, tart cedar . . ." Or rather: on the carrousel of the signifier, no one can say *what comes first*, Fourier's taste (for sugar, the negation of anything conflictual? for mixed fruits? for cooked food transformed into a semi-liquid consistency?) or the exaltation of a pure form, the composite-compote, the combinative. The signifier (Fourier is in full accord) is a non-originated, non-determined material, a text.

THE WEATHER

Antique rhetoric, especially the medieval, included a special topic, the *impossibilia* (*adunata* in Greek); the *adunaton* was a common site, a *topos*, based on the notion of an *over-abundance*: two naturally opposite, enemy elements (vulture and dove) were presented as peacefully living together ("The fire burns within the ice / The sun grows dark / I see the moon

---

[18] "Then compotes made up of one-fourth sugar will be lavished on children, because an equal measure of it will be cheaper than bread . . . ; man's pivotal nourishment must not be bread, a simple victual derived from one zone, but sugared fruit, a composed victual allying the produce of two zones" (IV, 19).

about to fall / This tree moves from its place," wrote Théo-phile de Viau); the impossible image served to stigmatize a hateful tense, a shocking *contra-naturam* ("We will have seen everything!"). Once again, Fourier inverts the rhetorical site; he uses the *adunaton* to celebrate the marvels of Harmony, the conquest of Nature by contra-natural means; for example, nothing is more incontestably "natural" (eternal) than the brackishness of the sea, whose water is undrinkable; Fourier, by the aromal action of the North Polar cap, turns it to lem-onade (tart cedar): a positive *adunaton*.

Fourier's *adunata* are many. They can all be reduced to the (very modern) conviction that man's farming modifies the climate.[19] For Fourier, human "nature" is not deformable (merely combinable), but "natural" nature is modifiable (the reason being that Fourier's cosmogony is *aromal*, tied to the notion of the sexual fluid, whereas his psychology is discon-tinuous, dedicated to arrangement, not to effluvium). This *topos* of the *impossible* abides by the categories of antique rhetoric:

I

Chronographies (temporal impossibilities). "We shall be witness to a spectacle to be seen once on each globe: the sudden passage from incoherence to social combination. . . . During this metamorphosis, each year will equal a century of existence," etc.

II

Topographies. Spatial impossibilities, very numerous, arise from what we call geography: (1) *Climatology:* (a) Fourier changes climates, makes the Pole into a new Andalusia and moves the pleasant temperature of Naples and Provence to the

[19] ". . . the air is a field, subject as is the earth to industrious exploitation" (III, 97).

coast of Siberia; (b) Fourier improves the seasons, hateful in civilized France (theme: *Spring has fled!*): "1822 had no winter, 1823 no spring at all. This confusion, which has gone on for ten years, is the result of an aromal lesion the planet is suffering because of the undue duration of chaos, civilized, barbarous and savage" (theme: *It's because of the Bomb*); (c) Fourier orders micro-climates: "The atmosphere and its protection are an integral part of our clothing. . . . In Civilization, no one ever dreamed of improving that part of the clothing we call atmosphere, with which we are perpetually in contact" (the theme of the phalanstery's corridors, heated and ventilated). (2) *Podology:* "[Crusaders of old shoes] . . . are carried off en masse to Jerusalem and brought out to cover over with good soil and plantations that Calvary where the Christians come to recite useless Our Father's; in three days, a fertile mountain has been created. Thus their religion consists in usefulness and agreeableness toward those countries to which our stupid piety brought only ravage and superstition." (3) *Physical Geography:* Fourier subjects the map of the world to a veritable plastic surgery: he moves continents, grafts climates, "lifts" South America (as we lift breasts), "lowers" Africa, pierces isthmuses (Suez and Panama), permutates cities (Stockholm is put in the place of Bordeaux, St. Petersburg of Turin), makes Constantinople the capital of the Harmonian world. (4) *Astronomy:* "Man is called upon to displace and replace the stars."

III

Prosographies: modifications of the human body: (a) *Stature:* "Mankind's height will increase 2 to 3 inches per generation, until it has attained the average of 84 inches or 7 feet for men." (b) *Age:* "Then the full span of life will be 144 years and vigor proportionate." (c) *Physiology:* "This multitude of meals is necessary for the ravenous appetite the New

Order will create. . . . Children raised in this way will acquire iron temperaments and will be subject to a renewal of appetite every 2 or 3 hours, due to the speedy digestion that will result from the delicacy of the food" (here again we touch on a Sadean theme: what in Fourier is the regulation of indigestion by digestion becomes inverted [or set right] in Sade, where indigestion rules the digestion—coprophagy requires good fecal matter). (d) *Sex:* "In order to confound the tyranny of men there must have existed for a century a third sex, male and female, stronger than man."

It is nugatory to stress the reasonable nature of these ravings, because certain of them are being implemented (acceleration of History, the modification of climate through agriculture or urbanization, the piercing of isthmuses, the transformations of soils, the conversion of desert sites into cultivated sites, the conquest of the heavenly bodies, the increase in longevity, the physical improvement of the race). The most insane (the most resistant) *adunaton* is not the one that upsets the laws of "Nature," but the one that upsets the laws of language. Neologisms are Fourier's *impossibilia*. It is easier to predict the subversion of "the weather" than to imagine, as does Fourier, a masculine form of a feminine word, *Fés* for *Fées:* the upheaval of a strange graphic configuration in which femininity has been sunk, there is the true *impossible:* the impossible garnered from sex and language: in "*matrones* (feminine) and *matrons* (masculine)," a new, monstrous, transgressor *object* has come to mankind.

1971

Writers, Intellectuals, Teachers

WHAT follows depends on the idea that there is a fundamental tie between teaching and speech. The idea is a very old one (did not the whole of our teaching spring from Rhetoric?) but it is possible today to consider it differently from yesterday: firstly, because there is a (political) crisis in teaching; secondly, because (Lacanian) psychoanalysis has shown the mechanism of the twists and turns of empty speech; lastly, because the opposition between speech and writing has become an obvious fact with effects that now need to be gradually drawn out.

Over against the teacher, who is on the side of speech, let us call a *writer* every operator of language on the side of writing; between the two, the intellectual, the person who prints and publishes his speech. Between the language of the teacher and that of the intellectual there is hardly any incompatibility (they often co-exist in a single individual); but the writer stands apart, separate. Writing begins at the point where speech becomes *impossible* (a word that can be understood in the sense it has when applied to a child).

From *Image-Music-Text*.

TWO CONSTRAINTS

Speech is irreversible: a word cannot be *retracted*, except precisely by saying that one retracts it. To cross out is here to add: if I want to erase what I have just said, I cannot do it without showing the eraser itself (I must say: *"or rather . . ."* *"I expressed myself badly . . ."*); paradoxically, it is ephemeral speech which is indelible, not monumental writing. All that one can do in the case of a spoken utterance is to tack on another utterance. The correcting and improving movement of speech is the wavering of a flow of words, a weave which wears itself out catching itself up, a chain of augmentative corrections which constitutes the favored abode of the unconscious part of our discourse (it is not by chance that psychoanalysis is linked to speech and not writing: dreams are spoken not written). The eponymous figure of the speaker is Penelope.

Nor is this all. We can only make ourselves understood (well or poorly) if we maintain a certain speed of delivery. We are like a cyclist or a film obliged to keep going so as to avoid falling or scratching. Silence and vacillation are equally forbidden: the articulatory speed binds each point of the sentence to what immediately follows or precedes (impossible to have the word "set off" toward distant and strange paradigms). Context is a structural given not of language but of speech and it is the very status of context to be reductive of meaning. The spoken word is "clear"; the banishment of polysemy (such banishment being the definition of "clarity") serves the Law— *all speech is on the side of the Law.*

Whoever prepares to speak (in a teaching situation) must realize the *mise en scène* imposed by the use of speech under the simple effect of a natural determination (stemming from the physical nature of articulatory breathing). This *mise en scène* develops as follows. Either the speaker chooses in all good faith a role of Authority, in which case it suffices to "speak well," in compliance with the Law present in every act of speech—without hesitation, at the right speed, clearly (which is what is demanded of good pedagogic speech: clarity, authority); the precise phrase is truly a sentence, a *sententia*, an act of penal speech. Or the speaker is bothered by all this Law that the act of speaking is going to introduce into what he wants to say, in which case, since it is impossible to alter the delivery (condemning one to "clarity") but possible to *excuse oneself* for speaking (for laying out the Law), he uses the irreversibility of speech in order to disturb its legality: correcting, adding, wavering, the speaker moves into the infinitude of language, superimposes on the simple message that everyone expects of him a new message that ruins the very idea of a message and, through the shifting reflection of the blemishes and excesses with which he accompanies the line of the discourse, asks us to believe with him that language is not to be reduced to communication. By all these operations, which come near the wavering movement of the Text, the imperfect orator hopes to render less disagreeable the role that makes every speaker a kind of policeman. Yet at the end of all this effort to "speak badly" another role is enforced, for the audience (nothing to do with the reader), caught in its own imaginary, receives these fumblings as so many signs of weakness and sends the speaker back the image of a master who is human, too human—*liberal*.

The choice is gloomy: conscientious functionary or free artist, the teacher escapes neither the theater of speech nor the Law played out on its stage: the Law appears *not in what is said but in the very fact of speech*. In order to subvert the Law (and not simply get around it), the teacher would have to undermine voice delivery, word speed, and rhythm to the point of *another* intelligibility. Or not speak at all; which, however, would be to rejoin other roles again—that of the great silent mind, mute with the weight of experience, or that of the militant who in the name of praxis dismisses all discourse as futile. Nothing to be done: language is always a matter of force, to speak is to exercise a will for power; in the realm of speech there is no innocence, no safety.

THE SUMMARY

Statutorily the discourse of the teacher is marked by the following characteristic: one can (one may) summarize it (a privilege it holds in common with the discourse of Members of Parliament). There is an exercise in our schools called *text reduction*,[1] a term which expresses nicely the ideology of the summary: on the one side the "thought," object of the message, element of knowledge, transitive or critical force; on the other the "style," ornament, province of luxury and leisure, and thus futility. To separate the thought from the style is in some sort to relieve the discourse of its sacerdotal robes, to secularize the message (hence the bourgeois conjuncture of the teacher and the Member of Parliament). "Form" is believed to be compressible and such compression is not judged essentially harmful—from a distance indeed, from our Western promontory, is the difference really so very great between the head of a living Jivaro and a shrunken Jivaro head?

It is difficult for a teacher to see the "notes" taken during his courses. He hardly wants to, either out of discretion (nothing more personal than "notes," despite the formal nature of the practice) or, more likely, from fear of contemplating himself in a reduced state, at once dead and substantial like a Jivaro treated by his fellows. No knowing whether what is taken (culled) from the flow of speech is scattered statements (formulae, sentences) or the gist of an argument, but in both cases what is lost is the supplement, the point of the advance

---

[1] ["*Réduction de texte*," i.e., a form of précis.]

of the state of language. The summary is a disavowal of writing.

In contrasting consequence, the term "writer" (a term which here always refers to a practice, not to a social value) may be applied to any sender whose "message" (thereby immediately destroying its very nature as message) cannot be summarized, a condition the writer shares with the madman, the chatterbox, and the mathematician but which precisely writing (namely a certain practice of the signifier) has as its task to specify.

THE TEACHING RELATIONSHIP

How can the teacher be assimilated to the psychoanalyst? It is exactly the contrary which is the case: the teacher is the person analyzed.

Imagine that I am a teacher: I speak, endlessly, in front of and for someone who remains silent. I am the person who says *I* (the detours of *one*, *we*, or impersonal sentence make no difference), I am the person who, under cover of *setting out* a body of knowledge, *puts out* a discourse, *never knowing how that discourse is being received* and thus forever forbidden the reassurance of a definitive image—even if offensive—which would *constitute me*. In the *exposé*, more aptly named than we tend to think, it is not knowledge which is exposed, it is the subject (who exposes himself to all sorts of painful adventures). The mirror is empty, reflecting back to me no more than the falling away of my language as it gradually unrolls. Like the Marx Brothers disguised as Russian airmen (in *A Night at the Opera*—a work which I regard as allegorical of many a textual problem), I am, at the beginning of my exposé, rigged out with a large false beard which, drenched little by little with the flood of my own words (a substitute for the jug of water from which the *Mute*, Harpo, guzzles away on the Mayor of New York's rostrum), I then feel coming unstuck piecemeal in front of everybody. Scarcely have I made the audience smile with some "witty" remark, scarcely have I reassured it with some progressive stereotype, than I experience all the complacency of such provocations; I regret the hysterical drive, would like to retract it, preferring too late an austere to a "clever" discourse (but in that contrary case it is the "severity" of the discourse that would seem hysterical to me). Should some smile answer my remark or some gesture of assent my stereotype of intimidation, I immediately persuade myself that these manifestations of complicity come from imbeciles or flatterers (I am here describing an imaginary process). It is I who am after a response and who let myself go as far as to provoke it, yet it suffices that I receive a response for me to become distrustful. If I develop a discourse such that it coldly averts any response, I do not thereby feel myself to be any more in *true* (in the musical sense), for I must then glory in the solitude of my speech, furnish it with the alibi of missionary discourses (science, truth, etc.).

Thus, in accordance with psychoanalytic description (Lacan's, the perspicacity of which in this respect any speaker can confirm), when the teacher speaks to his audience, the Other is always there, *puncturing* his discourse. Were the discourse held tightly fastened by an impeccable intelligence, armed with scientific "rigor" or political radicality, it would nevertheless be punctured: it suffices that I speak, that my speech flow, for it to flow away. Naturally however, though every teacher occupies the position of a person in analysis, no student audience can claim the advantage of the opposite situation: firstly, because the psychoanalytic silence has nothing pre-eminent about it; secondly, because it happens that a subject, carried away, emerges and rushes to burn on speech, to join in the oratorical promiscuity (and should the subject remain obstinately silent, this is simply to give voice to the obstinacy of his muteness). Yet for the teacher, the student audience is still the exemplary Other in that it *has an air* of not speaking—and thus, from the bosom of its apparent flatness, speaks in you so much the louder: its implicit speech, which is mine, touches me all the more in that I am not encumbered by its discourse.

Such is the cross borne in every public act of speech. Whether the teacher speaks or whether the listener urges the right to speak, in both cases we go straight to the analytic couch: the teaching relationship is nothing more than the transference it institutes; "science," "method," "knowledge," "idea" come indirectly, are given *in addition*—they are *left-overs*.

THE CONTRACT

"Most of the time, the relations between humans suffer, often to the point of destruction, from the fact that the contract established in those relations is not respected. As soon as two human beings enter into reciprocal relationship, their contract, generally tacit, comes into force, regulating the form of their relations, etc."
—BRECHT

Although the demand expressed in the community space of a course is fundamentally intransitive, as is natural in any transferential situation, it is nonetheless overdetermined and shelters behind other, seemingly transitive, demands. These latter constitute the conditions of an implicit contract between the teacher and the taught, a contract which is "imaginary," no way in contradiction with the economic determination which impels the student to be in search of a career and the teacher to fulfill the terms of an employment.

Here pell-mell (in the order of the imaginary there is no founding motive) is what the teacher demands of those taught: (1) to acknowledge him in whatever "role" it may be—authority, benevolence, militancy, knowledge, etc. (any newcomer who cannot be placed as to the *image* he asks of you is immediately disturbing); (2) to act as relay, to extend him, to spread his style and ideas far afield; (3) to let himself be seduced, to assent to a loving relationship (granting all the sublimations, the distances, the checks consonant with the social reality and the presentiment of the futility of the relationship); (4) to allow him to honor the contract he has himself entered into with his employer, with society: the person taught is the necessary part of a (remunerated) practice, the object of a job, the matter of a production (even if difficult to define).

From his side, here pell-mell is what the person taught demands of the teacher: (1) to help him to a good professional training; (2) to fulfill the roles traditionally devolving to the teacher (scientific authority, transmission of a capital of knowledge, etc.); (3) to reveal the secrets of a technique (of research, for passing an examination); (4) under the banner of the secular saint Method, to be an instructor in ascesis, a *guru*; (5) to represent a "movement of ideas," a School, a Cause, to be its spokesman; (6) to admit him, the student, into the complicity of a special language; (7) for those possessed by the fantasy of the thesis (a timid practice of writing, at once disfigured and shielded by its institutional finality), to guarantee the reality of that fantasy; (8) to lend service—the teacher signs registration forms, testimonials, and so on.

This is simply a topic, a fund of choices which are not necessarily all actualized at the same time in a particular individual. It is at the level of the contractual totality, however, that is decided the *comfort* of the teaching relationship: the "good" teacher, the "good" student are those who accept philosophically the plurality of their determinations, perhaps because they know that the truth of a relationship of speech is *elsewhere*.

RESEARCH

What is a piece of "research"? To find out, we would need to have some idea of what a "result" is. What is it that one finds? What is it that one wants to find? *What is missing?* In what axiomatic field will the fact isolated, the meaning brought out, the statistical discovery be placed? No doubt it depends each time on the particular science approached, but from the moment a piece of research concerns the text (and the text extends very much further than the literary work) the research itself becomes text, production: to it, any "result" is literally *im-pertinent*. "Research" is then the name which prudently, under the constraint of certain social conditions, we give to the activity of writing: research here moves on the side of writing, is an adventure of the signifier, an excess of exchange—impossible to maintain the equation of a "result" *for* a "piece of research." Which is why the discourse to which a piece of research must be submitted (in teaching it) has as specialty, besides its parenetic function (*"Write!"*), to recall the research to its epistemological condition: whatever it searches for, it must not forget its nature as language—and it is this which renders finally inevitable an encounter with writing. In writing, the enunciation deludes the enounced by the effect of the language which produces it, a good enough definition of the productive, dissatisfied, progressive, critical element which is indeed ordinarily granted to "research." Such is the historical role of research: teach the scientist or scholar *that he speaks* (but if he knew it, he would *write*—and the whole idea of science, the whole of scientificity would be changed thereby).

THE DESTRUCTION OF STEREOTYPES

Someone writes to me that "a group of revolutionary students is preparing a destruction of the structuralist myth." I am captivated by the stereotypic consistency of the expression. The destruction of the myth begins from the very announcement of its putative agents with the finest of myths, the "group of revolutionary students"—quite as good as "war widows" or "old soldiers."

Usually the stereotype is a sad affair, since it is constituted by a necrosis of language, a prosthesis brought in to fill a hole in writing. Yet at the same time it cannot but occasion a huge burst of laughter: it takes itself seriously, believes itself to be closer to the truth because indifferent to its nature as language. It is at once corny and solemn.

Setting the stereotype at a distance is not a political task, for political language is itself made up of stereotypes, but a critical task, one, that is, which aims to call language into crisis. Such an activity allows one first and foremost to isolate the speck of ideology contained in every political discourse and to attack it like an acid capable of dissolving the greasiness of "natural" language (that is to say, of language which feigns ignorance of the fact of its nature as language). It is a way, too, of breaking with the mechanistic conception of language as mere response to stimuli of situation or action, a way of opposing the production of language to its simple and fallacious utilization. Then again, it jolts the discourse of the Other and constitutes a permanent operation of preanalysis. Lastly, the stereotype is at bottom a form of opportunism: one conforms to the reigning language, or rather to that in language which seems to *govern* (a situation, a right, a struggle, an institution, a movement, a science, a theory, etc.); to speak in stereotypes is to side with the power of language, an opportunism which must (today) be refused.

But is it not possible to "transcend" stereotypes instead of "destroying" them? The wish is unrealistic; operators of language have no other activity at their command than that of emptying what is full: language is not dialectical—it allows only a movement in two stages.

THE CHAIN OF DISCOURSES

It is because language is not dialectical (does not allow the third term other than as pure oratorical flourish, rhetorical assertion, pious hope) that discourse (discursivity) moves, in its historical impetus, by *clashes*. A new discourse can only emerge as the *paradox* which goes against (and often goes for) the surrounding or preceding *doxa*, can only see the day as difference, distinction, working loose *against* what sticks to it. For example, Chomskyan theory is constructed *against* Bloomfieldian behaviorism; linguistic behaviorism once liquidated by Chomsky, it is then *against* Chomskyan mentalism (or anthropologism) that a new semiotics is being developed, while Chomsky himself, in quest of allies, is forced to *jump* over his immediate predecessors and go back as far as the Port-Royal *Grammar*. But doubtless it is in one of the greatest thinkers of dialectics, Marx, that it would be the most interesting to verify the undialectical nature of language: Marx's discourse is almost entirely *paradoxical*, the *doxa* being now Proudhon, now someone else, and so on. This twofold movement of separation and renewal results not in a circle but, according to Vico's great and beautiful image, in a spiral and it is in this *drift* of circularity (of paradoxical form) that historical determinations are articulated. Hence it is always necessary to establish what *doxa* an author is opposing (this can sometimes be a very minority *doxa*, holding sway over a limited group). A teaching may equally be evaluated in terms of paradox, provided it is built on the following conviction: that a system calling for corrections, translations, openings, and negations is more useful than an unformulated absence of system—one may then avoid the immobility of prattle and connect to the historical chain of discourses, the progress (*progressus*) of discursivity.

METHOD

. Some people talk avidly, demandingly of method; what they want in work is method, which can never be too rigorous or too formal for their taste. Method becomes a Law, but since that Law is devoid of any effect outside itself (nobody can say what a "result" is in "human sciences") it is infinitely disappointed; posing as a pure metalanguage, it partakes of the vanity of all metalanguage. The invariable fact is that a piece of work which ceaselessly proclaims its determination for method is ultimately sterile: everything has been put into the method, nothing is left for writing; the researcher repeatedly asserts that his text will be methodological but the text never comes. No surer way to kill a piece of research and send it to join the great waste of abandoned projects than Method.

The danger of Method (of a fixation with Method) is to be grasped by considering the two demands to which the work of research must reply. The first is a demand for responsibility: the work must increase lucidity, manage to reveal the implications of a procedure, the alibis of a language, in short must constitute a *critique* (remember once again that to *criticize* means *to call into crisis*). Here Method is inevitable, irreplaceable, not for its "results" but precisely—or on the contrary—because it realizes the highest degree of consciousness of a language *which is not forgetful of itself*. The second demand, however, is of a quite different order; it is that of writing, space of dispersion of desire, where Law is dismissed. *At a certain moment*, therefore, it is necessary to turn against Method, or at least to treat it without any founding privilege as one of the voices of plurality—as a *view*, a spectacle mounted in the text, the text which all in all is the only "true" result of any research.

QUESTIONS

To question is to want to know something. Yet in many intellectual debates the questions that follow the lecturer's talk are in no way the expression of a lack but the assertion of a plenitude. Under the cover of asking questions, I attack the speaker. *To question* then takes on its police sense: *to question* is to challenge, to interpellate. The person interpellated, however, must pretend to reply to the letter of the question, not to the manner in which it is posed. So a game is set up: although each person knows exactly what the intentions of the other really are, the game demands a reply to the content and not to the manner. If I am asked in a certain tone of voice *"What's the use of linguistics?"*, thereby signifying to me that it is of no use whatsoever, I must pretend to reply naïvely *"It helps to do this and that,"* and not, in accordance with the truth of the dialogue, "Why are you attacking me?" What I receive is the connotation; what I have to return is the denotation. In the space of speech, science and logic, knowledge and reasoning, questions and answers, propositions and objections are the masks of the dialectical relationship. Our intellectual debates are coded every bit as much as were the Scholastic disputations; we still have the stock roles (the "sociologistic," the "Goldmannian," the "Telquelian," etc.) but contrary to the *disputatio*, where such roles would have been ceremonial and have displayed the artifice of their function, our intellectual "intercourse" always gives itself "natural" airs: it claims to exchange only signifieds, not signifiers.

IN THE NAME OF WHAT?

I speak in the name of what? Of a function? A body of knowledge? An experience? What do I represent? A scientific capacity? An institution? A service? In fact, I speak only in the name of a language: I speak because I have written; writing is represented by its contrary, by speech. This distortion means that in writing *of* speech (on the subject of speech) I am condemned to the following aporia: denounce the imaginary of speech through the irreality of writing. Thus at this moment I am not describing any "authentic" experience, giving the picture of any "real" teaching, opening any "university" dossier. For writing can tell the truth on language but not the truth on the real (we are at present trying to find out what a real without language is).

THE STANDING POSITION

Can you imagine a more doubtful situation than that of talking for (or in front of) people who are standing up or who are visibly badly seated? What is being exchanged here? What is this discomfort the price of? What is my speech *worth*? How could the awkwardness of the hearer's position not lead to questions as to the validity of what is being heard? Is not the standing position eminently *critical*? And is it not thus, changing the scale, that political consciousness begins, in *un-ease*? Listening returns me the vanity of my own speech, its *price*, for, whether I like it or not, I am placed in a circuit of exchange; and listening is also the position of the person to whom I address myself.

FAMILIARITY

It sometimes happens, remnant of May '68, that a student speaks to a teacher in the familiar *tu* form, which gives us a strong, full sign, referring to the most psychological of signifieds: the will for militancy or mateyness—*muscle*. Since a morality of the sign is here imposed, it can be challenged in its turn and a subtler semantics preferred. Signs must be handled on a neutral ground and in French that ground is the polite *vous* form. The *tu* form can only break loose from the code in cases where it constitutes *a simplification of grammar* (as, for example, when talking to a foreigner with poor French). In such cases it is a matter of substituting a transitive practice for a symbolic attitude: instead of seeking to signify *just who* I think the other is (and so just who I think I am), I simply try to make myself clearly understood to him. But the strategy is also itself finally devious: the *tu* form is like all attitudes of flight; when a sign displeases me, when the meaning bothers me, I shift toward the operational, which becomes a censorship of the symbolic and thus the symbol of asymbolism. A great many political and scientific discourses are characterized by a shift of this kind (on which depends, notably, the whole of the linguistics of "communication").

AN ODOR OF SPEECH

As soon as one has finished speaking, there begins the dizzying turn of the image: one exalts or regrets what one has said, the way in which one said it, one *imagines oneself* (turns oneself over in image); speech is subject to remanence, it *smells*.

Writing has no smell: produced (having accomplished its process of production), it *falls*, not like a bellows deflating but like a meteorite disappearing; it will *travel* far from my body, yet without being something detached and narcissistically retained like speech; its disappearance holds no disappointment; it passes, traverses, and that's all. The time of speech exceeds the act of speech (only a jurist could have us believe that spoken words disappear, *verba volant*). Writing, however, has no past (if society obliges you to administer what you have written, you can only do it with the most profound boredom, the boredom of a false past). Which is why the discourse applied in commenting writing has a much less striking effect than that applied in commenting speech (though the stake is greater): I can *objectively* take account of the first for "I" am no longer there; the second, even if it is in praise, I can only try to get rid of, for it does no more than retighten the impasse of my imaginary.

(How is it then that this present text preoccupies me, that once completed, corrected, let go of, the text remains or returns in me as a state of doubt and, in a word, of fear? Is it not *written*, liberated by writing? I see that I cannot improve the piece, I have achieved the exact form of what I wanted to say; it is no longer a question of *style*. I conclude, therefore, that it is the very status of the piece which disturbs me, what plagues me in it is precisely that, dealing with speech, it cannot, *in writing itself*, fully liquidate speech. In order to write *of* speech (about speech) I am compelled to *refer* to illusions of experiences, memories, and feelings had by the subject I am when I speak, that I was when speaking: in such a writing the referential lingers on and it is that which smells to my own nostrils.)

OUR PLACE

Just as psychoanalysis, with the work of Lacan, is in the process of extending the Freudian topic into a topology of the subject (the unconscious is never there in *its* place), so likewise we need to substitute for the magisterial space of the past—which was fundamentally a religious space (the work delivered by the master from the pulpit above with the audience below, the flock, the sheep, the herd)—a less upright, less Euclidean space where no one, neither teacher nor students, would ever be *in his final place*. One would then be able to see that what must be made reversible are not social "roles" (is there any point in squabbling for "authority," for the "right" to speak?) but the regions of speech. Where is speech? In locution? In listening? In the *returns* of the one and the other? The problem is not to abolish the distinction in functions (*teacher/student*—after all, as Sade has taught us, order is one of the guarantees of pleasure) but to protect the instability and, as it were, the giddying whirl of the positions of speech. In the teaching space nobody should anywhere be in his place (I am comforted by this constant displacement: were I to *find my place*, I would not even go on pretending to teach, I would give up).

Yet is it not the case that the teacher has a fixed place, that of his *remuneration*, the place he occupies in the economy, in production? We come back to the same problem, our sole and continuing concern: the origin of a spoken discourse does not exhaust that discourse; once set off, it is beset by a thousand adventures, its origin becomes blurred, all its effects are not in its cause. It is this *excess* which here concerns us.

TWO TYPES OF CRITICISM

The mistakes that may be made in typing out a manuscript are so many meaningful incidents, incidents which by analogy help to shed light on the attitude it is necessary to adopt with regard to meaning when commenting a text.

Either the word produced by the mistake (if spoiled by a wrong letter) has no meaning, finds no textual contour, in which case the code is interrupted, creating an asemic word, a pure signifier; for example, instead of writing *officier* [officer] I write *offivier*, which is meaningless. Or the erroneous— mistyped—word, though not the word one intended to write, is a word identifiable in the lexicon, a word which means something: should I write *ride* [wrinkle] instead of *rude* [rude, rough], the new word exists in French and the sentence retains a meaning, even if eccentric. This is the choice (the voice?) of pun, anagram, semantic metathesis, spoonerism: there is a sliding *within the codes*—meaning remains but pluralized, cheated, without law of content, message, truth.

Each of these two types of mistake figures (or prefigures) a type of criticism. The first dismisses all meaning of the support text which is to lend itself only to a signifying efflorescence: its phonism alone is to be treated, but not interpreted; one associates, one does not decipher. Giving the reading *offivier* as opposed to *officier*, the mistake opens up for me the *right of association*—I am free to explode *offivier* toward *obvier* [obviate], *vivier* [fish stock], etc. It is not simply that the ear of this first criticism hears the cracklings of the phono pickup but rather that it desires to hear only them, making them into a new music. In the second type of criticism nothing is rejected by the "reading head"; it perceives both the meaning (the meanings) and its cracklings. The (historical) stake of these two types of criticism (I should like to be able to say that the field of the first is *signifiosis* and that of the second *signifiance*) is clearly different.

The first has in its favor the right of the signifier to spread out where it will (where it can?): what law, and what meaning, and with what basis, would restrain it? Once the philological (monological) law has been relaxed and the text eased open to plurality, why stop? Why refuse to push polysemy as far as asemy? In the name of what? Like any radical right, this one supposes a utopian vision of freedom: the law is lifted *all at once*, outside of any history, in defiance of any dialectic (hence the finally petit-bourgeois aspect of this style of demand). Yet the moment it evades all tactical reason while nevertheless remaining implanted in a specific (and alienated) intellectual society, the disorder of the signifier reverts into hysterical rambling: liberating reading from all meaning, it is ultimately *my* reading which I impose, for in *this* moment of History the economy of the subject is not yet transformed and the refusal of meaning (of meanings) falls back into subjectivity. At best, one can simply say that this radical criticism, defined by a foreclosure of the signified (and not by its slide), *anticipates* History, anticipates a new, unprecedented state in which the efflorescence of the signifier would not be at the cost of any idealist counterpart, of any closure of the person. To criticize, however, is to put into crisis, something which is not possible without evaluating the conditions of the crisis (its limits), without considering its historical moment. Thus the second type of criticism, that which applies itself to the division of meanings and the "trickery" of interpretation, appears (at least to me) more historically correct. In a society locked in the war of meanings and thereby under the compulsion of rules of communication which determine its effectiveness, the liquidation of the old criticism can only be carried forward *in* meaning (in the volume of meanings) and not outside it. In other words, it is necessary to practice a certain semantic enterism. Ideological criticism is today precisely condemned to operations of theft: the signified, exemption of which is the materialist task par excellence, is more easily "lifted" in the *illusion* of meaning than in its destruction.

TWO TYPES OF DISCOURSE

Let us distinguish two types of discourse:

Terrorist discourse is not necessarily bound up with the peremptory assertion (or the opportunist defense) of a faith, a truth, a certain justice; it can simply be the wish to accomplish the lucid adequation of the enunciation with the true violence of language, the inherent violence which stems from the fact that no utterance is able directly to express the truth and has no other mode at its disposal than the force of the word; thus an apparently terrorist discourse ceases to be so if, reading it, one follows the directions it itself provides, re-establishing in it the gap or dispersion, that is to say, the unconscious. Such a reading is not always easy: certain small-scale terrorisms which function above all by stereotypes themselves operate, like any discourse of good conscience, the foreclosure of the other scene; in short, these terrorisms *refuse writing* (they can be detected by something in them that remains rigid—the odor of seriousness given off by the commonplace).

Repressive discourse is not linked to declared violence but

to the Law. The Law here enters language as equilibrium: an equilibrium is postulated between what is forbidden and what is permitted, between commendable meaning and unworthy meaning, between the constraint of common sense and the probationary freedom of interpretations. Hence the taste shown by such discourse for motions of balance, verbal opposites, antitheses formulated and evaded, being *neither* for this *nor* for that (if, however, you do the double addition of the *neither* and *nors*, it will be seen that our *impartial, objective, human* speaker is *for* this, against *that*). Repressive discourse is the discourse of good conscience, liberal discourse.

THE AXIOMATIC FIELD

"All that is necessary," comments Brecht, "is to determine those interpretations of facts appearing within the proletariat engaged in the class struggle (national or international) which enable it to utilize the facts for its action. They must be synthesized in order to create an axiomatic field." Thus every fact possesses several meanings (a plurality of "interpretations") and among those meanings there is one which is proletarian (or at least which is of use to the proletariat in its struggle); by connecting the various proletarian meanings one constructs a revolutionary axiomatics. But who determines the meaning? According to Brecht, the proletariat itself (*"appearing within the proletariat"*). Such a view implies that class division has its inevitable counterpart in a division of meanings and class struggle its equally inevitable counterpart in a war of meanings: so long as there is class struggle (national or international), the division of the axiomatic field will be inexpiable.

The difficulty (despite Brecht's verbal assurance—*"All that is necessary"*) comes from the fact that a certain number of objects of discourse do not directly concern the proletariat (they find no interpretation within it) which cannot, however, remain indifferent to them, since they constitute, at least in advanced States which have wiped out both misery and folk-lore, the plenitude of the other discourse within which the very proletariat is compelled to live, nourish, and amuse itself. This discourse is that of culture (it is possible that in Marx's day the pressure of culture on the proletariat was weaker than it is now; in the absence of "mass communications," there was as yet no "mass culture"). How can you attribute a meaning for the struggle to something of no direct concern to you? How could the proletariat determine *within itself* an interpretation of Zola, Poussin, pop music, the Sunday sports paper, or the latest news item? To "interpret" all these cultural relays it needs *representatives*—those whom Brecht calls the "artists" or the "workers of the intellect" (a particularly malicious ex-pression, at least in French, where the intellect is so nearly off the top of the head), those who have at their command the language of the indirect, the indirect as language; in a word, *oblates* who devote themselves to the proletarian interpreta-tion of cultural facts.

Then begins, however, for these procurators of proletarian meaning, a real headache of a problem since their class situa-tion is not that of the proletariat: they are not producers, a negative situation they share with (student) youth—an equally unproductive class with whom they usually form an alliance of language. It follows that the culture from which they have to disengage the proletarian meaning brings them back round to themselves and not to the proletariat. How is culture to be *evaluated*? According to its origin? Bourgeois. Its finality? Bourgeois again. According to dialectics? Although bourgeois, this does contain progressive elements; but what, *at the level of discourse*, distinguishes dialectics from com-promise? And then again, with what instruments? Historicism, sociologism, positivism, formalism, psychoanalysis? Every one of them bourgeoisified. There are some who finally prefer to give up the problem, to dismiss all "culture"—a course which entails the destruction of all discourse.

In fact, even within an axiomatic field thought to be clarified by the class struggle, the tasks are various, occasionally contradictory, and, most importantly, established on different temporalities. The axiomatic field is made up of several specific axiomatics: cultural criticism proceeds *successively, diversely, and simultaneously* by opposing the Old with the New, historicism with sociologism, formalism with economism, psychoanalysis with logico-positivism, and then again, *by a further turn*, empirical sociology with monumental history, the New with the strange (the foreign), historicism with formalism, scientism with psychoanalysis, and so on. Applied to culture, critical discourse can only be a silk shot through with tactics, a tissue of elements now past, now circumstantial (linked to contingencies of fashion), now finally and frankly utopian. To the tactical necessities of the war of meanings is added the strategic conception of the new conditions which will be given the signifier when that war comes to an end. Cultural criticism, that is, must be *impatient*, it cannot be carried on without desire. Hence all the discourses of Marxism are present in its writing: the apologetic (glorify revolutionary science), the apocalyptic (destroy bourgeois culture), and the eschatological (desire and call for the undivision of meaning, concomitant on class undivision).

OUR UNCONSCIOUS

The problem posed is this: how can the two great *epistemes* of modernity, namely the materialist and the Freudian dialectics, be made to intersect, to unite in the production of a new human relation (it is not to be excluded that a third term may be hidden in the interdiction of the first two)? That is to say: how can we aid the interaction of these two desires—to change the economy of the relations of production and to change the economy of the subject? (For the moment psychoanalysis appears to be the force best fitted for the second of the tasks but other topics can be imagined, those of the East, for example.)

The path of this comprehensive work lies through the following question: what is the relation between class determination and the unconscious? By what displacement does this determination slip in between subjects? Certainly not by "psychology" (as though there were mental contents—bourgeois/proletarian/intellectual/etc.) but quite obviously by language, by discourse: the Other—who speaks, who is all speech—is social. On the one hand, the proletariat may well be *separated* but it is still bourgeois language, in its degraded petit-bourgeois form, which speaks unconsciously in the proletariat's cultural discourse; on the other, the proletariat may well be mute but it still speaks in the discourse of the intellectual, not as canonical founding voice but as unconscious. It suffices in this respect to see how it *knocks* on all our discourses (explicit reference by the intellectual to the proletariat in no way prevents the latter from occupying the place of the unconscious in our discourse). Only the bourgeois discourse of the bourgeoisie is tautological: the unconscious of bourgeois discourse is indeed the Other, but that Other is another bourgeois discourse.

WRITING AS VALUE

Evaluation precedes criticism. There is no putting into crisis without evaluation. Our value is writing, an obstinate reference which, apart from the fact that it must often irritate, seems in the eyes of some to involve a risk—that of developing a certain *mystique*. The reproach has its malice, for it reverses point by point the importance we attach to writing, regarded, in this tiny intellectual region of our Western world, as *the materialist field par excellence*. Though issuing from

Marxism and psychoanalysis, the theory of writing tries to displace—without breaking with—that place of origin: on the one hand, it rejects the temptation of the signified, that is the deafness to language, to the excessive return of its effects; on the other, it is opposed to speech in that it is not transferential and outplays—admittedly partially, in extremely narrow, particularist social limits even—the traps of "dialogue." There is in writing the beginnings of a mass gesture: against all discourses (modes of speech, instrumental writings, rituals, protocols, social symbolics), writing alone today, even if still in the form of luxury, makes of language something *atopical*, without place. It is this dispersion, this unsituation, which is materialist.

PEACEABLE SPEECH

One of the things that can be expected from a regular meeting together of speakers is quite simply *goodwill*, that the meeting figure a space of discourse divested of all sense of aggressiveness.

Such a divestiture arouses resistances. The first is of a cultural nature: the refusal of violence is commonly seen as a humanist lie, courtesy (minor mode of that refusal) as a class value and openness as a mystification related to the liberal idea of dialogue. The second resistance is of an imaginary order: many people want a conflictual discourse from motives of psychic liberation; the removal of confrontation is said to have something frustrating about it. The third resistance is of a political order: polemic is an essential arm in the struggle, any space of discourse must be splintered in order that its contradictions may emerge—it must be kept under scrutiny.

What is preserved in these three resistances, however, is ultimately the unity of the neurotic subject, which *comes together* in the forms of conflict. Yet we know that violence is always there (in language) and it is precisely this that can lead us to decide to bracket out its signs and thus to dispense with a rhetoric; violence must not be absorbed by the code of violence.

The first advantage of this would be to suspend or at least to delay the roles of speech—so that listening, speaking, replying, I never be the actor of a judgment, a subjection, an intimidation, the advocate of a Cause. No doubt peaceable speech will finally secrete its own role, since, whatever I say, the other continues to read me as an image; but in the time put into eluding such a role, in the work of language accomplished by the community week after week toward the abolition from its discourse of all stichomythia, a certain dispropriation of speech (from then on close to writing) may be attained—or again, *a certain generalization of the subject*.

Perhaps this is what is found in certain experiences with drugs (in the experience of certain drugs). Though not smoking oneself (if only because of bronchial inability to inhale the smoke), it is impossible to remain insensible to the general goodwill that pervades certain places abroad where cannabis is smoked. The movements, the (few) words spoken, the whole relationship of the bodies (a relationship nevertheless immobile and distant), everything is relaxed, disarmed (hence totally unlike drunkenness, the legal form of violence in the West); the space seems to be the product of a subtle ascesis (one can sometimes read in it a certain *irony*). A meeting for speech should, I think, aim at this *suspension* (no matter of what—the desire is for a form), try to rejoin an *art of living*, the greatest of all the arts according to Brecht (such a view is more dialectical than it appears, in that it compels the distinction and evaluation of the customs of violence). In short, within the very limits of the teaching space as given, the need is to work at patiently tracing out a pure form, that of a *floating* (the very form of the signifier); a floating which would not destroy anything but would be content simply to disorientate the Law. The necessities of promotion, professional obligations (which nothing then prevents from being scrupulously fulfilled), imperatives of knowledge, prestige of method, ideological criticism—everything is there, but *floating*.

1971

from *The Pleasure of the Text*

I AM offered a text. This text bores me. It might be said to *prattle*. The prattle of the text is merely that foam of language which forms by the effect of a simple need of writing. Here we are not dealing with perversion but with demand. The writer of this text employs an unweaned language: imperative, automatic, unaffectionate, a minor disaster of static (those milky phonemes which the remarkable Jesuit, van Ginnekin, posited between writing and language): these are the motions of ungratified sucking, of an undifferentiated orality, intersecting the orality which produces the pleasures of gastrosophy and of language. You address yourself to me so that I may read you, but I am nothing to you except this address; in your eyes, I am the substitute for nothing, for no figure (hardly that of the mother); for you I am neither a body nor even an object (and I couldn't care less: I am not the one whose soul demands recognition), but merely a field, a vessel for expansion. It can be said that after all you have written this text quite apart

The Pleasure of the Text, translated by Richard Miller (New York: Hill and Wang, 1975).

from bliss; and this prattling text is then a frigid text, as any demand is frigid until desire, until neurosis forms in it.

Neurosis is a makeshift: not with regard to "health" but with regard to the "impossible" Bataille speaks of ("Neurosis is the fearful apprehension of an ultimate impossible," etc.); but this makeshift is the only one that allows for writing (and reading). So we arrive at this paradox: the texts, like those by Bataille—or by others—which are written against neurosis, from the center of madness, contain within themselves, *if they want to be read*, that bit of neurosis necessary to the seduction of their readers: these terrible texts are *all the same* flirtatious texts.

Thus every writer's motto reads: *mad I cannot be, sane I do not deign to be, neurotic I am.*

The text you write must prove to me *that it desires me*. This proof exists: it is writing. Writing is: the science of the various blisses of language, its Kama Sutra (this science has but one treatise: writing itself).

Sade: the pleasure of reading him clearly proceeds from certain breaks (or certain collisions): antipathetic codes (the noble and the trivial, for example) come into contact; pompous and ridiculous neologisms are created; pornographic messages are embodied in sentences so pure they might be used as grammatical models. As textual theory has it: the language is redistributed. Now, *such redistribution is always achieved by cutting*. Two edges are created: an obedient, conformist, plagiarizing edge (the language is to be copied in its canonical state, as it has been established by schooling, good usage, literature, culture), and *another edge*, mobile, blank (ready to assume any contours), which is never anything but the site of its effect: the place where the death of language is glimpsed. These two edges, *the compromise they bring about*, are necessary. Neither culture nor its destruction is erotic; it is the seam between them, the fault, the flaw, which becomes so. The pleasure of the text is like that untenable, impossible, purely *novelistic* instant so relished by Sade's libertine when he manages to be hanged and then to cut the rope at the very moment of his orgasm, his bliss.

Whence, perhaps, a means of evaluating the works of our modernity: their value would proceed from their duplicity. By which it must be understood that they always have two edges. The subversive edge may seem privileged because it is the edge of violence; but it is not violence which affects pleasure, nor is it destruction which interests it; what pleasure wants is the site of a loss, the seam, the cut, the deflation, the *dissolve* which seizes the subject in the midst of bliss. Culture thus recurs as an edge: in no matter what form.

. . .

The stereotype is the word repeated without any magic, any enthusiasm, as though it were natural, as though by some miracle this recurring word were adequate on each occasion for different reasons, as though to imitate could no longer be sensed as an imitation: an unconstrained word that claims consistency and is unaware of its own insistence. Nietzsche has observed that "truth" is only the solidification of old metaphors. So in this regard the stereotype is the present path of "truth," the palpable feature which shifts the invented ornament to the canonical, constraining form of the signified. (It would be good to imagine a new linguistic science that would no longer study the origin of words, or etymology, or even their diffusion, or lexicology, but the progress of their solidification, their densification throughout historical discourse; this science would doubtless be subversive, manifesting much more than the historical origin of truth: its rhetorical, *languaging* nature.)

The distrust of the stereotype (linked to the bliss of the new word or the untenable discourse) is a principle of absolute instability which respects nothing (no content, no choice). Nausea occurs whenever the liaison of two important words *follows of itself*. And when something follows of itself, I abandon it: that is bliss. A futile annoyance? In Poe's story, M. Valdemar, hypnotized and moribund, is kept alive in a cataleptic state by the repetition of the questions put to him ("Are you asleep, M. Valdemar?"); however, this survival is untenable: the false death, the atrocious death, is what has no end, the interminable. ("For God's sake!—quick!—put me to sleep —or, quick—waken me!—quick!—I say to you that I am dead!") The stereotype is this nauseating impossibility of dying.

In the intellectual field, political choice is a suspension of language—thus a bliss. Yet language resumes, in its consistent stable form (the political stereotype). Which language must then be swallowed, without nausea.

Another bliss (other edges): it consists in de-politicizing what is apparently political, and in politicizing what apparently is not. —Come now, surely one politicizes what *must* be politicized, and that's all.

Nihilism: "superior goals depreciate." This is an unstable, jeopardized moment, for other superior values tend, immediately and before the former are destroyed, to prevail; dialectics only links successive positivities; whence the suffocation at the very heart of anarchism. How *install* the deficiency of any superior value? Irony? It always proceeds from a *sure* site. Violence? Violence too is a superior value, and among the best coded. Bliss? Yes, if it is not spoken, doctrinal. The most consistent nihilism is perhaps *masked*: in some way *interior* to institutions, to conformist discourse, to apparent finalities.

. . .

Why do some people, including myself, enjoy in certain novels, biographies, and historical works the representation of the "daily life" of an epoch, of a character? Why this curiosity about petty details: schedules, habits, meals, lodging, clothing, etc.? Is it the hallucinatory relish of "reality" (the very materiality of "*that once existed*")? And is it not the fantasy itself which invokes the "detail," the tiny private scene, in which I can easily take my place? Are there, in short, "minor hysterics" (these very readers) who receive bliss from a singular theater: not one of grandeur but one of mediocrity (might there not be dreams, fantasies of mediocrity)?

Thus, impossible to imagine a more tenuous, a more insignificant notation than that of "today's weather" (or yesterday's); and yet, the other day, reading, trying to read Amiel, irritation that the well-meaning editor (another person foreclosing pleasure) had seen fit to omit from this Journal the everyday details, what the weather was like on the shores of Lake Geneva, and retain only insipid moral musing: yet it is this weather that has not aged, not Amiel's philosophy.

Art seems compromised, historically, socially. Whence the effort on the part of the artist himself to destroy it.

I see this effort taking three forms. The artist can shift to another signifier: if he is a writer, he becomes a filmmaker, a painter, or, contrariwise, if he is a painter, a filmmaker, he works up interminable critiques of the cinema, painting, deliberately reduces the art to his criticism. He can also "dismiss" writing and become a scientist, a scholar, an intellectual theorist, no longer speaking except from a moral site cleansed of any linguistic sensuality. Finally, he can purely and simply scuttle himself, stop writing, change trades, change desires.

Unfortunately, this destruction is always inadequate; either it occurs outside the art, but thereby becomes impertinent, or else it consents to remain within the practice of the art, but quickly exposes itself to recuperation (the avant-garde is that restive language which is going to be recuperated). The awkwardness of this alternative is the consequence of the fact that destruction of discourse is not a dialectic term *but a semantic term*: it docilely takes its place within the great semiological "versus" myth (*white* versus *black*); whence the destruction of art is doomed to only *paradoxical* formulae (those which proceed literally against the *doxa*): both sides of the paradigm are glued together in an ultimately complicitous fashion: there is a structural agreement between the contesting and the contested forms.

(By *subtle subversion* I mean, on the contrary, what is not directly concerned with destruction, evades the paradigm, and seeks some *other* term: a third term, which is not, however, a synthesizing term but an eccentric, extraordinary term. An example? Perhaps Bataille, who eludes the idealist term by an *unexpected* materialism in which we find vice, devotion, play, impossible eroticism, etc.; thus Bataille does not counter modesty with sexual freedom but . . . with *laughter*.)

The text of pleasure is not necessarily the text that recounts pleasures; the text of bliss is never the text that recounts the kind of bliss afforded literally by an ejaculation. The pleasure of representation is not attached to its object: pornography is not *sure*. In zoological terms, one could say that the site of textual pleasure is not the relation of mimic and model (imitative relation) but solely that of dupe and mimic (relation of desire, of production).

We must, however, distinguish between *figuration* and *representation*.

Figuration is the way in which the erotic body appears (to whatever degree and in whatever form that may be) in the profile of the text. For example: the author may appear in his text (Genet, Proust), but not in the guise of direct biography (which would exceed the body, give a meaning to life, forge a destiny). Or again: one can feel desire for a character in a novel (in fleeting impulses). Or finally: the text itself, a diagrammatic and not an imitative structure, can reveal itself in the form of a body, split into fetish objects, into erotic sites. All these movements attest to a *figure* of the text, necessary to the bliss of reading. Similarly, and even more than the text, the film will *always* be figurative (which is why films are still worth making)—even if it represents nothing.

Representation, on the other hand, is *embarrassed figuration*, encumbered with other meanings than that of desire: a space of alibis (reality, morality, likelihood, readability, truth, etc.). Here is a text of pure representation: Barbey d'Aurevilly writes on Memling's Virgin: "She stands upright, very perpendicularly posed. Pure beings are upright. By posture and by movement, we know the chaste woman; wantons droop, languish and lean, always about to fall." Note in passing that the representative undertaking has managed to engender an art (the classical novel) as well as a "science" (graphology, for example, which deduces from the attenuation of a single letter the listlessness of the writer), and that it is consequently fair, without any sophistry, to call it immediately ideological (by the historical extent of its signification). Of course, it very often happens that representation takes desire itself as an object of imitation; but then, such desire never leaves the frame, the picture; it circulates among the characters; if it has a recipient, that recipient remains interior to the fiction (consequently, we can say that any semiotics that keeps desire within the configuration of those upon whom it acts, however new it may be, is a semiotics of representation. That is what representation is: when nothing emerges, when nothing leaps out of the frame: of the picture, the book, the screen).

No sooner has a word been said, somewhere, about the pleasure of the text, than two policemen are ready to jump on you: the political policeman and the psychoanalytical policeman: futility and/or guilt, pleasure is either idle or vain, a class notion or an illusion.

An old, a very old tradition: hedonism has been repressed by nearly every philosophy; we find it defended only by marginal figures, Sade, Fourier; for Nietzsche, hedonism is a pessimism. Pleasure is continually disappointed, reduced, deflated, in favor of strong, noble values: Truth, Death, Progress, Struggle, Joy, etc. Its victorious rival is Desire: we are always being told about Desire, never about Pleasure; Desire has an epistemic dignity, Pleasure does not. It seems that (our) society refuses (and ends up by ignoring) bliss to such a point that it can produce only epistemologies of the law (and of its contestation), never of its absence, or better still: of its nullity. Odd, this philosophical permanence of Desire (insofar as it is never satisfied): doesn't the word itself denote a "class notion"? (A rather crude presumption of proof, and yet noteworthy: the "populace" does not know Desire—only pleasures.)

So-called erotic books (one must add: of recent vintage, in order to except Sade and a few others) *represent* not so much the erotic scene as the expectation of it, the preparation for it, its ascent; that is what makes them "exciting"; and when the scene occurs, naturally there is disappointment, deflation. In other words, these are books of Desire, not of Pleasure. Or, more mischievously, they represent Pleasure *as seen by psychoanalysis*. A like meaning says, in both instances, that *the whole thing is very disappointing*.

(The monument of psychoanalysis must be traversed—not bypassed—like the fine thoroughfares of a very large city, across which we can play, dream, etc.: a fiction.)

There is supposed to be a mystique of the Text. —On the contrary, the whole effort consists in materializing the pleasure of the text, in making the text *an object of pleasure like the others*. That is: either relate the text to the "pleasures" of life (a dish, a garden, an encounter, a voice, a moment, etc.) and to it join the personal catalogue of our sensualities, or force the text to breach bliss, that immense subjective loss, thereby identifying this text with the purest moments of perversion, with its clandestine sites. The important thing is to equalize the field of pleasure, to abolish the false opposition of practical life and contemplative life. The pleasure of the text is just that: claim lodged against the separation of the text; for what the text says, through the particularity of its name, is the ubiquity of pleasure, the atopia of bliss.

Notion of a book (of a text) in which is braided, woven, in the most personal way, the relation of every kind of bliss: those of "life" and those of the text, in which reading and the risks of real life are subject to the same anamnesis.

Imagine an aesthetic (if the word has not become too depreciated) based entirely (completely, radically, in every sense of the word) on the *pleasure of the consumer,* whoever he may be, to whatever class, whatever group he may belong, without respect to cultures or languages: the consequences would be huge, perhaps even harrowing (Brecht has sketched such an aesthetic of pleasure; of all his proposals, this is the one most frequently forgotten).

.   .   .

In antiquity, rhetoric included a section which is forgotten, censored by classical commentators: the *actio*, a group of formulae designed to allow for the corporeal exteriorization of discourse: it dealt with a theater of expression, the actor-orator "expressing" his indignation, his compassion, etc. *Writing aloud* is not expressive; it leaves expression to the pheno-text, to the regular code of communication; it belongs to the geno-text, to significance; it is carried not by dramatic inflections, subtle stresses, sympathetic accents, but by the *grain* of the voice, which is an erotic mixture of timbre and language, and can therefore also be, along with diction, the substance of an art: the art of guiding one's body (whence its importance in Far Eastern theaters). Due allowance being made for the sounds of the language, *writing aloud* is not phonological but phonetic; its aim is not the clarity of messages, the theater of emotions; what it searches for (in a perspective of bliss) are the pulsional incidents, the language lined with flesh, a text where we can hear the grain of the throat, the patina of consonants, the voluptuousness of vowels, a whole carnal stereophony: the articulation of the body, of the tongue, not that of meaning, of language. A certain art of singing can give an idea of this vocal writing; but since melody is dead, we may find it more easily today at the cinema. In fact, it suffices that the cinema capture the sound of speech *close up* (this is, in fact, the generalized definition of the "grain" of writing) and make us hear in their materiality, their sensuality, the breath, the gutturals, the fleshiness of the lips, a whole presence of the human muzzle (that the voice, that writing, be as fresh, supple, lubricated, delicately granular and vibrant as an animal's muzzle), to succeed in shifting the signified a great distance and in throwing, so to speak, the anonymous body of the actor into my ear: it granulates, it crackles, it caresses, it grates, it cuts, it comes: that is bliss.

1973

from *Roland Barthes by Roland Barthes*

Actif/réactif — Active/reactive

In what he writes, there are two texts. Text I is reactive, moved by indignations, fears, unspoken rejoinders, minor paranoias, defenses, scenes. Text II is active, moved by pleasure. But as it is written, corrected, accommodated to the fiction of Style, Text I becomes active too, whereupon it loses its reactive skin, which subsists only in patches (mere parentheses).

. . .

La baladeuse — The caboose

There used to be a white streetcar that ran between Bayonne and Biarritz; in the summer, an open car was attached to it: the caboose. Everyone wanted to ride in that car: through a rather empty countryside, one enjoyed the view, the movement, the fresh air, all at the same time. Today neither the streetcar nor the caboose exists, and the trip from Biarritz is anything but a pleasure. This is not to apply a mythic embel-

Roland Barthes by Roland Barthes, translated by Richard Howard (New York: Hill and Wang, 1977).

lishment to the past, or to express regrets for a lost youth by pretending to regret a streetcar. This is to say that the art of living has no history: it does not evolve: the pleasure which vanishes vanishes for good, there is no substitute for it. Other pleasures come, which replace nothing. *No progress in pleasures*, nothing but mutations.

. . .

Et si je n'avais pas lu . . . — And if I hadn't read . . .

And if I hadn't read Hegel, or *La Princesse de Clèves,* or Lévi-Strauss on *Les Chats*, or *l'Anti-Œdipe*? —The book which I haven't read and which is frequently *told to me* even before I have time to read it (which is perhaps the reason I don't read it): this book exists to the same degree as the other: it has its intelligibility, its memorability, its mode of action. Have we not enough freedom to receive a text *without the letter*?

(Repression: not to have read Hegel would be an exorbitant defect for a philosophy teacher, for a Marxist intellectual, for a Bataille specialist. But for me? Where do my reading duties begin?)

The person who makes a practice of writing agrees cheerfully enough to diminish or to divert the acuity, the responsibility of his ideas (one must risk this in the tone one usually employs in saying: *What does it matter to me? don't I have the essentials?*): in writing there would be the pleasure of a certain inertia, a certain mental *facility*: as if I were more indifferent to my own stupidity when I write than when I speak (how often professors are more intelligent than writers).

. . .

Qu'est-ce que l'influence? — What is influence?

It is clear in the *Critical Essays* how the subject of the
writing "evolves" (shifting from an ethic of commitment to an
ethic of the signifier): he evolves according to the authors he
treats, in order. The inducing object, however, is not the author I am talking about but rather *what he leads me to say
about him*: I influence myself *with his permission*: what I say
about him forces me to think as much about myself (or not to
think as much), etc.

Hence there must be a distinction between the authors
about whom one writes, and whose influence is neither external nor anterior to what one says about them, and (a more
classical conception) the authors whom one reads; but what
comes to me from the latter group? A kind of music, a pensive
sonority, a more or less dense play of anagrams. (I had my
head full of Nietzsche, whom I had just been reading; but what
I wanted, what I was trying to collect, was a song of sentence-
ideas: the influence was purely prosodic.)

. . .

J'aime, je n'aime pas — I like, I don't like

I like: salad, cinnamon, cheese, pimento, marzipan, the
smell of new-cut hay (why doesn't someone with a "nose"
make such a perfume), roses, peonies, lavender, champagne,
loosely held political convictions, Glenn Gould, too-cold beer,
flat pillows, toast, Havana cigars, Handel, slow walks, pears,
white peaches, cherries, colors, watches, all kinds of writing
pens, desserts, unrefined salt, realistic novels, the piano,
coffee, Pollock, Twombly, all romantic music, Sartre, Brecht,
Verne, Fourier, Eisenstein, trains, Médoc wine, having
change, *Bouvard and Pécuchet*, walking in sandals on the

lanes of southwest France, the bend of the Adour seen from Doctor L.'s house, the Marx Brothers, the mountains at seven in the morning leaving Salamanca, etc.

I don't like: white Pomeranians, women in slacks, geraniums, strawberries, the harpsichord, Miró, tautologies, animated cartoons, Arthur Rubinstein, villas, the afternoon, Satie, Bartók, Vivaldi, telephoning, children's choruses, Chopin's concertos, Burgundian branles and Renaissance dances, the organ, Marc-Antoine Charpentier, his trumpets and kettledrums, the politico-sexual, scenes, initiatives, fidelity, spontaneity, evenings with people I don't know, etc.

I like, I don't like: this is of no importance to anyone; this, apparently, has no meaning. And yet all this means: *my body is not the same as yours.* Hence, in this anarchic foam of tastes and distastes, a kind of listless blur, gradually appears the figure of a bodily enigma, requiring complicity or irritation. Here begins the intimidation of the body, which obliges others to endure me *liberally,* to remain silent and polite confronted by pleasures or rejections which they do not share.

(A fly bothers me, I kill it: you kill what bothers you. If I had not killed the fly, it would have been *out of pure liberalism*: I am liberal in order not to be a killer.)

. . .

De l'écriture à l'oeuvre — From writing to the work

Snare of infatuation: to suggest that he is willing to consider what he writes as a work, an *"oeuvre"*—to move from the contingency of writings to the transcendence of a unitary, sacred product. The word *"oeuvre"* is already a part of the image-repertoire.

The contradiction is one between writing and the work (as for the Text, that is a magnanimous word: it shows no partiality to this difference). I delight continuously, endlessly, in writing as in a perpetual production, in an unconditional dispersion, in an energy of seduction which no legal defense of the subject I fling upon the page can any longer halt. But in our mercantile society, one must end up with a work, an "*oeuvre*": one must construct, i.e., *complete*, a piece of merchandise. While I write, the writing is thereby at every moment flattened out, banalized, made guilty by the work to which it must eventually contribute. How to write, given all the snares set by the collective image of the work? —Why, *blindly*. At every moment of the effort, lost, bewildered, and driven, I can only repeat to myself the words which end Sartre's *No Exit*: Let's go on.

Writing is that *play* by which I turn around as well as I can in a narrow place: I am wedged in, I struggle between the hysteria necessary to write and the image-repertoire, which oversees, controls, purifies, banalizes, codifies, corrects, imposes the focus (and the vision) of a social communication. On the one hand I want to be desired and on the other not to be desired: hysterical and obsessional at one and the same time.

And yet: the closer I come to the work, the deeper I descend into writing; I approach its unendurable depth; a desert is revealed; there occurs—fatal, lacerating—a kind of *loss of sympathy*: I no longer feel myself to be *sympathetic* (to others, to myself). It is at this point of contact between the writing and the work that the hard truth appears to me: *I am no longer a child*. Or else, is it the *ascesis* of pleasure which I am discovering?

· · ·

Projets de livres — Projected books

(These ideas are from different periods): *Journal of Desire* (Desire's daily entries, in the field of reality). *The Sentence* (ideology and erotics of the Sentence). *Our France* (new mythologies of today's France; or rather: am I happy/ unhappy to be French?). *The Amateur* (record what happens to me when I paint). *Linguistics of Intimidation* (of Value, of the war of meanings). *A Thousand Fantasies* (to write one's fantasies, not one's dreams). *Ethology of the Intellectuals* (quite as important as the behavior of ants). *The Discourse of Homosexuality* (or: the discourses of homosexuality, or again: the discourse of homosexualities). An *Encyclopedia of Food* (dietetics, history, economy, geography, and above all, *symbolics*). A *Life of Illustrious Men* (read a lot of biographies and collect certain features, biographemes, as was done for Sade and Fourier). A *Compilation of Visual Stereotypes* ("Saw a North African in dark clothes, *Le Monde* under his arm, paying court to a blond girl sitting in a café"). *The Book/Life* (take some classic book and relate everything in life to it for a year). *Incidents* (mini-texts, one-liners, haiku, notations, puns, everything that falls, like a leaf), etc.

. . .

La seiche et son encre — The cuttlefish and its ink

I am writing this day after day; it takes, it sets: the cuttlefish produces its ink: I tie up my image-system (in order to protect myself and at the same time to offer myself).

How will I know that the book is finished? In other words, as always, it is a matter of elaborating a language. Now, in every language the signs return, and by dint of returning they end by saturating the lexicon—the work. Having uttered the substance of these fragments for some months, what happens to me subsequently is arranged quite spontaneously (without forcing) under the utterances that have already been made: the structure is gradually woven, and in creating itself, it increasingly magnetizes: thus it constructs for itself, without any plan on my part, a repertoire which is both finite and perpetual, like that of language. At a certain moment, no further transformation is possible but the one which occurred to the ship *Argo*: I could keep the book a very long time, by gradually changing each of its fragments.

Projet d'un livre sur la sexualité
— A projected book on sexuality

A young couple comes into my compartment and sits down; the woman is blond, made up; she is wearing big dark glasses, reads *Paris-Match*; she has a ring on each finger, and each nail on both hands is painted a different color from its two neighbors; the nail of the middle finger, a shorter nail painted a deep carmine, broadly designates the finger of masturbation. From this—from the *enchantment* this couple casts upon me, so that I cannot take my eyes off them—comes the idea of a book (or of a film) in which there would be, in this way, nothing but secondary sex characteristics (nothing pornographic); in it one would grasp (would try to grasp) the sexual "personality" of each body, which is neither its beauty nor even its "sexiness" but the way in which each sexuality immediately lets itself be read; for the young blonde with the harlequin nails and her young husband with his tight pants and warm eyes were wearing their couple-sexuality like the legion-of-honor ribbon in a buttonhole (*sexuality* and *respectability* relating to the same kind of display), and this *legible* sexuality (as Michelet would certainly have read it) filled the compartment, by an irresistible metonymy, much more certainly than any series of coquetries.

Le sexy — Sexiness

Different from secondary sexuality, the sexiness of a body (which is not its beauty) inheres in the fact that it is possible to discern (to fantasize) in it the erotic practice to which one subjects it in thought (I conceive of this particular practice, specifically, and of no other). Similarly, distinguished within the text, one might say that there are *sexy sentences*: disturbing by their very isolation, as if they possessed the promise which is made to us, the readers, by a linguistic practice, as if we were to seek them out by virtue of a pleasure *which knows what it wants*.

. . .

Plus tard — Later

He has a certain foible of providing "introductions," "sketches," "elements," postponing the "real" book till later. This foible has a rhetorical name: *prolepsis* (well discussed by Genette).

Here are some of these projected books: a History of Writing, a History of Rhetoric, a History of Etymology, a new Stylistics, an Aesthetics of textual pleasure, a new linguistic science, a Linguistics of Value, an inventory of the languages of love, a fiction based on the notion of an urban Robinson Crusoe, a summa on the *petite bourgeoisie*, a book on France entitled—in the manner of Michelet—*Our France*, etc.

These projects, generally heralding a summative, excessive book, parodic of the great monument of knowledge, can only be simple acts of discourse (prolepses indeed); they belong to the category of the dilatory. But the dilatory, denial of reality (of the realizable), is no less alive for all that: these projects live, they are never abandoned; suspended, they can return to life at any moment; or at least, like the persistent trace of an obsession, they fulfill themselves, partially, indirectly, *as gestures*, through themes, fragments, articles: the History of Writing (postulated in 1953) engenders twenty years later the idea of a seminar on a history of French discourse; the Linguistics of Value, however remotely, orients this very book. *The mountain gives birth to a mouse?* This disdainful proverb must be reversed in a positive sense: the mountain is not any too much to make a mouse.

Fourier never describes his books as anything but the heralds of the perfect Book, which he will publish later (perfectly clear, perfectly persuasive, perfectly complex). The Annunciation of the Book (the *Prospectus*) is one of those dilatory maneuvers which control our internal utopia. I imagine, I fantasize, I embellish, and I polish the great book of which I am incapable: it is a book of learning and of writing, at once a perfect system and the mockery of all systems, a summa of intelligence and of pleasure, a vengeful and tender book, corrosive and pacific, etc. (here, a foam of adjectives, an explosion of the image-repertoire); in short, it has all the qualities of a hero in a novel: it is the one coming (the *adventure*), and I herald this book that makes me my own John the Baptist, I prophesy, I announce . . .

If he often foresees books to write (which he does not write), it is because he postpones until later what bores him. Or rather, he wants to write *right away* what it pleases him to write, and not something else. In Michelet, what makes him want to rewrite are those carnal themes, the coffee, the blood, the sisal, the wheat, etc.; thus one will construct a thematic criticism for oneself, but in order not to risk it theoretically against another school—historical, biographical, etc.—for the fantasy is too egoistic to be polemical, one declares that one is concerned with no more than a *precriticism*, and that the "real" criticism (which is that of other people) will come later.

Being incessantly short of time (or you imagine yourself to be), caught up in deadlines and delays, you persist in supposing that you are going to get out of it by putting what you have to do in order. You make programs, draw up plans, calendars, new deadlines. On your desk and in your files, how many lists of articles, books, seminars, courses to teach, telephone calls to make. As a matter of fact, you never consult these little slips of paper, given the fact that an anguished conscience has provided you with an excellent memory of all your obligations. But it is irrepressible: you extend the time you lack by the very registration of that lack. Let us call this *program compulsion* (whose hypomaniacal character one readily divines); states and collectivities, apparently, are not exempt from it: how much time wasted in *drawing up programs*? And since I anticipate writing an article on it, the very notion of program itself becomes a part of my program compulsion.

Now let us reverse all this: these dilatory maneuvers, these endlessly receding projects may be writing itself. First of all, the work is never anything but the metabook (the temporary commentary) of a work to come which, *not being written*, becomes this work itself: Proust, Fourier never wrote anything but such a "Prospectus." Afterward, the work is never monumental: it is a *proposition* which each will come to saturate as he likes, as he can: I bestow upon you a certain semantic substance to run through, like a ferret. Finally, the work is a (theatrical) *rehearsal*, and this rehearsal, as in one of Rivette's films, is verbose, infinite, interlaced with commentaries, excursuses, shot through with other matters. In a word, the work is a tangle; its being is the *degree*, the step: a staircase that never stops.

. . .

1975

from *A Lover's Discourse*

IN PRAISE OF TEARS

pleurer / crying

The amorous subject has a particular propensity to cry: the functioning and appearance of tears in this subject.

1. The slightest amorous emotion, whether of happiness or of disappointment, brings Werther to tears. Werther weeps often, very often, and in floods. Is it the lover in Werther who weeps, or is it the romantic?

Werther

It is perhaps a disposition proper to the amorous type, this propensity to dissolve in tears? Subjected to the Image-repertoire, he flouts the censure which today forbids the adult tears and by which a man means to protest his virility (Piaf's satisfaction and maternal tenderness: *"Mais vous pleurez, Milord!"*). By releasing his tears without constraint, he follows the orders of the amorous body, which is a body in liquid expansion, a bathed body: to weep

A Lover's Discourse, translated by Richard Howard (New York: Hill and Wang, 1978).

together, to flow together: delicious tears finish off the reading of Klopstock which Charlotte and Werther perform together. Where does the lover obtain the right to cry, if not in a reversal of values, of which the body is the first target? He accepts rediscovering the *infant body*.

Further, here, the amorous body is doubled by a historical one. Who will write the history of tears? In which societies, in which periods, have we wept? Since when is it that men (and not women) no longer cry? Why was "sensibility," at a certain moment, transformed into "sentimentality"? The images of virility are shifting; the Greeks as well as our audiences of the seventeenth century cried a great deal at the theater. St. Louis, according to Michelet, suffered at not having received the gift of tears; on the one occasion that he felt tears running gently down his face, "They seemed to him delectable and comforting, not only to the heart but to the tongue." (Similarly: in 1199, a young monk set out for a Cistercian abbey in Brabant in order to obtain, by the tears of its inmates, the gift of tears.)

(A Nietzschean problem: How do History and Type combine? Is it not up to the type to formulate—to form—what is out of time, ahistorical? In the lover's very tears, our society represses its own timelessness, thereby turning the weeping lover into a lost object whose repression is necessary to its "health." In Rohmer's film *The Marquise of O*, the lovers weep and the audience giggles.)

2.   Perhaps "weeping" is too crude; perhaps we must not refer all tears to one and the same signification; per-

SCHUBERT: *"Lob der Tränen"* (In Praise of Tears), poem by A. W. Schlegel.

haps within the same lover there are several subjects who engage in neighboring but different modes of "weeping." Which is that "I" who has "tears in my eyes"? Which is that other self who, on a certain day, was "on the verge of tears"? Who am I who pours out "all the tears in my body"? or who sheds, upon waking, "a torrent of tears"? If I have so many ways of crying, it may be because, when I cry, I always address myself to someone, and because the recipient of my tears is not always the same: I adapt my ways of weeping to the kind of blackmail which, by my tears, I mean to exercise around me.

3.   By weeping, I want to impress someone, to bring pressure to bear upon someone ("Look what you have done to me"). It can be—as is commonly the case—the other whom one thus constrains to assume his commiseration or his insensibility quite openly; but it can also be oneself: I make myself cry, in order to prove to myself that my grief is not an illusion: tears are signs, not expressions. By my tears, I tell a story, I produce a myth of grief, and henceforth I adjust myself to it: I can live with it, because, by weeping, I give myself an emphatic interlocutor who receives the "truest" of messages, that of my body, not that of my speech: "Words, what are they? One tear will say more than all of them."

Schubert

GOSSIP

potin / gossip

Pain suffered by the amorous subject when he finds that the loved being is the subject of "gossip" and hears that being discussed promiscuously.

SCHUBERT: *"Lob der Tränen."*

1.   On the road from Phalerum, a bored traveler catches sight of another man walking ahead of him, catches up and asks him to tell about the banquet given by Agathon. Such is the genesis of the theory of love: an accident, boredom, a desire to talk, or, if you will, a gossip lasting a little over a mile. Aristodemus has been to the famous banquet; he has described it to Apollodorus, who, on the road from Phalerum, tells the story of Glaucon (a man, it is said, without any philosophic culture) and thereby, by the book's mediation, tells it to us, who are still discussing it. The *Symposium* is therefore not only a "conversation" (we are discussing a question) but also a gossip (we are speaking together about others).

This work derives, then, from two different linguistic series, generally repressed—since official linguistics concerns itself only with the message. The first series would postulate that no question (*quaestio*) can be put without the texture of an interlocution; to speak of love, the guests not only speak together, *from image to image, from place to place* (in the *Symposium*, the arrangement of the couches has a great importance), but further imply in this general discourse the amorous links which bind them (or which they imagine bind the others): such would be the linguistics of "conversation." The second series would say that to speak is always to say something about someone; in speaking about the banquet, about Love, it is about Socrates, about Alcibiades, and about their friends that Glaucon and Apollodorus are talking: the "subject" comes to light by gossip. An active philology (that of the forces of language) would therefore include two necessary

SYMPOSIUM: Beginning.
SYMPOSIUM: Agathon: "Come here, O Socrates, take the couch next to mine, so that I might benefit by the wise thoughts that have struck you out there on the porch." And Alcibiades's entrance.

linguistic series: that of interlocution (speaking to another) and that of delocution (speaking about someone).

Werther

2.   Werther has not yet made Charlotte's acquaint-
ance; but in the carriage taking him to the ball (which is
to pass Charlotte on the way), a friend—the voice of
Gossip—discusses for Werther's benefit the woman whose
image will in a few seconds so delight him: she is already
engaged, he must not fall in love with her, etc. Thus gossip
summarizes and heralds the story to come. Gossip is the
voice of truth (Werther will fall in love with an object
belonging to another), and this voice is magical: the
friend is a wicked fairy who, under cover of admonish-
ment, predicts and enforces.

When the friend speaks, her discourse is insensitive (a
fairy has no pity): the gossip is light, cold, it thereby
assumes the status of a kind of objectivity; its voice, in
short, seems to double the voice of knowledge (*scientia*).
These two voices are reductive. When knowledge, when
science speaks, I sometimes come to the point of hearing
its discourse as the sound of a gossip which describes and
disparages lightly, coldly, and objectively what I love:
which speaks of what I love *according to truth*.

3.   Gossip reduces the other to *he/she*, and this reduction is intolerable to me. For me the other is neither *he*
nor *she*; the other has only a name of his own, and her
own name. The third-person pronoun is a wicked pronoun: it is the pronoun of the non-person, it absents, it
annuls. When I realize that common discourse takes possession of my other and restores that other to me in the
bloodless form of a universal substitute, applied to all the
things which are not here, it is as if I saw my other dead,

reduced, shelved in an urn upon the wall of the great mausoleum of language. For me, the other cannot be a *referent*: you are never anything but you, I do not want the Other to speak of you.

WHY?

pourquoi / why

Even as he obsessively asks himself why he is not loved, the amorous subject lives in the belief that the loved object does love him but does not tell him so.

1.   There exists a "higher value" for me: my love. I never say to myself: "What's the use?" I am not nihilistic. I do not ask myself the question of ends. Never a "why" in my monotonous discourse, except for one, always the same: *But why is it that you don't love me?* How can one not love this *me* whom love renders perfect (who gives so much, who confers happiness, etc.)? A question whose insistence survives the amorous episode: "Why didn't you love me?"; or again: *O sprich, mein herzallerliebstes Lieb, warum verliessest du mich?*—O tell, love of my heart, why have you abandoned me?

2.   Soon (or simultaneously) the question is no longer "Why don't you love me?" but "Why do you only love me *a little*?" How do you manage to love *a little*? What does that mean, loving "a little"? I live under the regime of *too much* or *not enough*; greedy for coincidence as I am, everything which is not total seems parsimonious; what I

Nietzsche

Heine

NIETZSCHE: "What does nihilism signify? *That the higher values are losing their value.* The ends are lacking, there is no answer to this question 'What's the use?' "
HEINE: "*Lyrisches Intermezzo.*"

want is to occupy a site *from which quantities are no longer perceived*, and from which all accounts are banished.

Or again—for I am a nominalist: Why don't you *tell me* that you love me?

Freud

3.   The truth of the matter is that—by an exorbitant paradox—I never stop believing that I am loved. I hallucinate what I desire. Each wound proceeds less from a doubt than from a betrayal: for only the one who loves can betray, only the one who believes himself loved can be jealous: that the other, episodically, should fail in his being, which is to love me—that is the origin of all my woes. A delirium, however, does not exist unless one wakens from it (there are only retrospective deliriums): one day, I realize what has happened to me: I thought I was suffering from not being loved, and yet it is because I thought I was loved that I was suffering; I lived in the complication of supposing myself simultaneously loved and abandoned. Anyone hearing my intimate language would have had to exclaim, as of a difficult child: *But after all, what does he want?*

(*I love you* becomes *you love me*. One day, X receives some orchids, anonymously: he immediately hallucinates their source: they could only come from the person who loves him; and the person who loves him could only be the person he loves. It is only after a long period of investigation that he manages to dissociate the two inferences: the person who loves him is not necessarily the person he loves.)

FREUD: "We must take into account the fact that the hallucinatory psychosis of desire not only . . . brings concealed or repressed desires to consciousness but, further, represents them in all good faith as realized."

RAVISHMENT

ravissement / ravishment

The supposedly initial episode (though it may be reconstructed after the fact) during which the amorous subject is "ravished" (captured and enchanted) by the image of the loved object (popular name: *love at first sight*; scholarly name: enamoration). Imagining himself dead, the amorous subject sees the loved being's life continue as if nothing had happened.

Djedidi

1.   Language (vocabulary) has long since posited the equivalence of love and war: in both cases, it is a matter of *conquering, ravishing, capturing,* etc. Each time a subject "falls" in love, he revives a fragment of the archaic time when men were supposed to carry off women (in order to ensure exogamy): every lover who falls in love at first sight has something of a Sabine Woman (or of some other celebrated victim of ravishment).

However, there is an odd turnabout here: in the ancient myth, the ravisher is active, he wants to seize his prey, he is the subject of the rape (of which the object is a Woman, as we know, invariably passive); in the modern myth (that of love-as-passion), the contrary is the case: the ravisher wants nothing, does nothing; he is motionless (as any image), and it is the ravished object who is the real subject of the rape; the *object* of capture becomes the *subject* of love; and the *subject* of the conquest moves into the class of loved *object*. (There nonetheless remains a public vestige of the archaic model: the lover—the one who has been ravished—is always implicitly feminized.)

DJEDIDI, *La Poésie amoureuse des Arabes*: in Arabic, for instance, *fitna* refers to both material (or ideological) warfare and the enterprise of sexual seduction.

This singular reversal may perhaps proceed from the fact that for us the "subject" (since Christianity) is *the one who suffers*: where there is a wound, there is a subject: *die Wunde! die Wunde!* says Parsifal, thereby becoming "himself"; and the deeper the wound, at the body's center (at the "heart"), the more the subject becomes a subject: for the subject is *intimacy* ("The wound . . . is of a frightful intimacy"). Such is love's wound: a radical chasm (at the "roots" of being), which cannot be closed, and out of which the subject drains, constituting himself as a subject in this very draining. It would suffice to imagine our Sabine Woman wounded to make her into the *subject* of a love story.

Parsifal

Ruysbroeck

2.   Love at first sight is a hypnosis: I am fascinated by an image: at first shaken, electrified, stunned, "paralyzed" as Menon was by Socrates, the model of loved objects, of captivating images, or again converted by an apparition, nothing distinguishing the path of enamoration from the Road to Damascus; subsequently ensnared, held fast, immobilized, nose stuck to the image (the mirror). In that moment when the other's image comes to ravish me for the first time, I am nothing more than the Jesuit Athanasius Kirchner's wonderful Hen: feet tied, the hen went to sleep with her eyes fixed on the chalk line, which was traced not far from her beak; when she was untied, she remained motionless, fascinated, "submitting to her vanquisher," as the Jesuit says (1646); yet, to waken her from her enchantment, to break off the violence of her Image-repertoire (*vehemens animalis imaginatio*), it was enough to

Athanasius Kirchner

RUYSBROECK: "The marrow of the bones wherein the roots of life reside is the center of the wound . . . The gaping thing which is deep within man does not readily close."

ATHANASIUS KIRCHNER: *Experimentum mirabile de imaginatione gallinae.*

tap her on the wing; she shook herself and began pecking in the dust again.

Freud

3.   The hypnotic episode, it is said, is ordinarily preceded by a twilight state: the subject is in a sense empty, available, offered unwittingly to the rape which will surprise him. In the same way Werther describes at some length the trivial life he leads at Wahlheim before meeting Charlotte: no mundanity, no leisure, only reading Homer, a kind of blank and prosaic daily round, lulling him (he has nothing but pease porridge). This "wondrous serenity" is merely a waiting—a desire: I never fall in love unless I have wanted to; the emptiness I produce in myself (and on which, like Werther, quite innocently, I pride myself) is nothing but that interval, longer or shorter, when I glance around me, without seeming to, looking for *who to love*. Of course love requires a release switch, just as in the case of animal rape; the bait is occasional, but the structure is profound, regular, just as the mating season is seasonal. Yet the myth of "love at first sight" is so powerful (something that falls over me, without my expecting it, without my wanting it, without my taking the least part in it) that we are astonished if we hear of someone's *deciding* to fall in love: for example, Amadour seeing Florida at the court of the Viceroy of Catalonia: "After having gazed at her a long while, *he determined upon loving her": se délibéra*. Indeed, shall I deliberate if I must go mad (is love, then, that madness *I want*?)?

4.   In the animal world, the release switch of the sexual mechanism is not a specific individual but only a form, a bright-colored fetish (which is how the Image-repertoire starts up). In the fascinating image, what impresses me (like a sensitized paper) is not the accumulation of its

Werther appears in the left margin alongside the paragraph, and *ameron* (Heptameron) appears in the left margin lower down.

details but this or that inflection. What suddenly manages to touch me (ravish me) in the other is the voice, the line of the shoulders, the slenderness of the silhouette, the warmth of the hand, the curve of a smile, etc. Whereupon, what does the aesthetic of the image matter? Something accommodates itself exactly to my desire (about which I know nothing); I shall therefore make no concessions to style. Sometimes it is the other's conformity to a great cultural model which enthralls me (I imagine I see the other painted by an artist of the past); sometimes, on the contrary, it is a certain insolence of the apparition which will open the wound: I can fall in love with a slightly vulgar attitude (assumed out of provocation): there are subtle, evanescent trivialities which swiftly pass over the other's body: a brief (but excessive) way of parting the fingers, of spreading the legs, of moving the fleshy part of the lips in eating, of going about some very prosaic occupation, of making one's body utterly idiotic for an instant, to keep oneself in countenance (what is fascinating about the other's "triviality" is just this, perhaps: that for a very brief interval I surprise in the other, detached from the rest of his person, something like a gesture of prostitution). The feature which touches me refers to a fragment of behavior, to the fugitive moment of an attitude, a posture, in short to a *scheme* (σχῆμα, *schema*, is the body in movement, in situation, in life).

Flaubert

etymology

5.   Stepping out of the carriage, Werther sees Charlotte for the first time (and falls in love with her), framed by the door of her house (cutting bread-and-butter for the

---

FLAUBERT: "And it seems that you are here, when I read love stories in books. —Everything that is taxed with being exaggerated, you have made me feel, Frédéric said. I understand how Werther could behave that way about Charlotte's bread-and-butter" (*Sentimental Education*).
ETYMOLOGY: *Trivialis*: to be found at every crossroads (*trivium*).

children: a famous scene, often discussed): the first thing
we love is *a scene*. For love at first sight requires the very

Lacan

sign of its suddenness (what makes me irresponsible, subject to fatality, swept away, ravished): and of all the arrangements of objects, it is the scene which seems to be
seen best for the first time: a curtain parts: what had not
yet ever been seen is discovered in its entirety, and then
devoured by the eyes: what is immediate stands for what
is fulfilled: I am initiated: the scene *consecrates* the object
I am going to love.

Anything is likely to ravish me which can reach me
through a ring, a rip, a rent: "The first time I saw X
through a car window: the window shifted, like a lens
searching out *who to love* in the crowd; and then—
immobilized by some *accuracy* of my desire?—I focused
on that apparition whom I was henceforth to follow for
months; but the other, as if he sought to resist this fresco
in which he was lost as a subject, whenever he was subsequently to appear in my field of vision (walking into the
café where I was waiting for him, for example) did so
with every precaution, *a minimo*, impregnating his body
with discretion and a kind of indifference, delaying his
recognition of me, etc.: in short, trying to keep himself out
of the picture."

Is the scene always visual? It can be aural, the frame can
be linguistic: I can fall in love with *a sentence spoken to
me*: and not only because it says something which manages to touch my desire, but because of its syntactical turn
(framing), which will inhabit me *like a memory*.

6.   When Werther "discovers" Charlotte (when the
curtain parts and the scene appears), Charlotte is cutting

LACAN: *Le Séminaire*, I.

Freud

bread-and-butter. What Hanold falls in love with is a woman walking (*Gradiva*: the one who comes toward him), and furthermore glimpsed within the frame of a bas-relief. What fascinates, what ravishes me is the image of a body *in situation*. What excites me is an outline in action, *which pays no attention to me*: Grusha, the young servant, makes a powerful impression on the Wolf-man: she is on her knees, scrubbing the floor. For the posture of action, of labor, guarantees, in a way, *the innocence of the image*: the more the other grants me signs of his occupation, of his indifference, of my absence, the surer I am of surprising him, as if, in order to fall in love, I had to perform the ancestral formality of rape, i.e., surprise (I surprise the other and thereby he surprises me: I did not expect to surprise him).

7.   There is a deception in amorous time (this deception is called: the love story). I believe (along with everyone else) that the amorous phenomenon is an "episode" endowed with a beginning (love at first sight) and an end (suicide, abandonment, disaffection, withdrawal, monastery, travel, etc.). Yet the initial scene during which I was ravished is merely reconstituted: it is *after the fact*. I reconstruct a traumatic image which I experience in the present but which I conjugate (which I speak) in the past:

Racine

Je le vis, je rougis, je pâlis à sa vue.
Un trouble s'éleva dans mon âme éperdue.
I saw him, blushed, turned pale when our eyes met.
Confusion seized my bewildered soul.

FREUD: *The Wolf-man.*
RACINE: *Phèdre.*

Love at first sight is always spoken in the past tense: it
might be called an *anterior immediacy*. The image is perfectly adapted to this temporal deception: distinct, abrupt,
framed, it is already (again, always) a memory (the nature of the photograph is not to represent but to memori-
alize): when I "review" the scene of the rape, I retrospectively create a stroke of luck: this scene has all the
magnificence of an accident: I cannot get over having had
this good fortune: to meet what matches my desire; or to
J.-L.B.   have taken this huge risk: instantly to submit to an unknown image (and the entire reconstructed scene functions like the sumptuous montage of an ignorance).

REGRETTED?

regretté / regretted

Imagining himself dead, the amorous subject sees the loved being's
life continue as if nothing had happened.

1.   Werther overhears Lotte and one of her friends
gossiping; they are talking quite indifferently about a dying
Werther   man: "And yet . . . if you were to die, if you vanished out
of their lives? . . . Would your friends even notice? How
deeply would they feel the loss? How long would your
disappearance affect their destiny? . . ."

Not that I imagine myself dying without leaving regrets
behind: the obituary is determined: rather that through
the mourning itself, which I do not deny, I *see* the lives of
others continuing, without change; I see them persevering
in their occupations, their pastimes, their problems, fre-
quenting the same places, the same friends; nothing would

J.-L.B.: Conversation.

change in the train of their existence. Out of love, the
delirious assumption of Dependence (I have an *absolute*
need of the other), is generated, quite cruelly, the adverse
position: no one has any real need of me.

J.-L.B.   (Only the Mother can regret: to be depressed, it is said, is
to resemble the Mother as I imagine her regretting me
eternally: a dead, motionless image out of the *nekuia*; but
the others are not the Mother: for them, mourning; for
me, depression.)

2.   What increases Werther's panic is that the dying
man (in whom he projects himself) is being *gossiped*
about: Charlotte and her friends are "silly women" speaking frivolously about death. I envision myself nibbled up
by others' words, dissolved in the ether of Gossip. And the
Gossip will continue without my constituting any further
part of it, no longer its object: a linguistic energy, trivial
and tireless, will triumph over my very memory.

"HOW BLUE THE SKY WAS"

rencontre / encounter

The figure refers to the happy interval immediately following the
first ravishment, before the difficulties of the amorous relationship
begin.

1.   Though the lover's discourse is no more than a dust
of figures stirring according to an unpredictable order, like
a fly buzzing in a room, I can assign to love, at least
retrospectively, according to my Image-repertoire, a settled course: it is by means of this *historical* hallucination

J.-L.B.: Conversation.

that I sometimes make love into a romance, an adventure. This would appear to assume three stages (or three acts): first comes the instantaneous capture (I am ravished by an image); then a series of encounters (dates, telephone calls, letters, brief trips), during which I ecstatically "explore" the perfection of the loved being, i.e., the unhoped-for correspondence between an object and my desire: this is the sweetness of the beginning, the interval proper to the idyll. This happy period acquires its identity (its limits) from its opposition (at least in memory) to the "sequel": the "sequel" is the long train of sufferings, wounds, anxieties, distresses, resentments, despairs, embarrassments, and deceptions to which I fall prey, ceaselessly living under the threat of a downfall which would envelop at once the other, myself, and the glamorous encounter that first revealed us to each other.

Ronsard

2. Some lovers do not commit suicide: it is possible for me to emerge from that "tunnel" which follows the amorous encounter. I see daylight again, either because I manage to grant unhappy love a dialectical outcome (retaining the love but getting rid of the hypnosis) or because I abandon that love altogether and set out again, trying to reiterate, with others, the encounter whose dazzlement remains with me: for it is of the order of the "first pleasure" and I cannot rest until it recurs: I affirm the affirmation, I begin again, without repeating.

(The encounter is radiant; later on, in memory, the subject will telescope into one the three moments of the

RONSARD: *"Quand je fus pris au doux commencement*
D'une douceur si doucettement douce . . ."

When I was caught up in the sweet beginning
Of a sweetness so deliciously sweet . . . ("*Doux fut le trait*")

amorous trajectory; he will speak of "love's dazzling tunnel.")

3.   In the encounter, I marvel that I have found someone who, by successive touches, each one successful, unfailing, completes the painting of my hallucination; I am like a gambler whose luck cannot fail, so that his hand unfailingly lands on the little piece which immediately completes the puzzle of his desire. This is a gradual discovery (and a kind of verification) of affinities, complicities, and intimacies which I shall (I imagine) eternally sustain with the other, who is thereby becoming "my other": I am totally given over to this discovery (I tremble within it), to the point where any intense curiosity for someone encountered is more or less equivalent to love (it is certainly love which the young Moraïte feels for the traveler Chateaubriand, greedily watching his slightest gesture and following him until his departure). At every moment of the encounter, I discover in the other another myself: *You like this? So do I! You don't like that? Neither do I!* When Buvard and Pécuchet meet for the first time, they marvel over the catalogue of their shared tastes: the scene, beyond all doubt, is a love scene. The Encounter casts upon the (already ravished) amorous subject the dazzlement of a supernatural stroke of luck: love belongs to the (Dionysiac) order of the Cast of the dice.

Chateau-
briand

Buvard and
Pécuchet

(Neither knows the other yet. Hence they must tell each other: "This is what I am." This is narrative bliss, the kind which both fulfills and delays knowledge, in a word,

R.H.

CHATEAUBRIAND: *Travels in Egypt, Palestine, Greece and Barbary.*
R.H.: Conversation.

restarts it. In the amorous encounter, I keep rebounding—
I am *light*.)

REVERBERATION

retentissement / reverberation

Fundamental mode of amorous subjectivity: a word, an image
reverberates painfully in the subject's affective consciousness.

1.   What echoes in me is what I learned with my body:
something sharp and tenuous suddenly wakens this body,
which, meanwhile, had languished in the rational knowledge of a general situation: the word, the image, the
thought function like a whiplash. My inward body begins
vibrating as though shaken by trumpets answering each
other, drowning each other out: the incitation leaves its
trace, the trace widens and everything is (more or less
rapidly) ravaged. In the lover's Image-repertoire, nothing
distinguishes the most trivial provocation from an au-
thentically consequent phenomenon; time is jerked forward (catastrophic predictions flood to my mind) and
back (I remember certain "precedents" with terror):
starting from a negligible trifle, a whole discourse of memory and death rises up and sweeps me away: this is the
kingdom of memory, weapon of reverberation—of what
Nietzsche called *ressentiment*.

(Reverberation comes from Diderot's "unforeseen incident which . . . suddenly alters the state of the characters": it is a *coup de théâtre*, the "favorable moment" of a
painting: pathetic scene of the ravaged, prostrated subject.)

2.　　The space of reverberation is the body—that imaginary body, so "coherent" (coalescent) that I can experience it only in the form of a generalized pang. This pang (analogous to a blush which reddens the face, with shame or emotion) is a sudden panic. In the usual kind of panic—the stage fright which precedes some sort of performance—I see myself in the future in a condition of failure, imposture, scandal. In amorous panic, I am afraid of my own destruction, which I suddenly glimpse, inevitable, clearly formed, in the flash of a word, an image.

Diderot

3.　　When his sentences ran dry, Flaubert flung himself on his divan: he called this his "marinade." If the thing reverberates too powerfully, it makes such a din in my body that I must halt any occupation; I stretch out on my bed and give in without a struggle to the "inner storm"; contrary to the Zen monk who empties himself of his images, I let myself be filled by them, I indulge their bitterness to the full. Depression has its own—encoded—*gestus*, then, and doubtless that is what limits it; for it suffices that at a given moment I can substitute another (even blank) gesture for this one (getting up, going to my desk, without necessarily working there, right away), to make the reverberation die down, giving way to no more than *ennui*. The bed (by day) is the site of the Image-repertoire; the desk is once again, and whatever one does there, reality.

Ruysbroeck

4.　　X tells me about a disagreeable rumor which concerns me. This incident reverberates within me in two ways: on the one hand, I receive the object of the message at point-blank range, outraged by its imposture, eager to

DIDEROT: "The word is not the thing, but a flash in whose light we perceive the thing."

deny it, etc.; on the other hand, I am perfectly conscious of the little impulse of aggression which has impelled X— without his being exactly aware of it himself—to pass on this wounding intelligence. Traditional linguistics would analyze only the message: conversely, active Philology would try especially to interpret, to evaluate the (here, reactive) force which directs (or attracts) it. Now, what is it that I do? I conjugate the two linguistic series, amplify them by each other: I establish myself, however painfully, in the very substance of the message (i.e., the content of the rumor), while I bitterly and mistrustfully scrutinize the force which warrants it: I lose on both counts, wounded on all sides. This is reverberation: the zealous practice of a perfect reception: contrary to the analyst (and with reason), far from "floating" while the other speaks, I listen *completely*, in a state of total consciousness: I cannot keep from hearing everything, and it is the purity of this reception which is painful to me: who can tolerate without pain a meaning that is complex and yet purified of any "noise" or interference? Reverberation makes reception into an intelligible din, and the lover into a monstrous receiver, reduced to an enormous auditive organ—as if listening itself were to become a state of utterance: in me, it is the ear which speaks.

AUBADE

réveil / waking

Various modes by which the amorous subject finds upon waking that he is once again besieged by the anxieties of his passion.

Werther 1.   Werther speaks of his exhaustion ("Let me suffer to the end: for all my exhaustion, I still have strength enough for that"). Amorous anxiety involves an expenditure which tires the body as harshly as any physical labor. "I suffered so much," someone said, "I struggled so hard all day with the image of the loved being, that I always slept very well at night." And Werther, shortly before committing suicide, goes to bed and sleeps very soundly.

S.S.

Werther

2.   Modes of waking: sad, wracked (with tenderness), affectless, innocent, panic-stricken (Octave comes to, after fainting: "All of a sudden his miseries were clear in his mind: one does not die of pain, or he was a dead man at that moment").

Stendhal

MAKING SCENES

scène / scene

The figure comprehends every "scene" (in the household sense of the term) as an exchange of reciprocal contestations.

1.   When two subjects argue according to a set exchange of remarks and with a view to having the "last word," these two subjects are *already* married: for them the scene is an exercise of a right, the practice of a language of which they are co-owners; *each one in his turn*, says the scene, which means: *never you without me*, and reciprocally. This is the meaning of what is euphemistically called *dialogue*: not to listen to each other, but to submit in common to an egalitarian principle of the distribution of language goods. The partners know that the confrontation in which they are engaged, and which will not separate them, is as inconsequential as a perverse

s.s.: Reported by S.S.
STENDHAL: *Armance*.

form of pleasure (the scene is a way of taking pleasure without the risk of having children).

With the first scene, language begins its long career as an agitated, useless thing. It is dialogue (the joust of two actors) which corrupted Tragedy, even before Socrates appeared on the scene. Monologue is thereby pushed back to the very limits of humanity: in archaic tragedy, in certain forms of schizophrenia, in amorous soliloquy (at least as long as I "keep" my delirium and do not yield to the desire to draw the other into a set contestation of language). It is as if the proto-actor, the madman, and the lover refused to posit themselves as hero of speech and to submit to adult language, the social language to which they are prompted by the wicked *Eris*: the language of universal neurosis.

2.   *Werther* is pure discourse of the amorous subject: the (idyllic, anguished) monologue is broken only once, at the end, just before the suicide: Werther pays a visit to Charlotte, who asks him not to come and see her again before Christmas Day, thereby signifying to him that he must visit less frequently and that henceforth his passion will no longer be "received": there follows a scene. The scene starts with a disagreement: Charlotte is embarrassed, Werther is excited, and Charlotte's embarrassment excites Werther all the more: thus the scene has only one subject, divided by a differential of energy (the scene is *electric*). So that this disequilibrium can *catch* (like a motor), so that the scene can get into its proper gear,

NIETZSCHE: "There already had existed something analogous in the exchange of remarks between the hero and the choryphaeus, but since the one was subordinate to the other, dialectical *combat* was impossible. But once two principal characters stood face to face, there was born, conforming to a profoundly Hellenic instinct, the battle of words and of arguments: amorous dialogue [what we mean by *the scene*] was unknown to Greek tragedy."

there must be a bait or decoy which each of the two partners tries to draw into his own camp; this bait is usually a fact (which one affirms and the other denies) or a decision (which one imposes and the other rejects: in *Werther*, to visit less frequently). Agreement is logically impossible insofar as what is being argued is not the fact or the decision, i.e., something which is outside language, but only precedes it: the scene has no object or at least very soon loses its object: it is that language whose object is lost. It is characteristic of the individual remarks in a scene to have no demonstrative, persuasive end, but only an origin, and this origin is never anything but immediate: in the scene, I cling to what has just been said. The (divided and yet mutual) subject of the scene is uttered in distichs: this is stichomythia, the archaic model of all the scenes in the world (when we are in a "state of scene," we speak in "rows" of words). Yet, whatever the regularity of this mechanism, the initial differential must be discoverable in each distich: thus Charlotte always turns her argument toward general propositions ("It's because it is impossible that you desire me at all"), and Werther always brings his argument back to contingence, god of amorous injury ("Your decision must have been made by Albert"). Each argument (each verse of the distich) is chosen so that it will be symmetrical and, so to speak, equal to its brother, and yet augmented with an additional protest; in short, with a *higher bid*. This bid is never anything but Narcissus' cry: *Me! And me! What about me!*

etymology

3.   The scene is like the Sentence: structurally, there is no obligation for it to stop; no internal constraint exhausts it, because, as in the Sentence, once the core is given (the

ETYMOLOGY: στίχος (*stichos*): row, file.

fact, the decision), the expansions are infinitely renewable. Only some circumstance external to its structure can interrupt the scene: the exhaustion of the two partners (that of only one would not suffice), the arrival of a third party (in *Werther*, it is Albert), or else the sudden substitution of desire for aggression. Unless these accidents are employed, no partner has the power to check a scene. What means might I have? Silence? It would merely quicken the *will to have* the scene; I am therefore obliged to answer in order to soothe, to erase. Reasoning? None is of such pure metal as to leave the other partner without something to say. Analysis of the scene itself? To shift from the scene to the metascene merely means opening another scene. Flight? This is the sign of a defection already achieved: the couple is *already* undone: like love, the scene is always reciprocal. Hence, the scene is interminable, like language itself: it is language itself, taken in its infinity, that "perpetual adoration" which brings matters about in such a way that since man has existed, *he has not stopped talking.*

(The good thing about X was that he never exploited the sentence that was given to him; by a kind of rare *askesis, he did not take advantage of language.*)

4.   No scene has a meaning, no scene moves toward an enlightenment or a transformation. The scene is neither practical nor dialectical; it is a luxury—and idle: As inconsequential as a perverse orgasm: it does not leave a mark, it does not sully. Paradox: in Sade, violence, too, does not leave a mark; the body is instantaneously restored—for new expenditures: endlessly lacerated, tainted, crushed, Justine is always fresh, whole, rested; the same is true of the scene's partners: they are reborn from the past scene

Sade

as if nothing had occurred. By the very insignificance of its tumult, the scene recalls the Roman style of vomiting: I tickle my uvula (I rouse myself to contestation), I vomit (a flood of wounding arguments), and then, quite calmly, I begin eating again.

5.   Insignificant as it is, the scene nonetheless struggles against insignificance. Each partner of a scene dreams of having the *last word*. To speak last, "to conclude," is to assign a destiny to everything that has been said, is to master, to possess, to absolve, to bludgeon meaning; in the space of speech, the one who comes last occupies a sovereign position, held, according to an established privilege, by professors, presidents, judges, confessors: every language combat (the *machia* of the Sophists, the *disputatio* of the Scholastics) seeks to gain possession of this position; by the last word, I will disorganize, "liquidate" the adversary, inflicting upon him a (narcissistically) mortal wound, cornering him in silence, castrating him of all speech. The scene passes with a view to this triumph: there is no question whatever that each remark should contribute to the victory of a truth, gradually constructing this truth, but only that the *last* remark be the right one: it is the last throw of the dice which counts. The scene bears no resemblance to a chess game, but rather to a game of hunt-the-slipper: yet here the game is inverted, for the victory goes to the one who manages to keep the slipper in his hand at the very moment the game stops: the slipper changes hands throughout the scene, and the victory goes to the player who captures that little creature whose possession assures omnipotence: the last word.

    In *Werther*, the scene is crowned with a blackmail: "Grant me only a little peace and everything will be settled," Werther says to Charlotte in a plaintive yet threat-

Werther

ening tone: which is to say: "You will soon be rid of me": a proposition marked with a certain voluptuous quality, for it is in fact hallucinated as a *last word*. In order that the subject of the scene be furnished with a truly peremptory last word, it requires no less than suicide: by the announcement of suicide, Werther immediately becomes *the stronger of the two*: whereby we see once again that only death can interrupt the Sentence, the Scene.

What is a hero? The one who has the last word. Can we think of a hero who does not speak before dying? To renounce the last word (to refuse to have a scene) derives, then, from an anti-heroic morality: that of Abraham: to the end of the sacrifice demanded of him, he does not speak. Or else, as a more subversive because less theatrical riposte (silence is always sufficient theater), the last word may be replaced by an incongruous pirouette: this is what the Zen master did who, for his only answer to the solemn question "What is Buddha?," took off his sandal, put it on his head, and walked away: impeccable dissolution of the last word, mastery of non-mastery.

rkegaard

"NO CLERGYMAN ATTENDED"

seul / alone

The figure refers, not to what the human solitude of the amorous subject may be, but to his "philosophical" solitude, love-as-passion being accounted for today by no major system of thought (of discourse).

1.   What do we call that subject who persists in an "error" against and counter to everyone, as if he had before himself all eternity in which to be "mistaken"? We

KIERKEGAARD: *Fear and Trembling.*

call him a *relapse*. Whether it be from one lover to the next or within one and the same love, I keep "falling back" into an interior doctrine which no one shares with me. When Werther's body is taken by night to a corner of the cemetery, near two lindens (the tree whose simple odor is that of memory and sleep), "no clergyman attended" (the novel's last sentence). Religion condemns in Werther not only the suicide but also, perhaps, the lover, the utopian, the class heretic, the man who is "ligatured" to no one but himself.

Werther

etymology

2.   In the *Symposium*, Eryximachus notes with some irony that he has read somewhere a panegyric of salt, but nothing on Eros, and it is because Eros is censured as a subject of conversation that the little society of the *Symposium* decides to make this the subject of its round table: rather like today's intellectuals reluctantly agreeing to discuss, precisely, Love and not politics, (amorous) Desire and not (social) Need. The eccentricity of the conversation derives from the fact that this conversation is systematic: what the guests try to produce are not proved remarks, accounts of experiences, but a doctrine: for each of them, Eros is a system. Today, however, there is no system of love: and the several systems which surround the contemporary lover offer him no room (except for an extremely devaluated place): turn as he will toward one or another of the received languages, none answers him, except in order to turn him away from what he loves. Christian discourse, if it still exists, exhorts him to repress and to sublimate. Psychoanalytical discourse (which, at least, describes his state) commits him to give up his Image-repertoire as lost. As for Marxist discourse, it has

Symposium

ETYMOLOGY: *Religare*, to tie together, to ligature.

nothing to say. If it should occur to me to knock at these doors in order to gain recognition *somewhere* (wherever it might be) for my "madness" (my "truth"), these doors close one after the other; and when they are all shut, there rises around me a wall of language which oppresses and repulses me—unless I *repent* and agree to "get rid of X."

("I have had that nightmare about a loved person who was sick in the street and begged the passers-by for help; but everyone refused him harshly, despite my own hysterical attempts to obtain medicine; the anguish of this loved person then became hysterical, for which I reproached him. I understood a little later that his person was myself —of course; who else is there to dream about?: I was appealing to all the passing languages (systems), rejected by them and pleading with all my might, *indecently*, for a philosophy which might 'understand' me—might 'shelter' me.")

3.   The lover's solitude is not a solitude of person (love confides, speaks, tells itself), it is a solitude of system: I am alone in making a system out of it (perhaps because I am ceaselessly flung back on the solipsism of my discourse). A difficult paradox: I can be understood by everyone (love comes from books, its dialect is a common one), but I can be heard (received "prophetically") only by subjects who have *exactly and right now* the same language I have. Lovers, Alcibiades says, are like those a viper has bitten: "They are unwilling, it is said, to speak of their misfortune to anyone except those who have been victims of it as well, as being the only ones in a position to conceive and to excuse all they have dared to say and do in the throes of their pain": paltry troupe of "Starved souls," the Suicides for love (how many times will not one

mposium

Ruysbroeck and the same lover commit suicide?), to whom no great language (save, fragmentarily, that of the passé Novel) lends its voice.

4.   Like the early mystic, scarcely tolerated by the ecclesiastical society in which he lived, as an amorous subject I neither confront nor contest: quite simply, I have no dialogue: with the instruments of power, of thought, of knowledge, of action, etc.; I am not necessarily "depoliticized": my deviation consists in not being "excited." In return, society subjects me to a strange, public repression: no censure, no prohibition: I am merely suspended *a humanis*, far from human things, by a tacit decree of insignificance: I belong to no repertoire, participate in no asylum.

5.   Why I am alone:

Tao

> "*Every man has his wealth,*
> *I alone appear impoverished.*
> *My mind is that of an ignorant man*
> *because it is very slow.*
> *Every man is clear-sighted,*
> *I alone am in darkness.*
> *Every man has a sharp wit,*
> *I alone have a clouded mind*
> *Which floats with the sea, blows with the wind.*
> *Every man has his goal,*
> *I alone have the dull mind of a peasant.*
> *I alone am different from other men,*
> *For I seek to suckle at my Mother's breast.*"

TAO: *Tao Te Ching.*

THE UNCERTAINTY OF SIGNS

signes / signs

Whether he seeks to prove his love, or to discover if the other loves him, the amorous subject has no system of sure signs at his disposal.

1.   I look for signs, but of what? What is the object of my reading? Is it: am I loved (am I loved no longer, am I still loved)? Is it my future that I am trying to read, deciphering in what is inscribed the announcement of what will happen to me, according to a method which combines paleography and manticism? Isn't it rather, all things considered, that I remain suspended on this question, whose answer I tirelessly seek in the other's face: *What am I worth?*

Balzac

2.   The power of the Image-repertoire is immediate: I do not look for the image, it comes to me, all of a sudden. It is afterward that I return to it and begin making the good sign alternate, interminably, with the bad one: "What do these abrupt words mean: you have all my respect? Was anything ever colder? Is this a complete return to the old intimacy? Or a polite way to cut short a disagreeable explanation?" Like Stendhal's Octave, I never know what is *normal*; lacking (as I well know) all reason, I would prefer, in order to decide on an interpretation, to trust myself to common sense; but common sense affords me no more than contradictory evidence: "After

Stendhal

BALZAC: "She was learned and she knew that the amorous character has its signs in what are taken for trifles. A knowledgeable woman can read her future in a simple gesture, as Cuvier could say, seeing the fragment of a paw: this belongs to an animal of such-and-such a size," etc. (*The Secrets of the Princess of Cadignan*).
STENDHAL: *Armance.*

all, it's not really normal to go out in the middle of the
night and to come home four hours later!" "After all, it's
only normal to go out and take a walk when you can't
sleep," etc. A man who wants the truth is never answered
save in strong, highly colored images, which nonetheless
turn ambiguous, indecisive, once he tries to transform
them into signs: as in any manticism, the consulting lover
must make his own truth.

3.   Freud to his fiancée: "The only thing that makes
me suffer is being in a situation where it is impossible for
Freud
me to prove my love to you." And Gide: "Everything in
her behavior seemed to say: Since he no longer loves me,
Gide
nothing matters to me. Now, I still loved her, and in fact I
had never loved her so much; but it was no longer possible
for me to prove it to her. That was much the worst thing
of all."

Signs are not proof, since anyone can produce false or
ambiguous signs. Hence one falls back, paradoxically, on
the omnipotence of language: since nothing assures language, I will regard it as the sole and final assurance: *I
shall no longer believe in interpretation.* I shall receive
every word from my other as a sign of truth; and when I
speak, I shall not doubt that he, too, receives what I say as
the truth. Whence the importance of *declarations*; I want
to keep wresting from the other the formula of his feeling,
and I keep telling him, on my side, that I love him: nothing is left to suggestion, to divination: for a thing to be
known, it must be spoken; but also, once it is spoken, even
very provisionally, it is true.

.   .   .

1977

FREUD: *Letters.*
GIDE: *Journal,* 1939.

Inaugural Lecture,
Collège de France

I SHOULD probably begin with a consideration of the reasons which have led the Collège de France to receive a fellow of doubtful nature, whose every attribute is somehow challenged by its opposite. For though my career has been academic, I am without the usual qualifications for entrance into that career. And though it is true that I long wished to inscribe my work within the field of science—literary, lexicological, and sociological—I must admit that I have produced only essays, an ambiguous genre in which analysis vies with writing. And though it is also true that very early on I associated my investigations with the birth and development of semiotics, it is true as well that I have scarcely any claim as its representative, so inclined was I to shift its definition (almost as soon as I found it to be formed) and to draw upon the eccentric forces of modernism, located closer to the journal *Tel Quel* than to many other periodicals which testify to the vigor of semiological inquiry.

Lecture in inauguration of the Chair of Literary Semiology, Collège de France, to which Barthes was elected. The lecture was delivered on January 7, 1977, and published as *Leçon* (Paris: Editions du Seuil) in 1978. Translated by Richard Howard.

It is then a patently impure fellow whom you receive in an establishment where science, scholarship, rigor, and disciplined invention reign. In the interests of discretion, then, and out of a personal inclination to escape intellectual difficulty through the interrogation of my own pleasure, I shall turn from the reasons which have induced the Collège de France to welcome me—for they are uncertain, in my view—and address those which make my entry here more joyful than honorific; for an honor can be undeserved—joy never is. It is my joy to encounter in this place the memory or presence of authors dear to me and who teach or have taught at the Collège de France. First, of course, comes Michelet, through whom, at the start of my intellectual life, I discovered the sovereign place of History in the study of man, and the power of writing, once scholarship accepts that commitment. Then, closer to us, Jean Baruzi and Paul Valéry, whose lectures I attended as an adolescent in this very hall. Then, closer still, Maurice Merleau-Ponty and Emile Benveniste. As for the present, allow me to exempt from the discretion and silence incumbent upon friendship the affection, intellectual solidarity, and gratitude which bind me to Michel Foucault, for it is he who kindly undertook to present this chair and its occupant to the Assembly of Professors.

Another kind of joy, more sober because more responsible, is mine today as well: that of entry into a place that we can strictly term *outside the bounds of power*. For if I may, in turn, interpret the Collège, I shall say that it is, as institutions go, one of History's last stratagems. Honor is usually a diminution of power; here it is a subtraction, power's untouched portion. A professor's sole activity here is research: to speak—I shall even say to dream his research aloud—not to judge, to give preference, to promote, to submit to controlled scholarship. This is an enormous, almost an unjust, privilege at a time when the teaching of letters is strained to the point of exhaustion between the pressures of technocracy's demands and of revolutionary desire, the desire of its students. To teach or even to speak outside the limits of institutional sanction is certainly not to be rightfully and totally uncorrupted by power; power (the *libido dominandi*) is there, hidden in any discourse, even when uttered in a place outside the bounds of power. Therefore, the freer such teaching, the further we must inquire into the conditions and processes by which discourse can be disengaged from all will-to-possess. This inquiry constitutes, in my view, the ultimate project of the instruction inaugurated today.

Indeed, it is power with which we shall be concerned, indirectly but persistently. Our modern "innocence" speaks of power as if it were a single thing: on one side those who have it, on the other those who do not. We have believed that power was an exemplarily political object; we believe now that power is also an ideological object, that it creeps in where we do not recognize it at first, into institutions, into teaching, but still that it is always one thing. And yet, what if power were plural, like demons? "My name is Legion," it could say; everywhere, on all sides, leaders, massive or minute organizations, pressure groups or oppression groups, everywhere "authorized" voices which authorize themselves to utter the discourse of all power: the discourse of arrogance. We discover then that power is present in the most delicate mechanisms of social exchange: not only in the State, in classes, in groups, but even in fashion, public opinion, entertainment, sports, news, family and private relations, and even in the liberating impulses which attempt to counteract it. I call the discourse of power any discourse which engenders blame, hence guilt, in its recipient. Some expect of us as intellectuals that we take action on every occasion against Power, but our true battle is elsewhere, it is against *powers* in the plural, and this is no easy combat. For if it is plural in social space, power is, symmetrically, perpetual in historical time. Exhausted, defeated here, it reappears there; it never disappears. Make a revolution to destroy it, power will immediately revive and flourish again in the new state of affairs. The reason for this endurance and this ubiquity is that power is the parasite of a trans-social organism, linked to the whole of man's history and not only to his political, historical history. This object in which power is inscribed, for all of human eternity, is language, or to be more precise, its necessary expression: the language we speak and write.

Language is legislation, speech is its code. We do not see the power which is in speech because we forget that all speech is a classification, and that all classifications are oppressive: *ordo* means both distribution and commination. Jakobson has shown that a speech-system is defined less by what it permits us to say than by what it compels us to say. In French (I shall take obvious examples) I am obliged to posit myself first as subject before stating the action which will henceforth be no more than my attribute: what I do is merely the consequence and consecution of what I am. In the same way, I must always choose between masculine and feminine, for the neuter and the dual are forbidden me. Further, I must indicate my relation to the other person by resorting to either *tu* or *vous*; social or affective suspension is denied me. Thus, by its very structure my language implies an inevitable relation of alienation. To speak, and, with even greater reason, to utter a discourse is not, as is too often repeated, to communicate; it is to subjugate: the whole language is a generalized *rection*.

I am going to quote a remark of Renan's. "French, ladies and gentlemen," he once said in a lecture, "will never be the language of the absurd; nor will it ever be a reactionary language. I cannot imagine a serious reaction having French as its organ." Well, Renan was, in his way, perspicacious. He realized that language is not exhausted by the message engendered by it. He saw that language can survive this message and make understood within it, with a frequently terrible resonance, something other than what it says, superimposing on the subject's conscious, reasonable voice the dominating, stubborn, implacable voice of structure, i.e., of the species insofar as that species speaks. Renan's error was historical, not structural; he supposed that French—formed, as he believed, by reason—compelled the expression of a political reason which, to him, could only be democratic. But language—the performance of a language system—is neither reactionary nor progressive; it is quite simply fascist; for fascism does not prevent speech, it compels speech.

Once uttered, even in the subject's deepest privacy, speech enters the service of power. In speech, inevitably, two categories appear: the authority of assertion, the gregariousness of repetition. On the one hand, speech is immediately assertive: negation, doubt, possibility, the suspension of judgment require special mechanisms which are themselves caught up in a play of linguistic masks; what linguists call modality is only the supplement of speech by which I try, as through petition, to sway its implacable power of verification. On the other hand, the signs composing speech exist only insofar as they are recognized, i.e., insofar as they are repeated. The sign is a follower, gregarious; in each sign sleeps that monster: a stereotype. I can speak only by picking up what *loiters* around in speech. Once I speak, these two categories unite in me; I am both master and slave. I am not content to repeat what has been said, to settle comfortably in the servitude of signs: I speak, I affirm, I assert *tellingly* what I repeat.

In speech, then, servility and power are inescapably intermingled. If we call freedom not only the capacity to escape power but also and especially the capacity to subjugate no one, then freedom can exist only outside language. Unfortunately, human language has no exterior: there is no exit. We can get out of it only at the price of the impossible: by mystical singularity, as described by Kierkegaard when he defines Abraham's sacrifice as an action unparalleled, void of speech, even interior speech, performed against the generality, the gregariousness, the morality of language; or again by the Nietzschean "yes to life," which is a kind of exultant shock administered to the servility of speech, to what Deleuze calls its reactive guise. But for us, who are neither knights of faith nor supermen, the only remaining alternative is, if I may say so, to cheat with speech, to cheat speech. This salutary trickery, this evasion, this grand imposture which allows us to understand speech *outside the bounds of power*, in the splendor of a permanent revolution of language, I for one call *literature*.

I mean by *literature* neither a body nor a series of works, nor even a branch of commerce or of teaching, but the complex graph of the traces of a practice, the practice of writing. Hence, it is essentially the text with which I am concerned—the fabric of signifiers which constitute the work. For the text is the very outcropping of speech, and it is within speech that speech must be fought, led astray—not by the message of which it is the instrument, but by the play of words of which it is the theater. Thus I can say without differentiation: literature, writing, or text. The forces of freedom which are in literature depend not on the writer's civil person, nor on his political commitment—for he is, after all, only a man among others—nor do they even depend on the doctrinal content of his work, but rather on the labor of displacement he brings to bear upon the language. Seen in this light, Céline is quite as important as Hugo, and Chateaubriand as important as Zola. By this I am trying to address a responsibility of form; but this responsibility cannot be evaluated in ideological terms—which is why the sciences of ideology have always had so little hold over it. Of these forces of literature, I wish to indicate three, which I shall discuss in terms of three Greek concepts: *Mathesis, Mimesis, Semiosis*.

Literature accommodates many kinds of knowledge. In a novel like *Robinson Crusoe* there is a historical knowledge, a geographical, a social (colonial), a technological, a botanical, an anthropological knowledge (Robinson proceeds from Nature to culture). If, by some unimaginable excess of socialism or barbarism, all but one of our disciplines were to be expelled from our educational system, it is the discipline of literature which would have to be saved, for all knowledge, all the sciences are present in the literary monument. Whereby we can say that literature, whatever the school in whose name it declares itself, is absolutely, categorically *realist*: it is reality, i.e., the very spark of the real. Yet literature, in this truly encyclopedic respect, displaces the various kinds of knowledge, does not fix or fetishize any of them; it gives them an indirect place, and this indirection is precious. On the one hand, it allows for the designation of possible areas of knowledge—unsuspected, unfulfilled. Literature works in the interstices of science. It is always behind or ahead of science, like the Bolognese stone which gives off by night what it has stored up by day, and by this indirect glow illuminates the new day which dawns. Science is crude, life is subtle, and it is for the correction of this disparity that literature matters to us. The knowledge it marshals is, on the other hand, never complete or final. Literature does not say that it knows something, but that it knows *of* something, or better, that it knows *about* something—that it knows about men. What it knows about men is what we might call the great *mess* of language, upon which men work and which works upon them. Literature can reproduce the diversity of sociolects, or, starting from this diversity, and suffering its laceration, literature may imagine and seek to elaborate a limit-language which would be its zero degree. Because it *stages* language instead of simply using it, literature feeds knowledge into the machinery of infinite reflexivity. Through writing, knowledge ceaselessly reflects on knowledge, in terms of a discourse which is no longer epistemological, but dramatic.

It is good form, today, to contest the opposition of sciences and letters, insofar as the number of relations, whether of model or method, uniting these two regions and often erasing their frontier is increasing, and it is possible that this opposition will appear one day to be a historical myth. But from the point of view of language, which is ours here, this opposition is pertinent; moreover it does not necessarily set up the opposition between the real and the fantastic, the objective and the subjective, the True and the Beautiful, but only different loci of speech. According to scientific discourse—or a certain discourse of science—knowledge is statement; in writing, it is an act of stating. The statement, the usual object of linguistics, is given as the product of the subject's absence. The act of stating, by exposing the subject's place and energy, even his deficiency (which is not his absence), focuses on the very reality of language, acknowledging that language is an immense halo of implications, of effects, of echoes, of turns, returns, and degrees. It assumes the burden of making understood a subject both insistent and ineffable, unknown and yet recognized by a disturbing familiarity. Words are no longer conceived illusively as simple instruments; they are cast as projections, explosions, vibrations, devices, flavors. Writing makes knowledge festive.

The paradigm I am proposing here does not follow the functional division: it is not aimed at putting scientists and researchers on one side, writers and essayists on the other. On the contrary, it suggests that writing is to be found wherever words have flavor (the French words for *flavor* and *knowledge* have the same Latin root). Curnonski used to say that in cooking "things should have the taste of what they are."

Where knowledge is concerned, things must, if they are to become what they are, what they have been, have that ingredient, the salt of words. It is this taste of words which makes knowledge profound, fecund. I know for instance that Michelet proposes much that is denied by historical scholarship. Nonetheless Michelet founded something on the order of an ethnology of France, and each time a historian displaces historical knowledge, in the broadest sense of the term and whatever its object, we find, quite simply, writing.

Literature's second force is its force as representation. From ancient times to the efforts of our avant-garde, literature has been concerned to represent something. What? I will put it crudely: the real. The real is not representable, and it is because men ceaselessly try to represent it by words that there is a history of literature. That the real is not representable, but only demonstrable, can be said in several ways: either we can define it, with Lacan, as the *impossible*, that which is unattainable and escapes discourse, or in topological terms we observe that a pluri-dimensional order (the real) cannot be made to coincide with a unidimensional order (language). Now, it is precisely this topological impossibility that literature rejects and to which it never submits. Though there is no parallelism between language and the real, men will not take sides, and it is this refusal, perhaps as old as language itself, which produces, in an incessant commotion, literature. We can imagine a history of literature, or better, say, of productions of language, which would be the history of certain (often aberrant) verbal *expedients* men have used to reduce, tame, deny, or, on the contrary, to assume what is *always* a delirium, i.e., the fundamental inadequation of language and the real. I said a moment ago, apropos of knowledge, that literature is categorically realist, in that it never has anything but the real as its object of desire; and I shall say now, without contradicting myself—

because I am here using the word in its familiar acceptation—
that literature is quite as stubbornly unrealistic; it considers
sane its desire for the impossible.

This function—perhaps perverse, therefore fitting—has a
name: it is the utopian function. Here we come back to History. For it is in the second half of the nineteenth century, one
of the grimmest periods of calamitous capitalism, that literature finds its exact figure, at least for us Frenchmen, in Mallarmé. Modernity—our modernity, which begins at this period
—can be defined by this new phenomenon: that *utopias of
language* are conceived in it. No "history of literature" (if
such is still to be written) could be legitimate which would be
content, as in the past, to link the various schools together
without indicating the gap which here reveals a new prophetic
function, that of writing. "To change language," that Mallarméan expression, is a concomitant of "To change the
world," that Marxian one. There is a *political* reception of
Mallarmé, of those who have followed him and follow him
still.

From this there follows a certain ethic of literary language,
which must be affirmed, because it is contested. We often
reproach the writer, the intellectual, for not writing "everyone's" language. But it is good that men, within the same
language—for us, French—should have several kinds of
speech. If I were a legislator (an aberrant supposition for
someone who, etymologically speaking, is an "an-archist"),
far from imposing a unification of French, whether bourgeois
or popular, I would instead encourage the simultaneous ap-
prenticeship to several French forms of speech, of various
function, promoted to equality. Dante seriously debates which
language he will use to write the *Convivio*: Latin or Tuscan?
Nor is it for political or polemical reasons that he chooses the
vulgar tongue: it is by considering the appropriateness of ei-

ther language to his subject. The two forms of speech—as for us, classical French and modern French, written French and spoken French—thus form a reservoir from which he is free to draw, *according to the truth of desire*. This freedom is a luxury which every society should afford its citizens: as many languages as there are desires—a utopian proposition in that no society is yet ready to admit the plurality of desire. That a language, whatever it be, not repress another; that the subject may know without remorse, without repression, the bliss of having at his disposal two kinds of language; that he may speak this or that, according to his perversions, not according to the Law.

Utopia, of course, does not save us from power. The utopia of language is salvaged as the language of utopia—a genre like the rest. We can say that no writer who began in a rather lonely struggle against the power of language could or can avoid being coopted by it, either in the posthumous form of an inscription within official culture, or in the present form of a mode which imposes its image and forces him to conform to expectation. No way out for this author than to shift ground—or to persist—or both at once.

To persist means to affirm the Irreducible of literature, that which resists and survives the typified discourses, the philosophies, sciences, psychologies which surround it, to act as if literature were incomparable and immortal. A writer—by which I mean not the possessor of a function or the servant of an art, but the subject of a praxis—must have the persistence of the watcher who stands at the crossroads of all other discourses, in a position that is *trivial* in relation to purity of doctrine (*trivialis* is the etymological attribute of the prostitute who waits at the intersection of three roads). To persist means, in short, to maintain, over and against everything, the force of drift and of expectation. And it is precisely because it persists that writing is led to shift ground. For power seizes upon the pleasure of writing as it seizes upon all pleasure, to manipulate it and to make of it a product that is gregarious, nonperverse, in the same way that it seizes upon the genetic product of love's pleasure, to turn it into soldiers and fighters to its own advantage. *To shift ground*, then, can mean: to go where you are not expected, or, more radically, to *abjure* what you have written (but not necessarily what you have thought), when gregarious power uses and subjugates it. Pasolini was thus led to "abjure" (as he said) his "trilogy of life" films because he realized that power was making use of them—yet without regretting the fact that he made them in the first place. "I believe," he said in a text published posthumously, "that *before* action we must never in any case fear annexation by power and its culture. We must behave as if this dangerous eventuality did not exist. . . . But I also believe that *afterward* we must be able to realize how much we may have been used by power. And then, if our sincerity or our necessity has been controlled or manipulated, I believe we must have the courage to abjure."

To persist and, at the same time, to shift ground relates, in short, to a kind of acting. We must therefore not be surprised if on the impossible horizon of linguistic anarchy—at that point where language attempts to escape its own power, its own servility—we find something which relates to theater. To designate the impossible in language, I have cited two authors: Kierkegaard and Nietzsche. Yet both have written. It was in each instance, however, in a reversal of identity, as a performance, as a frenzied gambling of proper names—one by incessant recourse to pseudonymity, the other by proceeding, at the end of his writing life, as Klossowski has shown, to the limits of the histrionic. We might say that literature's third force, its strictly semiotic force, is to *act* signs rather than to destroy them—to feed them into a machinery of language whose safety catches and emergency brakes have exploded; in short, to institute, at the very heart of servile language, a veritable heteronymy of things.

Which brings us to semiology.

First of all we must repeat that the sciences (at least those in which I have done any reading at all) are not eternal; they are values which rise and fall on an Exchange—the Exchange of History. In this regard, it suffices to recall the exchange fate of Theology, now a diminished area of discourse, yet once so sovereign a science as to be placed outside and above the Septenium. The fragility of the so-called human sciences derives perhaps from this: that they are *unforeseeing* sciences (whence the disappointments and the taxonomic discomfort of Economics)—which immediately alters the notion of science. Even the science of desire, psychoanalysis, must die one of these days, though we all owe it a great deal, as we owe a great deal to Theology: for desire is stronger than its interpretation.

Semiology, which we can canonically define as the science of signs, of all signs, has emerged from linguistics through its operational concepts. But linguistics itself, somewhat like economics (and the comparison is perhaps not insignificant), is, I believe, in the process of splitting apart. On the one hand, linguistics tends toward the formal pole, and, like econometrics, it is thereby becoming more formalized; on the other hand, linguistics is assimilating contents that are more and more numerous and remote from its original field. Just as the object of economics today is everywhere, in the political, the social, the cultural, so the object of linguistics is limitless. Speech, according to an intuition of Benveniste's, is the social itself. In short, either due to excessive ascesis or excessive hunger, whether famished or replete, linguistics is deconstructing itself. It is this deconstruction of linguistics that I, for my part, call *semiology*.

You may have noticed that in the course of my presentation I have surreptitiously shifted from language to discourse, in order to return, sometimes without warning, from discourse to language, as if I were dealing with the same object. I believe, indeed, that today, within the pertinence chosen here, language and discourse are undivided, for they move along the same axis of power. Yet initially this originally Saussurian distinction (the pairing was *Langue/Parole*) was very useful; it gave semiology the courage to begin. By this opposition, I could reduce discourse, miniaturize it into a grammatical example, and thereby hope to hold all human communication under my net, like Wotan and Loge securing Alberich transformed into a tiny toad. But the example is not "the thing itself," and the matter of language cannot be held or contained in the limits of the sentence. It is not only the phonemes, the words, and the syntactical articulations which are subject to a system of controlled freedom, since we cannot combine them arbitrarily; it is the whole stratum of discourse which is fixed by a network of rules, constraints, oppressions, repressions, massive and blurred at the rhetorical level, subtle and acute at the grammatical level. Language flows out into discourse; discourse flows back into language; they persist one above the other like children topping each other's fists on a baseball bat. The distinction between language and discourse no longer appears except as a transitory operation—something, in short, to "abjure." There has come a time when, as though stricken with a gradually increasing deafness, I hear nothing but a single sound, that of language and discourse mixed. And linguistics now seems to me to be working on an enormous imposture, on an object it makes improperly clean and pure by wiping its fingers on the skein of discourse, like Trimalchio on his slaves' hair. Semiology would consequently be that labor which collects the impurity of language, the waste of linguistics, the immediate corruption of the message: nothing less than the desires, the fears, the appearances, the intimidations, the advances, the blandishments, the protests, the excuses, the aggressions, the various kinds of music out of which active language is made.

I know how personal such a definition is. I know whereof it compels my silence: in one sense, and quite paradoxically, all of semiology, the semiology which is being studied and already acknowledged as the positive science of signs, which is developing in periodicals, associations, universities, and study centers. Nevertheless, it seems to me that the intention behind the establishment of a chair at the Collège de France is not so much the consecration of a discipline as the allowing for the continuance of a certain individual labor, the adventure of a certain subject. Now, semiology, so far as I am concerned, started from a strictly emotional impulse. It seemed to me (around 1954) that a science of signs might stimulate social criticism, and that Sartre, Brecht, and Saussure could concur in this project. It was a question, in short, of understanding (or of describing) how a society produces stereotypes, i.e., triumphs of artifice, which it then consumes as innate meanings, i.e., triumphs of Nature. Semiology (my semiology, at least) is generated by an intolerance of this mixture of bad faith and good conscience which characterizes the general morality, and which Brecht, in his attack upon it, called the Great Habit. *Language worked on by power:* that was the object of this first semiology.

Semiology then shifted ground, took on a different coloration, while retaining the same political object—for there is no other. This shift occurred because the intellectual community has changed, if only through the break of May '68. On the one hand, contemporary studies have modified and are modifying the critical image of the social subject and of the speaking subject. On the other hand, it has appeared that, insofar as the machinery of contestation was multiplying, power itself, as a discursive category, was dividing, spreading like a liquid leaking everywhere, each opposition group becoming in its turn and in its way a pressure group and intoning in its own name the very discourse of power, the universal discourse. Political bodies were seized with a kind of moral excitement, and even when claims were being made for pleasure, the tone was threatening. Thus we have seen most proposed liberations, those of society, of culture, of art, of sexuality, articulated in the forms of the discourse of power. We took credit for restoring what had been crushed, without seeing what else we crushed in the process.

If the semiology I am speaking of then returned to the Text, it is because, in this concert of minor dominations, the Text itself appeared as the very index of *nonpower*. The Text contains in itself the strength to elude gregarious speech (the speech which incorporates), even when that speech seeks to reconstitute itself in the Text. The Text always postpones— and it is this movement of *mirage* I have attempted to describe and to justify just now in speaking of literature. The Text procrastinates elsewhere, toward an unclassified, atopic site, so to speak, far from the topoi of politicized culture, "that obligation to form concepts, species, forms, ends, laws . . . that world of identical cases," of which Nietzsche speaks. Gently, transitorily, the text raises that cope of generality, of morality, of in-difference (let us clearly separate this prefix from the root), which weighs on our collective discourse. Literature and semiology thereby combine to correct each other. On one side, the incessant return to the text, ancient or modern, the regular plunge into the most complex of signifying practices, i.e., writing (since writing operates with ready-made signs), forces semiology to work on differences, and keeps it from dogmatizing, from "taking"—from taking itself for the universal discourse which it is not. And on the other side, semiotic scrutiny, focused on the text, forces us to reject the myth usually resorted to in order that literature may be saved from the gregarious speech surrounding and besetting it—from the myth of pure creativity. The sign must be thought—or re-thought—the better to be deceived.

The semiology I speak of is both *negative* and *active*. Someone bedeviled throughout life, for better and for worse, by language, can only be fascinated by the forms of its void—as against its emptiness. The semiology proposed here is there-fore negative—or better still, however heavy the term, *apophatic*—not in that it repudiates the sign, but in that it denies that it is possible to attribute to the sign traits that are positive, fixed, ahistoric, acorporeal, in short: scientific. This apophatic quality involves at least two consequences which directly concern the teaching of semiology.

The first is that semiology cannot itself be a metalanguage, though at its origin it was entirely so predisposed, since it is a language about languages. It is precisely in reflecting on the sign that semiology discovers that every relation of exteriority of one language to another is, *in the long run*, untenable. Time erodes my power of distance, mortifies it, turns this distance into sclerosis. I cannot function *outside* language, treating it as a target, and *within* language, treating it as a weapon. If it is true that the subject of science is that very subject which is not shown, and that it is ultimately this retention of the spectacle that we call "metalanguage," then what I am led to assume, in speaking of signs with signs, is the very spectacle of this bi-zarre coincidence, of that strange squint which relates me to the Chinese shadow-casters when they show both their hands and the rabbit, the duck, and the wolf whose silhouettes they simulate. And to those who take advantage of this condition to deny that active semiology, the semiology which writes, has anything to do with science, we must reply that it is by an epistemological abuse, *which in fact is beginning to crumble,* that we identify metalanguage and science, as if one were the necessary condition of the other, whereas it is only its historical, hence challengeable, sign. It may be time to distinguish the metalinguistic, which is a label like any other, from the scientific, whose criteria are elsewhere (perhaps, let it be said in passing, what is strictly scientific is the destruction of the science which precedes).

Semiology has a relation to science, but it is not a discipline (this is the second consequence of its apophatic quality). What relation? An ancillary relation: it can help certain sciences, can be their fellow traveler for a while, offering an operational protocol starting from which each science must specify the difference of its corpus. Thus, the best-developed part of semiology, the analysis of narrative, can be useful for History, ethnology, textual criticism, exegesis, and iconology (every image is, in a way, a narrative). In other words, semiology is not a grid; it does not permit a direct apprehension of the real through the imposition of a general transparency which would render it intelligible. It seeks instead to elicit the real, in places and by moments, and it says that these efforts to elicit the real are possible without a grid. It is in fact precisely when semiology comes to be a grid that it elicits nothing at all. We can therefore say that semiology has no substitutive role with regard to any discipline. It is my hope that semiology will replace no other inquiry here, but will, on the contrary, help all the rest, that its chair will be a kind of wheelchair, the wild card of contemporary knowledge, as the sign itself is the wild card of all discourse.

This negative semiology is an active semiology: it functions outside death. I mean by this that it does not rest on a "semiophysis," an inert naturalness of the sign, and that it is also not a "semioclasty," a destruction of the sign. Rather, to continue the Greek paradigm, it is a *semiotropy*; turned toward the sign, this semiology is captivated by and receives the sign, treats and, if need be, imitates it as an imaginary spectacle. The semiologist is, in short, an artist (the word as I use it here neither glorifies nor disdains; it refers only to a typology). He plays with signs as with a conscious decoy, whose fascination he savors and wants to make others savor and understand. The sign—at least the sign he sees—is always immediate, subject to the kind of evidence that leaps to the eyes, like a trigger of the imagination, which is why this semiology (need I specify once more: the semiology of the speaker) is not a hermeneutics: it paints more than it digs, *via di porre* rather than *via de levare*. Its objects of predilection are texts of the Image-making process: narratives, images, portraits, expressions, idiolects, passions, structures which play simultaneously with an appearance of verisimilitude and with an uncertainty of truth. I should like to call "semiology" the course of operations during which it is possible—even called for—to play with the sign as with a painted veil, or again, with a fiction.

This pleasure of the imaginary sign is conceivable now due to certain recent mutations, which affect culture more than society itself: the use we can make of the forces of literature I have mentioned is modified by a new situation. On one hand and first of all, the myth of the great French writer, the sacred depositary of all higher values, has crumbled since the Liberation; it has dwindled and died gradually with each of the last survivors of the *entre-deux-guerres*; a new *type* has appeared, and we no longer know—or do not yet know—what to call him: writer? intellectual? scribe? In any case, literary mastery is vanishing; the writer is no longer center stage. On the other hand and subsequently, May '68 has revealed the crisis in our teaching. The old values are no longer transmitted, no longer circulate, no longer impress; literature is desacralized, institutions are impotent to defend and impose it as the implicit model of the human. It is not, if you like, that literature is destroyed; rather *it is no longer protected*, so that this is the moment to deal with it. Literary semiology is, as it were, that journey which lands us in a country free by default; angels and dragons are no longer there to defend it. Our gaze can fall, not without perversity, upon certain old and lovely things, whose signified is abstract, out of date. It is a moment at once decadent and prophetic, a moment of gentle apocalypse, a historical moment of the greatest possible pleasure.

If then, in this teaching which, given its very location, expects no sanction other than the loyalty of its auditors, if method intervenes as a systematic procedure, it cannot be a heuristic method meant to result in decoding. Method can bear only upon language itself, insofar as it struggles to baffle any discourse *which takes*, which is why we can justly claim that method, too, is a Fiction—a proposition already advanced by Mallarmé when he thought of preparing a thesis in linguistics: "All method is a fiction. Language has appeared as the instrument of fiction; it will follow the method of language, language reflecting upon itself." What I hope to be able to renew, each of the years it is given me to teach here, is the manner of presentation of the course or seminar, in short, of "presenting" a discourse without imposing it: that would be the methodological stake, the *quaestio*, the point to be debated. For what can be oppressive in our teaching is not, finally, the knowledge or the culture it conveys, but the discursive forms through which we propose them. Since, as I have tried to suggest, this teaching has as its object discourse taken in the inevitability of power, method can really bear only on the means of loosening, baffling, or at the very least, of lightening this power. And I am increasingly convinced, both in writing and in teaching, that the fundamental operation of this loosening method is, if one writes, fragmentation, and, if one teaches, digression, or, to put it in a preciously ambiguous word, *excursion*. I should therefore like the speaking and the listening that will be interwoven here to resemble the comings and goings of a child playing beside his mother, leaving her, returning to bring her a pebble, a piece of string, and thereby tracing around a calm center a whole locus of play within which the pebble, the string come to matter less than the enthusiastic giving of them.

When the child behaves in this way, he in fact describes the comings and goings of desire, which he endlessly presents and represents. I sincerely believe that at the origin of teaching such as this we must always locate a fantasy, which can vary from year to year. This, I know, may seem provocative: how, in the context of an institution, however free it may be, dare we speak of a phantasmic teaching? Yet if we consider for a moment the surest of human sciences, if we consider History, how can we help acknowledging that it has a continuous relation with fantasy? This is what Michelet understood: History is ultimately the history of the phantasmic site par excellence, that of the human body. It was by starting from this fantasy, linked for him with the lyric resurrection of past bodies, that Michelet could make History into an enormous anthropology. Science can thus be born of fantasy. It is to a fantasy, spoken or unspoken, that the professor must annually return, at the moment of determining the direction of his journey. He thereby turns from the place where he is expected, the place of the Father, who is always dead, as we know. For only the son has fantasies; only the son is alive.

The other day, I reread Thomas Mann's novel *The Magic Mountain*. This book deals with a disease I know well, tuberculosis. By my reading, I held in consciousness three moments of this disease: the moment of the story, which takes place before World War I; the moment of my own disease, around 1942; and the present moment, when this disease, vanquished by chemotherapy, has no longer the same aspect it once had. Now, the tuberculosis I experienced is, down to virtually the last detail, the tuberculosis of *The Magic Mountain*. The two moments were united, equally remote from my own present. I then realized with stupefaction (only the obvious can stupefy) that *my own body was historical*. In a sense, my body is the contemporary of Hans Castorp, the novel's hero; my body, still unborn, was already twenty years old in 1907, the year when Hans entered and took up residence in "the country up there." My body is much older than I, as if we always kept the age of the social fears with which life has accidentally given us contact. Therefore, if I want to live, I must forget that my own body is historical. I must fling myself into the illusion that I am contemporary with the young bodies present before me, and not with my own body, my past body. In short, I must be periodically reborn. I must make myself younger than I am. At fifty-one, Michelet began his *vita nuova*, a new work, a new love. Older than he (you will understand that this parallel is out of fondness), I too am entering a *vita nuova*, marked today by this new place, this new hospitality. I undertake therefore to let myself be borne on by the force of any living life, forgetfulness. There is an age at which we teach what we know. Then comes another age at which we teach what we do not know; this is called *research*. Now perhaps comes the age of another experience: that of *unlearning*, of yielding to the unforeseeable change which forgetting imposes on the sedimentation of the knowledges, cultures, and beliefs we have traversed. This experience has, I believe, an illustrious and outdated name, which I now simply venture to appropriate at the very crossroads of its etymology: *Sapientia*: no power, a little knowledge, a little wisdom, and as much flavor as possible.

1977

Deliberation

I'VE never kept a journal—or rather I've never known if I should keep one. Sometimes I begin, and then, right away, I leave off—and yet, later on, I begin again. The impulse is faint, intermittent, without seriousness and of no doctrinal standing whatever. I guess I could diagnose this *diary disease*: an insoluble doubt as to the value of what one writes in it.

Such doubt is insidious: it functions by a kind of delayed action. Initially, when I write the (daily) entry, I experience a certain pleasure: this is simple, this is easy. Don't worry about finding *something to say*: the raw material is right here, right now; a kind of surface mine; all I have to do is bend over—I don't need to transform anything: the crude ore has its own value, etc. Then comes the second phase, very soon after the first (for instance, if I reread today what I wrote yesterday), and it makes a bad impression: the text doesn't hold up, like some sort of delicate foodstuff which "turns," spoils, becomes unappetizing from one day to the next; I note with discouragement the artifice of "sincerity," the artistic mediocrity of the "spontaneous"; worse still: I am disgusted and irritated to find a "pose" I certainly hadn't intended: in a journal situation,

"Délibération" was published in *Tel Quel*, No. 82, Winter 1979. Translated by Richard Howard.

and precisely because it doesn't "work"—doesn't get transformed by the action of work—*I* is a *poseur*: a matter of effect, not of intention, the whole difficulty of literature is here. Very soon, continuing my reperusal, I get tired of these verbless sentences ("Sleepless night. And the third in a row," etc.) or sentences whose verb is carelessly condensed ("Passed two girls in the Place St-S.")—and try as I will to re-establish the propriety of a complete form ("I passed . . ." "I spent a sleepless night"), the matrix of any journal, i.e., the reduction of the verb, persists in my ear and exasperates me like a refrain. In a third phase, if I reread my journal pages several months, several years after having written them, though my doubt hasn't dissipated, I experience a certain pleasure in rediscovering, thanks to these lines, the events they relate, and even more, the inflections (of light, of atmosphere, of mood) they bring back. In short, at this point no literary interest (save for problems of formulation, i.e., of phrasing), but a kind of narcissistic attachment (faintly narcissistic—let's not exaggerate) to *my* doings (whose recall is inevitably ambiguous, since to remember is also to acknowledge and to lose once again what will not recur). But still, does this final indulgence, achieved after having traversed a phase of rejection, justify (systematically) keeping a journal? Is it *worth the trouble*?

I am not attempting any kind of analysis of the "Journal" genre (there are books on the subject), but only a personal deliberation, intended to afford a practical decision: should I keep a journal *with a view to publication*? Can I make the journal into a "work"? Hence I refer only to the functions which immediately come to mind. For instance, Kafka kept a diary in order to "extirpate his anxiety," if you prefer, "to find salvation." This motive would not be a natural one for me, or at least not a constant one. Nor would the aims traditionally attributed to the intimate Journal; they no longer seem pertinent to me. They are all connected to the advantages and the prestige of "sincerity" (to express yourself, to explain yourself, to judge yourself); but psychoanalysis, the Sartrean critique of bad faith, and the Marxist critique of ideologies have made "confession" a futility: sincerity is merely a second-degree Image-repertoire. No, the Journal's justification (as a work) can only be *literary* in the absolute, even if nostalgic, sense of the word. I discern here four motives.

The first is to present a text tinged with an individuality of writing, with a "style" (as we used to say), with an idiolect proper to the author (as we said more recently); let us call this motive: poetic. The second is to scatter like dust, from day to day, the traces of a period, mixing all dimensions and proportions, from important information to details of behavior: don't I take great pleasure in reading Tolstoy's journal to discover the life of a Russian nobleman in the nineteenth century? Let us call this motive: historical. The third is to constitute the author as an object of desire: if an author interests me, I may want to know the intimacy, the *small change* of his time, his tastes, his moods, his scruples; I may even go so far as to prefer his person to his work, eagerly snatching up his Journal and neglecting his books. Hence I can attempt—making myself the author of the pleasure others have been able to afford me—I can attempt in my turn to seduce, by that swivel which shifts from writer to person, and vice versa; or, more seriously, I can attempt to prove that "I am worth more than what I write" (in my books): the writing in my Journal then appears as a *plus power* (Nietzsche: *Plus von Macht*), which it is supposed will compensate the inadequacies of public writing; let us call this motive: utopian, since it is true that we are never done with the Image-repertoire. The fourth motive is to constitute the Journal as a workshop of sentences: not of "fine phrases," but of correct ones, exact language: constantly to refine the exactitude of the speech-act (and not of the speech), according to an enthusiasm and an application, a fidelity of intention which greatly resembles passion: "Yea, my reins shall rejoice, when thy lips speak right things" (Proverbs 23, xvi). Let us call this motive: amorous (perhaps even: idolatrous—I idolize the Sentence).

For all my sorry impressions, then, the desire to keep a Journal is conceivable. I can admit that it is possible, in the actual context of the Journal, to shift from what at first seemed to me improper in literature to a form which in fact rallies its qualities: the individuation, the scent, the seduction, the fetishism of language. In recent years, I have made three attempts; the first and most serious one—because it occurred during my mother's last illness—is the longest, perhaps because it corresponded in some degree to the Kafkaesque goal of extirpating anxiety by writing; each of the other two concerned only one day: they are more experimental, though I can't reread them without a certain nostalgia for the day that has passed (I give only one of these, the second one involving others besides myself).

I

U——, July 13, 1977

Madame ***, the new cleaning woman, has a diabetic grandson she takes care of, we are told, with devotion and expertise. Her view of this disease is confused: on the one hand, she does not admit that diabetes is hereditary (which would be a sign of inferior stock), and on the other, she insists that it is fatal, absolving any responsibility of origin. She posits disease as a social image, and this image is beset with pitfalls. The Mark certainly appears as a source of pride and of pain: what is was for Jacob-Israel, dislocated, disconnected by the Angel: delight and shame of being re-marked.

Depression, fear, anxiety: I see the death of a loved one, I panic, etc. Such an imagination is the very opposite of faith. For constantly to imagine the inevitability of disaster is constantly to accept it: to utter it is to assert it (again the fascism of language). By imagining death, I discourage the miracle. In Ordet *the madman did not speak, refused the garrulous and peremptory language of inwardness. Then what is this incapacity for faith? Perhaps a very human love? Love, then, excludes faith? And vice versa?*

Gide's old age and death (which I read about in Mme van Rysselberghe's Cahiers de la petite dame*) were surrounded by witnesses. But I do not know what has become of these witnesses: no doubt, in most cases, dead in their turn: there is a time when the witnesses themselves die without witnesses. Thus History consists of tiny explosions of life, of deaths without relays. Our human impotence with regard to transition, to any science of degrees. Conversely, we can attribute to the classical God the capacity to see an infinity of degrees: "God" as the absolute Exponential.*

(Death, real death, is when the witness himself dies. Chateaubriand says of his grandmother and his great-aunt: "I may be the only man in the world who knows that such persons have existed": yes, but since he has written this, and written it well, we know it too, insofar, at least, as we still read Chateaubriand.)

July 14, 1977

A little boy—nervous, excited, like any number of French kids, who so quickly pretend to be grown up, is dressed up as a musical-comedy grenadier (red and white); doubtless he will precede the band.

Why is Worry harder to bear here than in Paris? —This Village is a world so natural, so exempt from any extrava-

gance, that the impulses of sensibility seem entirely out of place. I am excessive, hence excluded.

It seems to me I learn more about France during a walk through the village than in whole weeks in Paris. Perhaps an illusion? The realist illusion? The rural, village, provincial world constitutes the traditional raw material of realism. To be a writer meant, in the nineteenth century, to write from Paris about the provinces. The distance makes everything signify. In Paris, in the street, I am bombarded with information—not with signification.

July 15, 1977

At five in the afternoon, how calm the house is, here in the country. Flies. My legs ache a little, the way they did when I was a child and had what was called growing pains—or when I was getting the grippe. Everything is still, peaceful, asleep. And as always, the sharp awareness, the vivacity of my own "seediness" (a contradiction in terms).

X visits: in the next room, he talks endlessly. I do not dare close the door. What disturbs me is not the noise but the banality of the conversation (if at least he talked in some language unknown to me, and a musical one!). I am always amazed, even flabbergasted by the resistance of others: for me, the Other is the Indefatigable. Energy—and especially verbal energy—stupefies me: this is perhaps the only time (aside from violence) when I believe in madness.

July 16, 1977

Again, after overcast days, a fine morning: luster and subtlety of the atmosphere: a cool, luminous silk. This blank moment (no meaning) produces the plenitude of an evidence: that it is worthwhile being alive. The morning errands (to the *grocer, the baker, while the village is still almost deserted) are something I wouldn't miss for anything in the world.*

Mother feeling better today. She is sitting in the garden, wearing a big straw hat. As soon as she feels a little better, she is drawn by the house, filled with the desire to participate; she puts things away, turns off the furnace during the day (which I never do).

This afternoon, a sunny, windy day, the sun already setting, I burned garbage at the bottom of the garden. A complete course of physics to follow; armed with a long bamboo pole, I stir the heaps of paper, which slowly burn up; it takes patience —who would have guessed how long paper can resist the fire? On the other hand, the emerald-green plastic bag (the garbage bag itself) burns very fast, leaving no trace: *it literally vanishes. This phenomenon might serve, on many an occasion, as a metaphor.*

Incredible incidents (read in the Sud-Ouest *or heard on the radio? I don't remember): in Egypt, it has been decided to execute those Moslems who convert to another religion. In the U.S.S.R., a French agent was expelled because she gave a present of underwear to a Soviet friend. Compile a* contemporary *dictionary of intolerance (literature, in this case Voltaire, cannot be abandoned, so long as the evils subsist to which it bears witness).*

July 17, 1977

As if Sunday morning intensifies the good weather. Two heteroclite intensities reinforce each other.

I never mind doing the cooking. I like the operations *involved. I take pleasure in observing the changing forms of the food as they occur (colorations, thickenings, contractions, crystallizations, polarizations, etc.). There is something a little* perverse about this observation. On the other hand, what I can't do, and what I always do badly, are proportions and schedules: I put in too much oil, afraid everything will burn; I leave things too long on the fire, afraid they won't be cooked through. In short, I'm afraid because I don't know (how much, how long). Whence the security of a code (a kind of guaranteed knowledge): I'd rather cook rice than potatoes because I know it takes seventeen minutes. This figure delights me, insofar as it's precise (to the point of being preposterous); a round number would seem contrived, and just to be certain, I'd add to it.

July 18, 1977

Mother's birthday. All I can offer her is a rosebud from the garden; at least it's the only one, and the first one since we're here. Tonight, M. is coming for dinner and will cook the dinner itself: soup and a pimento omelette; she brings champagne and almond cookies from Peyrehorade. Mme L. has sent flowers from her garden, delivered by one of her daughters.

Moods, in the strong, Schumannian sense: a broken series of contradictory impulses: waves of anxiety, imaginations of the worst, and unseasonable euphorias. This morning, at the core of Worry, a crystal of happiness: the weather (very fine, very light and dry), the music (Haydn), coffee, a cigar, a good pen, the household noises (the human subject as caprice: such discontinuity alarms, exhausts).

July 19, 1977

Early in the morning, coming back with the milk, I stop in the church to have a look around. It has been remodeled according to the prescribed New Look: now it resembles nothing so much as a Protestant establishment (only the wooden *galleries indicate a Basque tradition); no image, the altar has become a simple table, no candle of course. Too bad, isn't it?*

Around six in the evening, I doze on my bed. The window is wide open, the gray day has lifted now. I experience a certain floating euphoria: everything is liquid, aerated, drinkable *(I drink the air, the moment, the garden). And since I happen to be reading Suzuki, it seems to me that I am quite close to the state that Zen calls* sabi; *or again (since I am also reading Blanchot), to the "fluid heaviness" he speaks of apropos of Proust.*

July 21, 1977

Some bacon, onions, thyme, etc.: simmering, the smell is wonderful. Now this fragrance is not that of food as it will be served at table. There is an odor of what is eaten and an odor of what is prepared (observation for the "Science of Motley," or "diaphorology").

July 22, 1977

For some years, a unique project, apparently: to explore my own stupidity, or better still: to utter *it, to make it the object of my books. In this way I have already* uttered *my "egoist" stupidity and my "lover's" stupidity. There remains a third kind, which I shall someday have to get on paper: political stupidity. What I think of events politically (and I never fail to think something), from day to day, is stupid. It is a stupidity which I should now* utter *in the third book of this little trilogy: a kind of* Political Diary. *It would take enormous courage, but maybe this would exorcise that mixture of boredom, fear, and indignation which the Politician (or rather Politics) constitutes for me.*

"I" is harder to write than to read.

Last night, at Casino, *the Anglet supermarket, with E.M., we were fascinated by this Babylonian Temple of Merchandise. It is really the Golden Calf: piles of (cheap) "wealth," gathering of the species (classified by types), Noah's ark of things (Swedish clogs to eggplants), predatory stacking of carts. We are suddenly convinced that people will buy anything (as I do myself): each cart, while parked in front of the cash register, is the shameless chariot of manias, impulses, perversions, and cravings: obvious, confronting a cart proudly passing before us, that there was no* need *to buy the cellophane-wrapped pizza ensconced there.*

I'd like to read (if such a thing exists) a History of Stores. What happened before Zola and Le Bonheur des dames?

> *August 5, 1977*

Continuing War and Peace, *I have a violent emotion, reading the death of old Prince Bolkonsky, his last words of tenderness to his daughter ("My darling, my friend"), the Princess's scruples about not disturbing him the night before, whereas he was calling her; Marie's feeling of guilt because for a moment she wanted her father to die, anticipating that she would thereby gain her freedom. And all this, so much tenderness, so much poignance, in the midst of the crudest scuffles, the arrival of the French, the necessity of leaving, etc.*

Literature has an effect of truth much more violent for me than that of religion. By which I mean, quite simply, that literature is like *religion. And yet, in this week's* Quinzaine, *Lacassin declares peremptorily: "Literature no longer exists except in textbooks." Whereby I am dismissed, in the name of . . . comic strips.*

> *August 13, 1977*

This morning, around eight, the weather was splendid. I had an impulse to try M.'s bicycle, to go to the baker's. I haven't ridden a bike since I was a kid. My body found this operation very odd, difficult, and I was afraid (of getting on, of getting off). I told all this to the baker—and as I left the shop, trying to get back on my bike, of course I fell off. Now by instinct I let myself fall excessively, *legs in the air, in the silliest posture imaginable. And then I understood that it was this silliness which saved me (from hurting myself too much):* I accompanied *my fall and thereby turned myself into a spectacle, I made myself ridiculous; but thereby, too, I diminished its effect.*

All of a sudden, it has become a matter of indifference to me whether or not I am modern.

(. . . And like a blind man whose finger gropes along the text of life and here and there recognizes "what has already been said.")

II

Paris, April 25, 1979

Futile Evening:

Yesterday, around seven in the evening, under a cold rain in a bad spring, I ran to catch the No. 58 bus. Oddly, there were only old people on the bus. One couple was talking very loudly about some History of the War *(which? you can't tell anymore):* "No distance, no perspective," *the man was saying admiringly,* "only details." *I got off at the Pont Neuf. Since I was early, I lingered a little along the Quai de la Mégisserie. Workmen in blue smocks (I could smell how badly paid they were) were brutally stacking big cages on dollies where ducks and pigeons (all fowls are so stupid) were fluttering in hysterics, sliding in heaps from one side to the other. The shops were closing. Through the door, I saw two puppies: one was teasing the other, which kept rebuffing him in a very human* manner. Once again, I had a longing to have a dog: I might have bought this one (a sort of fox terrier), which was irritated and showed it in a way that was indifferent and yet not haughty. There were also plants and pots of kitchen herbs for sale. I envisioned myself (both longingly and with horror) stocking up on the lot before going back to U., where I would be living for good, coming to Paris only for "business" and shopping. Then I walked down the deserted and sinister rue des Boudonnais. A driver asked me where the BHV was: oddly enough, he seemed to know only the abbreviation, and had no idea where or even what the Hôtel de Ville was. At the (crumbling) Galerie de l'Impasse, I was disappointed: not by D.B.'s photographs (of windows and blue curtains, taken with a Polaroid camera), but by the chilly atmosphere of the opening: W. wasn't there (probably still in America), nor R. (I was forgetting: they've quarreled). D.S., beautiful and daunting, said to me: "Lovely, aren't they?" "Yes, very lovely" (but it's thin, there's not enough here, I added under my breath). All of which was pathetic enough. And since, as I've grown older, I have more and more courage to do what I like, after a second quick tour of the room (staring any longer wouldn't have done more for me), I took French leave and indulged in a futile spree, from bus to bus and movie house to movie house. I was frozen, I was afraid of having caught bronchitis (this happened to me several times). Finally, I warmed up a little at the Flore, ordering some eggs and a glass of Bordeaux, though this was a very bad day: an insipid and arrogant audience: no face to be interested in or about which to fantasize, or at least to speculate. The evening's pathetic failure has impelled me to begin, at last, the reformation of my life which I have had in mind so long. Of which this first note is the trace.

(On rereading: this bit gave me a distinct pleasure, so vividly did it revive the sensations of that evening; but curiously, *in reading it over, what I remembered best was what was not written, the interstices of notation: for instance, the gray of the rue de Rivoli while I was waiting for the bus; no use trying to describe it now, anyway, or I'll lose it again instead of some other silenced sensation, and so on, as if resurrection always occurred alongside the thing expressed: role of the Phantom, of the Shadow.)*

However often I reread these two fragments, nothing tells me they are publishable; nothing tells me, on the other hand, that they are not. Which raises a problem that is beyond me— the problem of "publishability"; not: "is it good or is it bad?" (a form every author gives to his question), but "is it publishable or not?" This is not only a publisher's question. The doubt has shifted, slides from the text's quality to its image. I raise for myself the question of the text from the Other's point of view; the Other is not the public, here, or any particular public (this is the publisher's question); the Other, caught up in a dual and somehow personal relation, is *anyone who will read me.* In short, I imagine that my Journal pages are put in front of "whom I am looking at," or under the silence of "whom I am speaking to." —Is this not the situation of any text? —No. The text is anonymous, or at least produced by a kind of *nom de guerre,* that of the author. This is not at all true of the Journal (even if its "I" is a false name): the Journal is a "discourse" (a kind of *written word* according to a special code), not a text. The question I raise for myself: *"Should I keep a journal?"* is immediately supplied, in my mind, with a nasty answer: *"Who cares?",* or, more psychoanalytically: *"It's your problem."*

All I have left to do is analyze the reasons for my doubt. Why do I suspect, *from the point of view of the Image,* Journal writing? I believe it is because this writing is stricken, in my

eyes, as though with an insidious disease, with negative characteristics—deceptive and disappointing, as I shall try to say.

The Journal corresponds to no *mission*. Nor is this word
laughable. The works of literature, from Dante to Mallarmé,
Proust, and Sartre, have always had, for those who wrote
them, a kind of social, theological, mythic, aesthetic, moral
end. The book, "architectural and premeditated," is supposed
to reproduce an order of the world, it always implies, I believe, a monist philosophy. The Journal cannot achieve the
status of the Book (of the Work); it is only an Album, to
adopt Mallarmé's distinction (it is Gide's life which is a
"work," not his Journal). The Album is a collection of leaflets
not only interchangeable (even this would be nothing), but
above all *infinitely suppressible*: rereading my Journal, I can
cross out one entry after the next, to the complete annihilation
of the Album, with the excuse that "I don't like this one": this
is the method of Groucho and Chico Marx, reading aloud and
tearing up each clause of the contract which is meant to bind
them. —But can't the Journal, in fact, be considered and practiced as that form which essentially expresses the inessential of
the world, the world as inessential? —For that, the Journal's
subject would have to be the world, and not me; otherwise,
what is uttered is a kind of egotism which constitutes a screen
between the world and the writing; whatever I do, I become
consistent, confronting the world which is not. How to keep a
Journal without egotism? That is precisely the question which
keeps me from writing one (for I have had just about enough
egotism).

Inessential, the Journal is unnecessary as well. I cannot
invest in a Journal as I would in a unique and monumental
work which would be dictated to me by an incontrovertible
desire. The regular writing of the Journal, a function as daily
as any other physiological one, no doubt implies a pleasure, a
comfort, but not a passion. It is a minor mania of writing,

whose necessity vanishes in the trajectory which leads from the entry produced to the entry reread: "I haven't found that what I've written so far is particularly valuable, nor that it obviously deserves to be thrown away" (Kafka). Like any subject of perversion (I am told), subjected to the "yes, but," I know that my text is futile, but at the same time (by the same impulse) I cannot wrest myself from the belief that it exists.

Inessential, uncertain, the Journal is also inauthentic. I don't mean by this that someone who expresses himself in one is not sincere. I mean that its very form can only be borrowed from an antecedent and motionless Form (that, precisely, of the intimate Journal), which cannot be subverted. Writing my Journal, I am, by status, doomed to simulation. A double simulation, in fact: for every emotion being a copy of the same emotion one has read somewhere, to report a mood in the coded language of the Collection of Moods is to copy a copy: even if the text was "original," it would already be a copy; all the more so, if it is familiar, worn, threadbare: "The writer, by his pains, those dragons he has fondled, or by a certain vivacity, must set himself up, in the text, as a witty histrion" (Mallarmé). What a paradox! By choosing the most "direct," the most "spontaneous" form of writing, I find myself to be the clumsiest of ham actors. (And why not? Are there not "historic" moments when one must be a ham actor? By practicing to the bitter end an antiquated form of writing, do I not say that I love literature, that I love it in a harrowing fashion, at the very moment when it is dying? I love it, therefore I imitate it—but precisely: not without complexes.)

All of which says more or less the same thing: that the worst torment, when I try to keep a Journal, is the instability of my judgment. Instability? Rather its inexorably descending curve. In the Journal, Kafka pointed out, the absence of a notation's value is always recognized too late. How to transform what is written at white heat (and take pride in the fact) into a nice cold dish? It is this waste, this dwindling which constitutes the Journal's uneasiness. Again Mallarmé (who moreover did not keep one): "Or other verbiage become just that, provided it is exposed, persuasive, pensive and true when one confides it in a whisper": as in that fairy tale, under the effect of a curse and an evil power, the flowers that fall from my mouth are changed into toads. "When I say something, this thing immediately and definitively loses its importance. When I write it here, it also loses it, but sometimes gains another importance" (Kafka). The difficulty proper to the Journal is that this secondary importance, liberated by writing, is not certain: it is not certain that the Journal recuperates the word and gives it the resistance of a new metal. Of course writing is indeed that strange activity (over which, hitherto, psychoanalysis has had little hold, understanding it with difficulty), which miraculously arrests the hemorrhaging of the Image-repertoire, of which speech is the powerful and pathetic stream. But precisely: however "well written," is the Journal "writing"? It struggles, swells, and stiffens: am I as big as the text? Never! you aren't even close. Whence the depressive effect: acceptable when I write, disappointing when I reread.

At bottom, all these failures and weaknesses designate quite clearly a certain defect of the subject. This defect is existential. What the Journal posits is not the tragic question, the Madman's question: "Who am I?", but the comic question, the Bewildered Man's question: "Am I?" A comic—a comedian, that's what the Journal keeper is.

In other words, I never get away from myself. And if I never get away from myself, if I cannot manage to determine what the Journal is "worth," it is because its literary status slips through my fingers: on the one hand, I experience it, through its facility and its desuetude, as being nothing more

than the Text's limbo, its unconstituted, unevolved, and imma-
ture form; but on the other hand, it is all the same a true scrap
of that Text, for it includes its essential torment. This torment,
I believe, consists in this: that literature is *without proofs*. By
which it must be understood that it cannot prove, not only
what it says, but even *that* it is worth the trouble of saying it.
This harsh condition (Play and Despair, Kafka says) achieves
its very paroxysm in the Journal. But also, at this point, everything turns around, for out of its impotence to prove, which
excludes it from the serene heaven of Logic, the Text draws a
*flexibilit*y which is in a sense its essence, which it possesses as
something all its own. Kafka—whose Journal is perhaps the
only one that can be read without irritation—expresses this
double postulation of literature to perfection: Accuracy and
Inanity: ". . . I was considering the hopes I had formed for
life. The one which appeared the most important or the most
affecting was the desire to acquire a way of seeing life (and,
what was related, of being able, by writing, to convince others) in which life would keep its heavy movement of rise and
fall, but would at the same time be recognized, and with a no
less admirable clarity, as a nothing, a dream, a drifting state."
Yes, that is just what the ideal Journal is: at once a rhythm
(rise and fall, elasticity) and a trap (I cannot join my image):
a writing, in short, which tells the truth of the trap and guarantees this truth by the most formal of operations, rhythm. On
which we must doubtless conclude that I can rescue the Journal on the one condition that I labor it *to death*, to the end of
an extreme exhaustion, like a *virtually* impossible Text: a
labor at whose end it is indeed possible that the Journal thus
kept no longer resembles a Journal at all.

1979